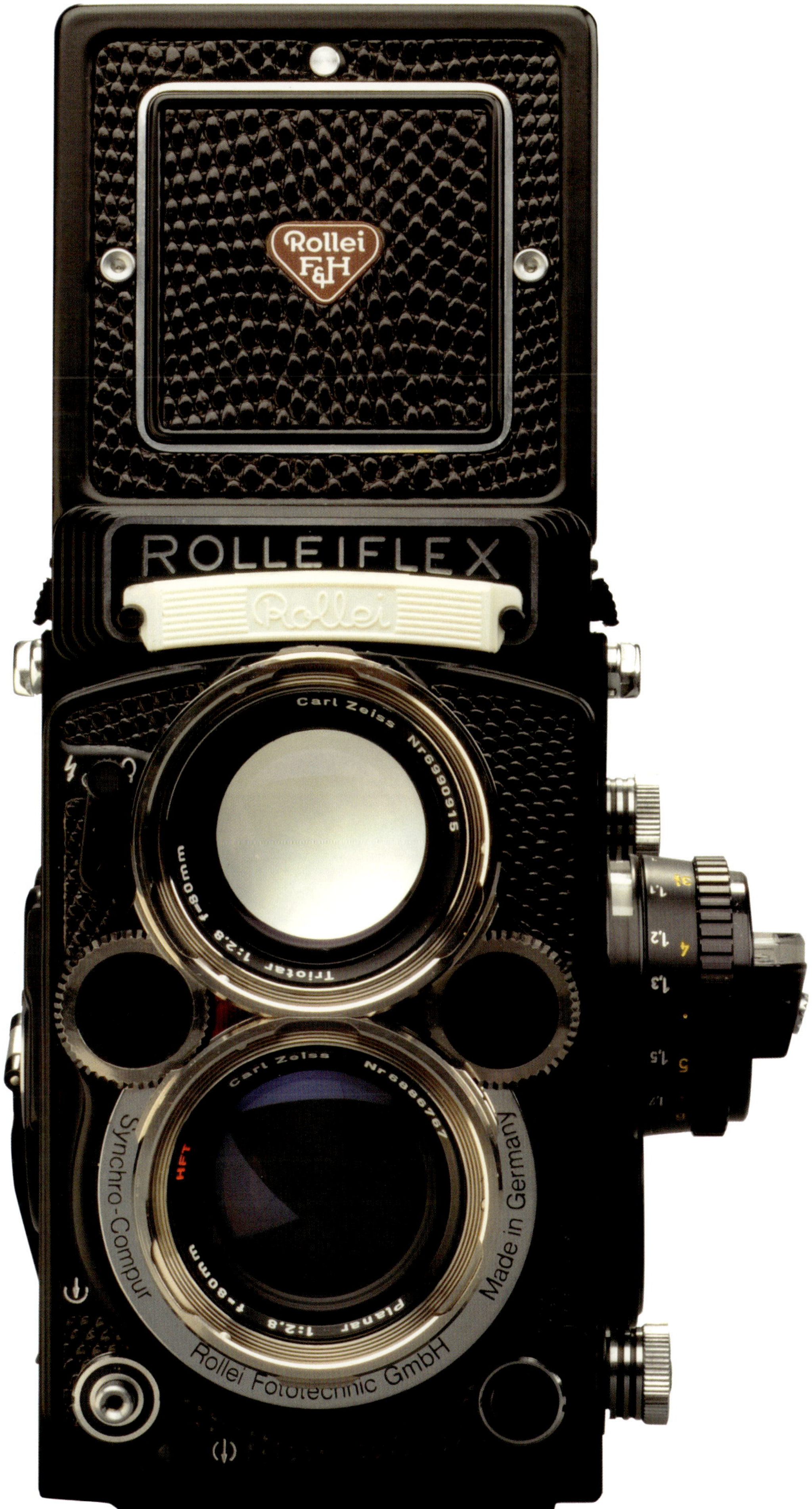
Rollei
F&H
ROLLEIFLEX
Rollei
Carl Zeiss
Carl Zeiss
Synchro-Compur
Made in Germany
Rollei Fototechnic GmbH

Publication of this book was made possible by the generous support of the Judy and Steven Gluckstern Family through their Lucky Star Foundation and the Robin and Danny Greenspun Family through their Culture Dog Foundation.

For reasons of economy and speed, this volume has been printed from camera-ready copy furnished by the author, who assumes full responsibility for its contents.

Printed in China
First edition, 2009

♾ The paper used in this book meets the minimum requirements of ANSI/NISO Z39.48-1992 (R1997) (Permanence of Paper).

Library of Congress Cataloging-in-Publication Data

Flukinger, Roy, 1947–
Fritz Henle : in search of beauty / Roy Flukinger. — 1st ed.
p. cm. — (Harry Ransom Center Photography Series)
Includes bibliographical references and index.
ISBN 978-0-292-71972-9 (cloth : alk. paper)
1. Photography, Artistic. 2. Henle, Fritz, 1909–1993 I. Henle, Fritz, 1909–1993 II. Title.
TR653.F587 2009
779.092—dc22

2008034261

Photo Opposite: Maria and Fritz Henle, Diego Conde.

Book and jacket design by DJ Stout and Julie Savasky, Pentagram Design, Austin, Texas

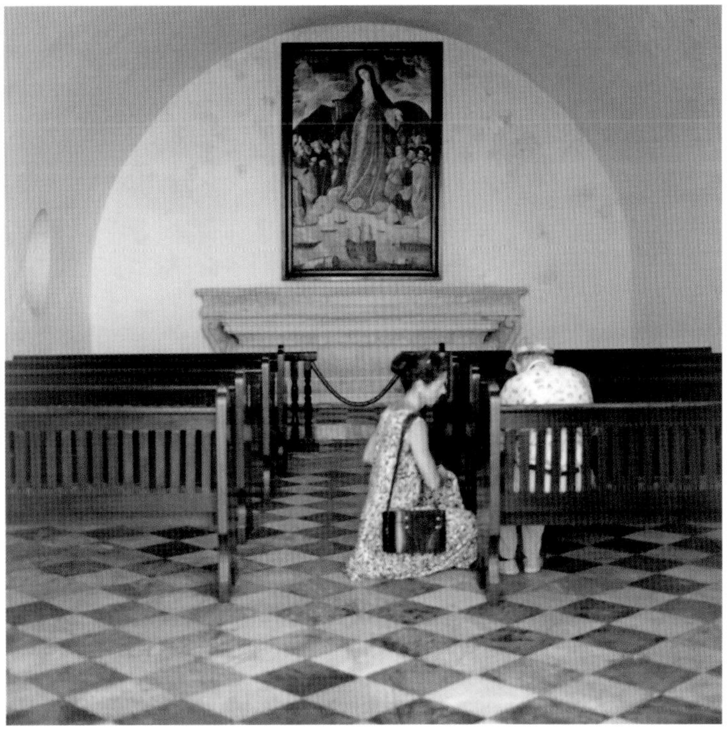

FOR FRITZ AND MARIA

DIRECTOR'S FOREWORD

In one sense, I think Fritz Henle gave me my first course in photography, which is not to say that he was didactic, but his words captured the essence of his images and taught me a great deal about the medium. Henle was the first world-class photographer I had ever met. In our earliest conversations, we discussed the relationship between the printed photograph and the taken photograph, how printing was, in a way, the realization of the image. From there, we talked about his New Orleans photographs, which I admire greatly, and his images of Europe, and especially Germany, in the 1930s. There is a haunting quality that emerges from those images of Europe on the eve of World War II and the rise of the Fascist state, whether they be of a silent street on a rainy evening or a Nazi parade in the midday sun. Indeed, those images evoke the essence of time and place in the same way as does the film directed by Sir Carol Reed of Graham Greene's *The Third Man.* Henle's evocation of place is less "misty" but equally haunting.

I think Fritz Henle had a genius for catching the most arresting detail in rendering an epiphanic scene. He gave great texture to his photographs, as one can see in his images of the rippling sands of the desert or the crumbling stones of a pyramid. His photographs were full of movement, whether they captured a fisherman casting his net or cowboys riding through an oil field. One must admit, as well, his eye for beauty. There are more than 1,300 prints by Fritz Henle at the Ransom Center, not including the two that are hanging on the walls of my office, gifts to me from Henle. My favorite is his portrait of Harry S. Truman. It is a portrait that captures the fortitude and determination that was so characteristic of Truman. Henle is the only photographer whose work is featured twice on my office walls.

We are proud at the Ransom Center to showcase Fritz Henle's remarkable work in an exhibition, greatly pleased to offer this published volume, and deeply grateful to the Lucky Star and Culture Dog foundations for enabling us to do both. I would also like to thank Roy Flukinger for so brilliantly portraying the spirit of Henle's work in the exhibition and this catalog.

THOMAS F. STALEY
September 2008

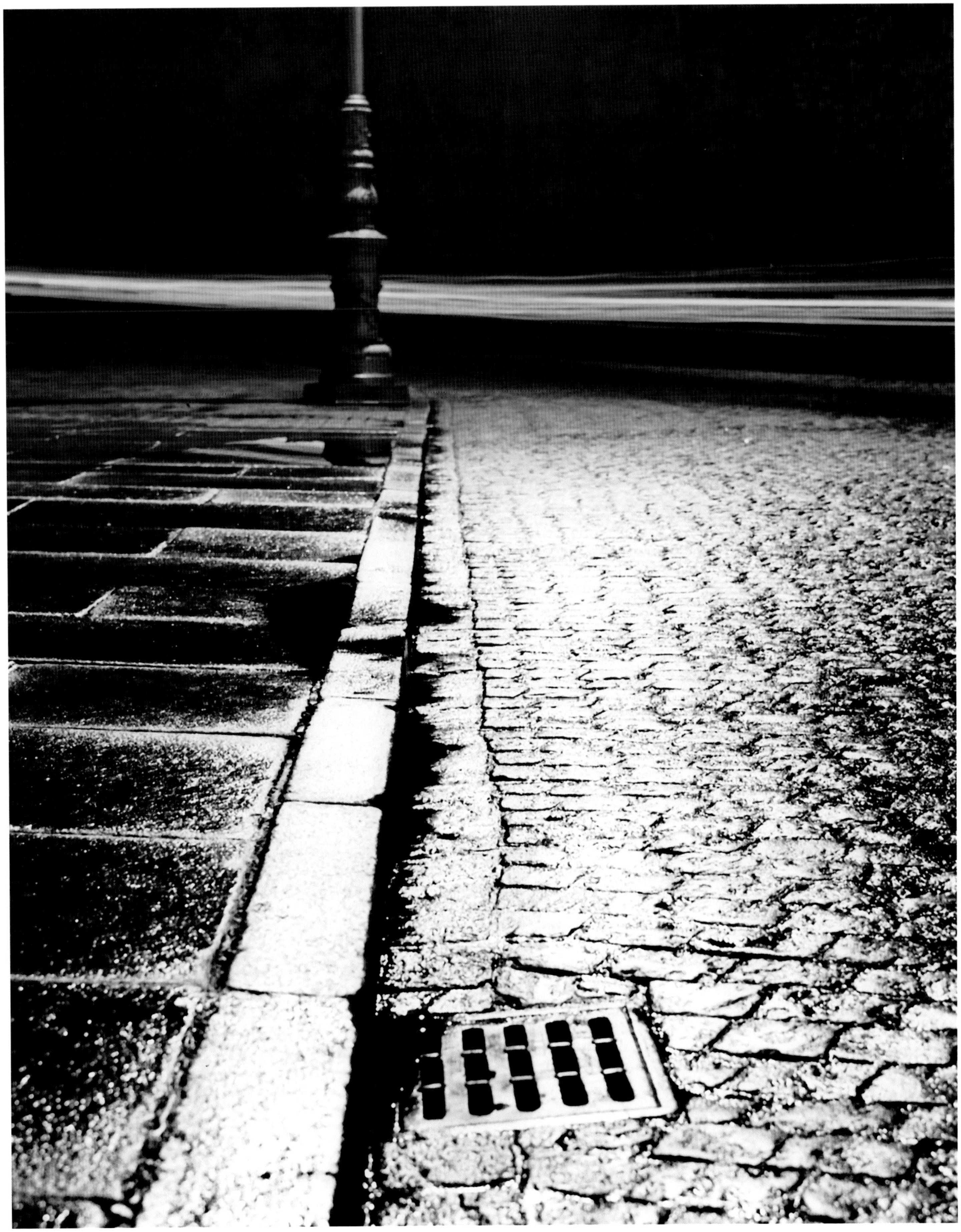

Rainy Night at the English Garden, Munich. 1931.

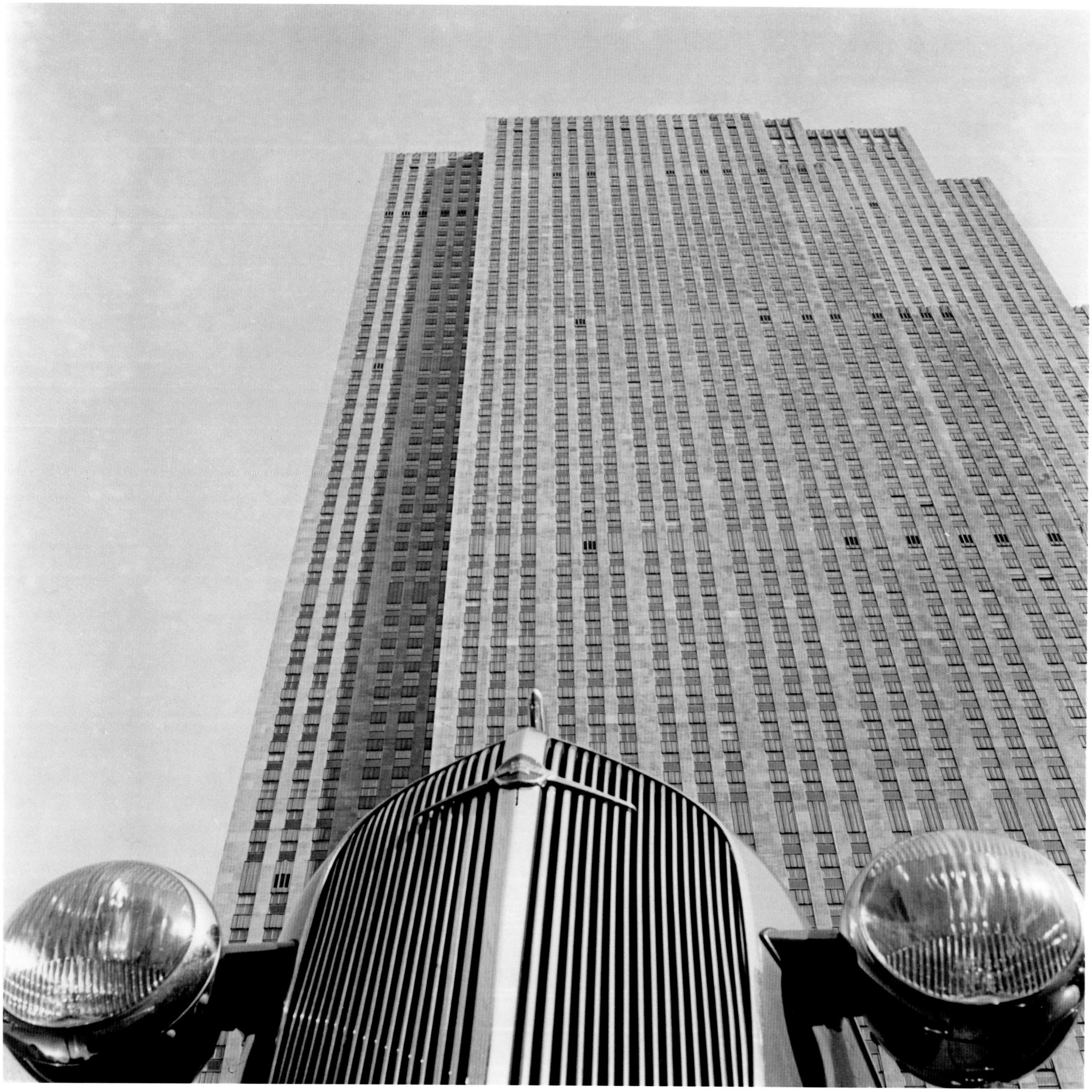

RCA Building and Chevrolet Grill, New York City. 1937.

FRITZ HENLE

ROY FLUKINGER

IN SEARCH OF BEAUTY

UNIVERSITY OF TEXAS PRESS, AUSTIN
HARRY RANSOM CENTER

One thing an artist can do in this world is to remind people that there is so much beauty that you only have to see it.

FRITZ HENLE

THE MORE ONE TALKED with Fritz Henle about his art and his career the more one noticed that he always returned to one particularly defining moment in his life. In 1927 the teenaged Henle had gone on a holiday in his native Germany, hiking the hills and valleys of Franken and exploring the medieval town of Rothenberg. For the vacation he had borrowed his father Adolf's Icarette camera and had returned with many undeveloped rolls of film.

On the heels of the trip Fritz persuaded his father to let him build a darkroom in their Dortmund home. He and his mother found an ideal location in the basement that provided ample darkness and, being located next to the laundry room, a good water source. With the help of a carpenter from his father's medical clinic he fashioned a light-tight work space of wood and cardboard about the size of a telephone booth that was clean, orderly, and up and running within a few short days. It was in that space that Henle first taught himself photographic chemistry and learned both the hard work and the art of securing a fine print.

Certainly the richest experience and influence of that newly constructed space came not from its function but rather from its location. As it happened the section of the basement that housed Fritz's darkroom was located directly beneath the family's music room — one of the most active spaces in the Henle family home. Adolf, among his many community interests, also served as director of the Dortmund Philharmonic Society, and as a result, the room was always in use, whether by his string quartet or by notably famous visiting European musicians who utilized the room for practice and intimate performances.

It was a fruitful arrangement for Fritz, who had studied the violin briefly but felt that musical performance was not where his talents lay. He would spend many days and evenings in this darkroom studying, exploring and testing the wonders of his new art while listening to the live music of Mozart and many other classical masters drifting into his work space from the seeming firmament above. As he would later reflect upon the magical complement of these arts: "Ever since I taught myself to develop my films and print my photographs, music has become an integral part of my life. I began to realize that for me there was a close relationship and I believe that with my great love for music I was able to develop a much keener sense for the true meaning of my desire to express myself with pictures." [2]

It was in that music-saturated darkness and under the glow of the red-filtered developing lamp that Henle would spend many days and nights, learning how to process films and how to coax the optimum sharpness, brightness, contrast and luminosity out of the various photographic printing papers of the day. At the end of his first two years in that intimate space of personal creativity, he himself was transformed, even as he discovered how to transform his vision into tangible and beautiful prints. The experience proved to be a fortuitous one — learning the basics and refinements of the art of photography while also being immersed in the equally eloquent art of music. The experience became a deeply affecting and profound one, and music would continue to suffuse Fritz Henle's personal and professional life from that time forward. It entered his language whenever he discussed any aspect of the visual arts and became the focus of the experience of his being. Throughout the remainder of his days he would always be shaped by the photographer's song.

The arc of Fritz Henle's life and career throughout the twentieth century — his having been born in its first decade and departing with its final decade — is as complex as his contributions to the art of photography. A direct, honest and openly optimistic individual, he rolled with the blows that life tried to throw at him, all the while being consistent in pursuing and enriching the muse that drove him ever forward. His idealism was never false or naïve but rather grew out of the realism with which he faced each day of his life. The resulting fine photographs, which he produced with eloquent creativity and consistent excellence, serve, now that he has passed on, not only as a record of countless people, places and events but even more so as an undying testament to the humanity that can resonate through the finest art.

Throughout Fritz Henle's professional career his photography was recognized repeatedly for its artistry, eloquence and insightfulness. Although his loyalty toward Rollei cameras at times still distracts some technophiles and critics toward the camera instead of the artist wielding it, Fritz's position never wavered and his message to professionals and amateurs alike was always consistent: "Any camera can be used for any picture story...provided the photographer is thoroughly familiar with his camera and its operation is automatic and almost intuitive. The camera's role is secondary. The photographer's principal role is vision and understanding of life's beauty, drama, poetry or even ugliness."[3]

Fritz Henle's imagery has always proved, as the photohistorians Beaumont and Nancy Newhall once denoted, that his consistent excellence was "not the production of an instrument, but the record of [his] personal and sensitive vision..."[4] Norman Hall, one of Britain's most famous photography editors from the mid-twentieth century, would label him the "*maestro* of the Rollei"[5] while acknowledging that he "has become one of the best-known photographers of the present time."[6] Decades later the critic/editor Herbert Keppler would describe him as the "greatest living exponent of the Twin-lens reflex camera"[7] — a sentiment that would be echoed later by a fellow editor, Norman Rothschild, who would declare him "a true 'Old Master' of the reflex camera."[8] And, in a summary of Henle's career, the photohistorian Helmut Gernsheim paid him the ultimate compliment of calling him "the last classic freelance photographer."[9]

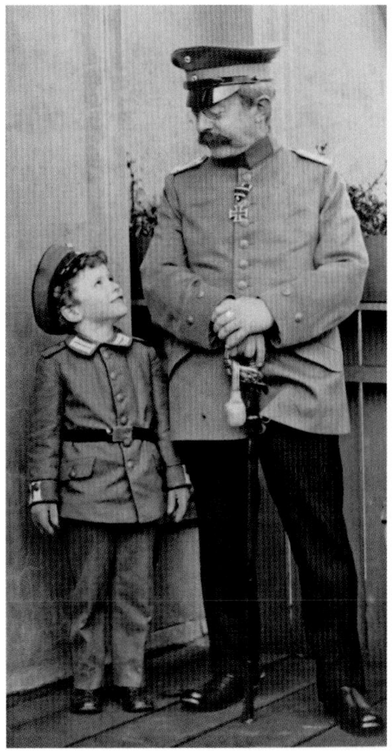

Photographer Unidentified.
Fritz Henle and his father, Adolph, in military uniforms. Dortmund, Germany. 1915. Adolph was home on leave from the German army. Although Fritz had been photographed by his father from early on, this image was taken on the occasion when he said he first became aware of photography.

1 "Fritz Henle, Artistry on Exhibition." *The St. Croix Avis*, February 1982: [1p.].

2 Ibid: 5.

3 Irving Desfor. "Camera Angles." Associated Press, 1975.

4 Beaumont Newhall. "Fritz Henle." *Infinity*, March 1968: 5.

5 [Norman Hall.] *Photography*, December 1956: [24].

6 [Norman Hall.] "One Man and a Rolleiflex: Fritz Henle." *Photography*, December 1956: 29.

7 H[erbert] K[eppler]. "Books in Review." *Modern Photography*, September 1965: 40.

8 Norman Rothschild. "Portfolio Review in Brief — The American Virgin Islands." *Popular Photography*, February 1973: [1p.].

9 Helmut Gernsheim. "Henle, Fritz." In: Colin Naylor, ed. *Contemporary Photographers*, 1988: 436–7.

Adolf and Tina Henle. [Family album of the Henle Family. Dortmund, ca. 1910–1922.] Various pages.

Not surprisingly, some of the best insight into Fritz Henle's early life comes from viewing his family photograph albums. Assembled throughout the last decades of the nineteenth century and the early years of the twentieth century, they reveal the faces and home life of his parents, Adolf and Tina (née Lange) Henle, and follow on through the childhood and youth of Fritz Jacob Henle (born on June 9, 1909) and his siblings — his older sister, Annemarie, and his younger brother, Werner. Indeed, Henle's earliest memory of photography was being dressed up and made to pose before the unblinking lens of Adolf's tripod-mounted portrait camera. Filled primarily with amateur portraits and his parents' domestic and vacation snapshots, the family albums contain a vivid, personal glimpse of both the family and the upper-class German life into which Fritz was born and raised.

Adolf Henle was a successful surgeon in the industrial German city of Dortmund and, as the albums tend to reveal, afforded his wife and children with a comfortable home and lifestyle for the period. He obviously provided his family with a fine level of domestic and societal refinements that were comparable with his professional career and position in Dortmund society. In fact, it seems that the only serious challenge to their lives would prove to be a monumental one for most Europeans of that era — the First World War.

When World War I broke out the family was on holiday in Switzerland. Adolf returned his family to blacked-out Dortmund and, after he saw to their security, assumed a critical position as Surgeon General for the German Army. He would spend the next four years traversing between the front lines and working long hours in his own clinic near his home. Tina became the children's full-time parent and was able to maintain some semblance of uniformity over the children's education and family life. Although Adolf's visits home became sporadic, Fritz would recall each one as being memorable despite its often terrible brevity.

They were not the only bad memories that Fritz would carry with him from that war. His impressions of the war's effect upon his homeland were those of a sensitive child who grew from five to nine in the interval, and it is not surprising to realize that many of those memories would remain strongly visual. The sights of uniformed youths in the windows of the troop trains, the shortages in foodstuffs in the Dortmund shops, the nights without lights, the glum and worried expressions on familiar faces, the gunfire flashes of French occupational forces and the bodies of townspeople in the dark city streets, and the absence of laughter — all became sharp moments that impressed themselves upon his young and active mind.

With his father's return at the war's end and with the gradual restoration of a reasonably regular daily life and recovering society for the Ruhr Valley, the Henle family began its return to normalcy. Adolf's home and clinic remained secure, and he was quickly able to

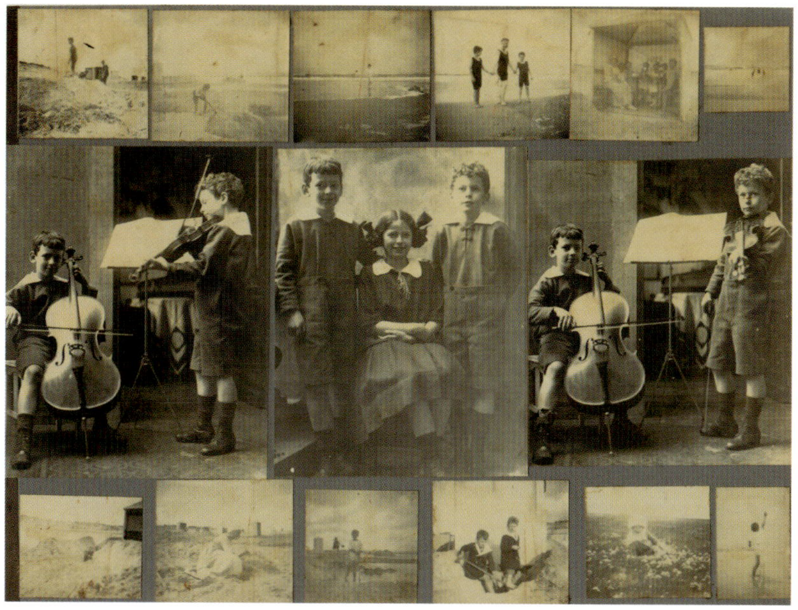

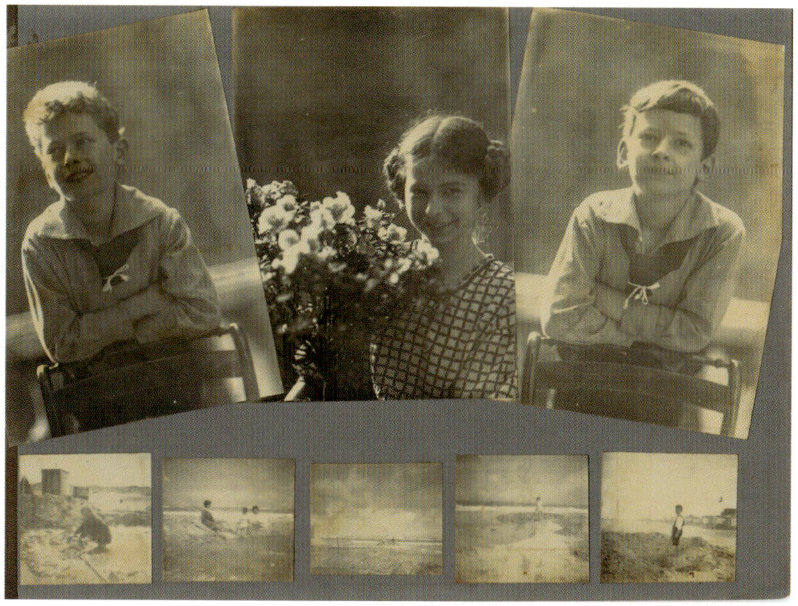

resume his practice. And, as the family albums also attest, he was able to maintain the stability of their domestic life within the ever-changing society of the Weimar Republic of 1920s Germany.

The albums are important not only because of what they are able to show us about the life of Fritz and his family, but also because they remain the essential repository for the imagery that Adolf created through his primary hobby — photography. It is significant that the majority of the photographs in the albums were generated by, or under the direction of, Adolf Henle and reflect the degree of his fascination with and expertise in that continuing avocation. He was a precise and careful amateur who obviously took patient care in directing family and friends in front of his lens. With the aid of an elderly assistant, the negatives and subsequent prints were developed at the nearby lab and, finally, carefully arranged on the gray leaves of the albums.

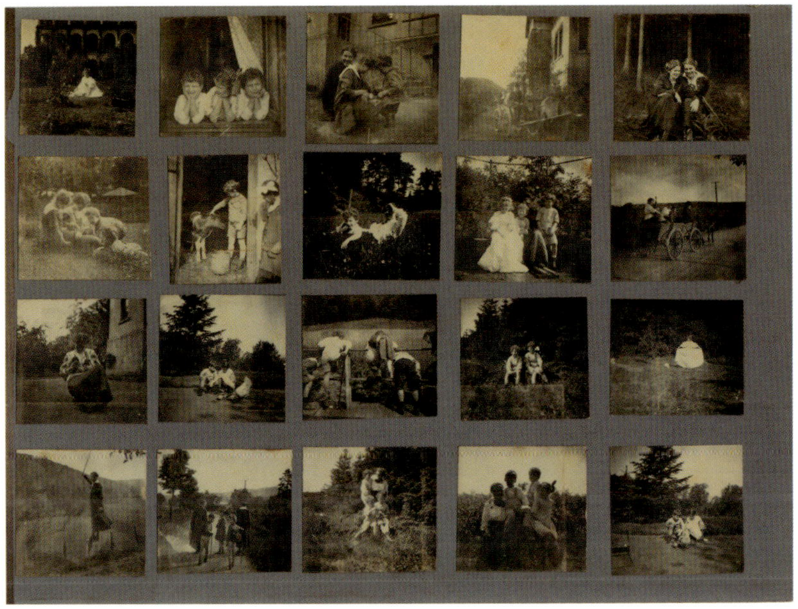

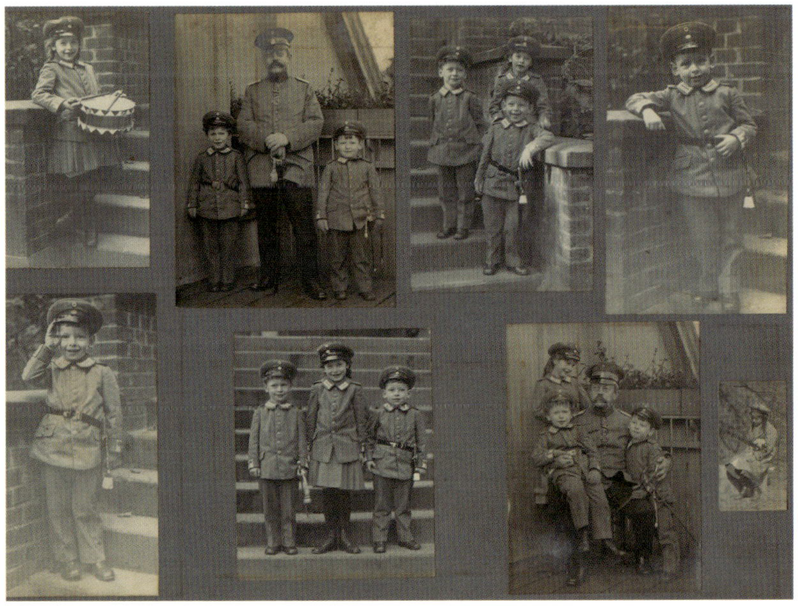

Adolf and Tina Henle. [Family album of the Henle Family. Dortmund, ca. 1910–1922.] Single page: Henle children and family activities.

Adolf and Tina Henle. [Family album of the Henle Family. Dortmund, ca. 1910–1922.] Single page: Henle family in military uniforms, ca. 1915.

Although Adolf remained the active hobbyist during those years, his passion soon attracted the attention of his older son, and by the age of fifteen, Fritz was asking permission to borrow his father's small Icarette camera. Adolf instructed his son in the basic operation of the instrument, loaded it with a roll of film, and encouraged him in his efforts. When the roll was processed and prints generated, he was pleased enough with the results to offer Fritz the continued use of the camera whenever he wished.

For the father it must have seemed that sharing the hobby marked the formation of an additional bond with his son. For Fritz it became the awakening of a destiny. As he would later recall: "Life had become a sequence of sad and disturbing memories which never left me. As yet, I could behold them only in my mind but slowly there formed an opinion in myself — I would try to do what my father's lab assistant with the scarred hands managed to do — keep my memories on small sheets of some special paper. It was [like] showing our images after my father had used a camera with a big lens. I felt my memories could be shown the same way..."[10]

Following his elementary education, Fritz Henle entered the Stadt Gymnasium in Dortmund in 1920 and remained an above-average student until his graduation in 1929. And it would be through the school that his next developments in photography would evolve. In 1927 he arranged to accompany the school's French instructor, "Abu" Becker, on a spring holiday to Franken. He again borrowed his father's Icarette, and following his return home and the building of his basement darkroom beneath the home's music room, he processed the film rolls and printed his photographs of the mountains, the countryside, and most especially the medieval town of Rothenberg. It was at that instant, holding the tangible evidence of the richness of his vision in his hands, that he became convinced that a camera must be his constant companion throughout his life.

In 1928 he also had his first opportunity to seriously explore the challenges of industrial photography — a not altogether surprising subject, with Dortmund's physical location and prominent importance in the development of Germany's industrial Ruhr Valley. His photographs of the blast furnace in the Hoesch AG steel plant in Dortmund were shared with Heinrich Butzer, a schoolmate whose father was a major figure in ship construction. Fritz was dispatched to the port city of Bremen to photograph the shipyards and the building of the German superliners, *Europa* and *Bremen*, as they were nearing completion. The resulting images, besides satisfying Herr Butzer, displayed a combination of straightforward clarity mixed with avant-garde compositions that went beyond the conventionally romanticized styles of the day. With his natural curiosity and technical expertise, Fritz Henle was already experimenting with different ways of seeing.

A final, significant achievement preceded Henle's graduation from Gymnasium. Rebelling against the conventionally preferred classical language education of his classmates, Henle decided that it would be very important for him in the modern world to learn English. During his last years in school, he sought out an elderly British couple in Dortmund and had them instruct him, chiefly through conversation, in their native language. It would be a wise decision in view of the way that events in his own life were soon to turn out, and as a result, he received his diploma in 1929 as the only Gymnasia student whose second language requirement was fulfilled by English.

The paternal side of the Henle family tree was populated by a vast number of doctors and scientists, of whom the most famous was probably Fritz's grandfather, the noted anatomist Jacob Henle.[11] It was a tradition in which the men of the family were supposed to follow, and Adolf was expecting the same of his sons. Excellence, in

10 Fritz Henle. *Time—Exposures.* Typescript, ca. 1984–1993: 4. Henle Family Archive.

11 See: Victor Robinson. *The Life of Jacob Henle.* New York, Medical Life Company, 1921; and, Friedrich Siegmund Merkel. *Jacob Henle: Ein Deutsches Gelehrtenleben.* Braunschweig, 1891.

both education and one's medical career, was a driving force in the Henle family, with sons expected to follow and exceed their fathers. However, while Werner was fully planning to follow his father into the medical profession,[12] Fritz had awakened a passion in an entirely different direction and was recognizing that the discipline of photography was beckoning. It therefore probably did not come as a total surprise to Adolf when his eldest son requested to delay going to university for a year and proposed instead to apprentice himself to a master photographer in Dortmund. The father reluctantly agreed, hoping that Fritz would then come around to a much more satisfying professional career choice among the sciences.

Fritz would recall his year of apprenticeship to a local photographer named Schnieding with mixed emotions. He was introduced to a variety of camera and film formats, chiefly the studio and large plate cameras that were the workhorses of the commercial trade — and, as the assistant, he was often the individual who had to carry them and their cumbersome tripods, handle the setups, and break down and transport the equipment back to the studio. He spent a great deal more of his time in the darkroom (absent any music), mixing large amounts of chemicals and processing both larger sheet film and glass dry plates. Forsaking the folding roll film Icarette, he began working with newer glass plate cameras — first a "Perka" Spiegel reflex model and then a 9 x 12 Linhoff — while also learning the art of making bromoil prints.[13] Fritz even saw the first exhibition of some of his imagery in the front window showcase of the shop. His work hours were long and his duties were numerous, but he did learn much about the technical requirements, artistic conventions, and organizational and operational demands of running a photographic business.

Fritz Henle. Rothenberg. 1927.

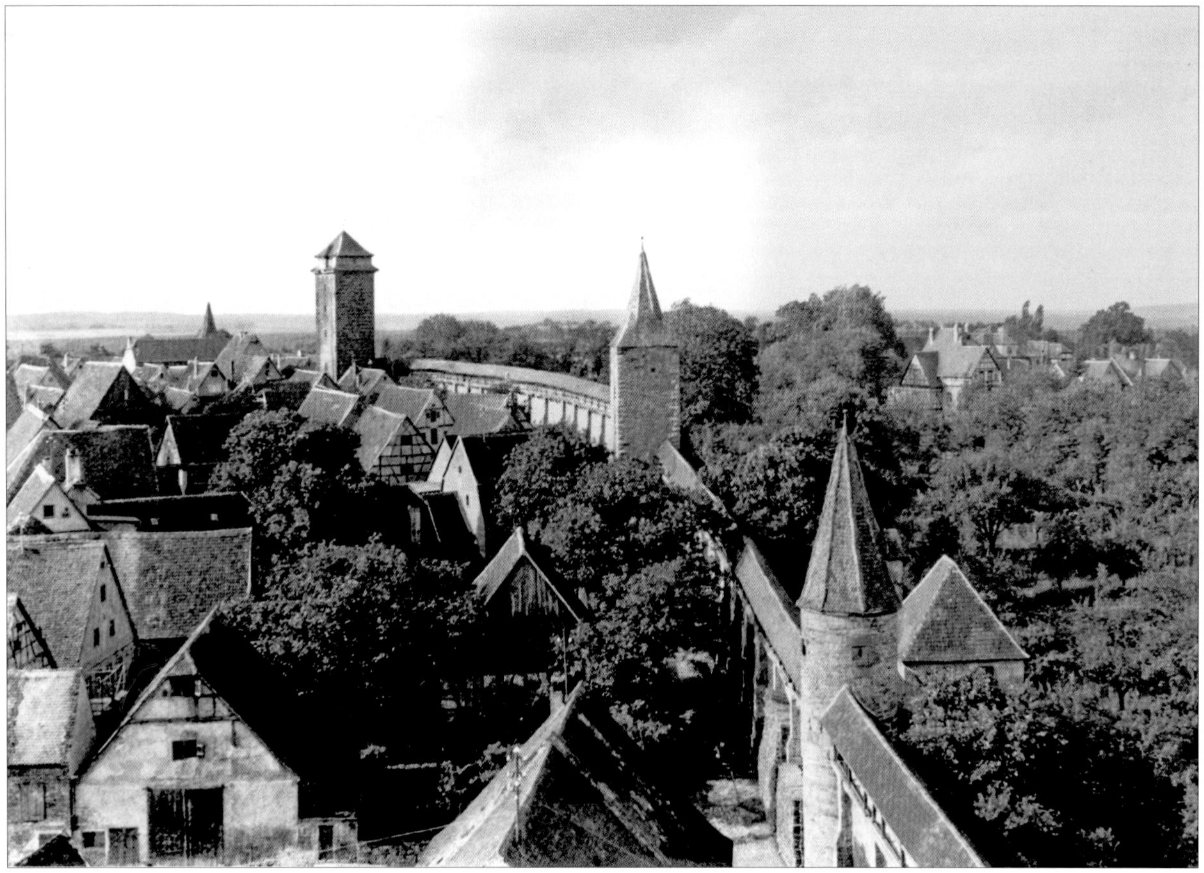

Schnieding, however, represented a conventional "old school" of European photography, based firmly in the late nineteenth century styles and techniques that were becoming outdated by the early decades of the twentieth century. His Pictorialist style and traditional practices accommodated an increasingly obsolescent fashion, which was being replaced by the rise of a new Modernist culture that was gaining popularity rapidly after World War I.[14] In all factions of the contemporary arts — theater, music, dance, the visual arts, architecture, literature, and so forth — a new progressive era was attracting the youth and challenging the old ways. Fritz Henle was in his twentieth year and an exciting world of possibilities and challenges was opening before his eyes. As he would recall: "My first steps in photography were to follow the trend. Soon my mind revolted."[15] At the end of his year of apprenticeship he had learned his greatest lesson to date — that while he still wanted to be a photographer he did not wish to be a limited commercial one like his current master.

In the interim Adolf Henle had become director of the Städtischen Krankenanstalten, the State Hospital, in Heidelberg and had moved his family to a new home there at Hainsbachweg 6, on the Bergstrasse overlooking the Neckar River. The basement of the house contained a large darkroom and, of course, the town was the seat of one of Europe's oldest and most prestigious universities. By the spring of 1930 Fritz had said farewell to his apprenticeship with Herr Schnieding and, together with a large portfolio of his best photographic prints, was living in the new family home in Heidelberg.

At first he kept his promise to his father and entered the University of Heidelberg to study the sciences in preparation for a traditional family career. However, he found the classes too large and crowded, and his mind drifted away from studies that did not hold any attraction for him. Within a month he had convinced Adolf to send him to the University of Munich. The educational conditions were better — he had smaller classes to attend but did not have to share a desk or sit on the floor — but the study of physics and chemistry continued to bore him. What did attract Henle was in the nearby suburb of Schwabing: the Bayerische Staatslehranstalt für Lichtbildwesen, or Bavarian Institute of Photography, Germany's finest school for traditional photography.

In the summer of 1930 Fritz Henle gathered up his portfolio and, overcoming his innate shyness, sought out the Institute's most notable teacher, Hanna Seewald. His determination, coupled with the technical excellence of his body of work, soon convinced her of his serious intent. Together they persuaded the Institute's director, a professor named Sprol, that Henle should be enrolled that fall. Fritz was even so bold as to convince them that, based upon his apprenticeship and accumulated expertise, he be permitted to jump the First Class (first year) and enter the Second Class (second year) of the two-year degree program. That same determination also must have been evident to Adolf, for despite the fact that upper-class German society would regard photography only as a mere trade rather than a serious profession, he too finally if reluctantly was convinced that this was the career path that his eldest son desired. By September Fritz had taken rooms at 26 Clemensstrasse (diagonally across the street from the School of Photography at 33 Clemensstrasse) and was supporting himself by developing and processing customers' prints above a local drugstore.

By the late 1920s Munich had become the cultural capital of the Weimar Republic. While Berlin remained the seat of government and Dortmund could lay claim to being in the heart of industrial Germany, Munich flourished as the center for Modernism, a radical new cultural and artistic movement that had emerged in the post–World War I state. New ideas arose and became prevalent not only in the educational institutions but also through the city. Innovation and experimentation brushed up against decadence and revolution, resulting in new contributions to the institutions of art, theater and music. The city began to attract a more youthful population, and the young Henle began to experience more of that firsthand with his fellow students and friends. They would debate the current affairs and discuss possible solutions for German society while fostering their dreams and making their own plans. As Henle would later reflect upon that era: "In our class were 7 boys and 35 girls; when we were not busy learning how to take pictures and develop them, we had a gay time. Some of us used to see a guy named Hitler in the Hofgarten Café, but none asked the man, who looked alien and sinister, to sit for his portrait. We were all ambitious and had serious work to do."[16]

The single most profound influence upon Fritz Henle's photographic career also occurred at that time — but it did not take place at the Institute. Located strategically across Clemensstrasse from the school was the camera shop of a Herr Letzgus. The store provided much of the apparatus, chemicals and associated supplies for the photography students across the street. And it was there, in the front display window of Photo Letzgus, that Fritz would first lay eyes upon the camera that would change his life forever — the Rolleiflex twin-lens reflex.

The Rolleiflex was manufactured in Braunschweig, Lower Saxony, by a firm that bore the names of its founders, Paul Franke and Reinhold Heidecke. Originally established in 1920 as manufacturers of fine stereographic cameras, Franke and Heidecke quickly developed a reputation for well-manufactured high-end cameras. However, the apparatus that secured their greatest fame and economic success was the development in 1929 of a premier line of medium format twin-lens reflex roll-film cameras — the professional Rolleiflex and, a bit later, the amateur Rolleicord.

The professional Rolleiflex that Henle purchased in 1930 had become, in little more than a year on the international market, a favorite of photographers from all disciplines of the profession. A compromise between cameras that required either larger or smaller film sizes, the popular Rolleiflex would come in one of two standard sizes and, taking a multiple-exposure roll of film, produced square negatives of either a Sports model 4 x 4 cm. (1½ x 1½ inches) or a Standard model 6 x 6 cm. (2¼ x 2¼ inches) size. By utilizing any available fine-grain film, the resulting matrix would rival the quality of the larger format negatives but in a camera whose portability and flexibility could compete with that of the Leica and other 35mm cameras that had just premiered a half-decade earlier in the 1920s. The fixed lenses, chiefly a 7.5 Zeiss or 8.0 Schneider, had excellent sharpness and bokeh, which also added to the potential quality of the resulting negatives. In addition, its shutter was placed between its lenses, thus making it possible to enjoy superior flash synchronicity that utilized either a standard flash or a speedlight synchronization at all speeds. A number of revolutionary design elements also attracted working and future professionals like Henle: a reduced weight, a brighter viewfinder, a mechanical wind mechanism that made loading fast and accurate, and a revolutionary internal mirror mechanism.

Although not as compact in body design as the competing 35mm cameras, the Rollei line of twin-lens reflex cameras were lightweight and flexible and, in the hands of an accomplished professional like Henle, would handle most shooting situations with excellent clarity. Combined with the camera's superior optics and his outstanding technical proficiency, Henle's resulting negatives[17] were of such excellent resolution and tonality that their subsequent prints were often assumed to have been generated by 4 x 5– or 8 x 10–inch cameras. In fact, during his first years working as a professional in New York City, Henle would often provide 8 x 10–inch enlarged prints to his art directors and agents in order to make them assume that he was working with larger format cameras. Contact sheets of the 2¼-inch roll film negatives would have revealed that he had been using the Rolleiflex, which was considered taboo by the major periodical magazines of the mid-1930s. Indeed, it was in part due to the high quality of Henle's work that minds were changed and the Rolleiflex quickly became an accepted professional instrument in photojournalism and commercial photography by the end of that decade.

When Henle began utilizing his new Rolleiflex, many of his fellow students joked about his "toy" camera, but his resulting prints would soon make more than one convert to the system within his class. Franke and Heidecke had produced a superior and revolutionary

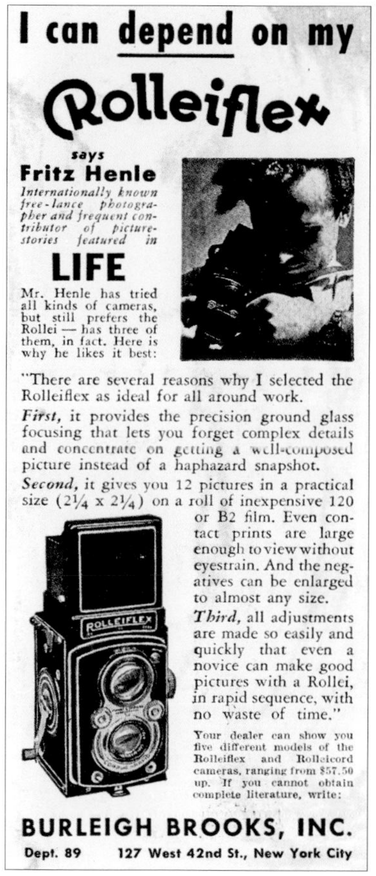

Advertisement: Burleigh Brooks, Inc. "I can depend on my Rolleiflex says Fritz Henle..." *LIFE*. ca. 1938.

12 Indeed, Werner Henle and his wife, Gertrude, would become some of America's most noted cancer researchers. Their papers are housed at the U.S. National Library of Medicine.

13 That was the only time in his life that Fritz would practice and produce prints made by any of the earlier non-silver photomechanical processes of the late nineteenth and early twentieth century. Apparently none of those works have survived.

14 The only works that Henle recalls seeing from that time were the bromoil prints of Hugo Erfurth and volumes of the German photographic annual *Das Deutsche Lichtbild*.

15 Terri Guttilla. "Interview with Fritz Henle." *ASMP Bulletin*, August 1990: 10.

16 Fritz Henle. "Fritz Henle on Shooting Color Roll Film." *Popular Photography*, December 1948: 74.

17 Henle's first Rolleiflex took the smaller, 4 x 4 size roll film. The earliest 6 x 6 size format negatives do not appear in his archive until his 1936–37 hiatus in Mexico — pointing to the fact that he may have purchased the larger Rollei specifically for that journey. Regardless, it is that larger format Rolleiflex that would eclipse the 4 x 4 and soon become his primary camera.

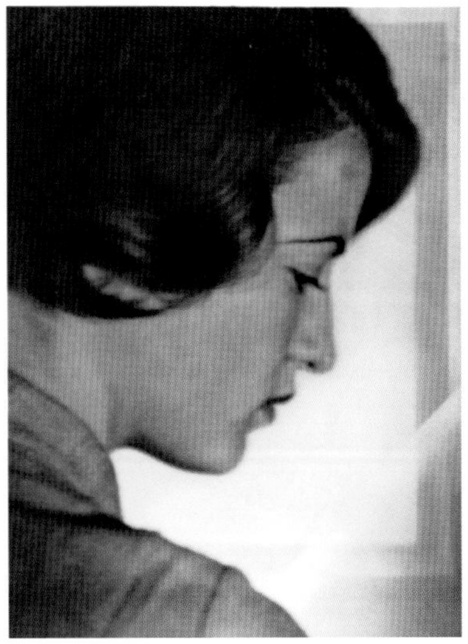

Fritz Henle. Ruth. 1930. Gelatin silver print from a copy negative. Henle cited the lost original print of this image as his first portrait.

camera that would prove to be both successful and proficient for many generations of photographers to come.[18] As James Abbe, Jr., would later sum up its excellence: "The reflex is a versatile camera, above all else. The number of photographers doing a large part, if not all of their work with it, attests to that. Action, still-life, posed or candid fashions, portraits, illustration — all are done with reflex cameras, every day."[19]

In the historical evolution of photographic aesthetics and technology, it would be Fritz's exuberant advocacy for the Rolleiflex that would do so very much "in breaking down the old prejudice against the square picture."[20] As he was able to convert photojournalists and editors to the square format, so he would also lead the way for its acceptance in other photographic dimensions, ranging from the fine arts to commercial work. Henle's message — for both novice and professional alike — was marked by the aesthetic consistency that would be discovered throughout all his imagery: "From my point of view, it is simpler and easier to become the master of one camera, rather than to collect a dozen or more different ones, each for a special purpose. The photographer must be the master of his tools; they must never hold the advantage..."[21]

Although Henle never hesitated to utilize a wide variety of cameras and techniques — including cropping the equilateral frame itself — he always felt that the Rollei's square imagery allowed for the richest possibilities for both professional and amateur photographers. As later generations of 2¼-inch camera artists — from Bill Brandt and Diane Arbus to Keith Carter and O. Rufus Lovett — would find, the square image provided one of the brightest and clearest screens for composition, detail, flexibility and creative expression.

For more than six prolific decades, Fritz Henle made his Rolleis the mainstay of his professional career — Gernsheim once declared him "the man with the four sharp eyes."[22] He would, for the remainder of his long life, view the world on the Rollei's ground glass — "I have learned to see in squares...I try to make each shot count and seldom shoot two pictures of any one picture angle."[23] Indeed, he would champion the Franke and Heidecke line of photographic apparatus so successfully that he would eventually obtain the informal but universal nickname of "Mr. Rollei." It was a distinctive moniker that he would always carry with pride.

Hanna Seewald proved to be an inspirational influence on her young student, encouraging Fritz in the use of his new Rolleiflex. Most importantly, as his primary teacher she eschewed the traditional technological and chemical bases of the other faculty in favor of developing and invigorating the aesthetic and creative possibilities of the art of photography for her students. While she and her students were not greatly influenced by the Modernist movements of the Bauhaus artists (established in Weimar and Dessau in the 1920s), she clearly took them far beyond the Institute's photography-as-craft traditions.

Seewald's approach seems to have been more closely akin to the contemporaneous *Neue Sachlichkeit*, or *New Objectivity*, movement and most directly from its discipline of concentration on form and line that had begun evolving with the photographer Albert Renger-Patzsch during the previous decade. Although the Institute failed to acknowledge any aspect of that major artistic movement — and, indeed, had as late as 1929 organized an exhibition in opposition to it — Renger-Patzsch's advocacy of photography as an independent medium of creative expression would be innovative and exciting to at least some of Seewald's students. The publication of his 1928 milestone book, *Die Welt Ist Schön (The World Is Beautiful)*, would call the old tenets of Pictorialism into question while challenging others to see anew what was true and beautiful in the world. In the end it would be a search for beauty that would engage equally sensitive artists like Henle throughout their lives.

The Munich Institute's excellent reputation was derived mainly from producing superior commercial and technologically advanced professionals, and in the end, neither of those major artistic movements appears to have played a significant part in the school's curriculum. While most of the faculty was concerned with instructing students in the photochemical and technological basics of photography — many of which Henle had skipped by entering in the second level — only Hanna Seewald and a few other faculty sought to instruct the students in the art of creative photography. As Seewald's existing photographs demonstrate, she was very much a straightforward artist who could consistently challenge her students to grow from within.[24] Henle would recall: "Her concept and my vision and ability to grasp her ideas brought me to the threshold of success. Most of my photographs were still in the then prevailing mood of 'Avant Garde.' Of course, we could not at that time relate any pictures to that term. It was simply our way of seeing, and Hanna Seewald never lost much time to bore us with philosophical explanations — golden rules and theories, which were of little importance to the creative mind. Her aim in teaching us was to make us see. This was an approach I had been longing for and I realized that our aims were identical."[25]

In the end she also saved his academic neck. During his student days, Fritz had begun to investigate other professional dimensions of photography. In 1931 he saw the first publication of his photography in a periodical, when Fritz Goro, then editor of the *Münchner Illustrierte*, purchased and ran his photograph of a policeman in the rain on the Odeons-Platz. In March Fritz was approached by the North German Lloyd steamship line and hired to photograph a two-week Mediterranean tour. He decided to take the risk of skipping out of school, trading the cold and rain of Munich to explore the sunny world

18 Among the many contemporaneous and future photographers who specialized — though not with Henle's exclusivity — in Rollei imagery would be such masters as Phillipe Halsman, Arthur Rothstein, Ewing Krainin, Ozzie Sweet, Andreas Feininger, Werner Bischof, Brett Weston, Joseph Breitenbach, Joe Munroe, Toni Schneiders, Peter Gowland, Ernst Haas, Peter Basch, David Bailey, Richard Avedon and Helmut Newton.

19 James Abbe, Jr. "The Reflex Is Versatile." *U.S. Camera*, August 1951: 76.

20 Fritz Henle. *Fritz Henle's Guide to Rollei Photography*. New York & London, The Studio Publications Inc. in association with Thomas Y. Crowell, 1956: 55.

21 H.M. Kinzer. "Fritz Henle's Figure Studies." *Photography*, May 1954: 132.

22 Helmut Gernsheim. "Fritz Henle." Typescript translation of his article for *Foto Magazin*, 1989: [2].

23 Herbert Keppler. "How Peter Basch and Fritz Henle use creative Composition and Cropping." *Modern Photography*, April 1956: 61.

24 *Hanna Seewald*. Munich, Bayerische Staatslehranstalt für Photographie, 1989.

25 *Op. cit.: Time—Exposures*: 10.

of the Near East and the Mediterranean. He departed from Genoa and traveled for two weeks in Egypt, the Middle East and Greece, depicting life aboard the luxury liner as well as photographing many new sights of Old World lands and peoples, including Jerusalem, the Great Pyramid and the Acropolis.[26] He returned with a sizeable paycheck, great memories of distant places, an overwhelming desire to make travel photography a significant aspect of his future profession and, most importantly, an expanded portfolio of outstanding prints.

He also returned to big trouble. His unexcused absence of a number of weeks had been discovered and landed him in danger of immediate expulsion from the Institute. He was swiftly called into Director Sprol's office and asked to explain himself. Seewald supported her prize pupil and suggested that in his own defense he show his new photographs from the liner tour. The portfolio, together with her persuasive argument, saved Henle, and he was permitted to complete his studies. On July 15 he graduated at the top of his class, receiving the *Preis-Diplom* from the Institute.

Even as Fritz was finishing up his studies, fate intervened, when his sister, Annemarie, met and showed his photographs to the eminent art historian Clarence Kennedy.[27] An avid photographer and student of light and sculpture,[28] Kennedy, besides being on the art history faculty of Smith College, was also the school's director of its division of graduate studies in Europe. He and his wife, Ruth, were the recipients of a Guggenheim Fellowship for 1931–32 to photograph classical sculptures and architecture in Florence and around the Toscana region of Italy. As it happened Kennedy was looking for a photographer-assistant to head up his team, and based upon the quality and vision demonstrated in Fritz's photographs of the Great Pyramid in Egypt and the Acropolis in Athens, he offered the new graduate that important position.

By the early autumn Fritz Henle was in Florence, living in the tower of an old *podere* (farmhouse), the Poggio Imperiale — which was also the home of the Kennedys — on the Via San Felice a Ema, on the southern hill overlooking the city. More than a mere documentarian, Clarence Kennedy was a precise and careful artist — working chiefly with an 11 x 14–inch view camera in order to capture every exquisite detail of classical sculptures, friezes and facades. He would examine each piece in detail, judging what new detail or viewpoint he wished to capture, erecting whatever scaffolding and specialized lighting might be needed, cleaning all surfaces, and then, taking all other aspects of framing, focusing and exposure into account, he would create innovative renderings that no previous photographer had ever captured successfully. Henle worked right at his side, studying his techniques and learning the infinite patience (exposures could often last up to an hour or more) that such methodical but exciting work could engender. Fritz also supervised the two native lab assistants (from whom he also learned his fourth language, Italian) and oversaw all the negative processing and print production firsthand. In order to assist Ruth Kennedy with her work on the painter Alesso Baldovinetti, he also became expert at copying paintings and frescoes as well.

While Clarence Kennedy's perfectionism and artistry aided Henle's maturity, he was most impressed with the historian's kindness and humanity, which he felt also added to the special vitality of his photographs.[29] The Kennedys were stimulating conversationalists as well as enthusiastic and well-educated teachers. (Henle always recalled that the first time he heard the music of Stravinsky was when it came wafting into his *podere* from the windows of the Kennedys' rooms.) Evenings were spent largely with dinner and conversation with their friends and other art students. One of the students, a Mrs. Scoville, gave Henle his first prints sales when she saw his work at the Kennedy home and arranged to purchase more than 80 prints. He also met and briefly romanced another art student, Margaret Arnstein, whose father, the American philanthropist Leo Arnstein, would soon prove to be of important assistance to the young photographer.

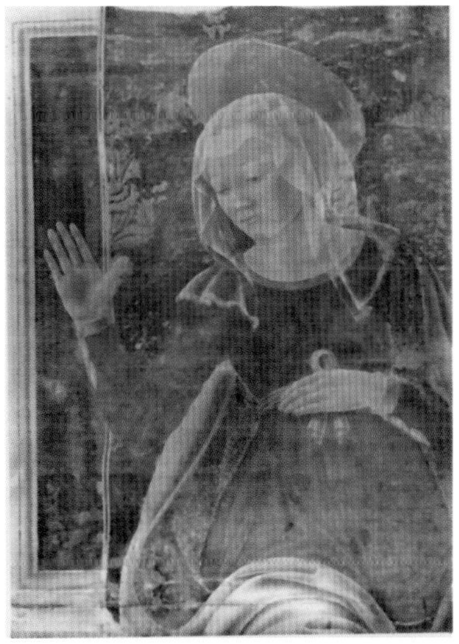

Fritz Henle. Copy of a detail of the Madonna from a work by Baldovinetti in the Basilica della Santissima Annunziata, Florence. 1931. An example of the fine precision copy work that Henle and his team did for Ruth and Clarence Kennedy.

On weekends or days off, Fritz never rested. He and his new Rolleiflex were often out touring the city or the surrounding countryside. He purchased a bicycle, christened it *Giovanni* — the name of Florence's patron saint — and pedaled off as far as a day's round-trip travels could take him. At other times he also was able to talk the housekeeper into letting him ride along with her on her motorbike as she ran errands around the region. He was even able to print some of his local views and sell them to such major Italian periodicals as *Illustrazione Toscana*. And, shortly before his time was up, Henle also arranged to travel to Rome, adding photographs of both the old and the new city to his ever-growing portfolio.

As the Smith College/Guggenheim program drew to a close, Fritz said farewell to his mentors and friends. The year with the Kennedys had become a second education for him, as he not only was exposed to a new land and culture but also was able to expand his knowledge and experience in art and art history, photographic technique, and the Italian language. He also made many new friends and future contacts and, of course, created with his Rolleiflex some more outstanding photographs in the bargain. As he departed for home he "began to realize how interrelated the art forms are with my own concept to express myself. Without the harmony of music, life seemed empty to me... Photography is a medium which can be learned by millions. But to master the medium with all its intricacy and to relate to it with one's deep emotions — this shows the master."[30]

The directness and clarity of his photographic vision, which he had recognized during his disappointing apprenticeship under Schnieding, had been reinvigorated by his years with Seewald and

26 The firm would publish a number of his photographs later that year in its book, *Kreuzfahrt in Mittelmeer*, as well as a number of the company's advertising brochures.

27 Annemarie Henle, who would receive her doctorate in art history in 1932 from the University of Heidelberg, was at that time in the process of becoming a postgraduate exchange student in the museum program taught by Paul Sachs at Harvard University's Fogg Art Museum.

28 Kennedy's 1924 Ph.D. dissertation from Harvard was entitled *The Effect of Lighting on Greek Sculpture*.

29 Years later Henle's works would be included in both their publications: Clarence Kennedy's seven volume masterwork, *Studies in the History and Criticism of Sculpture*, and Ruth Kennedy's book, *Alesso Baldovinetti: A Critical and Historical Study*.

30 *Op. cit.: Time — Exposures*: 14–15.

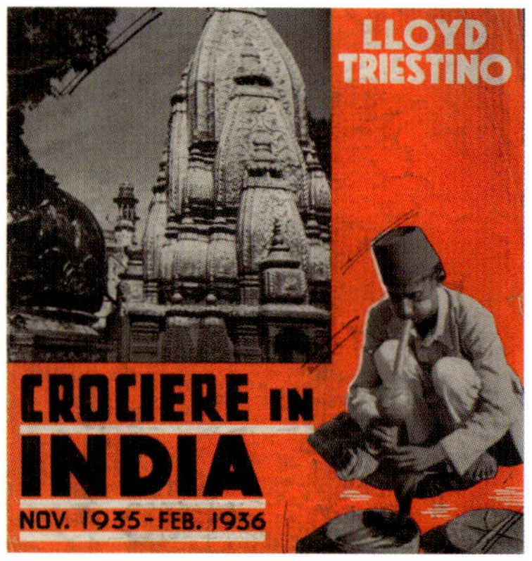

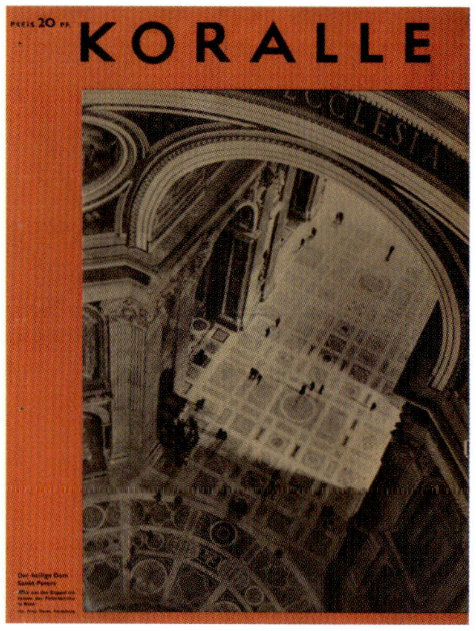

Lloyd Triestino. *Crociere in India. Nov. 1935 – Feb. 1936.* Advertising brochure. 1935. Front cover, featuring Henle's photographs from an earlier season's voyage.

Fritz Henle. "Der Helige Dom Sankz Peters." *Koralle.* Paris. ca. 1934. Front cover.

Kennedy. He was leaving old traditions behind and discovering newer levels of luminosity and simplicity upon which he could build in the future: "...Photographers, whose acquaintance I had made, were buried in a bewildering kind of romanticism and unrealism. Their pictures were exquisitely composed and lighted and their technic was without any fault. But those pictures were not photographs. By every means of softening, by strange looking paper surfaces and rather complicated printing technics their pictures were made to resemble etchings or soft-colored paintings. Photography since its first start, when Octavio Hill [David Octavius Hill] and [Eugene] Atget made their beautifully simple pictures, had lost its way by force methods.

"To me these methods led to a dead end as they were dishonest and weak. But there were new ways for discovery after this period of romantic photography which were leading to entirely new finds and back to reality and the manifold but simple ways of life."[31]

Although Henle would return to his family and friends in Heidelberg, the Florence fellowship of 1931–32 would mark the beginning of what he would come to call his *Wander-Jahre*. In comparison with the revolutionary culture of Munich or the classical elegance of Florence, Heidelberg must have seemed a much more staid and traditional old university town. Whether to satisfy his youthful exuberance or just to have an affordable means of transportation, Fritz purchased his first automobile, an open four-seat Baby Austin upon which he bestowed the name of his old Italian bicycle, *Giovanni*. In the process of learning to drive he would become quite the terror of the residents of the lower Bergstrasse; years later he would refer to this particularly youthful personality manifestation as the "Death-defying race driver of Heidelberg."

He continued to practice his art locally and to make many more prints from the negatives he had produced on his earlier travels. He would see his first photographs to be published in books — Heinrich Kreisel's *Deutsche Land, Deutsche Kunst* (1934) and Manfred Schneider's *Rom* (1935). Even more significantly, however, he rediscovered the illustrated German and European press — which had undergone a revival starting in the 1920s, reflecting a public thirst for more and more photographs. Until the rise of Nazism would turn the German picture press into a much more propagandist medium in the later 1930s, Henle was quite successful in marketing his travel photographs — whether as single images or brief picture stories — to a growing number of photo-illustrated magazines and newspapers.[32] And, as his list of contributions to those publications grew, so did his name and reputation as a dependable and highly creative master of the camera.

While Fritz Henle's *Wander-Jahre* may have been naturally motivated by his youthful confusion over which of the seemingly endless dimensions of the photographic profession to pursue, he was also growing more alarmed about the state of affairs in his own country. By 1933 Hitler had become chancellor of Germany and the Nazi party was on the rise. Henle and his family did not wish to see their nation decline into chaos, and it was perhaps inevitable that the photographer should set his sights abroad in the hope of getting away from the worsening political situation in his home nation.

As a temporary solution he worked from 1934 to 1936 as a photographer in advertising and promotion for the Lloyd Triestino line, while continuing to freelance and publish his photographs in the German illustrated press. In late 1934 he traveled on its newest ship, *Victoria*, on a four-month trip to India and Ceylon, photographing not only the boat and its passengers but, because his images would ultimately be used to sell the destination as well as the passage, the views and people of those ancient lands. With the close assistance of Narendra Naik, a very good Hindu friend who also had been his fellow classmate at the Munich Institute, he was able to travel throughout the country and gain access to the entire spectrum of Indian life, from the grandest palaces and sacred temples to the smallest villages and homes of the native people. Naik and Henle cemented their old friendship, and despite the fact that the photographer never was able to return, they remained faithful correspondents for many years to come.

Lloyd Triestino was very pleased with Henle's work, employed many of his images throughout the company's 1935 advertisements and brochures, and planned upon using him again in the next travel season to show off the latest travel package to the land of Germany's newest ally, Japan. In order to prepare for the assignment Henle had to deal with the growing bureaucracy that the Nazis were employing throughout the nation. He was able to obtain the new *Deutsches Reich Reisepass*, which enabled German citizens to travel outside of the country (and which he first tested out with shorter assignment work and holidays in Switzerland and northern Italy). He also renewed his visa to visit British India and finally obtained a six-month Japanese transient visa from Tokyo.

By the late fall of that year he had made the passage on the Lloyd liner, journeying through Singapore and on to Tokyo. He would spend the next four months first exploring Japan and then extending his visit on to China[33] and briefly into Korea. His fascination and curiosity carried him past most language and cultural barriers in both nations, as his Rolleis — which also attracted a great deal of attention — carefully recorded and interpreted all aspects of both the ancient and the modern Orient. He was able to gain access to everything — from ancient temples to modern military schools, and into both public bathhouses and private shrines — and he produced "hundreds of pictures without the assistance and advice of editors and art directors. I followed my own ideas and impressions and the people never refused this rather young man with the

31 Fritz Henle. "Pattern and Photography." *U.S. Camera*. April 1941: 45.

32 Examples in Fritz Henle's clippings books from that era number in the hundreds.

33 Adolf Henle had, as a young doctor, worked for years in China, and Fritz had always been curious to see the nation that had figured in some of his early tales.

small black box."[34] He was even able to arrange and make large (40 x 40 inches) prints for his first one-man exhibition at the Mitsubishi Department Store in Tokyo.

Upon his return from China, his gracious hosts in Tokyo, the photographer Yônosuke Natori[35] and his German-born wife, had to deliver him the cable bearing the sad news that his father had died. Henle canceled his travel plans for Bali, immediately arranged passage, and returned to Heidelberg, knowing that he would never again be able to share his new photographs and his travel stories with Adolf. The romance and adventure of his *Wander-Jahre* seemed to be concluding on a very sad note, and he knew that he had to see to family duties involving his father's estate and his mother's future. Even more alarmingly, he was returning to a homeland that was becoming more alien and hostile to him than many of the foreign lands he had visited during those years.

By 1936 Nazi Germany was transforming itself into a militaristic power on the world stage. German life was becoming more restricted and regulated, and for Henle, to whom Freedom had become his guiding principle, the situation was becoming more and more intolerable. Worse still, the Nazis' Nuremberg Laws of 1935 were in effect, attempting to define just who was and was not a true Aryan and broadening the restrictions upon Jews and other disfavored minorities. Although Henle had been raised in the Christian faith of his mother, he knew that there was Jewish blood on his late father's side of the family, and by 1936 the Nazi race theorists were debating what degree of mixed ancestry constituted a *Mischlinge* and what should be done with them in order to protect the purity of the race. For Henle the dangers of possibly being drafted into the German army or, even worse, being subject to the tide of growing racial and religious prejudice was too horrible to contemplate. As his sister and brother had already done, he resolved to find a way out of Germany; as it would turn out, photography would supply him with the solution.

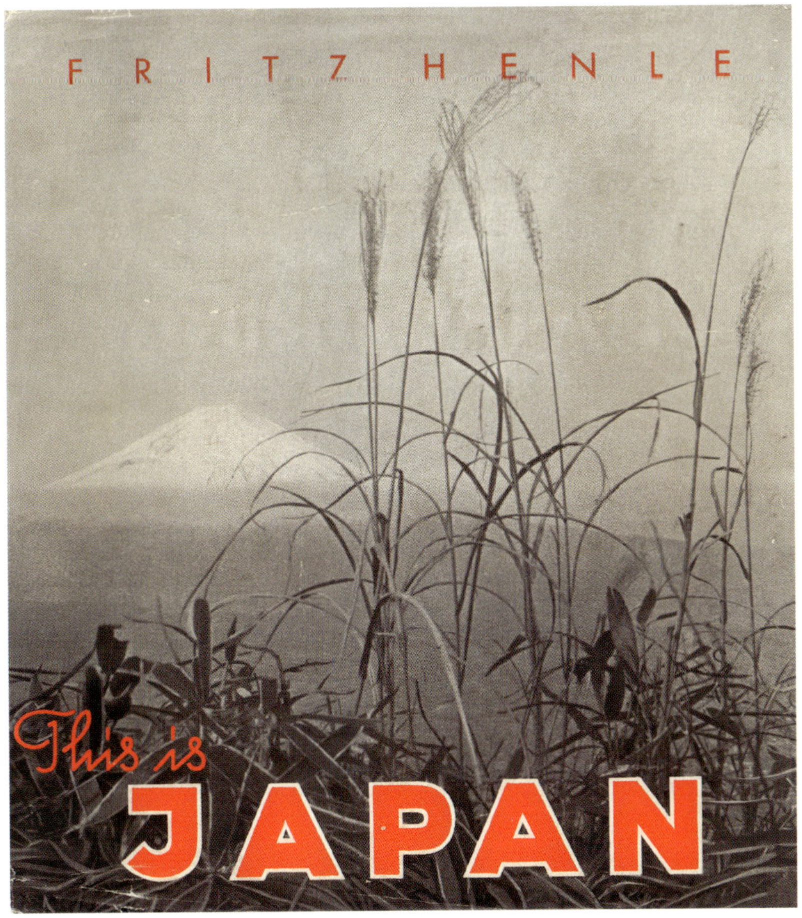

As soon as he was able, Fritz Henle set out for Braunschweig, where he personally introduced himself and his photographs to Paul Franke and Reinhold Heidecke. The portfolio of his elegant prints taken all over the world with their very own Rolleiflex cameras excited them both, and Franke immediately decided to publish some of the work. He covered all expenses for the publication and contacted an old friend, Dr. Walter Heering, who headed up his own publishing firm in Harzburg. Within three months Fritz Henle had published the first major book of his work, *Das Ist Japan*, with an American edition scheduled to follow in the next year.

The Japan book would become a solid, critical success and help establish Henle as a rising photographer. As the prestigious *Magazine of Art* would observe, the book was "...really a visual survey of the country and its people... But...it is the interpretation of the thing surveyed which changes. Henle's survey is not simply a collection of 'views' on the order of post cards, nor is it a collection of pictures of 'spots' that the tourist might be expected to visit and admire. It is a survey of the land and the people, and as usual the Germans have a word for it: *Kulturlandschaft*, the cultural landscape in its broadest sense... In this type of survey the interpretation of the characters and the scenes is of greatest importance: for it is in the unconscious gesture, of the deftly chosen and delineated character that the deepest aspirations of individuals and their culture are expressed most clearly."[36]

Great reviews aside, however, *Das Ist Japan* would have an even more significant value for the photographer. For, with that new tangible record of his talent and accomplishments, Fritz, tapping into the firm's interest in a larger American market, next was able to secure an agreement with Franke and Heidecke to publish a second volume, to be called *Life in America*. And that meant that Fritz Henle, published author and photographer, now had the backing of a major German industrial firm and a legitimate commission to travel to the United States of America.

The departure for America was a busy undertaking. First, Henle saw to the safety and security of his mother, Tina, and the family home in Heidelberg.[37] In August he obtained a temporary visitor visa from the American Embassy in Berlin. Although the bureaucracy of obtaining a six-month travel visa from the Nazi au-

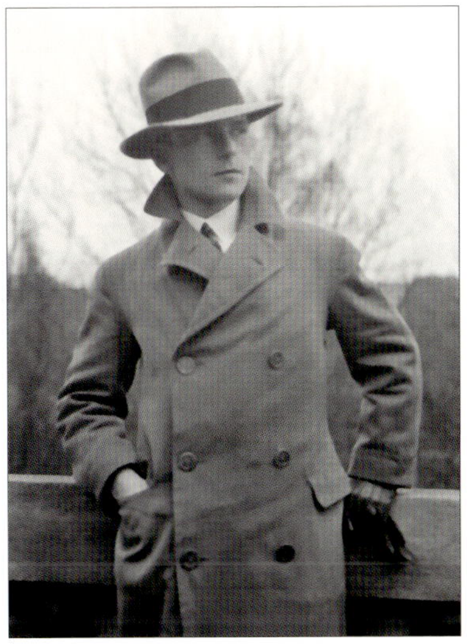

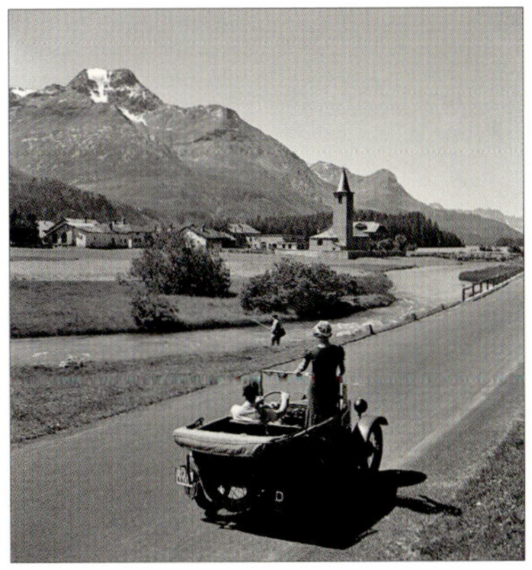

This Is Japan. English Edition. Harzburg: 1937. Front dust jacket.

Fritz Henle. Self-portrait as the young gentleman-photographer, ca. 1933.

Photographer Unidentified. Fritz Henle in his Austin in Germany, ca. 1934.

34 *Op. cit.: Time — Exposures*: 23.

35 Natori also had been a student in Munich, which was probably where he and Henle first met. Although he worked in Japan as a photojournalist throughout his life, the sale of his 1936 Berlin Olympic photographs to *LIFE* would make him that magazine's first Japanese contract photographer.

36 F.A. Gutheim. "Shadows on Celluloid." *Magazine of Art*, March 1937: 169.

37 The old university town was judged to be an important historical city and throughout World War II would be spared the later Allied bombing that blanketed the surrounding industrial cities of the Ruhr Valley. Tina Henle and the family home would be unharmed.

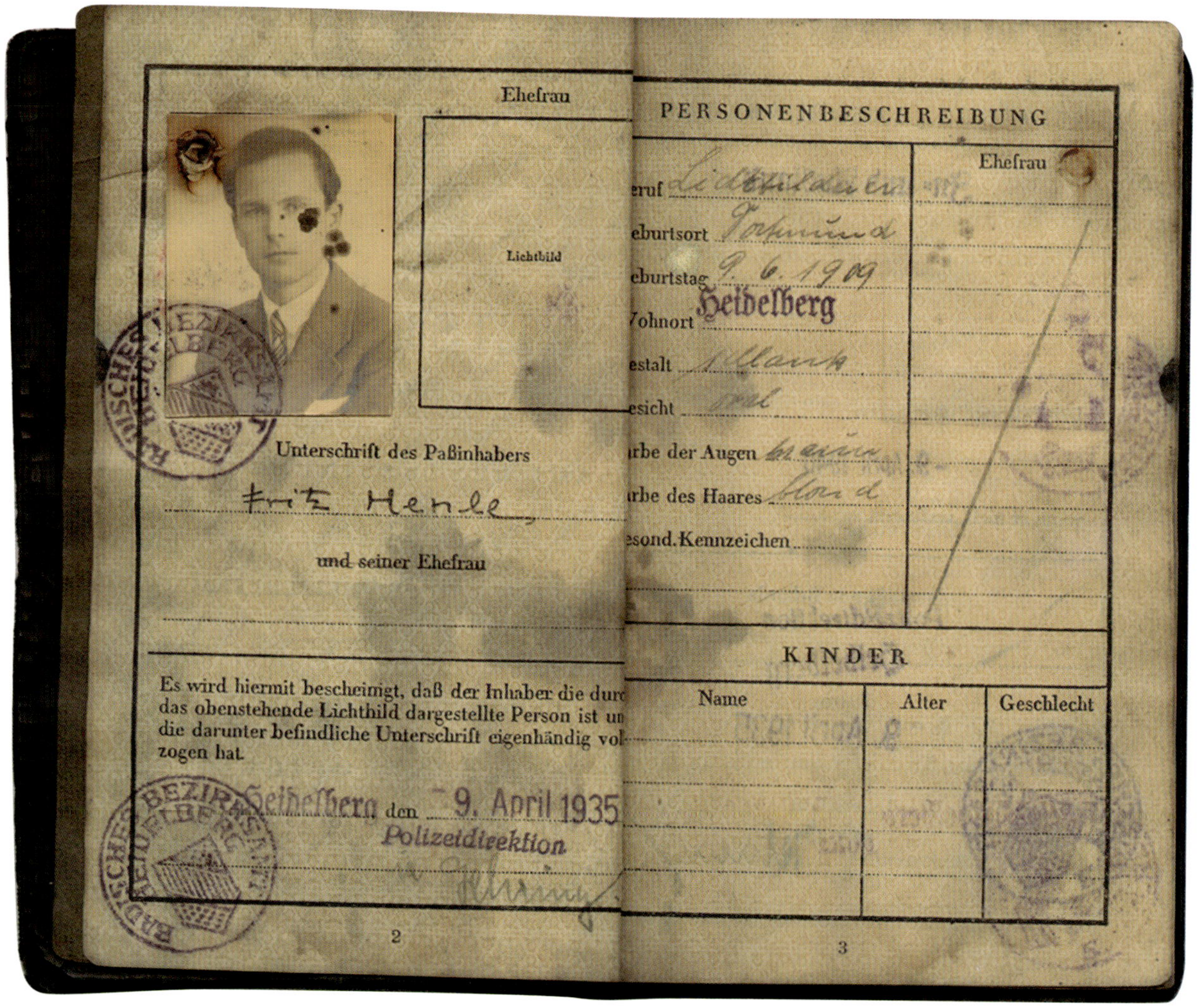

Deutsches Reich. Reisepass Nr. 420, issued to Fritz Henle, April 9, 1935.

thorities in Heidelberg included a somewhat terrifying inquisitional interview. Fritz, with his Japan book in hand and the official backing of Franke and Heidecke, was able to secure all the proper papers. He bade his mother farewell and set sail on the North German Lloyd liner *Europa* from Hamburg in early September. It was not until the ship had pulled away from the dock and was sailing out of the port that Henle felt the tears of relief fill his eyes.

It is amazing to contemplate all that Fritz Henle would accomplish in the next few months following his arrival in New York City on September 11, 1936. Despite the fact that the United States was in the midst of fighting off the Great Depression, it was almost as if the energy and industry of Henle's new home was immediately absorbed into his very being. With only fifty dollars in his pocket "and a lot of hope"[38] he secured a small apartment on Bank Street in the Village. Bearing copies of the new September issue of *Fortune* — a special edition featuring many of his photographs of Japan — Henle worked his way into editorial offices and began receiving assignments. In addition, he accepted a private commission from Margaret Arnstein's aid organization to travel to Logan, West Virginia, and document the poor working and living conditions for miners and their families in the coalfields.

He joined the Black Star picture agency[39] and obtained the only agent he would ever have, Kurt Kornfeld, with whom he would remain until 1942.[40] The agency, though only a year old, was an energetic one, employing a number of young photographers and keeping them on daily around-the-clock picture assignments. Andreas Feininger, who lasted only a year with the organization, called it "a brutal job...the hardest possible school for any young photographer — a sink or swim proposition...."[41] In contrast, Henle found the agency work invigorating and had no trouble staying with the firm for more than half a decade. To further facilitate his work, Fritz also solved his immediate problem of having accessible studio and darkroom facilities by becoming a member of a consortium of ten photographers, organized by Ewing Krainin, that shared common work spaces encompassing the entire top floor of a skyscraper at 538 Fifth Avenue.

He even found time to organize and mount two exhibitions: his photographs of India at the Cleveland Art Museum, and his photographs of Japan and China in the lobby galleries at Rockefeller Center. The latter show, entitled Photographs of the East by F.J. Henle, was his first one-person exhibition in New York City, and he utilized the small publication that accompanied the show to state, in the third person, his philosophy: "Clarity, simplicity, reality: one must use some such portmanteau catchwords to evoke the essence of F.J. Henle's photographic art. Here there is no retouching, no exaggeration, no distortion, for Henle believes that to the seeing eye and the obedient lens Nature provides forms strange and wonderful enough in their immediate simplicity. His methods are 'usual'; his results unusual in their combination of integrity with precision... The best of his work uncovers psychological depths, particularly in the treatment of the human face and figure, and projects a message to the emotions of the beholder."[42]

In the big city for less than two months, Fritz Henle was energetically establishing his name and building his professional career in America. In addition to the commercial opportunities that were available for a vigorous and creative photographer, there was the ever-changing face of New York City itself. Henle's enthusiasm for that urban canvas was marked by his enchantment with its people and places, and in later years he would still reflect that "Lower Manhattan has always had a fascination for me because of its incredible contrasts...it is almost impossible to keep my usual fast pace... There is a beauty in this immense contrast."[43] The new immigrant celebrated his attraction by hitting the streets to meet the people and drink in every aspect of the city's life and culture. And, of course, everywhere he went he took photographs.

During that period of intense work he, nonetheless, kept his focus upon becoming a permanent resident of his new land. He filed all the necessary application forms to begin his process for U.S. citizen-

38 *Op. cit.*: Newhall.

39 Black Star Publishing Co., 420 Lexington Ave., New York, N.Y.

40 Black Star was founded in 1935 by Kornfeld and two other fellow German émigrés, Ernest Mayer and Kurt Zafransky, all of whom had also fled the rise of Nazism.

41 Andreas Feininger. *Andreas Feininger, Photographer.* New York, Harry N. Abrams, 1986: 76.

42 *Photographs of the East by F.J. Henle.* New York City: Burleigh Books and Black Star Publishing, [1936]: unpaged.

43 Fritz Henle. "Travel & Camera." *U.S. Camera*, July 1956: 50.

ship, obtaining an affidavit of support from Clarence Kennedy and the official sponsorship of Leo Arnstein, Margaret's highly influential father. With the clock ticking away on his temporary visa and the process of immigration into the U.S. requiring him to begin a six-month residency outside of the country, Henle was determined not to return to Germany. In November he purchased a Ford V-8 (which he christened *Narendra*, after his Hindu friend), found a traveling companion — a British banker from Wall Street named Norman Pickels — and set off on an adventure-filled road trip across the American South. On November 30 he left Texas and entered Mexico at the border town of Nuevo Laredo.

While Pickels quickly had enough of the journey and returned to Wall Street shortly after they reached Mexico City, Fritz became instantly fascinated with nation and, as he had done on all his previous travels, began to absorb the views and experiences of the country. He would traverse the country, visiting its larger cities as well as small villages, learning Spanish, and taking photographs of everything that attracted his hungry eye. In Coyoacan he sought out and befriended Diego Rivera and Frida Kahlo, photographing them and their home and studios, and traveling with them to various other sites. Although he never joined their more radical circle, he made many contacts and friends among the artistic community of Mexico and found that the time away from the United States passed quickly. On July 2 he and *Narendra* re-entered Texas at Laredo with a new U.S. Immigration Visa and immediately headed back East.

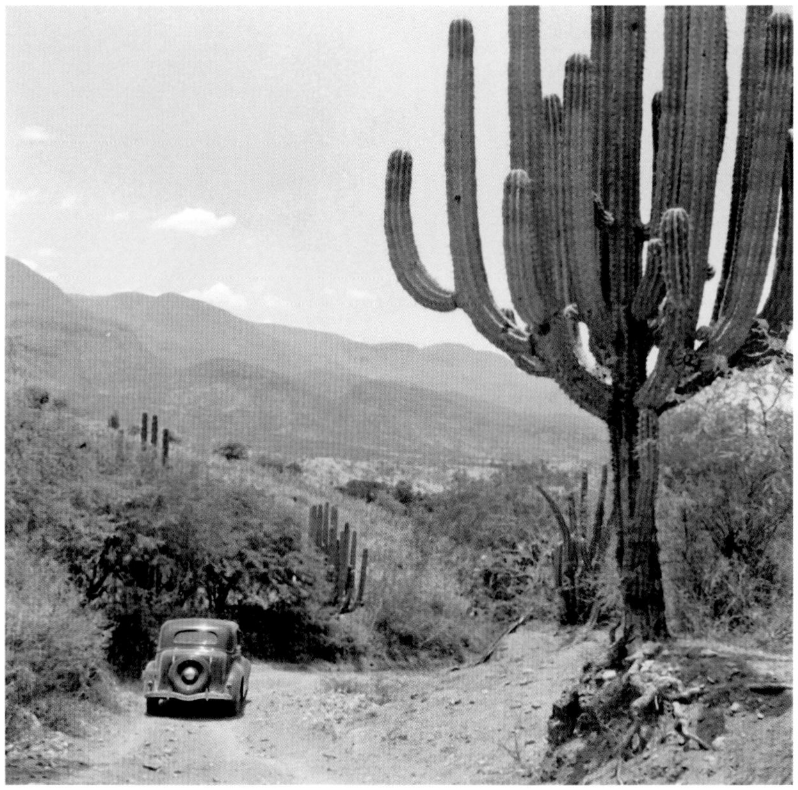

New York would become Henle's home for most of the next two decades, as well as the focal point of his professional photographic career. He would remain a freelancer for nearly all that time, preferring to work on a contracted assignment or commission rather than joining any permanent staff. In part that was because he always wanted to control the use and marketing of his work and, as a result, be able to utilize the vast body of his rapidly growing archive of imagery. He had determined from early on that his passion for photography would help guide his career and that he wanted always to be free to explore and take advantage of all avenues of the use and distribution of his works. Independence often comes with a high price, but Henle felt that it was worth paying that cost so that he could always follow his guiding principle of Freedom. In order to remain faithful to his art and also make a living, he would practice all forms of photography. For Fritz Henle the highest form of artistic expression lay within the constancy of his vision rather than adopting a false allegiance to any one particular style, discipline, or subject matter.

When he returned to New York City in the autumn of 1937, Henle began to pick up where he left off. Krainin had kept his place open in the photographers' consortium. He remained an active member of Black Star and accepted a number of independent assignments from Kornfeld. While developing his editorial contacts among many magazines throughout the city he was also able to sell many American and Mexican images to the picture press in Europe. Perhaps most exciting was the purchase of four of his prints by Beaumont Newhall, the new curator of photography at the Museum of Modern Art, for inclusion in MOMA's inaugural photography exhibition, Photography 1839–1937. It would mark the first acquisition of Henle's works by a major art museum.

As one would expect of any energetic and resourceful photographer, Henle was attracted to America's rising new magazine, *LIFE*, which had been founded in the previous year. Utilizing his 1936 work for *Fortune* to gain access to its parent company, he approached *LIFE*'s picture editors, Daniel Longwell and Joe Thorndike, and laid out his portfolio for their inspection. The picture magazine was growing rapidly in popularity and sales and was employing a number of notable photographers either on its staff or as associates, including fellow German and European refugees such as Alfred Eisenstaedt, Fritz Goro, Herbert Matter, Roman Vishniac and Andreas Feininger. Longwell and Thorndike admired Henle's work and agreed to hire him under his condition that he remain an associate photographer — working by assignment, paid per contract, and able to retain the copyright to all his work. Fritz would maintain an active association with the magazine for four years, seeing his work published primarily from August 1937 through August 1941 and participating in more than 50 picture stories and five front covers for his rapidly expanding résumé.

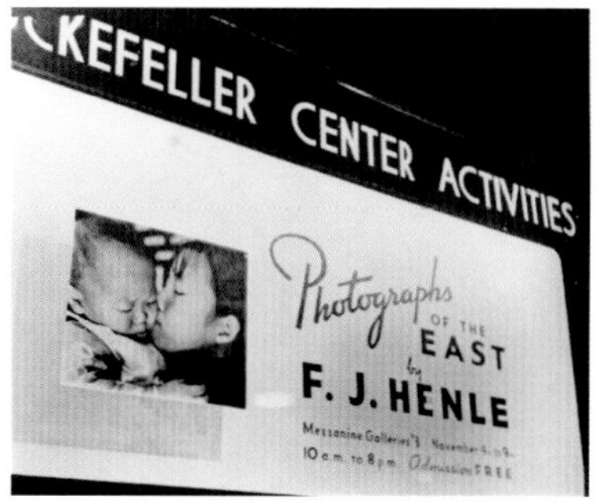

Fritz Henle. My Ford V8 in Mexico. 1937.

Fritz Henle. Title signage for Henle's first American one-man show at Rockefeller Center. November 1936.

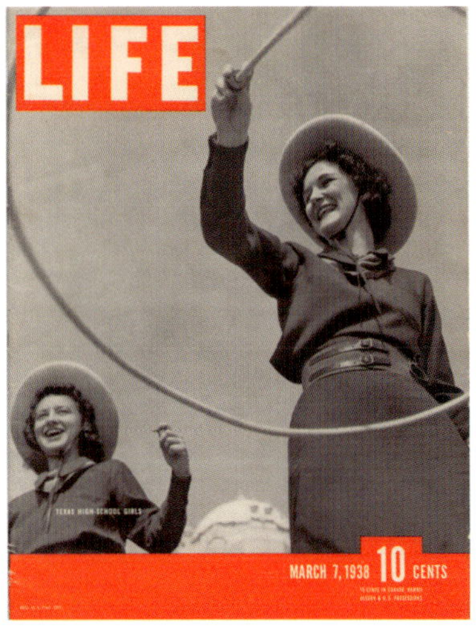

"Texas High-School Girls." *LIFE*. March 7, 1938. Front cover.

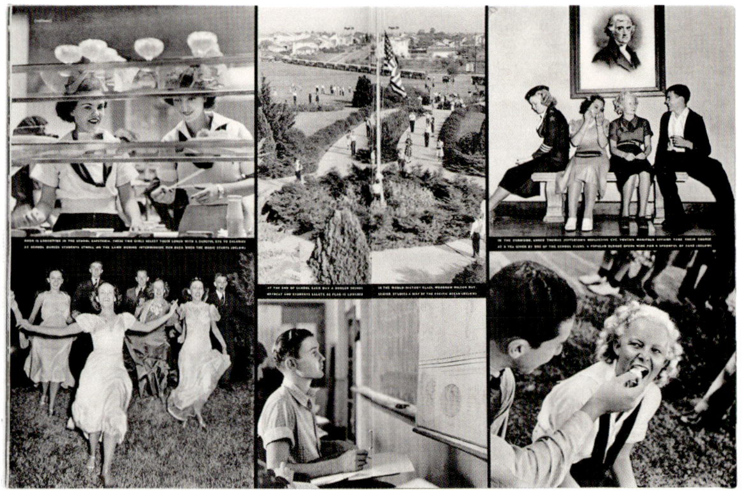

"One American High School...." *LIFE*. March 7, 1938. pp. 28–29.

Fritz Henle. *Atty Van Den Berg, Dancing "The Happy Maiden" Role*. 1939. One of a series of dance poses that Henle made for publicity purposes for his new wife, this particular photograph would see multiple publications in periodicals as varied as *Harper's Bazaar* and *U.S. Camera*.

Although many of his *LIFE* assignments were the customary light news or society fluff that typified a significant portion of every issue of the magazine, Henle also turned out some major picture stories for the editors during those years. As a newly arrived American immigrant he was assigned to document impressions from his perspective of a cross section of Manhattan by photographing people and scenes along the entire length of 52nd Street.[44] Early in the next year he journeyed to San Antonio, Texas, to depict the life of a typical American high school.[45] A joint fashion shoot with Alfred Eisenstaedt in 1938 — in which the photographers moved their models to an outdoor location at a Connecticut farm — proved to be highly successful and marked the rapid adoption of outdoor fashion work by other photographers.[46] Only an attempt to make him *LIFE*'s Hollywood photoreporter proved to be unsatisfactory. Henle's desire for freedom of coverage did not match the limited-access, press agent–controlled influence that the movie business sought over the picture magazines, and he was glad to see his six-month sojourn on the West Coast come to an end.[47] On any number and variety of other subjects throughout the United States, Fritz became known as a photographer who could deliver the goods with professionalism, consistent artistry and an unstoppable level of energy. Many years later he was still characterized as "Never still, never satisfied..."[48] On the streets of the city he may have cut a modestly distinctive figure — "Slight and boyish, he wanders among New York's skyscrapers hatless and with camera slung over his shoulder," as one editor characterized him[49] — but he continued to find himself in increasingly greater demand.

In 1938 Henle proposed to *LIFE*'s new picture editor, Wilson Hicks, that he be sent to Paris to photograph the city before Europe was plunged into war. The story was quickly and enthusiastically approved, and in May Henle departed on the British liner *Mauretania* for France. Although the *LIFE* Paris office was not excited by the project and did not assign a writer to him as it customarily should have, he took a room in an old city hotel and used the bathroom at night to develop the Rolleiflex's rolls of 120 film. The results were exciting, and for nearly three weeks Henle roamed the city, depicting the faces and scenes of a lifestyle and a culture that were fated soon to be changed. The richness of the resulting prints was equally striking, and he soon had the difficult but enviable task of editing the vibrant body of work down to a manageable number of prints for submission to the New York office.

When he returned in August he and Kornfeld were dumbfounded to find that the work was rejected and the story had been killed by *LIFE*. There was no explanation. No letter or editorial assessment accompanied the returned prints. It was a shattering experience for Henle and one for which he would never receive a satisfactory explanation, although he continued to contribute to *LIFE* until 1941. The package of prints and negatives of a vanishing Paris went into his safe. Years later Fritz could only reflect that: "Magazine photography, in the span of a few years, had become like a yo-yo, a tricky game in which I was never a good actor. My best weapon, as I learned through the years, was always my concept and the quality of my photography."[50]

Nonetheless, Fritz Henle and his émigré peers would have a profound impact upon American photojournalism by the midpoint of the twentieth century. Fellow photographers such as Eisenstaedt, André Kertész, Robert Capa, Cornell Capa, Andreas Feininger and

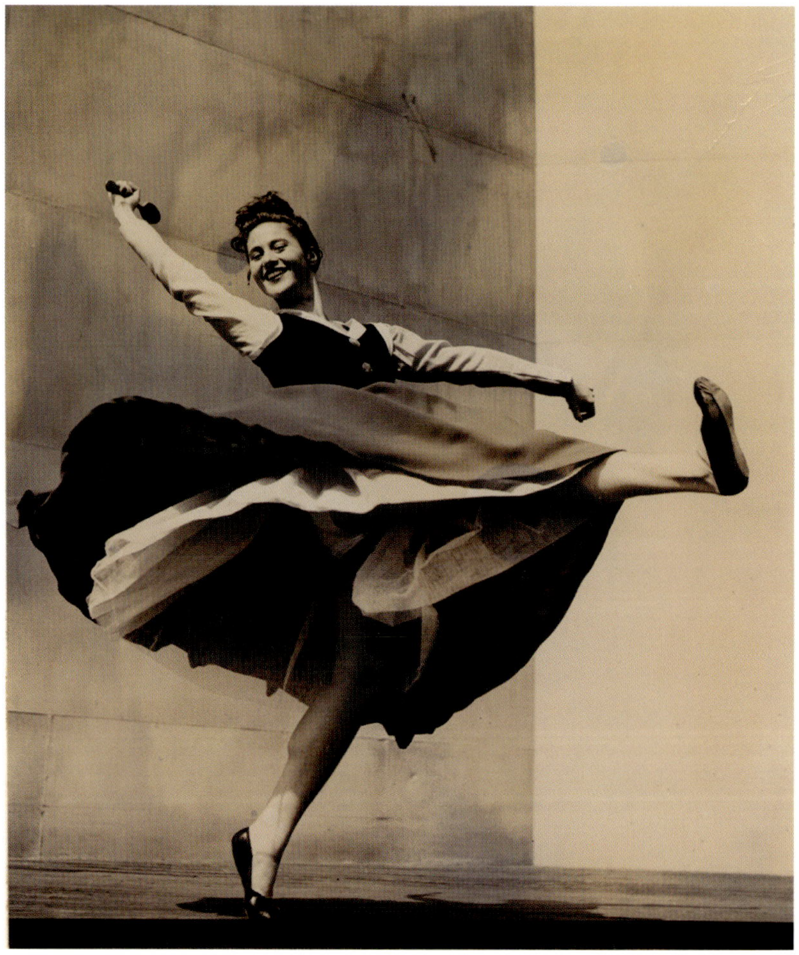

44 "Memo To: Walter Wanger, Subject: 52nd Street: Photographs for *LIFE* by Fritz Henle." *LIFE*, November 29, 1937: 64–67.

45 "One American High School: The Thomas Jefferson of San Antonio." *LIFE*, March 7, 1938: 22–29. For years afterward Wilson Hicks, who was Henle's later picture editor at *LIFE*, would use the high school shoot as a key example of an outstanding feature picture story.

46 Throughout his career Henle was often credited with creating outdoor and on-location fashion photography, but he was always careful to acknowledge the photographer who inspired him and first did it successfully — Martin Munkacsi.

47 The Hollywood beat would have the opposite effect upon other *LIFE* photographers; in fact, Henle's sometime-collaborator, Alfred Eisenstaedt, would thrive on such motion picture assignments.

48 "Henle's Best Over 40 Years In Album." *The St. Croix Avis*, April 3, 1974: [1 p.].

49 "Editor's Guest Book." *Harper's Bazaar*, August 1940: [1 p.].

50 *Op. cit.*: *Time — Exposures*: 31.

others had been exposed to the teaching, styles and news periodicals in post–World War I Europe. They brought those sensibilities to bear on the United States publishers and editors who employed them and were soon swiftly enriched by their experiences. The American revolution in pre–World War II photojournalism, fueled by the rise of many bold and distinctive picture magazines, thrived throughout the mid-twentieth century, and Fritz would become one of its most active and versatile participants. Henle was celebrated as "one of that group of European photographers who brought so much of photo-journalism, of interpretative reportage photography to this country in the 30's. He was in on the early developments in the technique of the picture story and his competence is shown by his all around camera ability."[51]

One important benefit that did arise from his *LIFE* work at that time came while he was on assignment in Hollywood, photographing the corps of the Joos European Ballet and Ballet Russe. While documenting the rehearsals and performances Henle met, courted and in 1938 married a Dutch ballerina, Atty Van Den Berg. They would move into a flat on Sutton Place, and Atty would quickly become one of Fritz's fashion and nude figure models. And she would eventually teach him his fifth language, Dutch.

Although Fritz's work with *LIFE* was gradually waning with the onset of the coming war, his professional résumé and portfolio always gained him many new assignments. As one exuberant American photo magazine would put it: "His first pictures...brought him instant recognition from critics and magazine editors. Here was a prophet of photography's coming of age. His pictures are free of bombastic photo-ideas and stereotyped composition rules."[52] Although the modest Fritz would often find such praise to be personally embarrassing, his impact on the American photography scene had become significant during that critical period.

Henle always turned down offers to join the photographic staff of any number of American magazines but his desire for independence in his work never resulted in the diminishment of assignments. Among the many periodicals that carried his work at that time were *Mademoiselle*, *Town and Country*, *Harper's Bazaar*, *Saturday Evening Post*, *Holiday*, *House & Garden*, *Collier's*, *Dance*, *Better Living*, *Glamour*, *Look*, and *Theatre Life*. And, with a number of front covers and articles, he also began contributing to the rapidly rising tide of American contemporary photography magazines, such as *U.S. Camera* and *Popular Photography*. As a 1942 survey on the young German émigré would note: "Fritz Henle's pictures appear time and again in magazines of major importance, never fail to catch one's eye by their vitality and freshness of approach. They give the feeling that the picture was taken at the right time, in the right place, by the right photographer."[53]

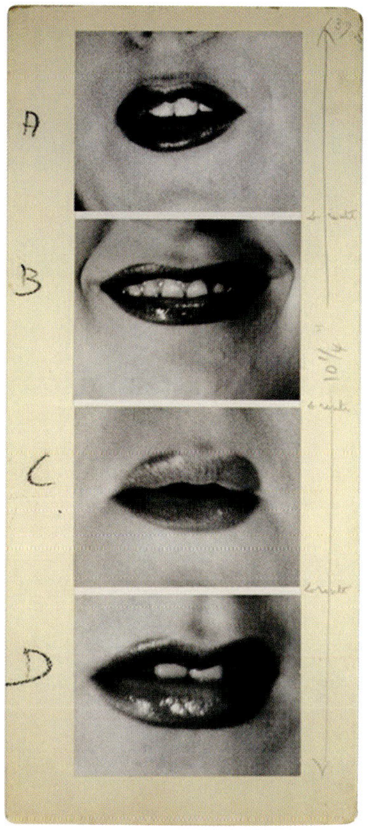

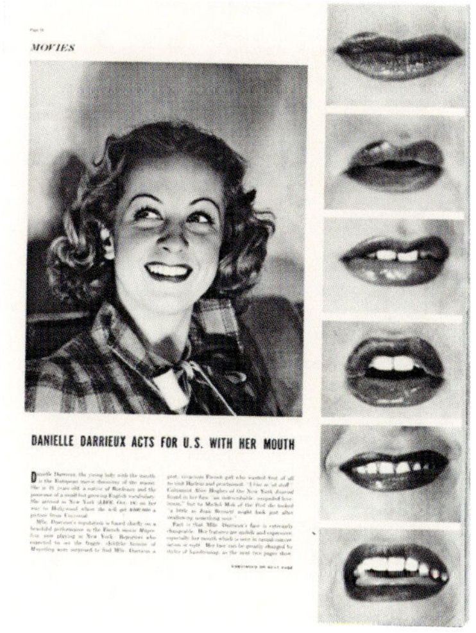

Fritz Henle. *The Lips of Danielle Darrieux I (A-D)*. 1937.

"Danielle Darrieux Acts for U.S. with Her Mouth." *LIFE*. October 25, 1937. p. 59.

Feeling that he must contribute to the war effort of his future homeland, Henle made the momentous decision in 1942 to suspend his freelance career. He left Black Star and Kurt Kornfeld, moved Atty into a new home in the suburban Westchester community of Millwood, New York, and joined the Office of War Information in Washington, D.C.[54] The OWI evolved out of the Farm Security Administration, Roy Stryker's legendary government agency that created some of the most outstanding photodocumentary work of America in the late 1930s. Utilizing the talents of such photographers as Carl Mydans, Russell Lee, Walker Evans and Dorothea Lange, Stryker's FSA had created an extensive and historic documentary portrait of America at the end of the Great Depression.

With the onset of World War II the agency evolved into the OWI and altered its mandate, becoming much more propagandistic in recording the life and times of an America that was changed by its entry into war. As it would be reported at the time, "More than any single group of people in the country the Office of War Information photographers have been watching this change... Their main job...is to present a factual story with the most factual medium that man has at his disposal. And within the limits of this responsibility they have, like all good members of their craft, given a certain individuality to their pictures, interpreted the story as through their own eyes."[55]

Fritz Henle joined a roster of other notable OWI photographers, such as Jack Delano, Esther Bubley, Gordon Parks, Howard Liberman and Howard R. Hollem, who would crisscross the country from coast to coast, continuing to build an historic photographic archive of the nation engaged in yet another critical era of change.

Just as he was embarking upon federal service, Fritz Henle received the extremely important news that he had become an American citizen. On December 2, 1942, the Justice Department issued the German émigré a Certificate of Naturalization, making him a full citizen of the United States of America. Even though his former homeland was engaged in a world war with his new one, Fritz had no doubts about the correctness of his decision and the six years of hard work that it had taken him to achieve his goal. He had attained a final measure of

51 Jacquelyn Judge, "Men Who Love Paris," *Popular Photography*, January 1947: 94.

52 "Simplicity is Henle's Keynote," *Minicam Photography*, May 1942: 57.

53 "Fritz Henle Photo-Globe-Trotter Settles for Fashion And The American Scene" ["Aces" series], *U.S. Camera*, February 1942: 59.

54 The coordinator of information at OWI, Frank Zachary, apparently knew Kurt Zafransky at Black Star. It is not known if Henle may have tapped into that network in order to obtain the OWI position, but he and Zachary must have had some sort of professional relationship, because both would end up working with Alexey Brodovitch at *Harper's Bazaar* after World War II.

55 Fred Knoop, "Photographers for Victory... The O.W.I. Photographers Show Democracy Working and Fighting," *Minicam Photography*, January 1943: 50.

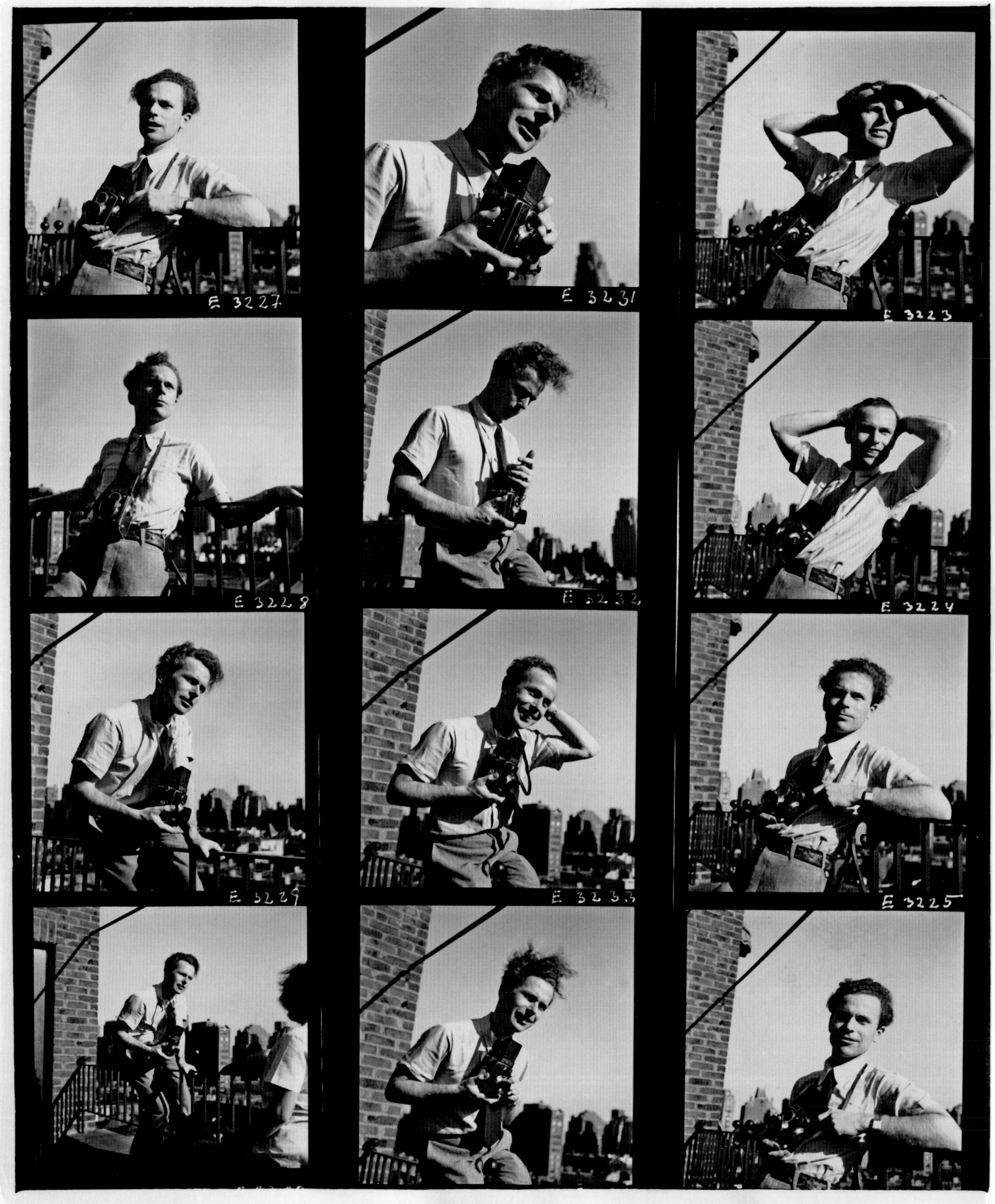

Hansel Mieth. Contact sheet of Fritz Henle in Manhattan. 1938.

the freedom he had long dreamt of and was resolved to continue to serve his new country throughout her time of great strife.

Between 1942 and 1945 Fritz Henle, OWI staff photographer, journeyed across America from assignment to assignment in his Buick station wagon, armed with his Rolleis and an extensive supply of film and gas coupons. His assignments ranged from victory gardens in New England to industrial plants in the West — with some of the shoots having a more precise focus than others. Many of his stories — such as those about nursing schools, family farms or a few on Mexico's military preparedness and industrial growth (which included some of his earliest color work) — resulted in insightful bodies of imagery, which he believed "like most of my work, has a lasting purpose."[56]

For the most part, however, Fritz saw the OWI years as ones of "great agony." Weeks of loneliness separated from Atty were often combined with many hours of driving and far too brief time periods in which he was forced to hurriedly finish one assignment and then depart to make another. His health suffered and he no longer slept as soundly. Perhaps worst of all was that, unlike with his other professional work, he had to send his undeveloped film back to Washington for processing. He frequently was unable to see his own work for months at a time — thereby lacking any visual feedback and being

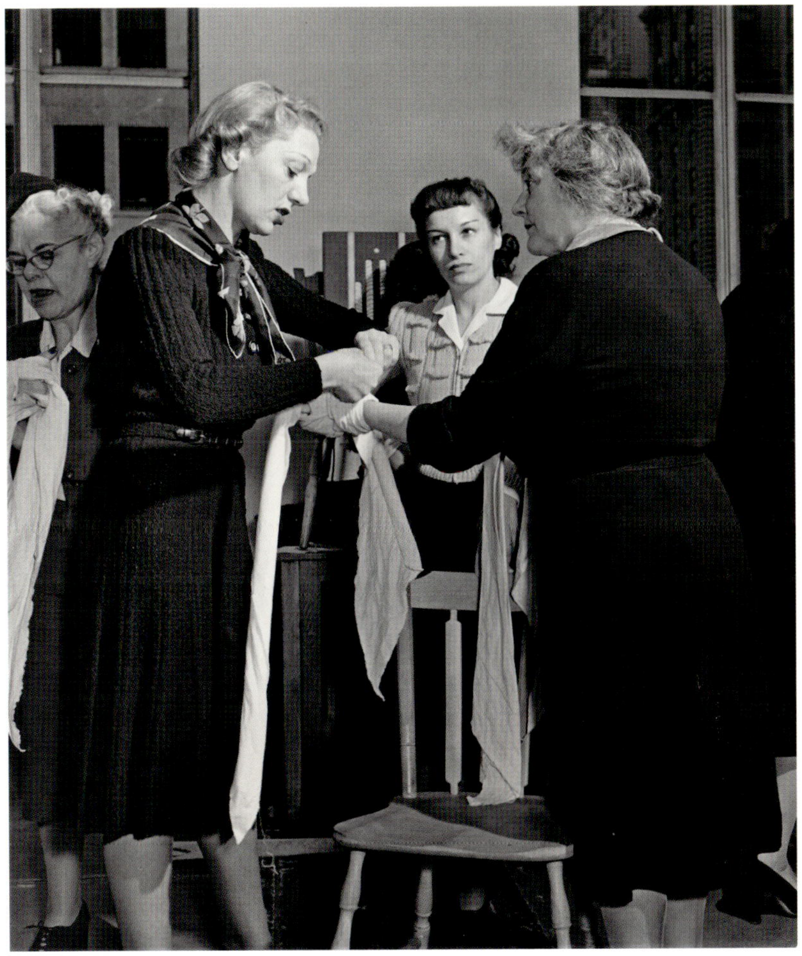

unable to play any part in its editorial use. The three years of government work resulted in some singularly fine images — including such classics as his *Grand Canyon* and the iconic masterpiece *Freedom: Yucca Plant*. In fact, the desert plant photograph remains his all-time favorite image, not for its beauty alone but also because it came to symbolize his desire to survive: "I was able to express my hope and ability to overcome near desperation."[57] In the final analysis, Henle was relieved to complete his service with the OWI at the close of World War II.

Fritz Henle's tenure with the OWI has often been overlooked by most photohistorians — and not infrequently by the photographer himself — as insignificant in comparison with the larger oeuvre of his entire career. It has also been used as conclusive evidence that he was not a social documentarian, unlike others who had preceded him in the FSA. Such summaries, however, belie the insightful work that he did earlier for Margaret Arnstein among the West Virginia coal miners or such key OWI photo-essays as that on the education of nurses during the war. Nor do they account for the cultural shift within that government agency itself, for the OWI had adopted a much more overtly propagandistic agenda than its FSA predecessor. In retrospect it does not seem all that surprising that the nature of that style of survey work would have caused far greater levels of tension and exhaustion for the independent-minded Henle.

Fritz's best work on all varieties of subjects, from the industrial to the social, was founded upon two absolute requirements: the need to know the broad guidelines around to which to organize a story and the time required in any level of storytelling to establish a bond with his subjects. Shooting fashions could be managed speedily — and, in fact, Henle had a reputation among fashion editors as being a very fast shooter. While he frequently shot quickly and economically, he rarely took more than one or two 12-exposure rolls of film for each documentary situation or fashion setup. But getting to truly know the people he was going to photograph at a calm and natural pace was always Fritz's primary methodology for producing memorable portraits and for subsequently telling the stories of the individuals whose lives, work and even dreams were important to relate to any and all viewers. Mood and character — as well as the necessary time to find and record them — were among the critical elements that he required in order to establish his story and build an effective photo sequence of images. The pace and superficial requirements that OWI demanded of its photographers did not match the talents of a photographer who would later assess himself thusly: "I'm not a great explorer... And I don't just happen to find my pictures."[58]

There were a few bright moments during that relatively dark period. Nineteen forty-three would see the publication of his second book, *China*, incorporating the images he made while on his 1935–36

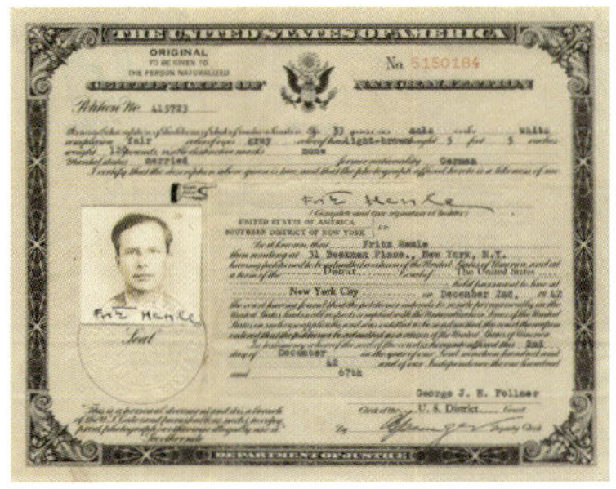

Fritz Henle. OWI: Gertrude Lawrence Applying Bandages in a First Aid Class, New York City. ca. 1943.

U.S. Department of Justice. Certificate of Naturalization No. 5150184, issued to Fritz Henle, December 2, 1942.

56 "Fine Pictures." T.J. Maloney, ed. *The U.S.A. at War: U.S. Camera 1944. Photographs selected by Commander Edward Steichen, U.S.N.R.* New York, ca1943: 92.

57 *Op. cit.*: Guttilla: 12.

58 Barnett Bildersee. "The Camera Eye: On making photo-essays." [Periodical unidentified.] 1948: unpaged.

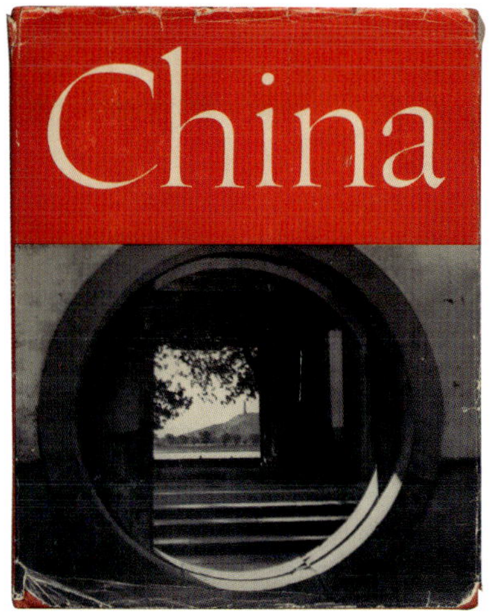

China. New York: 1943.
Front dust jacket.

commission for Lloyd Triestino. Even more significantly, at least to his wounded heart, was a communication he received in New York City in August of 1944. The news from France was that General Charles de Gaulle was preparing to enter Paris with victorious Allied Forces, and Hélène Lazareff, a Parisian refugee from the war now serving as an editor for the *New York Times Magazine*, was inquiring about Fritz's 1938 photographs of the capital city before the outbreak of the war. The photographer spent a sleepless night reprinting more than 150 of his photographs and by 10 o'clock the next morning was spreading them out in Lazareff's office. His shock at seeing her burst into tears was superseded only by a greater shock when she immediately asked to feature several of them in that Sunday's magazine in celebration of the freeing of the city from the German occupation. It had taken six years, but Henle's stunning work was at last vindicated over *LIFE*'s earlier rejection of the story.

The years following World War II became more positive and optimistic for America, and with the end of his darker OWI years, Fritz Henle quickly rebounded. He would return to Atty and the Millwood house in the country, which rapidly became his home, "the place where I have my roots and where my plans grow for ever new safaris."[59] And, in the process, he proceeded to become one of the nation's most successful and well-known photographers. To memorialize that renewed spirit, both artistically and symbolically, he returned to New York City in time to celebrate the end of the city's blackouts. On the first night that the lights were turned on again all over the city, he ascended to the top floor of a building at Fifth Avenue and 42nd Street and from a balcony on the north side created his famous "New York at Night" series.

In late 1944 he would journey back to Ewing Krainin's old consortium studio on Fifth Avenue, where, on the evening of October 12, he joined with a dozen other photographers — among them Krainin, W. Eugene Smith, Philippe Halsmann, Fritz Goro, Arthur Rothstein, Andreas Feininger and William Vandivert — and the columnist/critic/photography editor for the *New York Post*, John Adam Knight, in the formation of the American Society of Magazine Photographers.[60] The ASMP, organized to protect professional photographers against such injustices as speculative assignments, censorship, and copyright abuse,[61] was destined to become the most important consortium of professional photographers in the nation, and Henle was one of the first nine trustees during its earliest and most critical years following World War II.[62]

In addition to re-establishing his friendships with his old friends and fellow photographers, Henle opened a new studio, at 667 Madison Avenue, a medical building in which he would joke that he was always surrounded by doctors. He also signed with a new picture agency, Monkmeyer Press,[63] in order to increase his print sales. Perhaps most significantly he found that he had not been forgotten by the chief picture editors and large magazines, and he began to obtain many challenging assignments.

Although fashion magazines had, since the nineteenth century, always met with important social and commercial success in America, they have customarily seemed to enjoy a particular boom with the periods of renewed prosperity following the twentieth century's major wars. In the twenties and thirties periodicals such as Condé Nast's *Vogue* and *Vanity Fair* turned to such artists as Edward Steichen and Cecil Beaton to help set the styles and produce important imagery for the American public. Following World War II, American periodicals also concentrated on forgetting the war years and celebrating the return of peace and prosperity throughout the land. It was in that epoch of flourishing fashion photography for such magazines as *Harper's Bazaar*, *House & Garden*, *McCalls* and *Mademoiselle* that an important generation of picture editors would create a new and flourishing aesthetic.

Henle and his contemporaneous commercial and fashion photographers evolved in that era to expand the roles of advertising and marketing styles, taste and glamour for the postwar rise of the new consumer culture. Their energy and talent, along with that of a similar generation of news photographers — Dorothea Lange labeled both groups "the new breed" — would set them apart as influential and vigorous artists "who were discovering life anew, and, in the process, their own potentials as image makers."[64] It would be this exceptional body of men and women who would ultimately provide a major impetus and foundation for the worldwide popularization of photography as well as its embrace as an art form in the immediate decades that followed.

For Fritz Henle there was no limitation on creativity or personal expression to be found within the parameters of fashion photography. While always attentive to the needs of his editors and the requirements of their clients, the photographer approached each assignment with the same consistency of creativity and expressiveness that he brought to all other dimensions of his art. The pose and expression of Henle's models were always natural, the lighting consistently effective and persuasive, and the combinations of fashion and setting always working in fine support of one another. Based upon his customary technical excellence, his final portfolios were as expressive and unique in their artistry as those of any of his closest rivals.

Of most significant importance during that era, Fritz Henle became closely associated with the premiere fashion magazine of the time, *Harper's Bazaar*, and its powerful editor, Carmel Snow. Henle had been published in the magazine in the years before the war, of course, but now in the postwar American culture that required style mixed with a bit of dash, Snow and her already legendary art direc-

59 Fritz Henle. "Travel & Camera." *U.S. Camera*, March 1956: 30.

60 Toni Ficalora. "The ASMP at 25 Years." In: R. Smith Schuneman, ed., *Photographic Communication*. New York, Hastings House, 1972: 232.

61 Arnold Newman. "A Personal Perspective." In: *10,000 Eyes*. New York, 1991: 15.

62 The saga of the founding of the ASMP (now renamed the American Society of Media Photographers) is colorful and varied, and many of the variations on the tale are available in the published reminiscences of its founders and earliest members. A number can be found on the Society's website: www.asmp.org/about/history

63 Monkmeyer Press Photo Service, 225 Fifth Ave., New York, N.Y.

64 Jacob Deschin. "A Quarter Century in Photography, 1942–1967." In: Tom Maloney, ed. *U.S. Camera World Annual 1968*. New York (1967): 70.

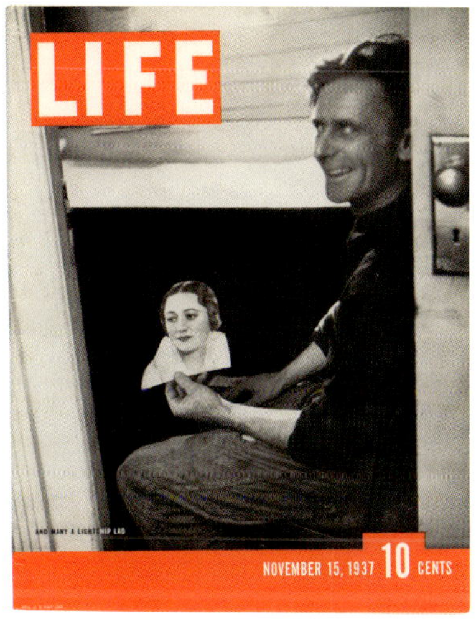

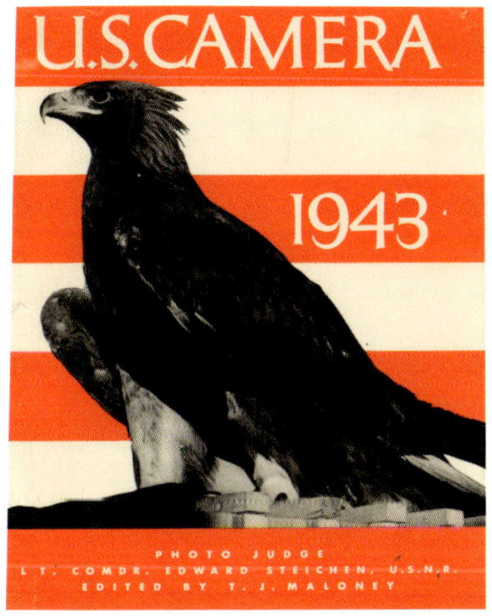

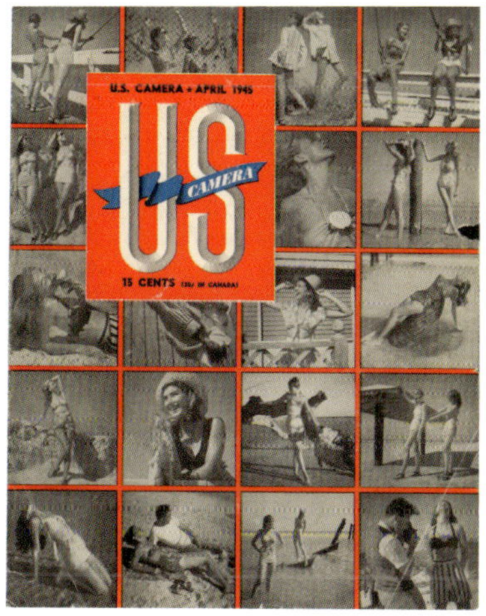

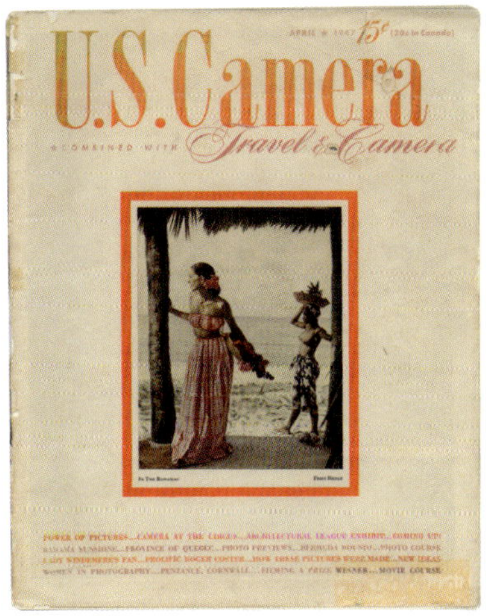

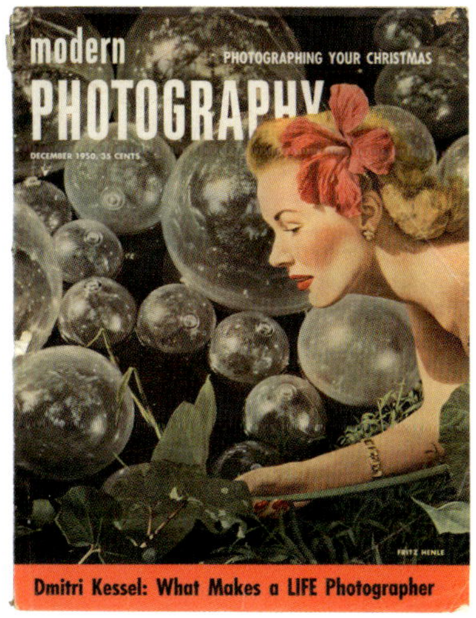

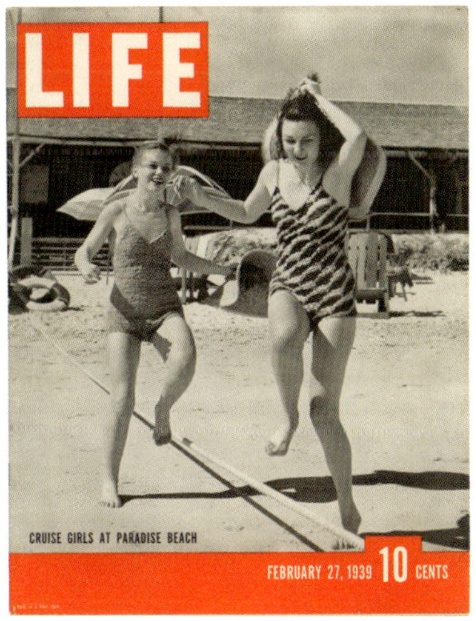

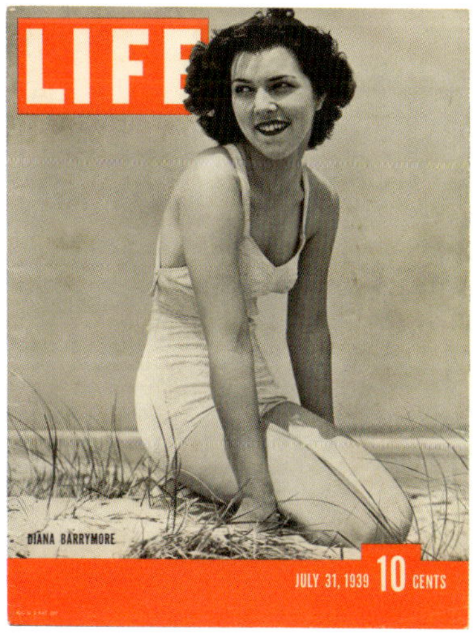

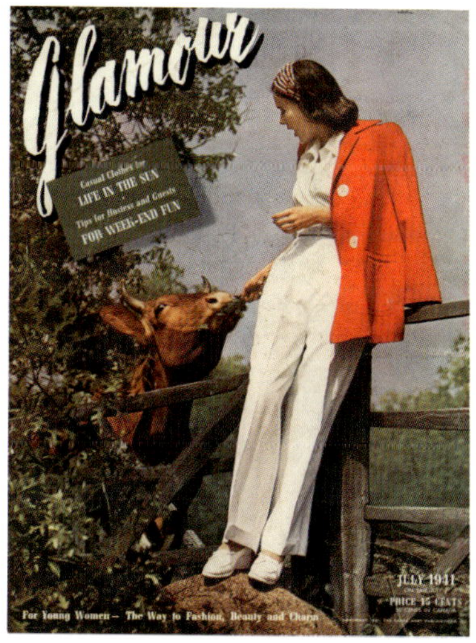

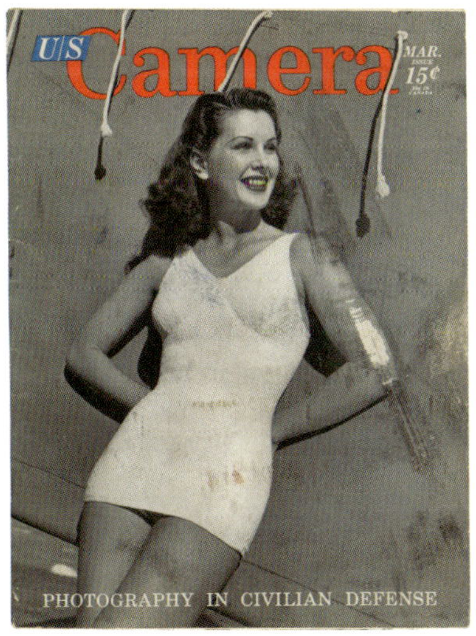

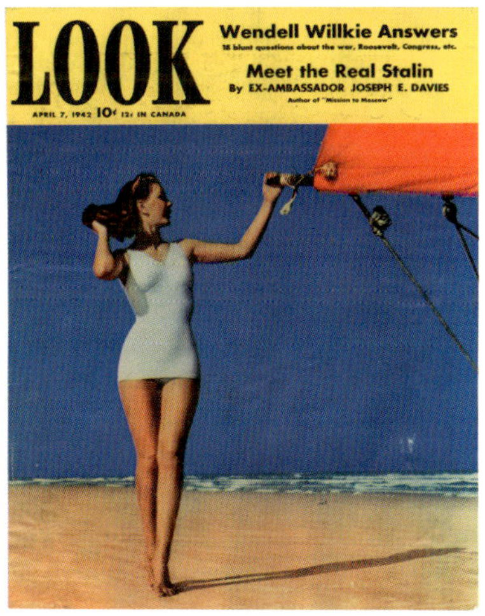

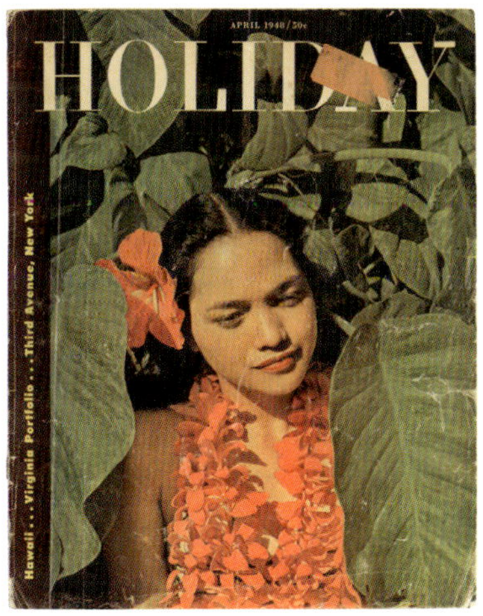

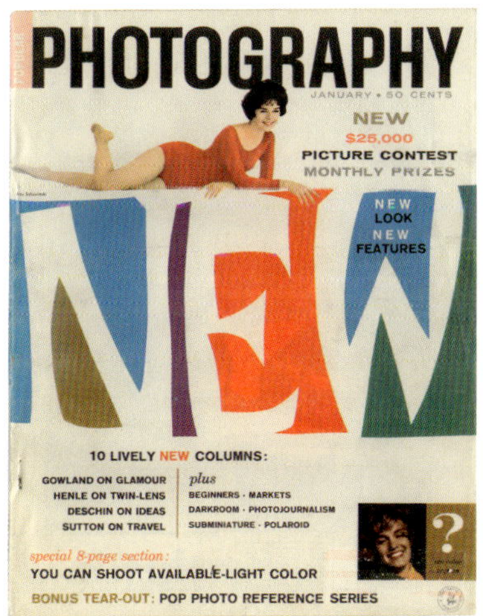

Fritz Henle. "And Many A Lightship Lad." *LIFE*. November 15, 1937. Front cover. This photograph of a merchant mariner brandishing a clipping of Wallace Simpson became Henle's first front cover for *LIFE* magazine. Unfortunately, the editors attributed the image to a different photographer and were forced to correct their error in the next week's issue.

Fritz Henle. "Golden Eagle." *U.S. Camera Annual* 1943. 1942. Front cover.

Fritz Henle. *U.S. Camera*. April 1945. Front cover. The issue's cover was designed to mimic a contact sheet, with shots of various models in beachwear plus one of Fritz in action in the lower right frame.

Fritz Henle. "In the Bahamas." *U.S. Camera*. April 1947. Front cover.

Fritz Henle. [Mexico Beauty.] *Modern Photography*. December 1950: Front cover.

Fritz Henle. "Cruise Girls at Paradise Beach." *LIFE*. February 27, 1939. Front cover.

Fritz Henle. "Diana Barrymore." *LIFE*. July 31, 1939. Front cover.

Fritz Henle. [Model with Cow.] *Glamour*. July 1941. Front cover.

Fritz Henle. [Evelyn Frye.] *U.S. Camera*. March 1942. Front cover.

Fritz Henle. [Evelyn Frye.] *Look*. April 7, 1942. Front cover. One of Henle's first models, Frye scored two front magazine covers in the spring of 1942. As was his custom, Henle used both color and black and white film for the same shoot, thereby doubling his opportunity to sell his swimwear photographs to two different major magazines.

Fritz Henle. [Hawaiian Beauty.] *Holiday*. April 1948: Front cover.

Popular Photography. January 1960. Front cover. Fritz was one of several new columnists to receive front billing as he initiated his monthly column, "Twin Lens," in the magazine.

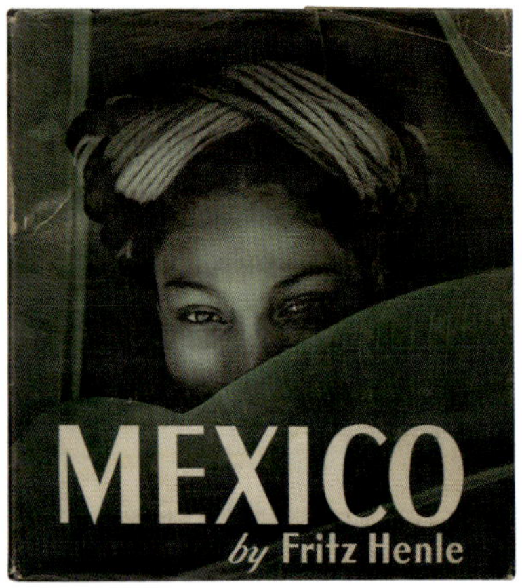

Mexico. Chicago & New York: 1945. Front dust jacket.

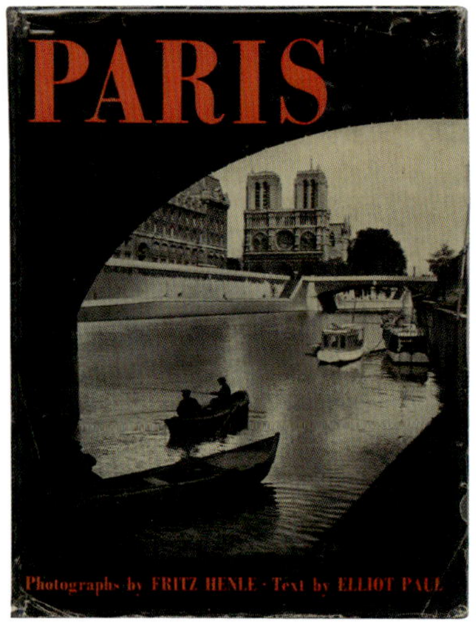

Paris. Chicago & New York: 1947. Front dust jacket.

tor, Alexey Brodovitch, were building a team of dynamic artists and photographers and felt that Henle would fit the bill nicely. Although Fritz would not give up his total independence to become an official staff photographer, he quickly numbered among the magazine's most important contributing professionals for the next seven years.

In particular the relationship between Brodovitch, the Russian émigré, and Henle, the German émigré, led to a long professional association and friendship. The art director found Henle's art always to be innovative and original, while the photographer in turn felt that Brodovitch was his greatest teacher (with the possible exception of Hanna Seewald) as well as someone who had a profound impact upon all who worked with him. As Fritz would later recall: "Alexey Brodovitch got photography out of a strait jacket [*sic*] that it had been in for many years. He broke the ground for unusual and mature photographers who otherwise might never have found an audience. He had the vision and, as art director...he had the power to put that vision into effect."[65] Throughout his career Henle would continue to honor the legendary art director as "...an inspiration. There are human beings who have the kind of vibrations that carry over... He could work with the best to bring out the best. There is no one to compare him to."[66]

Finally, besides his work on all of Henle's contributions to *Harper's Bazaar*, Brodovitch also encouraged him to publish more of his bodies of work and even did the innovative design layouts for the photographer's next two books, *Mexico* (1945), and in an edition of 15,000 copies, *Paris* (1947). Both volumes, supported by Brodovitch's boldly dramatic design work, were critical successes.[67] *Mexico*, a relatively larger scale photo book, which also featured the then innovative concept of having English and Spanish texts throughout, would have two printings, with a hefty 20,000 copies within a little more than a year.[68]

Paris, based upon the earlier *Sunday New York Times Magazine* publication, would enjoy significant advance sales even before it came out in early 1947,[69] in addition to being named one of the three outstanding photographic books of 1948 by the National Arts Club. As one critic, realizing what the *LIFE* editors had missed years earlier, would comment: "Henle's Paris is not only the stuff of centuries... Obviously, he wanted to talk about something more — the inhabitants — the types, the faces, the work, the pleasures, the infinite variety of pursuits; the worker, aristocrat, priest, housewife. In the larger sense, it is a symbol of the city..."[70] Years later the editors of *Popular Photography* would list *Paris* as a classic and note that the "Closest and most perceptive examiner of Parisians since Atget was the pre–World War II Henle. His well-publicized Rollei looked with utter candor into the visages of the City of Light in the 1930's."[71]

The postwar years became a golden, productive era for Fritz Henle. Beyond all the magazine and fashion work, his freelance work also continued to expand and prosper. In 1947 a large commission from the Matson Lines provided him and Atty with the opportunity to spend several weeks in the Hawaiian Islands. That first tropical experience captivated him, and by the following year he made two additional trips there on assignment for United Airlines. Fritz found that *Mexico* and *Paris* "opened many doors to him in Hawaii, and he got a lot of shots that he wouldn't have if folks hadn't liked the way he portrayed other people and places."[72] As a result he again amassed a large body of personal work — especially among the rarely photographed native Hawaiians — and was able to publish a book, *Hawaii*, by the end of that year. As Jacob Deschin would note in his review of the work: "Rather than record objectively, in the manner of the conventional traveler-photographer, [Henle] tries to get into his pictures something of what he sees, feels, and understands about the island and its people. And as the reader leafs through the pictures... he gets to know them too."[73]

Additionally in 1947 the Museum of Modern Art handed him a prestigious assignment by sending him to Paris to photograph Georges Braque for its future catalogue to accompany the painter's exhibition. The profession also began to acknowledge Henle, as *Popular Photography* presented him with the first of many awards in 1948. In the next year, Roy Pinney, one of *U.S. Camera*'s major columnists, named him one of the ten best all-around magazine photographers.[74] Most significantly, in 1948 he and Atty celebrated the birth of their son, Jan.

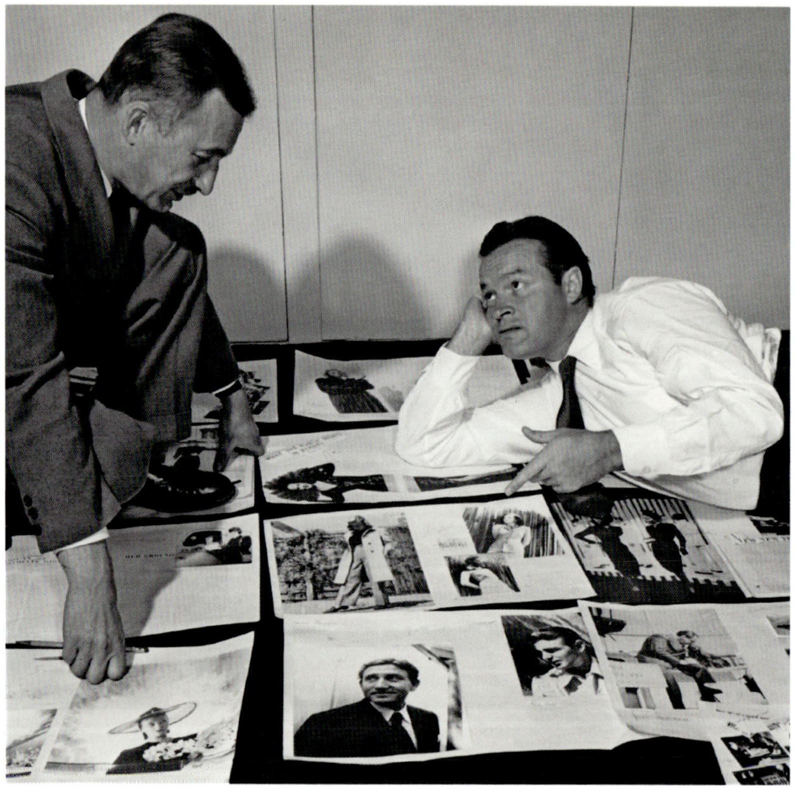

Fritz Henle. Alexey Brodovitch and Bob Hope discussing a layout for *Harper's Bazaar.* 1942. The image was part of a larger series that Henle produced to accompany Hope's comic article on serving as editor-for-a-day at *Harper's Bazaar.*

65 "Photographers on Brodovitch." *Popular Photography*, December 1961: 87.

66 Ellen Wallenstein. "[The] Medium Is The Message: Fritz Henle's Perspective." *Photo District News*, May 1985: 67.

67 It is interesting how Brodovitch influenced Henle's way of seeing. When one examines the scrapbook albums in the photographer's archive it becomes obvious how Fritz began using oblique angles and overlapping pages to compile at that time the clippings and tearsheets that he glued onto the leaves.

68 Mary Ellen Slate. "The Magazines." *Popular Photography* XVII, 6, December 1945: 110.

69 Robert Fuhrings. "The Magazines." *Popular Photography*, July 1947: 142.

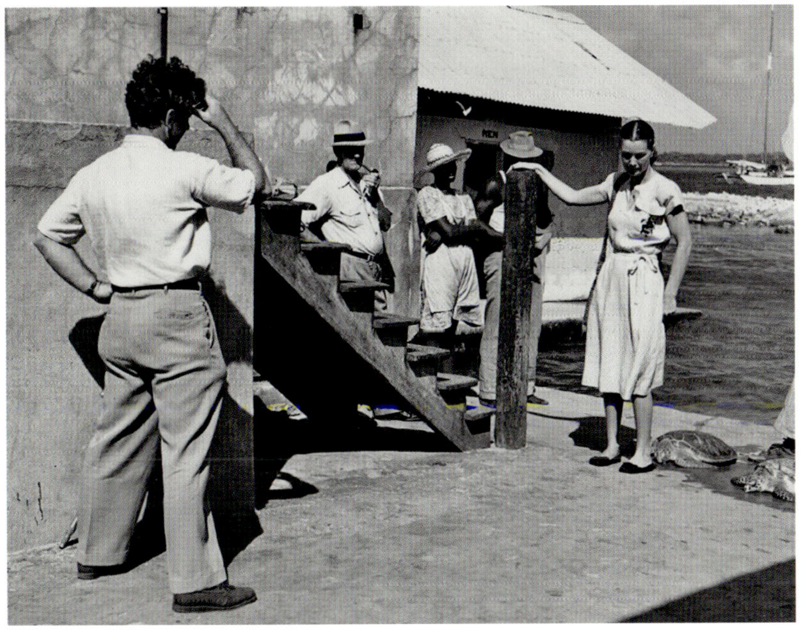

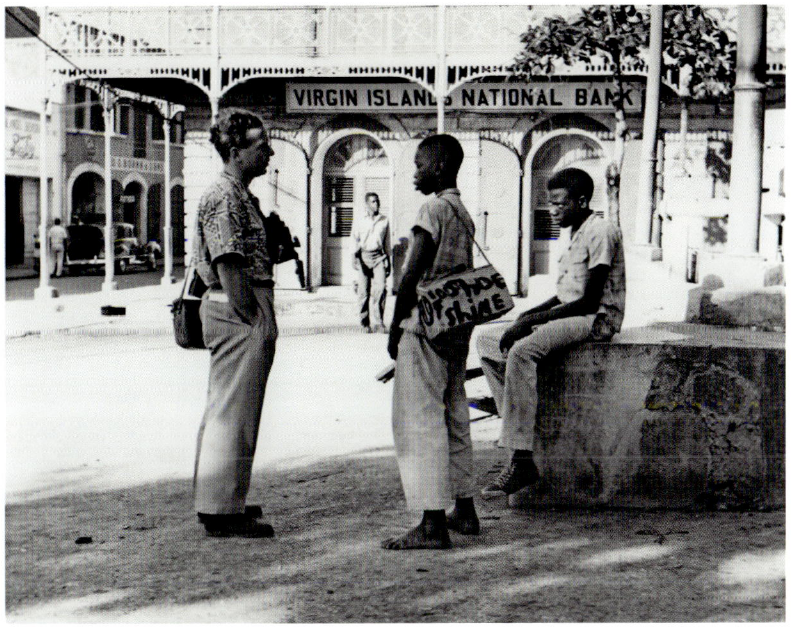

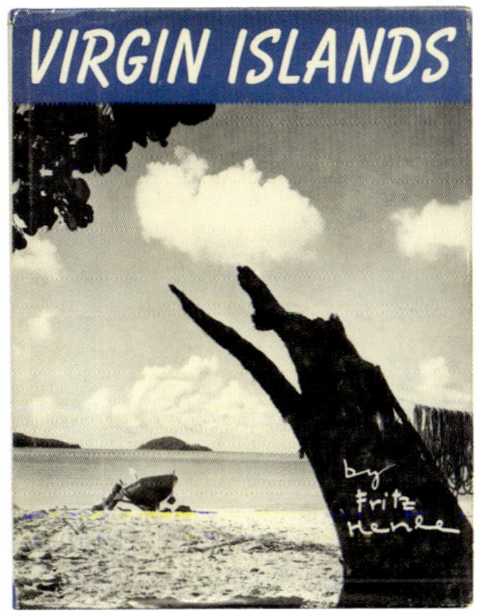

Freddie Maura. Fritz Henle solving a composition problem during a McMullen & Co. fashion shoot in Nassau, Bahamas. 1947.

Photographer Unidentified. Fritz Henle talking with Crucians during his first visit to St. Croix, U.S. Virgin Islands. January 1948.

Virgin Islands. New York: 1949. Front dust jacket.

Family aside, the most important development in Fritz's life during those years would have nothing to do with awards or publications; rather it grew out of a fashion shoot for *Holiday* that almost was cancelled. A fierce New York City snowstorm in late December of 1947 delayed the departure of Henle, his models and their entourage for a flight to Caracas, Venezuela. The company was able to depart the next day, but when they arrived in San Juan, Puerto Rico, they found that a revolution in the Venezuelan capital had forced the airline to cancel the remainder of their flight. Faced with a possible further delay, Henle consulted a map, found a place called the Virgin Islands, and had the pilots fly his group to its chief island, St. Thomas. He found a tropical island with almost limitless landscapes and was ultimately able to conduct the entire shoot on the picturesque white sands of the surrounding beaches.

The Virgin Islands are a string of three islands — St. Croix, St. Thomas and St. John — that are part of a large underwater mountain chain lying south of Puerto Rico in the Caribbean Sea initially discovered by Christopher Columbus on his second voyage to the New World in 1493. Their tropical beauty was renowned through the Americas, and their native population was subsequently subjected to more than four hundred years of European settlement. Finally, in 1917 the chain was purchased from the Danes and became an official U.S. Territory, thereafter placing the islands under American laws and affording its residents full U.S. citizenship. Beyond the beauty of the land and sea itself, there was a harmonious blending of the old European and New World cultures that particularly attracted Henle from the very first. Even on this initial visit to the islands he found himself greatly overwhelmed by this easy mixing of the people and cultures of the West Indies with those of a Western European background: "...the Islands he found to be as beautiful as any place he had ever seen... The climate is lovely, warm with a cool breeze from the Trades, and the atmosphere Fritz found especially invigorating — no racial prejudices."[75] Henle would become quickly intoxicated with this very unique cultural mix.

Walking the beaches of the Virgin Islands reminded Fritz of his Hawaiian assignment from earlier that year, and he became so captivated that he resolved to learn more about the place. As a result, after the remainder of his company for the *Holiday* shoot returned home he arranged to stay for a few days into the new year of 1948 in order to visit and explore the larger island, St. Croix (his guide, Wilhelm, had at the time the only taxi on the island) — and permit himself the dream of perhaps one day trading the snows of New York for the sunshine of the Caribbean. Years later he would find the words to describe that experience: "To arrive on an island is always a thrill. There is the promise of the unknown and at the same time there is a limitation. The sea borders all around, and within hours, sometimes within minutes, a feeling of closeness and intimacy is being created — it has become our island."[76] He resolved to return and, with some careful planning, gradually adjusted his entire working schedule to include fashion shoots on the island every winter. As one magazine columnist noted in 1949, the Virgin Islands were "an area about which Henle gets lyrical, both in telephone conversations with us, and in his pictures."[77]

Although his work in fashion photography, especially with *Harper's Bazaar*, would continue until 1952, Henle was obviously finding higher levels of creativity and challenge in industrial and travel photography before the close of the 1940s.[78] As he continued to produce significant work while reappraising his career, his desire for freedom led him in other directions as well. By the early 1950s he

70 Ralph Samuels. "To photographer Fritz Henle — Paris Is People." *Minicam Photography*, October 1947: 60.

71 "Yesterday's Classics." *Popular Photography*, May 1963: 58.

72 Robert Fuhring. "The Magazines." *Popular Photography*, October 1947: 153.

73 Jacob Deschin. "Picture Books. Travel Photography by Henle—Other Guides." *The New York Times*, September 12, 1948: [1 p.].

74 The other nine to share the honor were: Margaret Bourke-White, Ralph Crane, Herbert Gehr, George Karger, Joe Costa, Hans Knopf, Jack O'Reilly, Frank Scherschel and W. Eugene Smith.

75 A.P. Sutherland, Jr. "The Magazines." *Popular Photography* 23, 2, August 1948: 146.

76 Fritz Henle. "The Virgin Islands." *Camera*, June 1969: 2.

77 Doris Birnbaum. "The Magazines." *Popular Photography* 25, 5, November 1949: 18.

78 For example, in 1948–49 Henle found himself in a humorous, informal monthly competition with Eliot Elisofon, *LIFE's* famous globe-trotting photojournalist, whose beat was also all four corners of the world. For details of the "Henle-Elisofon international marathon," see many of Doris Brinbaum's columns in a number of the late 1940s issues of *Popular Photography*.

Fritz Henle. Contact sheet: Views of airplanes, models and sites of Henle's first trip to the U.S. Virgin Islands. December 1947. The first roll of exposures Fritz made on the trip to San Juan and St. Thomas for the *Holiday* shoot that would introduce him to the U.S. Virgin Islands.

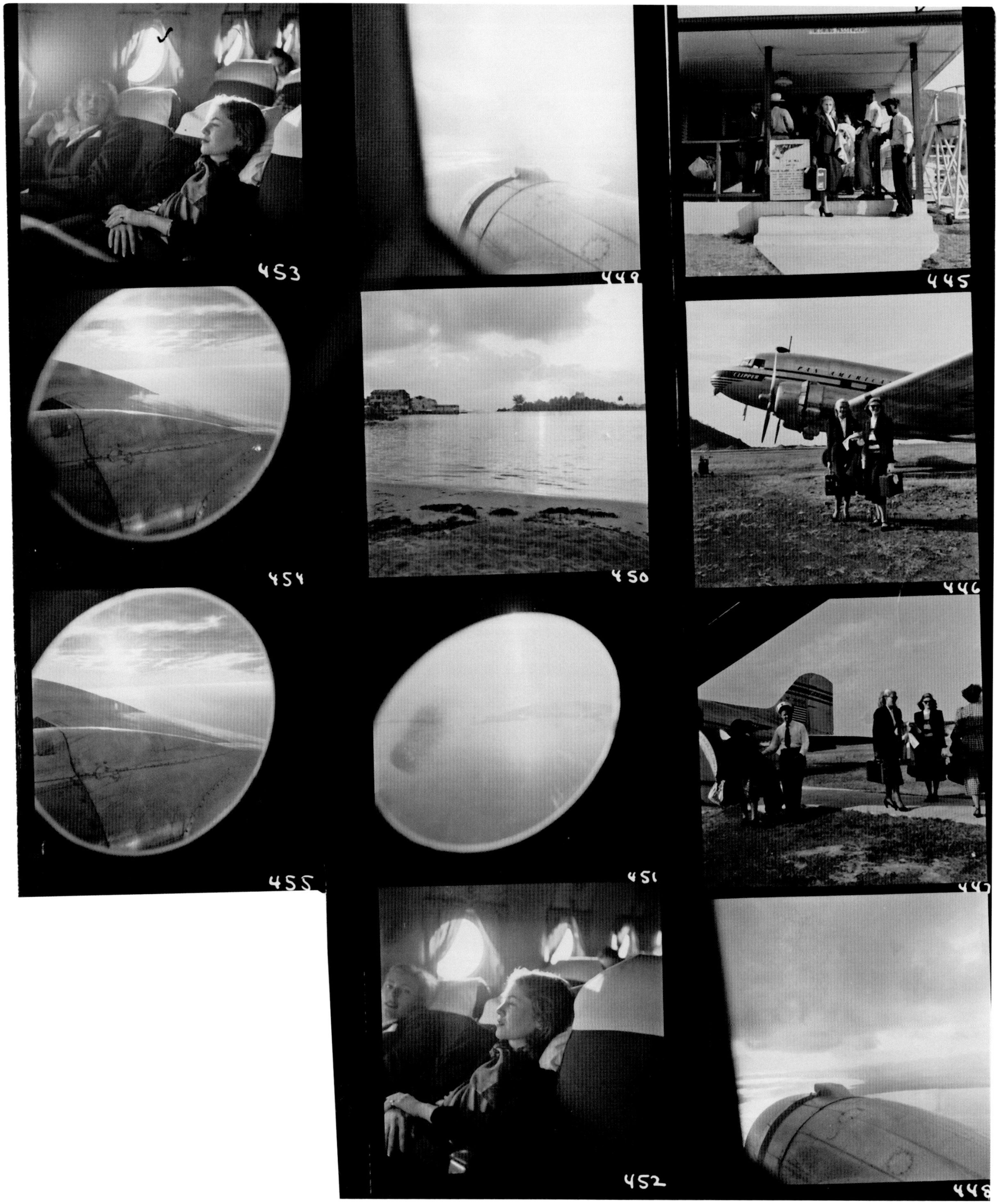

had published his first book on the Virgin Islands and, surprisingly, also his first motion picture — a travel film about the islands entitled *The American Virgin Islands* and starring Atty and Jan. Other short films based upon life in the Caribbean islands were produced and distributed in short order, but his filmmaking career would end in 1953 with his commercial movie for the National Biscuit Company, entitled *Crackers by the Billion*. Although he never returned to the production of motion pictures, Henle always contended that working with moving pictures helped him improve his still photography.[79]

In 1950–51 he undertook a massive ten-week project for the United States Steel Corporation — which was celebrating its fiftieth anniversary in 1951 — traveling some 20,000 miles to more than 30 company plants across the nation. It would prove to be a remarkable body of work, involving a tight and complicated shooting schedule and working in the often-hazardous conditions of industrial plants and near blast furnaces that were so hot that within seconds the metal of his camera bodies became too hot to hold. Focusing on Mr. Rollei's apparatus, the editors of *U.S. Camera* "...believed that Henle's exclusive use of this type camera for the USS assignment marks the first time that a job as big as this has been handled completely in the 2¼ x 2¼ format."[80] The resulting photographs, totaling 4,000 black and white and 500 color images, were edited and published in a special edition entitled *Steel Serves the Nation*.[81]

In 1952 he was honored to be one of the invited photographers to have his works included in The World Exhibition of Photography

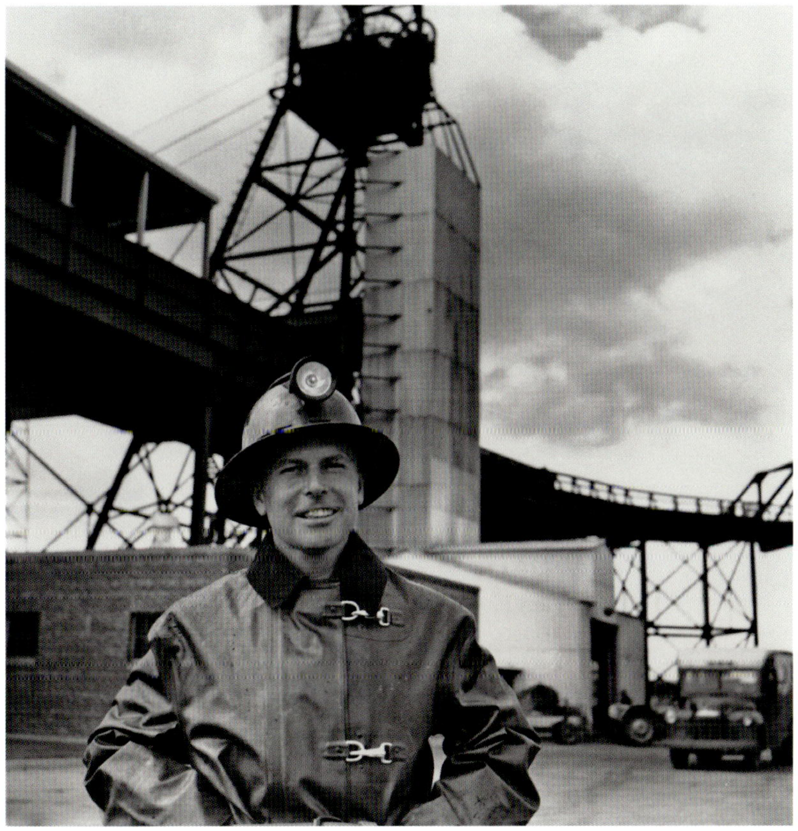

— the first international celebration of photography — which was held in Lucerne, Switzerland. The exhibition's review in *Camera* would describe Henle as "intelligent, alive, capable, [a photographer] who captured the stillness of the New Mexico desert lands with the same penetration as he depicts everyday people in all walks of life..."[82] Finally, he also took his first steps into publishing comprehensive picture books — 1950's *Fritz Henle's Rollei* — and how-to magazine articles, which took advantage of the exploding interest in amateur photography throughout the United States and, eventually, the world.

Based upon his photographic assignments documenting the oil industry in the late 1940s and early 1950s, Fritz Henle continued to find a strong attraction to industrial work. Following upon his work on the Cities Service annual report for 1950, he accepted a commission from Nick Parrino, the director of the organization's Photo Library, to serve part time as the chief photographer for the oil company. Initially he was sent on an extensive photographic tour of the company's far-flung facilities, searching out picture possibilities for a multiyear survey. He "returned from the assignment with hundreds of black and white and color pictures, proclaiming, 'There are terrific pictures wherever you look!'"[83]

He would make room in his work schedule to spend a number of months each spring and summer, traveling around the nation and documenting and interpreting all aspects of the Cities Service vast enterprise. In the process he and Parrino set up a comprehensive program of photographic documentation that would employ a number of diverse photographers, including Charles Rotkin, Russell Lee, David Peskin, Nelson Morris, James Hampson and Tony Linck, among many others.[84] At his busiest Henle could log up to 50,000 miles a year, providing thousands of photographs for the organization's annual reports, picture library, and promotional department. As the survey progressed Fritz's photographs continued to be marked by his freedom of styles, ranging from on-the-job portraits of employees to abstract compositions that celebrated both the mechanical and the human aspects of the industry. The work satisfied the huge demands of the company, which was proud to point out that "Mr. Henle's achievement is further proof that industrial photography is high art."[85] The Cities Service project would become Fritz's longest commission, ending only in 1959 after his final relocation to the Virgin Islands.

As Henle's career was expanding and blossoming, his personal life began to change dramatically. Perhaps it was due to the demands of his profession and the long weeks and even months away from home, but for whatever reason his marriage was failing. While Atty remained at home raising Jan, Fritz was finding more reasons — his photography, the books, his films, a commission from Lawrence

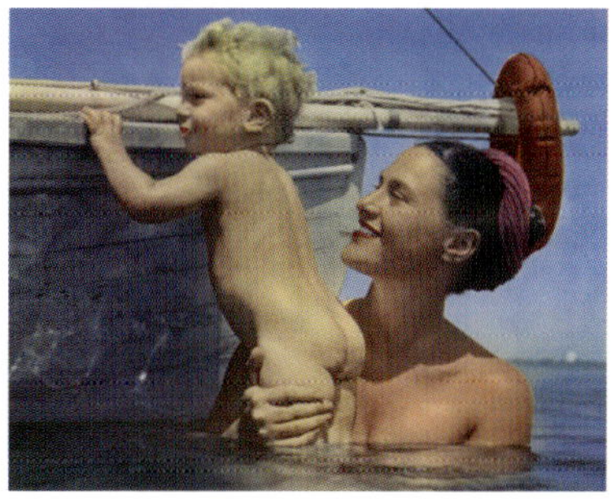

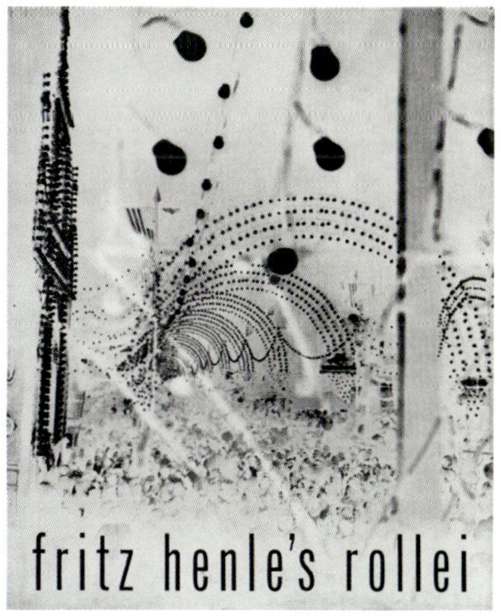

Photographer Unidentified. Fritz Henle on assignment for U.S. Steel. 1952.

Fritz Henle. Jan and Atty at Nantucket, Rhode Island. 1950. Fritz's wife and son, besides being favorite subjects for his Rollei, were soon to be featured in his first motion picture as they "discovered" the people and places of *The American Virgin Islands*.

Fritz Henle's Rollei. New York: 1950. Front dust jacket.

79 For an excellent analysis of his early motion picture work, see: Jacquelyn Judge. "Henle's First Movie..." *Modern Photography*, November 1952: 90–92, 94, 96, 100.

80 "U.S. Camera Presents......a portfolio of outstanding industrial photographs made by Fritz Henle on special assignment for a 50th anniversary picture record of United States Steel Corporation." *U.S. Camera*, September 1951: 57.

81 *Ibid.*: 57–62, 103.

82 Max A. Wyss. "Grosse Namen in der Photographe / Great names in photography / Les grands noms de l'art photographique." *Camera*, June/July 1952: 237.

83 Bill Cannon. "Picture File on Oil." *U.S. Camera*, November 1952. 51.

84 Ibid: 106; Roy Pinney. "Magazine & Advertising Photography." *U.S. Camera*, August 1950: 10.

85 "The Camera Artist Strikes OIL." *Service*, April 1950: 17.

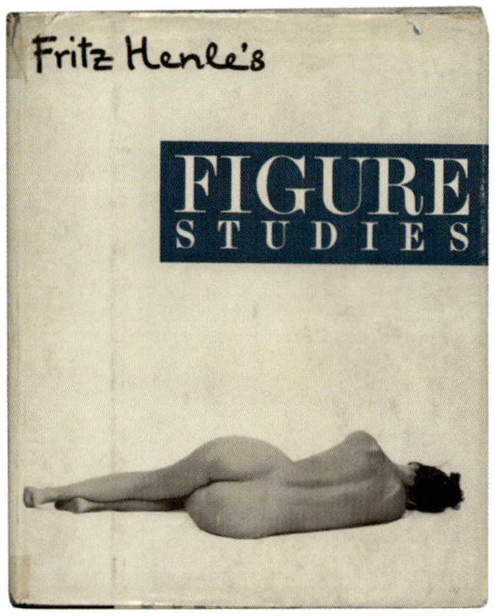

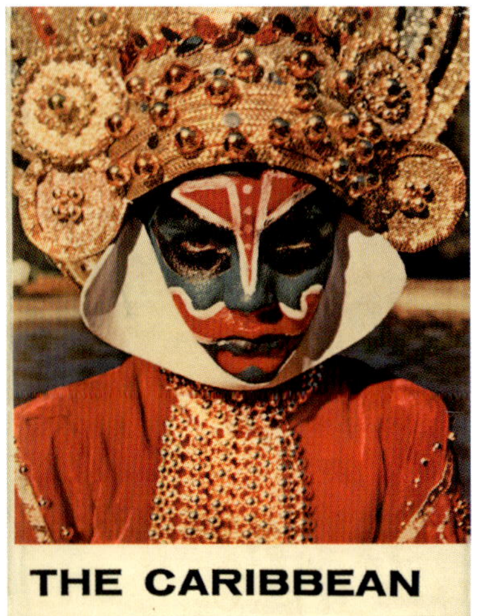

Fritz Henle's Figure Studies. New York & London: 1954. Front dust cover.

The Caribbean: A Journey with Pictures. New York. 1957. Front cover.

Fritz Henle. *Portrait of Marguerite*. New York City. 1953.

Rockefeller to assist with his plans to establish a national park on St. John — to visit the Virgin Islands and stay as long as he could. To complicate his life further, in 1953 Fritz met a vacationing couple, Bill and Marguerite Schrader, at Spratt Hall, a tourist beach on the west end of St. Croix. He found himself immediately attracted to the wife, received her husband's permission to photograph her, and eventually began a long-distance relationship. As it would happen, both couples were involved in marriages that were winding down into mutual unfaithfulness and grief. After a long and painful period of separation, both Fritz and Marguerite were divorced from their spouses by 1954 and were free to marry later that same year.

Marguerite became many things to Fritz: wife, lover, model, inspiration, partner, and eventually mother to their three children. He had found a true soulmate to share his remaining years with and theirs became an active and loving relationship. In addition, Marguerite would prove to be his most elegant model, inspiring him to create in the first few years of their marriage some of the most profound nudes and figure studies in the history of photography. The whole series became for Fritz "an expression of absolute beauty" based on "no intent, only pure intuition."[86] In both marriage and before the lens of his Rolleis, Marguerite became a true collaborator, nurturing his fierce independence and encouraging his eloquent creativity. Their resulting book, *Fritz Henle's Figure Studies* (New York & London, 1954), became a remarkable celebration of their intense collaboration. With a fine introduction by Jacquelyn Judge,[87] it would become his most successful publication up to that time, going through two editions and three printings in its first eight years.

The period of great transition that began with his marriage to Marguerite and the figure studies that she had inspired would carry on throughout the remainder of the 1950s. A commission to photograph the Caribbean for Alcoa, including its bauxite mining facilities in Venezuela,[88] would eventually lead to a series of distinctive advertisements as well as a fine color volume, *The Caribbean* (1957). More significantly, the commission would also provide them with the opportunity to investigate all the real possibilities of moving their home, as well as supplying the additional funds to purchase some land on Little Princess Hill overlooking the town of Christiansted on St. Croix. Professionally the islands were only a few hours away from New York City by airplane, and daily direct flights could keep Henle in relatively quick contact with all his business interests in the city. In addition, and of essential importance to Henle's unwavering loyalty to America, the Virgin Islands were an official territory of the United States and he and his family would be able to remain full U.S. citizens. Offering a quiet tenor of life and unmatched tropical beauty, the Islands were far from primitive, did offer modern facilities and were still relatively unspoiled by their rising tourist trade. As Fritz would later describe St. Croix: "This island is poetry...moments of quiet peace, great natural beauty and a feeling of life that is almost untranslatable."[89] He was destined to spend the remaining decades of his life using his Rolleis to, if not visually translate, then at least celebrate that poetry. For the remainder of his days it would become "...a microcosm of the world, but happily a spot where the hope of becoming Paradise is greater than the threat of becoming Hades."[90]

In addition, his family life was beginning to expand rapidly. He and Marguerite would have three children during this same half decade: a daughter, Maria, born in 1955, a second daughter, Tina, born three years later in 1958, and a son, Martin, born in 1961. In his late forties, Fritz Henle was again becoming a family man, and he wished to scale down and modify his professional career, reduce his number of far-flung multiple assignments, and have the time to build a new home and family life on his new island home. In 1957 he began planning his home site on the hill above Christiansted. He turned to a new picture agency, Photo Researchers, to handle and increase the distribution and sales of his works. He also closed down his Madison Avenue studio and moved the vast majority of his negatives to the studio of Julius and Pat Motal, his favorite printers. Henle had always preferred to do his own printing throughout his career, but as he began to spend longer portions of the postwar years away from New York City he was forced to entrust more of his printing requirements to outside firms. The Motals, refugees from Czechoslovakia and by that time very good friends, were precise and elegant printers and the Motal Custom Darkroom[91] maintained one of the finest reputations in the city. Fritz Henle, now often characterized as

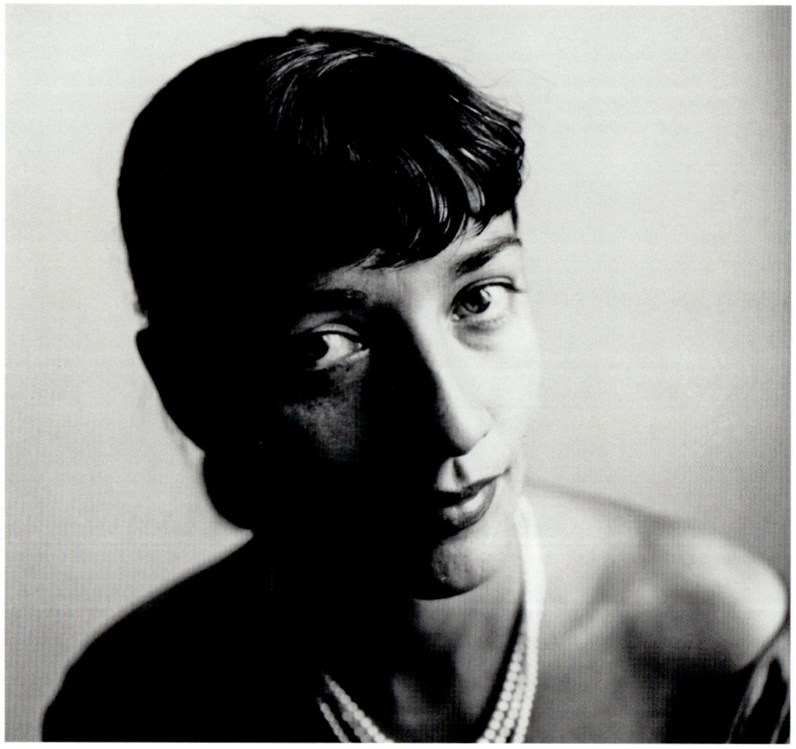

86 Mike Cox. "'Decisive moment' key to photo success." *Austin American-Statesman*, [May?] 1980: [1 p.].

87 Jacquelyn Judge met Henle when she was hired as one of the first staffers for the fledgling ASMP. One of the major writers, editors and critics during the remarkable growth of mid-twentieth century American photography magazines, she eventually served for many years as chief editor for *Modern Photography*.

88 By the 1970s Alcoa would become so successful that the company expanded and took over the Harvey Alumina [later Martin Marietta] aluminum manufacturing facilities on St. Croix.

89 Evelyn Kieran. "Curable case of islomania." *PSA, The California Magazine*, May 1976: 16.

90 Unknown author. "Fritz Henle: The Photographer Who 'Documents Happiness' in the Virgin Islands." Typescript, ca. 1973: 5. Henle Family Archive.

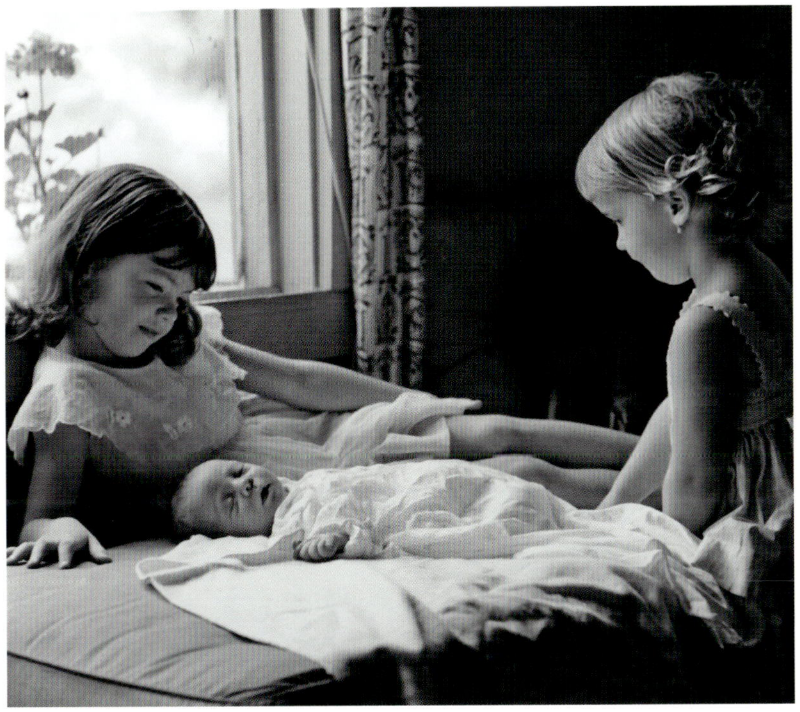

chiefly a "fashion" or "advertising" photographer, would be honored in 1959 with a prestigious career award from the Art Directors Guild celebrating his professional career to date, but by that time he was once more changing the direction of his photographic life.

The process of this transition continued when he sold his suburban New York home and completed construction of his St. Croix home in 1958. The Henles' new home, though relatively small, proved to be wonderful for their growing family, situated along the hillside above Christiansted with unparalleled views of the town and the blue waters of the Caribbean. By 1959 Fritz had ended most of his fashion work as well as his long-term relationship with Cities Service, and he and Marguerite embarked upon two world tours to begin photography for many future publications on travel photography and photo guides for amateurs and professionals. Despite the demands upon his family life and work schedules, he still maintained a strong enthusiasm for travel photography and that "...while I'm hard at work I'm also enjoying myself every minute. I like traveling, and taking pictures as I go seems the most natural thing in the world."[92]

Perhaps the most important aspect of those trips was that he was finally able to end his long alienation from his German homeland. The wounds were deep, starting with his experiences in Germany during the rise of the Nazis in the 1930s. He had also lost many friends and relatives, including his beloved Uncle Fritz, to the devastation of the Holocaust's concentration camps. So deep was his anger that Henle had resolved never to speak his native tongue again — a promise he kept until his return in 1959. He made two long visits to his mother, Tina, at their family's old Heidelberg home, introducing her to Marguerite and reviving many old family memories. In the end his mother was able to have a positive effect upon his reconciliation with his native land before she passed away in 1960.

He also became an active participant in photography's rapid rise in popularity and acceptance as a major art form in the 1950s and 1960s. His newest books were *Fritz Henle's Guide to Rollei Photography* (1956) and the popular amateur guide, *Photography for Everyone* (1959 and 1960) — which would enjoy multiple printings and a German language edition and be praised by Arthur Goldsmith because it "...emphasizes the fun and the creative aspects of photography with scarcely a technical word in the book."[93] Featuring clear instruction into the hows and whys of the art, it was a critical and popular success: "For the beginner in photography it would be hard to find a better way to start..."[94] Based upon those publications he would also become an active contributor for America's most predominant photo magazine, *Popular Photography*, writing a monthly column entitled "Twin Lens," which ran successfully for nearly five years, from 1960 to 1964.[95] He found himself increasingly sought out for his critical and aesthetic expertise and became a frequent contributor of both images and words to a wide variety of American and European photography books, annuals and periodicals. He would also be an active participant in a number of major group exhibitions, whose curators would include such notable figures as Edward Steichen and Ivan Dmitri.

Fritz Henle's relationship with Franke and Heidecke would also be transformed during the 1960s. His final handbook, *A New*

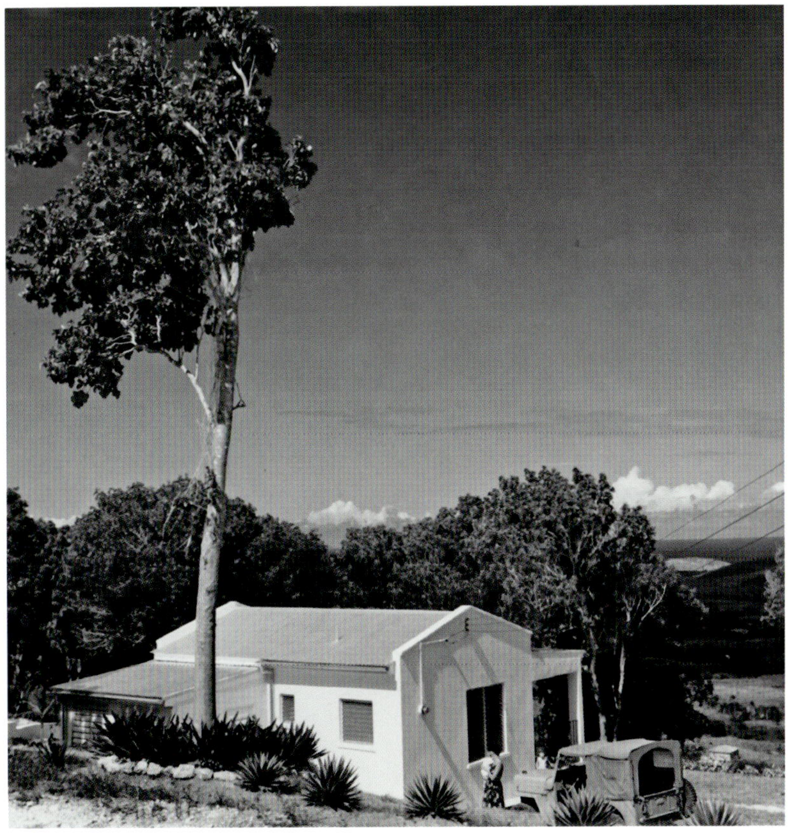

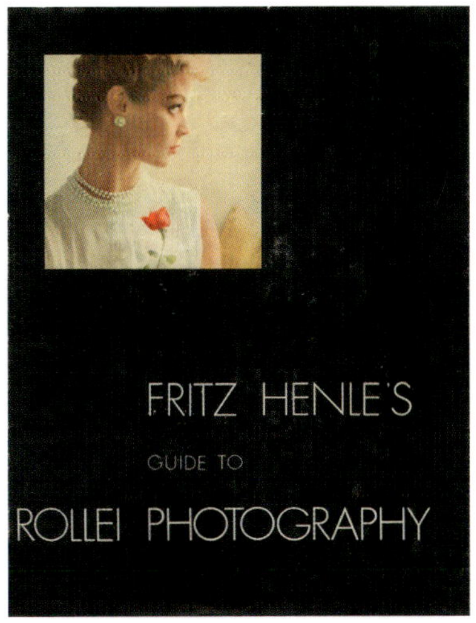

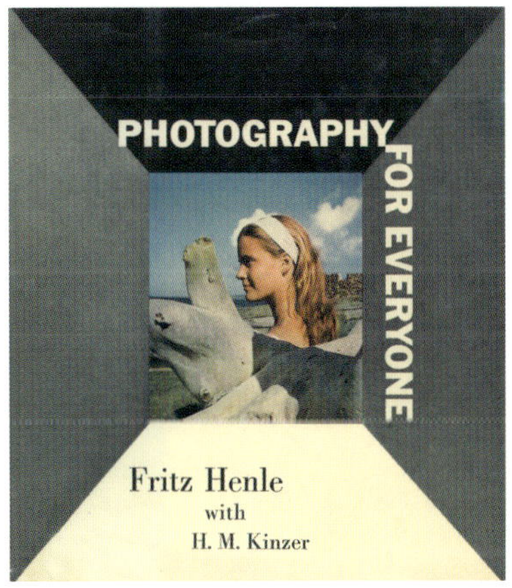

Fritz Henle. Marguerite and Fritz's children: Maria, Martin and Tina. Christiansted, St. Croix, U.S. Virgin Islands. 1961.

Fritz Henle. View of the newly-built Henle family home on Little Princess Hill. Christiansted, St. Croix, U.S. Virgin Islands. 1958.

Fritz Henle's Guide to Rollei Photography. New York & London: 1956. Front dust jacket.

Photography for Everyone. New York: 1959. Front dust jacket.

91 Also later known as Motal Custom Photography.

92 Fritz Henle. "Fritz Henle on Travel." *Popular Photography*, November 1960: 94.

93 Arthur Goldsmith. "For Beginners: Good Photo Books for Beginners." *Popular Photography*, April 1960: 36.

94 C[harles] R[eynolds]. "Books: Photography for Everyone." *Popular Photography*, December 1960: 148.

95 Actually, "Twin Lens" was Fritz's second column for an American photographic periodical. In 1955–56 Henle and photographer Ray Atkeson alternated on the writing of a column, "Travel & Camera," for the monthly *U.S. Camera*; when Henle opted not to continue, his semimonthly contributions were taken over by photographer Roy Pinney.

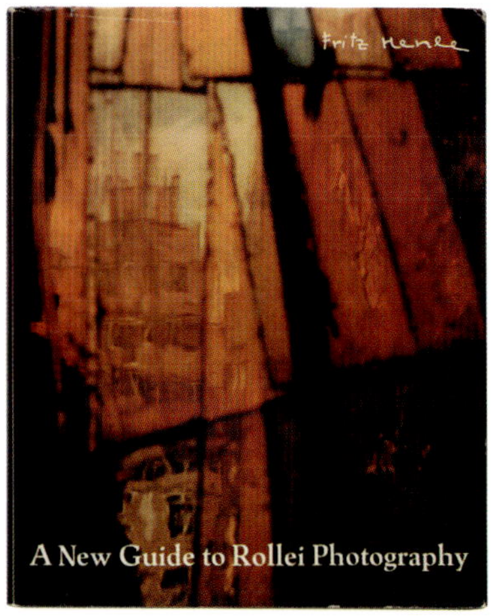

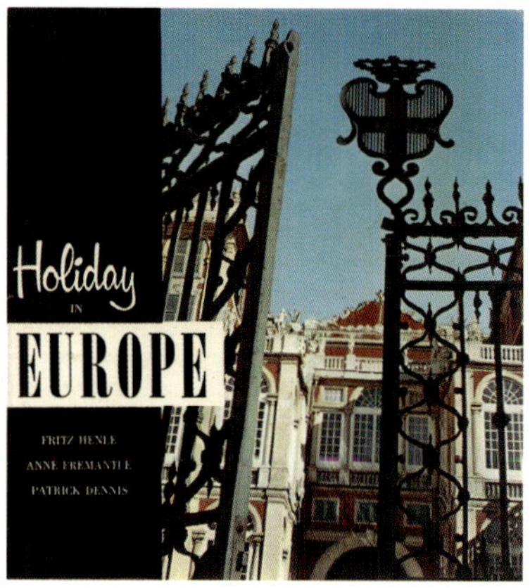

A New Guide to Rollei Photography. New York: 1965. Front dust jacket.

Holiday in Europe. Canada: 1963. Front dust jacket.

Photographer Unidentified. Marguerite and Fritz Henle at Castle Lichtenstein, Germany. 1962.

Guide to Rollei Photography — a compilation of his *Popular Photography* "Twin Lens" columns of the previous five years — came out in 1965, on the cusp of an era of major transitions for the firm. Although the company was always appreciably grateful to "Mr. Rollei" and his commitment to their Rolleiflexes, the firm had, with the death of its founders, passed into new corporate hands in the early 1960s. The new company, Rollei-Werke, believed that it had to change with the demands of the times as well.[96] In 1966, after experimenting with miniature and 35mm format cameras, the firm came out with a new 6 x 6 roll film camera. The SL66 continued to take 120 roll film, but it was now a single lens reflex camera with the capacity to handle a variety of interchangeable lenses. In addition, Fritz had been instrumental in getting the firm to adopt interchangeable backs as well — eliminating his longtime practice of having had to simultaneously carry two of the older Rolleiflexes, one each for color and black and white films. The company provided Henle with a complete system and, after a period of initial experimentation, he delivered his verdict: "When I held it in my hands for the first time, I was surprised. It looked quite different from what I had imagined. (In the fifties I had played with the idea of an interchangeable front, with different focal lengths, but still with twin lenses.) Then, after a few minutes of experimenting, I was enthusiastic. A few hours were enough to adjust the costly instrument to my eyes, and make it fit snugly into my hands... Since that time I seldom use the TLR."[97]

The months of journeying all over Western Europe culminated in 1963 with the publication of Fritz Henle's final classic travel book, *Holiday in Europe.* Filled with more than 200 of Henle's new and vibrant color and black and white images that he had produced — while often carrying up to four Rolleis and a Veriwide — throughout the previous two years' journeys, the book was a popular seller. The Travel Book Club marketed it as the "gayest, freshest, and most colorful of travel books... A delightful and unusual guidebook before you go — and a nostalgic memory book after you return."[98] The book was published in five countries and in four language editions. And, while it did not end Fritz's globetrotting or his fascination with the world, it provided a fitting coda to his nearly three decades of innovative and often revolutionary travel imagery.

By the end of the 1960s Fritz Henle would begin to direct his energies in new directions. He and Marguerite had three future teenagers yet to raise and a new and exciting world of the Virgin Islands to explore and enjoy as their final home. He had a large body of imagery for which he had kept his copyrights to review and continually draw upon for future sales. His career had been exemplary — "4 Decades at the Top" as Julia Scully, the editor of *Modern Photography,* would characterize it in her definitive 1970 article[99] — and as he was approaching 60 he was attaining an age at which he could be permitted to retire with satisfaction. Personal odysseys, however, are often not so simply and neatly concluded. And this after all was Fritz Henle, who would later reflect that: "The power of creativity was my strongest asset and as in all the years before, I found myself confronted by challenges. I was looking for them by creating constantly for myself. This drive has never left me, and there were periods in my life when rather than wait for an assignment I went out and created them myself."[100]

To begin with, he started to focus much of his attention and energies upon his new home, the Virgin Islands. In 1965 he undertook industrial work for Hess Oil, which, on St. Croix's southern shore, had erected one of the hemisphere's largest refineries. Simultaneously but in very marked contrast, he also continued to add to his black and white portrait of the islands and their people and, in 1969, received the first of many awards of funding to enable him to document them in color as well. He played an active role in local movements to help preserve the ecology and culture of his islands and participated in both native celebrations as well as the international festival celebrating their Danish heritage. When the annual conference of the U.S. National Governors Association was convened in the Virgin Islands in 1967, Fritz edited and illustrated a booklet for all the participants. He also expanded his program of exhibiting and selling his work locally and decided to present a greater variety of photographs of his islands to the world at large. Starting in 1969 he produced a large traveling show of his black and white photographs, which was circulated over the next two years to major museums in Denmark, Germany and the United States.

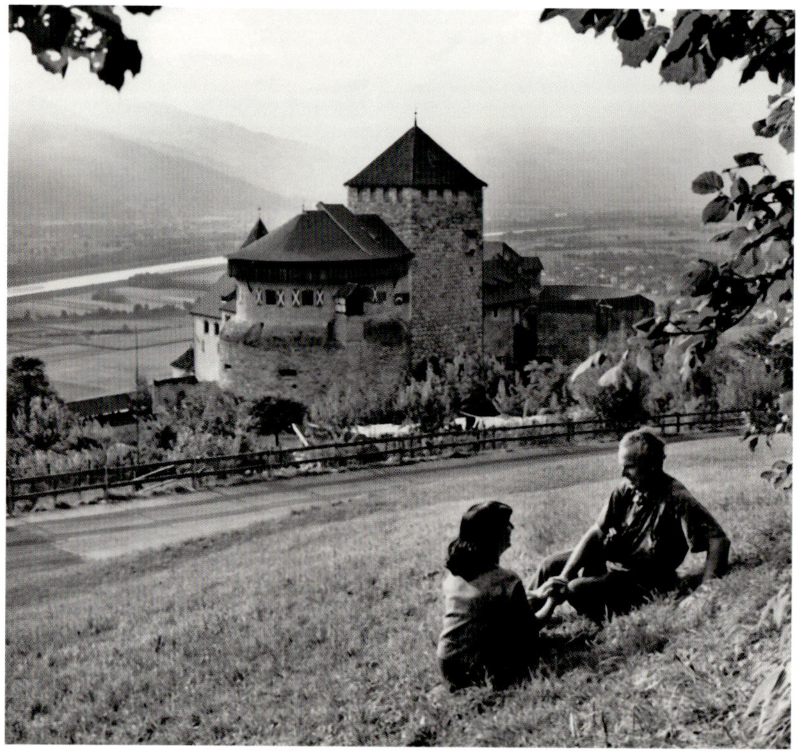

96 In just the past few years of the twenty-first century the company has been purchased, divided, and re-sold in part by a number of investors, including at one time Samsung and later a Danish investment group. As of this writing Rollei Fototechnic is diversifying into multimedia and IT industries, while Franke & Heidecke GmbH continues, as an independent company, to produce photographic apparatus that retains the historical names of Rolleiflex and Rolleivision.

97 "Fritz Henle's New Perspectives, 'Mr. Rollei' and the SL 66: Credo of a 'Convert.'" Rollei-Werke advertising brochure, 1967: unpaged.

98 Travel Book Club advertisement, *Popular Photography,* ca. 1963: [1 p.].

99 Julia Scully, "Fritz Henle: 4 Decades at the Top," *Modern Photography,* March 1970: [62]–71, 107.

100 *Op. cit.: Time — Exposures*: 116.

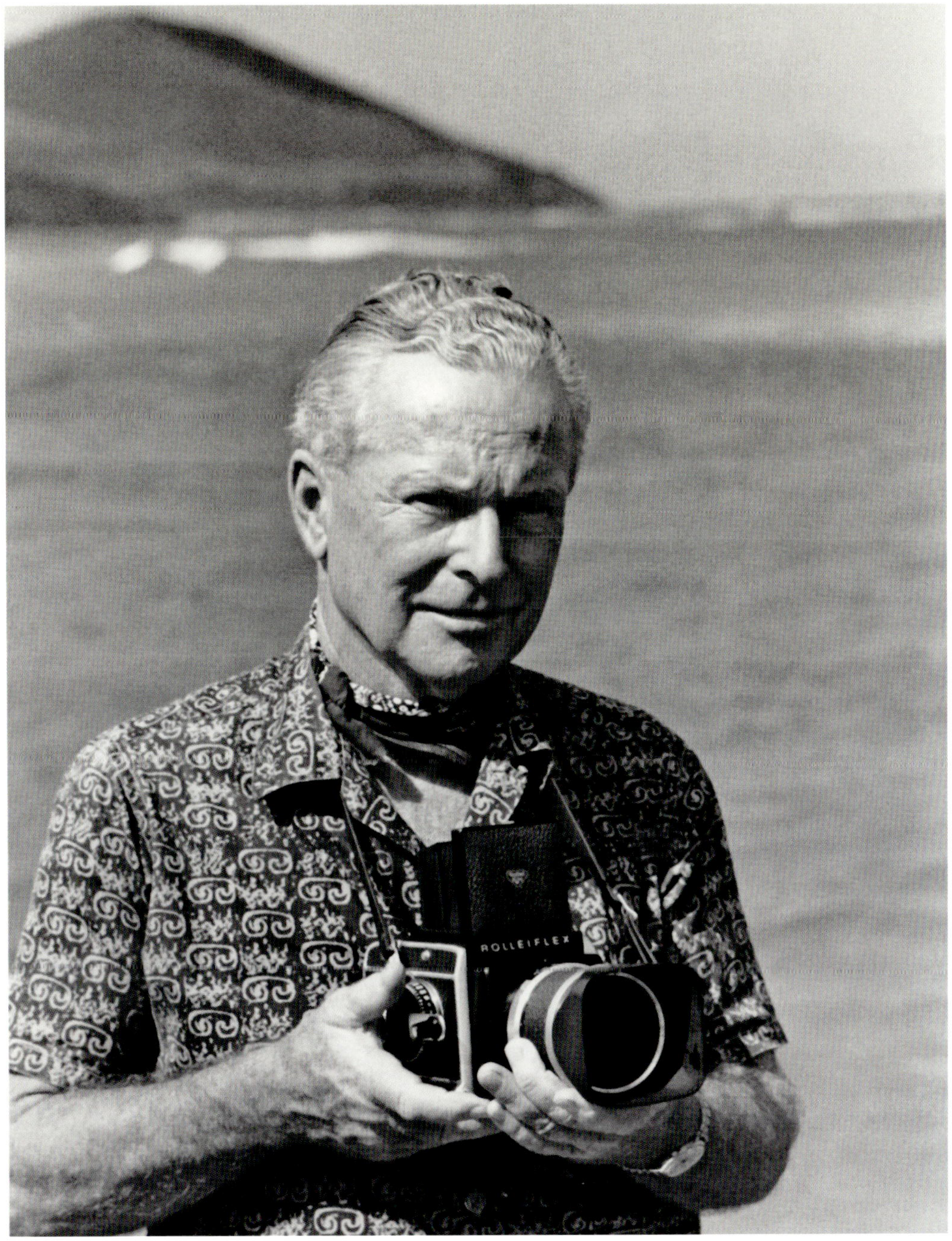

In 1971 he met and impressed another island resident, the wealthy businessman and philanthropist Fairleigh Dickinson. They began an active and far-reaching friendship that would last until Dickinson's death. Dickinson was able to help fund Henle's expansion of his color work to such a degree that new and larger exhibitions, now incorporating significant color imagery as well, continued to tour the world through 1973. To memorialize these Virgin Island exhibitions, he helped finance a large format portfolio, *The American Virgin Islands: A Photographic Essay*. In order for the prints to be displayed to their maximum effect, the plates were printed in heliogravure by C.J. Bucher, Ltd., and to assure their quality, Fritz himself traveled to Lucerne, Switzerland, to personally supervise their printing. As Norman Rothschild would later note in his review "...no matter which Rollei is found in the hands of Henle, the results are always technically clean and visually inspiring... [he] reminds us that the 'straight' camera has great value in helping us remember, or introducing us to, some inspiring scenes of nature and of people."[101]

Dickinson was so impressed with the final production that he and Fritz decided to do another magnum opus, this time featuring two dozen of the photographer's finest works from throughout his long career. Henle was required to re-examine nearly 50 years of work and face the near-impossible editing task of honing them down to only 24 images that could in some fashion capture the range of his styles and subject matters while also giving his audience a sense of his never-ending quest for beauty. The volume, simply titled *Fritz Henle*, was similar in size and design to the earlier large-format Virgin Islands book and featured rotogravure plates that were again printed by Bucher under Fritz's direct supervision. Henle's son Jan, already on his way to becoming an established artist himself, assisted his father with the volume's layout. The texts included an introduction by Alan Porter, the editor of *Camera*, notes on the photographs by the photographer himself, and a brief dedication to Dickinson. When the book was released in 1973, it would prove to be the largest scaled and finest printed of the more than 20 Henle books that had preceded it.

For Fritz Henle no book or poster reproduction could ever match up with the actual experience of viewing a genuine print of his work. He had come to realize once again, through the experience of mounting and circulating the Virgin Island exhibitions, just how important it now was to share both his vision and his realization of that vision by putting more of his actual prints out into the worldwide public arena. In the process he resolved to devote a large portion of his energy and creativity to that commitment.[102]

Therefore, throughout the last more than 20 years of his life, Fritz became an almost one-man exhibition designer, distributor and promoter of his own works. While some of the more notable shows would have specific themes and contents — such as his American retrospective, America: Theme and Variations, or his reprinting of the 1938 *Paris* work — a number of others were often designed for specific institutions and borrowers. Wherever possible he would utilize existing American organizations, such as the U.S. Information

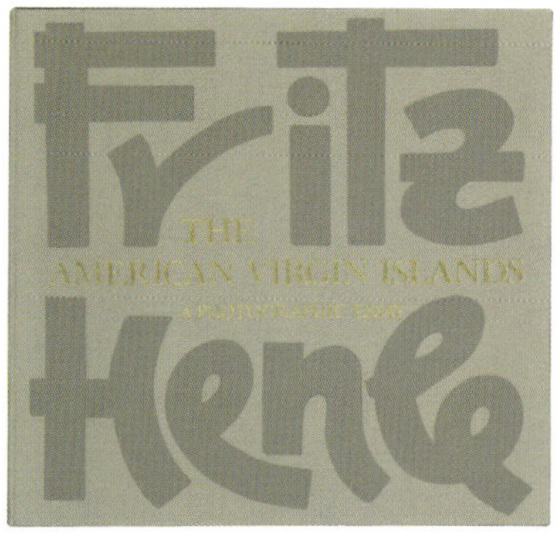

Photographer Unidentified. Fritz Henle on St. Croix. 1970. Henle is holding the Rollei SL66, the single-lens reflex camera that eventually replaced his twin-lens Rolleiflexes.

The American Virgin Islands: A Photographic Essay. New York: 1971. Front cover.

Fritz Henle. Christiansted: 1973. Front cover.

101 *Op. cit.*: Rothschild.

102 Even a hard fall that he took in 1973 failed to slow him down. Although it resulted in painful spinal damage and a long recovery period, Henle embraced his daily walking therapy, assisted by Marguerite, while continuing his work on the project.

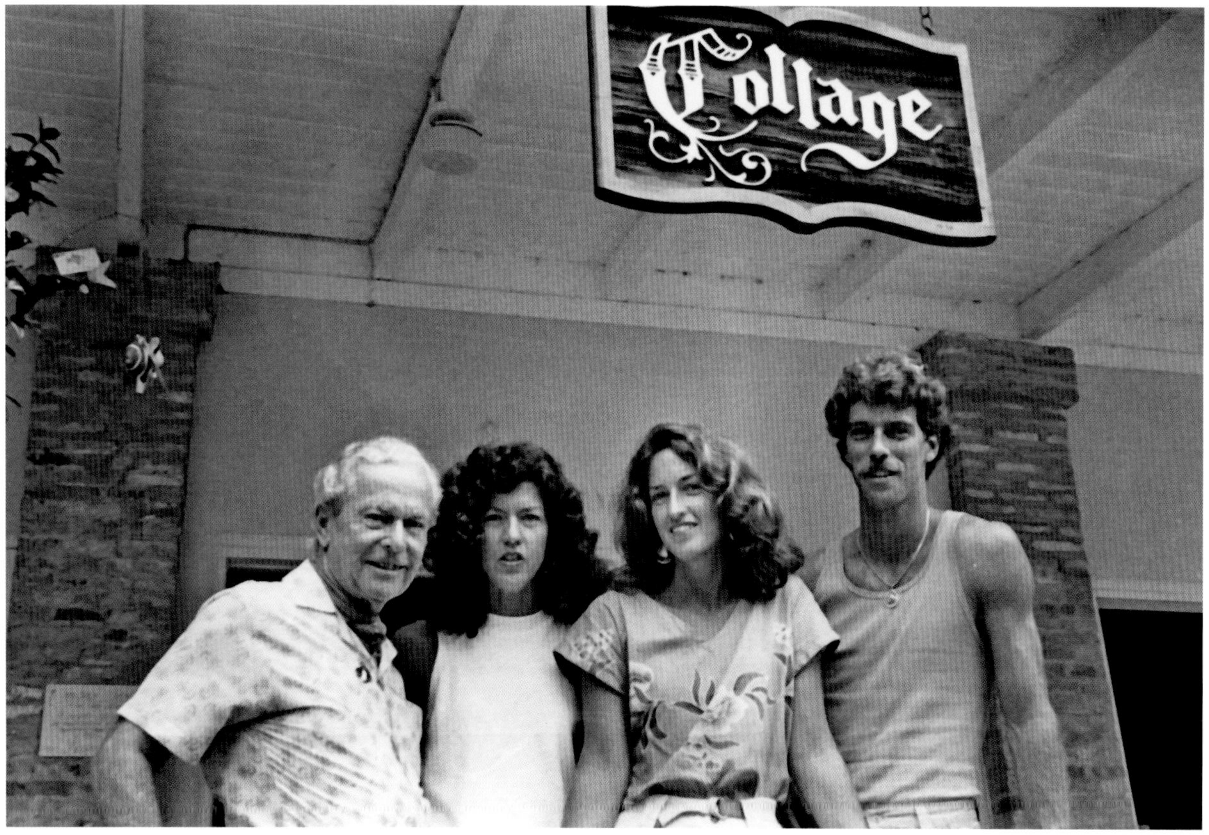

Photographer unknown. Fritz and his children, Maria, Tina and Martin, at their four-person show in Christiansted, St. Croix, U.S. Virgin Islands. 1984.

Agency, the International Exhibitions Foundation, and various U.S. embassies around the globe, to help him find support and venues for his shows. In many instances, however, he relied upon his own networking to discover interested institutions and to design specific exhibitions for them. He brought to bear the same organization and attention to detail that he had employed so vigorously throughout his career as an active photographer, now substituting the creative challenge of taking photographs with an equally creative one of attempting to share his vision through their exhibition before audiences around the world.[103] His enterprise was so successful that there was no year between 1969 and his death, in 1993, in which Fritz Henle did not have a least one show — and frequently many more — traveling to some major museum or other art institution around the world.

His exhibitions also provided him with even further ways to engage with the world and to find newer audiences that were not familiar with him or his work. In 1973 he was surprised to be honored by the Virgin Islands Academy of Arts and Letters for his outstanding contribution to the cultural heritage of the Islands. In 1978 a retrospective of his work at Trinity University in San Antonio, Texas, led him to The University of Texas at Austin and his first meeting with the photohistorian Helmut Gernsheim — whom he had never met despite the fact that both had graduated (two years apart) at the top of their respective classes from the Bayerische Staatslehranstalt für Lichtbildwesen in Munich. The association would further lead to exhibits in Austin and San Antonio in future years and to the eventual housing of his archive and the establishment of his Master Print Project at the Harry Ransom Humanities Research Center at The University of Texas at Austin. Also in 1980 he compiled a massive retrospective exhibition at America's most important private photography gallery, the Witkin Gallery in New York City. The Henle show would become the new gallery's most successful undertaking up to that time, with a record 35 print sales being made in the course of its monthlong run. And, to cap the year off, Henle also had been awarded his first ever Photographer's Fellowship from the National Endowment for the Arts.

After a fashion Fritz Henle was also finally able to keep his commitment to Paul Franke and Reinhold Heidecke, who had vouchsafed his departure from Germany in 1936 by actively supporting the photographer's plan to do a picture book on the United States of America. In 1984 the Rollei firm honored the photographer and its classic twin lens reflex camera by issuing a special edition of the Rolleiflex 2.8 F model. Produced in a numbered limited edition of 500 instruments, the Platin Edition of the Rolleiflex, sporting a Carl Zeiss Planar 2.8/80mm lens, was issued in a special wooden case to collectors and photographers worldwide.

In response, by 1986 Henle was able to review the archives of his early American work in order to curate and produce his retrospective exhibition entitled Fritz Henle: Amerika, Ein Thema mit Variationen. Produced by the American Embassy in Bonn, with the assistance of Dieter Lommel, the program coordinator, and the support of Karl Steinorth of Kodak AG, the traveling exhibition premiered at the Museum für Kunst und Kulturgeschichte in Henle's hometown of Dortmund. From there the show next traveled to Fritz's later home city of Heidelberg, where, in October, the photographer was personally honored at the opening by the city and its mayor. Bringing images of America back to his two hometowns completed a cycle for him —

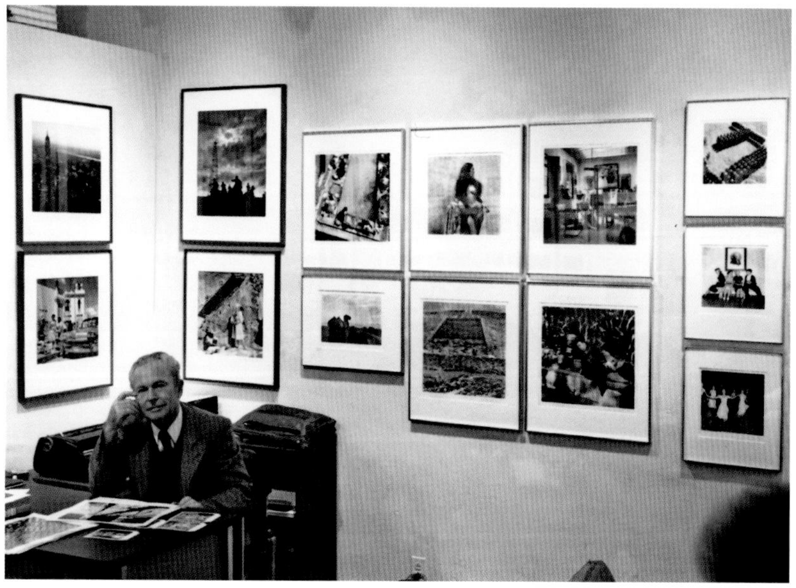

Photographer Unidentified. Fritz Henle at the opening of his retrospective exhibition at the Witkin Gallery, New York City. April 1980.

103 Henle's son Martin would often assist in the operation and recalled many days filled with the matting, framing, rematting, reframing and crating of entire shows. He also recalled the daily or even more frequent runs down from the house on Princess Hill to and from the St. Croix post office. Interview with Martin Henle, July 11, 2007.

an honored "homecoming," if you will — and brought Henle a final emotional repatriation to the country he had fled exactly fifty years earlier. The exhibition, one of his most successful, would tour Germany for more than three years, and Henle made certain that one of its primary venues, in honor of his late patrons Franke and Heidecke, would be the Rollei Fototechnik in Braunschweig.

In 1987 a very different sort of dream was realized, as Fritz and Marguerite's three children — all by now established or rising artists in their own right and working independently from their father — were able to collaborate on a joint family exhibition with him in Christiansted. Maria had become an award-winning painter and etcher in New York City, while Tina and Martin were both accomplished photographers. It was heartwarming for Fritz to see the family tradition, already well begun with his first son, Jan, being carried on so strongly by his other offspring. As Maria would later joke: "I think we all have little camera-shaped cells in our blood... The disease has manifested itself."[104]

In 1989 Henle would repeat the success of his Amerika exhibition with another successful tour — that of his pre–World War II journey through Paris. Entitled Fritz Henle: Paris 1938, the show was sponsored by the Goethe Institute and, after its premiere in Dortmund, would travel to more than 20 venues in Germany and Europe. The exhibition again met critical success and even engendered an illustrated catalogue — both of which served to renew yet once more Henle's initial faith in his intuition and vision about the Paris project. Finally, at the time of his death in 1993, Henle was also actively engaged in the organization of a retrospective exhibition of his life's work — again for the Museum für Kunst und Kulturgeschichte in Dortmund. The exhibition, now titled Fritz Henle: 1909–1993, was mounted in conjunction with a posthumous publication in 1994.

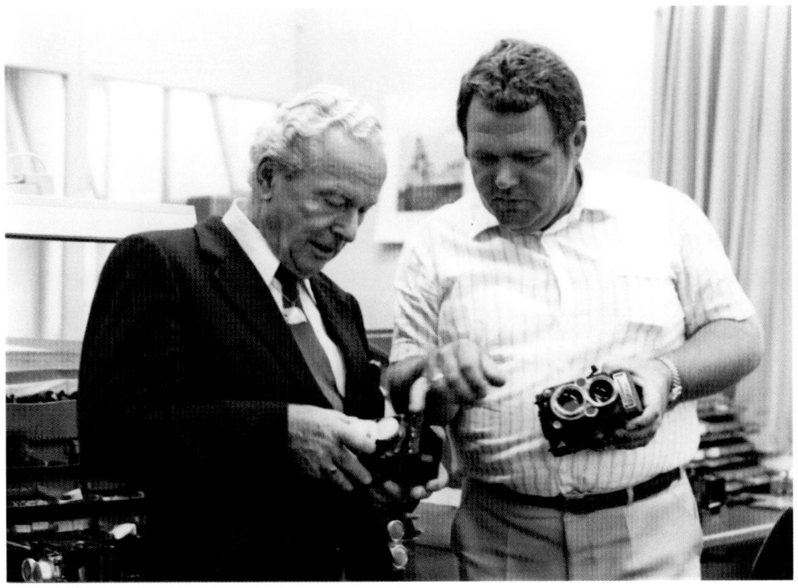

Photographer Unidentified. Fritz Henle with camera technician Bob Bacon discussing the repair of his Rolleiflexes. Austin, Texas. 1985.

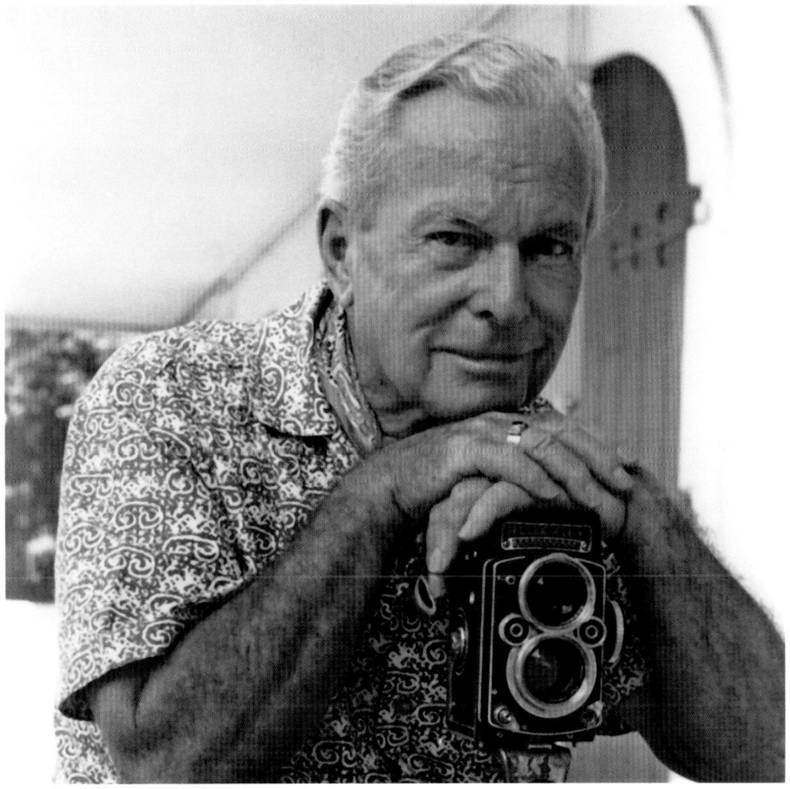

Nils Fritzner. Fritz Henle with his old 2.8 Rolleiflex. St. Thomas, U.S. Virgin Islands. March 1984.

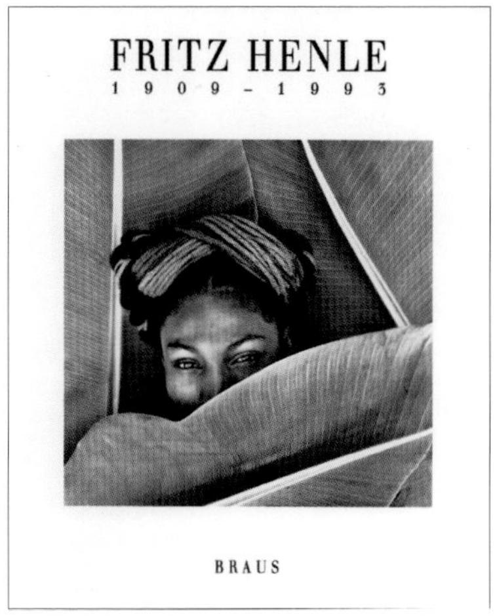

Fritz Henle (1909–1993): Die Quadratur der Schönheit. Retrospektive für den Fotografen Fritz Henle. Dortmund and Heidelberg: 1994. Front cover.

Looking back over his life and fashioning publications and exhibitions over more than 50 years would bring Fritz into deep consideration of the future of his entire archive of prints, negatives, publications and memorabilia. Above all else he was seeking an opportunity to revisit his entire oeuvre, select the works that he felt were his very best, and make a final definitive print of them on modern photochemical papers — which he felt were far superior to the papers he had used previously throughout his professional life.[105] By the early 1980s he moved his negative archive into the processing lab of Walter Lenoir, a master printer in Austin, Texas. With funding from his old friend Fairleigh Dickinson he began what we would christen the Fritz Henle Master Print Project — a program that helped him select and print up to 200 prints per year for inclusion into the permanent collection of the Harry Ransom Center. When the torrential rains from the aftermath of a 1982 hurricane struck Austin, Lenoir was able to rescue all of Henle's imagery from his flooding lab. Henle approached Decherd Turner, then director at the Ransom Center, to see that his entire archive was safely moved into a secure room in its building. From that new base Fritz, always accompanied by one or more of his children, continued to return almost annually to the Ransom Center, where he would work with the staff on the ongoing Master Print Project. Maria, Tina and Martin were able at various times to put aside their growing artistic careers and accompany their father to Austin to assist him with the production of the prints as well as with the equally important task of helping Fritz arrange and catalog his entire archive. At the end of each visit Henle would personally approve, title

104 Venetia Harvey, "Art is a part of life for the Henle family," *The Virgin Islands Daily News*, January 24, 1987: 1.

105 To his credit, Fritz did understand the current art market and the much higher values that it placed upon his rarer vintage prints. Nonetheless, he would always claim that the prints he was producing late in life with modern papers and chemicals were far superior, both technically and artistically, to the earlier renditions from the same negatives.

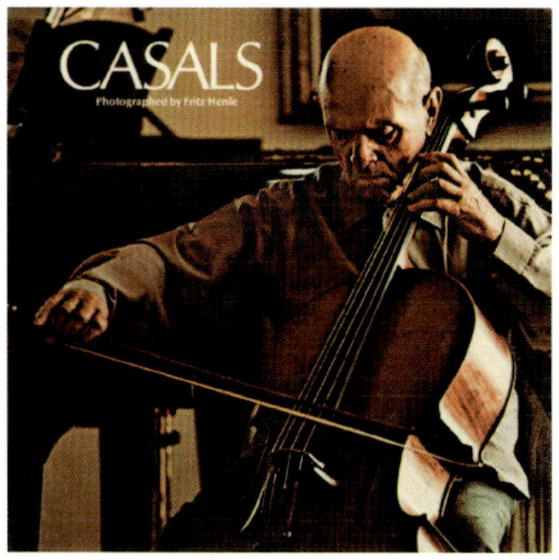

Casals. Garden City, NY: 1975. Front dust jacket.

Marguerite Henle. Pablo Casals and Fritz Henle looking over the print of *Concentration* that Casals has just signed. 1972.

and sign each finished master print, and his subsequent final review — laced with personal recollections and anecdotes — remained a particularly rewarding experience for us all.

It is important to note that, throughout all his exhibition and archival endeavors during those final decades, Fritz Henle never abandoned his first love of making new photographs as well. At various times and in any number of interviews he was looking to the future, planning to do a big book on his homeland of Germany or to perhaps journey back once more to photograph the people and sights of modern Japan and China. When Hurricane Hugo cut a devastating path across St. Croix on the night and early morning of September 16th and 17th, 1989, Fritz, Marguerite and Martin weathered the storm from their family home on Little Princess Hill. Throughout the very next days, after seeing to the stability of the house and the safety of the family, Fritz was out and about with his Rolleis, photographing the terrible beauty within the aftermath of one of the Caribbean's worst storms of that century.

It was also during those final years that he continued to conceptualize and make images for a mammoth project entitled *The Story of Life*. He envisioned the final book and exhibition as an interpretive study of the faces and figures of all humanity, covering a very broad spectrum of subjects — including representative images of most races, cultures and creeds and photographs ranging from birth to death, from babies to the very elderly, from portraits to nude figure studies. It remained largely unfinished at the time of Henle's passing, on January 31, 1993, but the surviving images and sequences are most intriguing and do give us some sense of the intense levels of creativity and op-

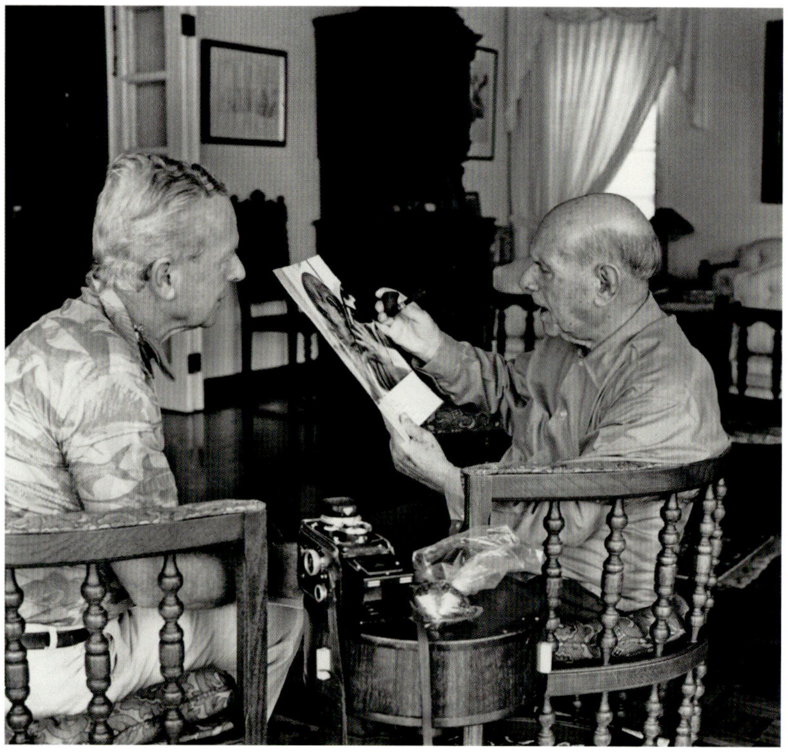

timism that he engendered even into his final days. Not surprisingly, even while his magnificent heart was failing him Fritz was speculating on when he would be well enough to get up from his hospital bed, grab his constant Rollei and take more photographs.

Clearly, however, the most invigorating and fully realized body of work from this final period goes back to 1971 — and provided Fritz Henle with the opportunity to hear once more the photographer's song that he first heard in his small darkroom beneath the music room of his Dortmund home. For it was in that year that he met and came to photograph one of the world's greatest musicians, Pablo Casals.[106] Journeying to the Casals home on the nearby island of Puerto Rico, Fritz and Marguerite were first drawn to the music of his cello coming from the open front door. Henle clicked away with his Rollei's soft shutter while the transported master completed his morning practice session, after which he and Marguerite met Casals and his wife, Martita, and swiftly formed a close friendship. For the next year Henle would have unparalleled access to the maestro, visiting his home often and photographing the world-famous cellist at practice and in repose. They would also spend many hours in conversation ranging from art to world politics, and Fritz gained profound insight once more into the intricate relationship of music and photography as well as into his own creativity.

To translate and elevate that emotional relationship into photographs would prove to be a most challenging enterprise, but Henle was committed to succeeding, and when he finally displayed his images to Don Pablo he was rewarded with his subject's enthusiastic response — "This is beyond photography!" — and an even more moving response — "When he saw it later he become so excited that he went to the piano immediately and played some music."[107] Casals even signed a print of his favorite image from Henle's series, *Concentration*, for the photographer.

From the first, Fritz knew that he had to create a publication to celebrate their collaboration. As he envisioned it: "It is a book different from any ever done about a great artist. People think a book about a man should be a biography. Actually, this will be a poem which I have photographed."[108] The final book, *Casals*, would be published in 1975, followed by eight additional foreign publications running through 1983. The resulting series of volumes was published in far too small a scale to do justice to the richness of Henle's photographs, but the elegant intimacy of the editions was praised and most of the versions did enjoy healthy sales.[109] More to the point, Fritz continued to use traditional larger prints of the work, both in his later retrospective exhibitions and in the series of shows that he would circulate exclusively about Casals in the 1980s and 1990s. And, packaged with each exhibition was Casals's own statement about his great friend: "Fritz Henle is an artist whose pictures effect

106 Henle photographed many others from the world of music — chiefly his friend and fellow Crucian resident Victor Borge. However, he made only random portraits of them throughout his life, none of which approached the inspired elegance of his complete series on Casals.

107 Jacob Deschin. "Fritz Henle on Pablo Casals." *The Photo Reporter*, June 1974: 2.

108 Freck Hart. "Henle's Casals Album To Be Photographic Poem." *The San Juan Star*, October 28, 1973: 32.

109 Another project that Henle was not able to realize before his death was his plan to reissue the *Casals* book in a much larger format in order to do greater justice not only to his photographs but also to Casals himself.

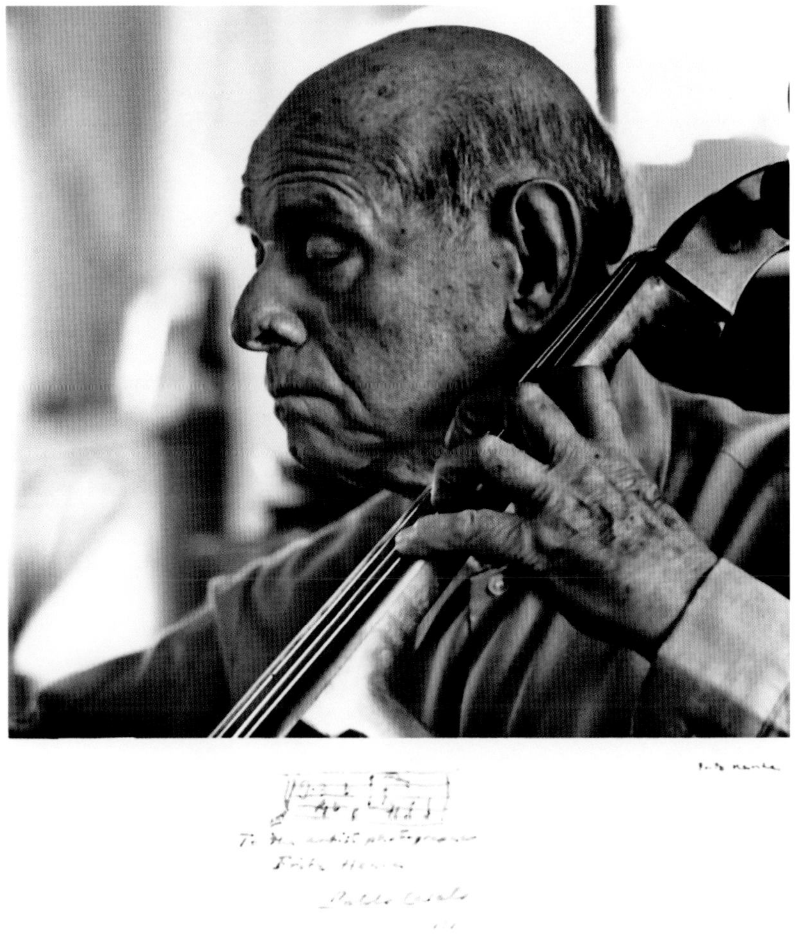

Fritz Henle. *Concentration.* 1972. Gelatin silver print with original ink manuscript and signature by Pablo Casals.

[*sic*] me deeply. They are not just photographic images, but expressions created by deep feeling. His Photography is as much a creative art to him as Music is to me."[110]

Throughout the remainder of his life, Fritz Henle would remain deeply affected by his close friendship with Pablo Casals. Whether it was their age, their successes in their separate fields, or the mutual respect that one artist can have for another remains unclear, but the results that the relationship had on Henle's work were important to his art. As a singular body of work the Pablo Casals portfolio of his images transports a strong emotional impact, and the musical feelings that it ultimately captures, seen but unheard, are as tangibly complex as the images of the master cellist that are preserved by Henle's Rolleis. As he did through his photographic interpretation and rendering of so many subjects over so many years and throughout so many lands, Fritz Henle not only secured the music of the spheres but also provided his viewers with the profound opportunity to experience them anew and forever.

By closely studying the photographs of Fritz Henle — and most especially what he and many others have written about them over the years — one becomes aware of just how varied has been the range of his art. Many descriptive terms have been employed to describe and categorize his photographs. In the course of this research, they have included freelance, romantic, reportorial, pictorial, picturesque, travel, fashion, commercial, portrait, feature, journalistic, documentary, celebrity, straight, modernist, avant garde, symbolic, metaphorical, industrial, landscape, urban, lyrical, cultural, sociological, interpretive and inspirational.[111]

It becomes quickly obvious that the entire oeuvre of Fritz Henle's photographic world is not easy to categorize. In fact, unlike nearly all of his contemporaries, he was not driven to specialize in one or two dominant styles or types of photography throughout the more than 60 years of his professional life. As one critic would summarize it, "Fritz is possessed of great sensitivity, and his desire to see and record beauty with his camera is a reflection of his own deep-seated longing for perfection. It is hard to separate the man from his photographs. His pictures are true representations of himself, and in them one can always find beauty, even though the subject is inherently depressing or ugly...the subject acquires a tenderness and beauty that transcends the sadness of the situation. Such ability is the hallmark of the creative photographer."[112]

Henle did not limit himself to particular subject areas or schools of photography — his usual response being that "too many things interest me"[113] — and perhaps that lack of easy categorization is what has kept him out of any form of simple art historical categorization or has made him a difficult artist to pigeonhole into the general surveys of the history of photography. As Jacquelyn Judge would observe: "Most photographers begin with a fresh spirit. Soon their imaginations dull, and they improve only technically. Henle had such a thorough grounding in technique that he could not get much better technically. His growth has been in approach. 'I can hardly limit myself as far as subject matter is concerned,' he says. 'There are many things which I would have overlooked ten years ago which I find fascinating today.'"[114] The answer to Fritz was at once both simple and yet completely fundamental: "To him photography is one field — and the separate categories provide a file clerk's nomenclature, nothing more."[115]

To Henle great photography was above all else that which engaged in the emotional aspects of life — and was thus capable of being discovered in almost any style of expression or subject from the panoply of human experience.[116] As one editor would put it, "Fritz Henle is a man who uses not only a camera, but his heart."[117] For the most part Fritz's vision was grounded in a clarity and directness that made his subjects easy to identify or describe superficially. If, however, one had the opportunity to discuss his photographs with him for any period of time, it became evident that he did not see their interpretation in so simplistic a light. As Freedom, and all that it implied, remained the guiding force in this life, so Beauty remained his constant goal.

The eternal quest for the Beautiful in Art revolves around not only the Good but also the True. And for artists of Henle's caliber

110 Pablo Casals. In: Fritz Henle. *Pablo Casals*, 1973: unpaged.

111 For years there was an old family saying that "Fritz has done everything except underwater photography."

112 Willard Clark. "Fritz Henle, Master of Twin-Lens Reflex." *U.S. Camera*, February 1956: [70].

113 *Op. cit.*: Fuhrings, July 1947.

114 Jacquelyn Judge. "The World and Fritz Henle." *Photography*, Fall 1947: 64.

115 Jacquelyn Judge. "Fritz Henle — What Makes Him Click." *Popular Photography*, May 1950: 37.

116 One sense of this comes from the fact that the fellow photographers whom he most consistently admired were a tremendously diverse group, including Andreas Feininger, Alfred Eisenstaedt, Henri Cartier-Bresson, W. Eugene Smith and Edward Weston.

117 "Notes on the Picture Section." *Popular Photography*, June 1947: 84.

Photographer Unidentified. Fritz Henle supported by his Bavarian assistant on the cliff edge while photographing Neuschwanstein Castle. Germany. 1974.

Tina Henle. Portrait of Fritz. April 1979.

that Truth was to be found not in an idealization of what could be but rather in the discovery and celebration of things as they are. Far beyond any mere stylistic devices, Fritz's photography achieved a profound sensibility that was eloquent in its embrace of Beauty's nuance and wonder. Indeed, it was no coincidence that whenever Fritz spoke of that Beauty that he strove to secure, he would frequently use the language of music — employing emotional terms such as harmony, tone, balance, interpretation, performance, or even abstracts such as love and hope — in order to try to convey the power and clarity that he had originally experienced in securing each photograph.[118]

To understand Henle's artistic sensibilities, one must first recognize that the foundation of his success in creating so many stunning photographs lay in his remarkable technical achievements. He always pushed for the greatest clarity in his negatives and transparencies in order that he could then achieve the highest quality of luminosity and brilliance in their subsequent prints. Only in that fashion did he feel that he could do full justice to both his subjects and his own vision. From early on in his professional career he established a reputation as an outstanding printer — undoubtedly built upon the strong foundation of his two years of experimentation and practice that evolved in the music-filled darkroom of his early Dortmund home. His subsequent and continuous success served the needs of his viewers and collectors while also inspiring his contemporaries. Herb Giles, a fellow founder of the ASMP, typified the attitudes of so many when he noted, "I was using Fritz Henle's film because I admired his prints as being the finest grain and the loveliest stuff."[119] As most reviewers and critics so frequently acknowledged "...every Henle photograph can be

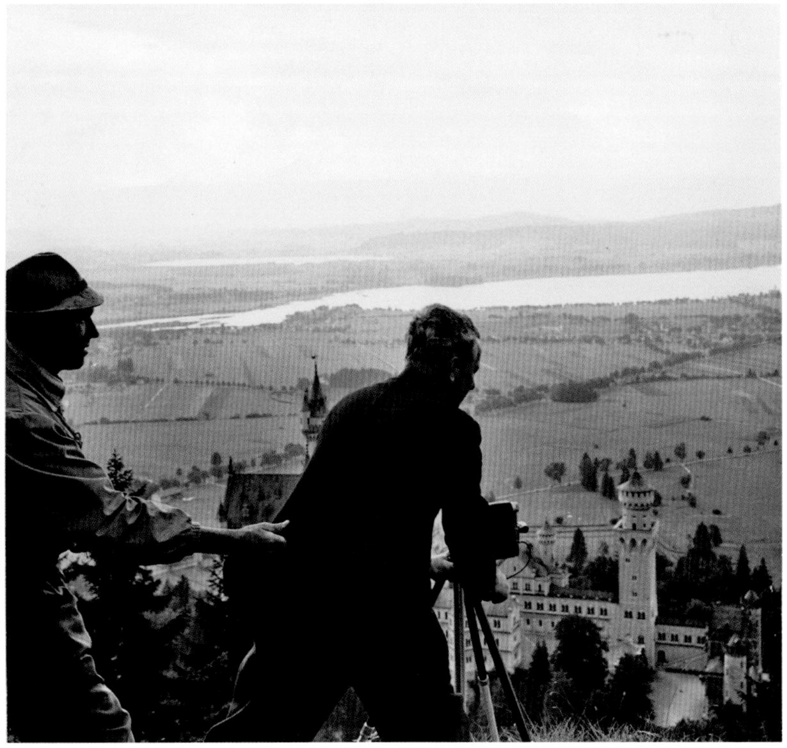

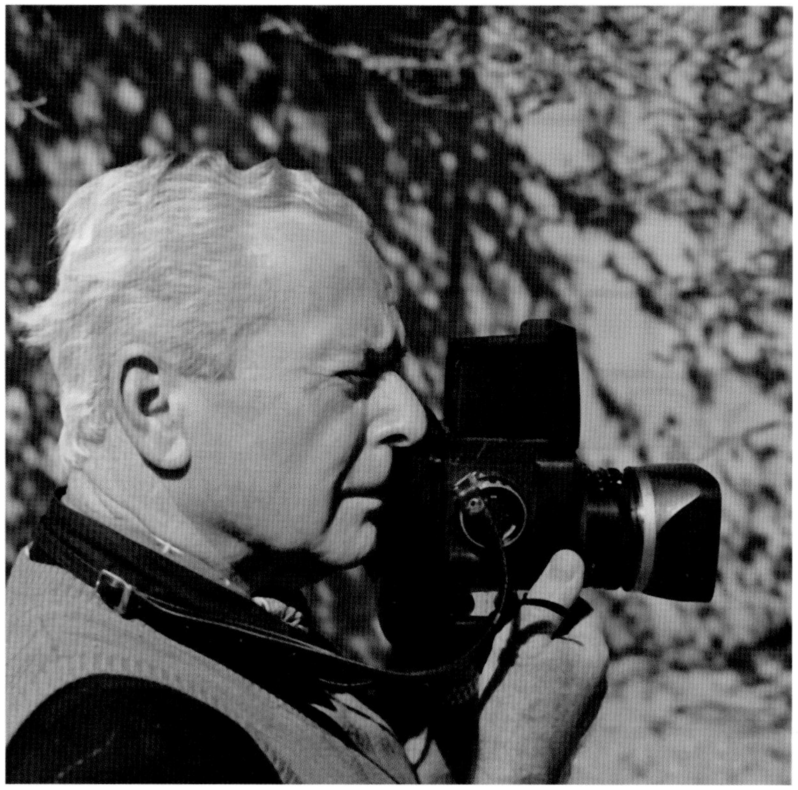

counted on to have what appears to be an unhurried elegance of composition, great sharpness in depth, and fine image quality. His prints are masterpieces of subtle shading and exquisitely crisp detail."[120]

In addition, the simplicity and directness of Henle's vision was also representative of his equipment and how he chose to employ it. Fritz's strong commitment to a single camera system, the Rollei and its square film format, lay in opposition to the practice of most of his fellow professionals, who always found security in owning a wide variety of cameras and support apparatus. Henle packed lightly — "Spartan simple," as one writer would characterize it[121] — worked flexibly and moved quickly, generally with two Rolleiflexes (one for black and white and the other for color), plus a tripod (which he employed consistently for nearly 90 percent of his work) and his reserve of film. And that was it. Period. As Alan Porter would acknowledge: "It was men like Henle who persevered in their belief that the small camera was not only a necessary tool, [and] who convinced us that its convenience and portability would change our old belief in making images."[122]

For Henle, nonetheless, apparatus would always be secondary and only supplemental to seeing: "But personally, I prefer a very straight approach, which definitely is never the easy way. Simplicity is a very hard goal to reach."[123] At its purest Fritz Henle's vision remains remarkable and rare for one fundamental reason: his stunning ability to think photographically regardless of all the other factors that enter into the making of a photograph. His ceaseless exploration for a certain freedom of life and creativity would lead Fritz to clarify the world about him with a vigorous assuredness of purpose and

118 The family also recalls many after-dinner conversations during which Fritz would sit at the table and engage in discussions while absentmindedly tapping out the rhythm of a silent song with his hands on the tabletop. When it was pointed out, he would say, "I have a song in my head." Telephone interview with Tina Henle, March 31, 2008.

119 [Maria Henle.] "Retrospective: Photographer Fritz Henle 1909–1993." *Art Fusion*, Spring–Summer 2007: 13. Giles stated that the fine-grain black and white film that he found Henle preferred at that time was Ansco Supreme ASA 50. See also: www.asmp.org/60th/interview_herb_giles.php.

120 "Meet the Rollei's Master." [Publication unknown.] ca. 1989: 73.

121 *Op. cit.*: "Simplicity is Henle's Keynote": 57.

122 Alan Porter. "Eye of Truth." In: *Fritz Henle*. Christiansted, 1973: unpaged.

123 Freck Hart. "Lensman Was Always in Focus." *The San Juan Star*, February 6, 1972: 27.

124 *Op. cit.*: [Hall.] "One Man and A Rolleiflex: Fritz Henle." 30.

125 *Ibid.*: 28.

126 *Op. cit.*: Judge. "The World and Fritz Henle." 62.

127 *Op. cit.*: Newhall. 5.

technique: "In photography, he says, you will spend the rest of your life learning to see light. It will not take long to learn all about the camera, but you will never come to the end of discovering about the effects of light itself. The only rule is to watch the world about you, all the time, even when you have not got a camera in your hand, and notice the behaviour of light."[124]

There is, finally, in Fritz Henle's unending quest for beauty an overwhelming sense of hope for all of humanity. For him photography would remain, first and always, a "tremendously effective medium to show people beauty, and I am obsessed by showing them beauty. Too few people do that these days."[125] In our present era of cynicism and doubt his message may seem woefully naïve and out of place. But then again, "Henle's camera is an optimistic one… It is as if Henle said 'The world is a wonderful place' — and then proceeded to prove it."[126] As he himself would characterize it to the Newhalls, "my way of seeing has never been able to change from a positive approach and the deep love of the beauty of life itself."[127]

The tangible evidence of this state of mind and heart is, of course, the powerful corpus of photographs that he has left us — and the inherent beauty that he strove to find and preserve within each and every print. As he once reflected, "It seems like a constant struggle to reach out for the infinite — for the ability to comprehend and to translate one's vision of beauty."[128] In some sense it was an impossible challenge but one that he, like centuries of artists before him, unfailingly accepted throughout all his days. In likening it to music he perhaps foreswore any further attempt to define precisely what beauty was, but by encouraging all of us to listen to the photographer's song he also recognized that its quest was the final goal for all humankind.

Herbert Matter. Fritz Henle. New York. 1938. Fritz always called this publicity photograph the "camera on my nose" shot.

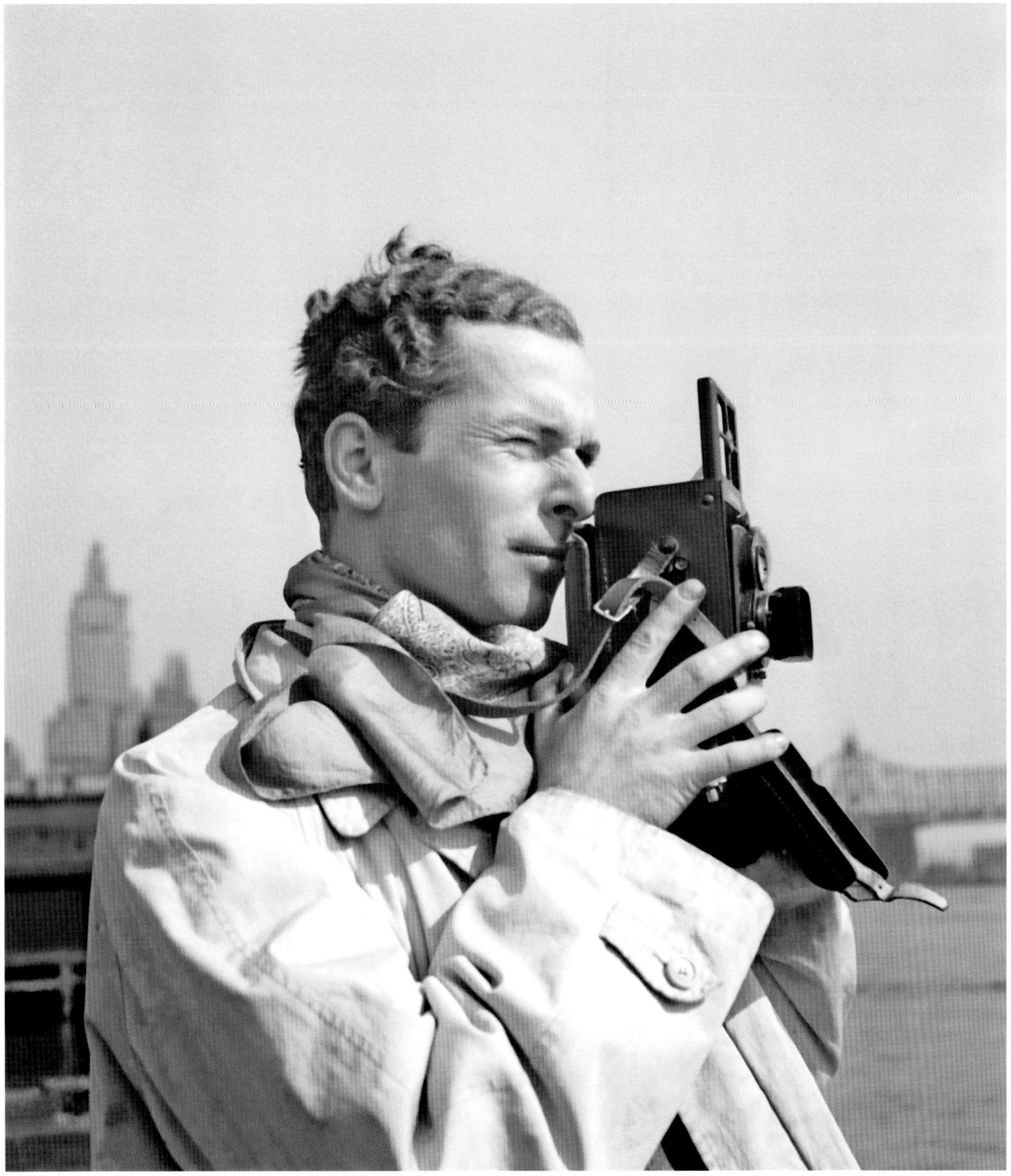

Early in his professional American career, in the late 1930s, Fritz Henle was on assignment when he found himself the subject of an anonymous reporter's article in an unidentified Colorado newspaper. The correspondent would describe the *LIFE* photographer thusly: "Short and wiry, he seems to be possessed of a limitless amount of energy. He puts his whole being into his work and like most successful people, loves the work that he is doing."[129] It would prove to be both accurate and prescient for Fritz's entire career.

Indeed, even toward the end, in 1989 the legendary photohistorian L. Fritz Gruber defined Henle with words that were as simple and direct as Fritz's own imagery: "Basically Fritz Henle is still a man who is in love with Photography."[130] It encapsulates with profound clarity Henle's great hope that "emotion [could be] translated through creativity and technique into photographs that enable the viewer to share the photographer's vision."[131] Perhaps that remains Henle's providential message: that through the music and majesty of photography lies the simple, direct, nurturing, honest and fundamental path by which all of us can continue to commit to life itself and thus must never completely forsake the search for its beauty.

128 Fritz Henle. Untitled manuscript. Typescript, October 8, 1978: 2. Henle Family Archive.

129 "Colorado Mountains Delight Photographer Sent By Life Magazine On Glacier Trip." [Periodical unidentified], ca. 1939: [1 p.].

130 L. Fritz Gruber. "Laudatio." Translation by Fritz Henle from the Vernissage of the Paris 1938 exhibition in the Museum für Kunst und Kulturgeschichte in Dortmund — June 23, 1989. Manuscript, undated: [1]. Henle Family Archive.

131 *Op. cit.*: "Fritz Henle: The Photographer Who 'Documents Happiness' in the Virgin Islands.": 6.

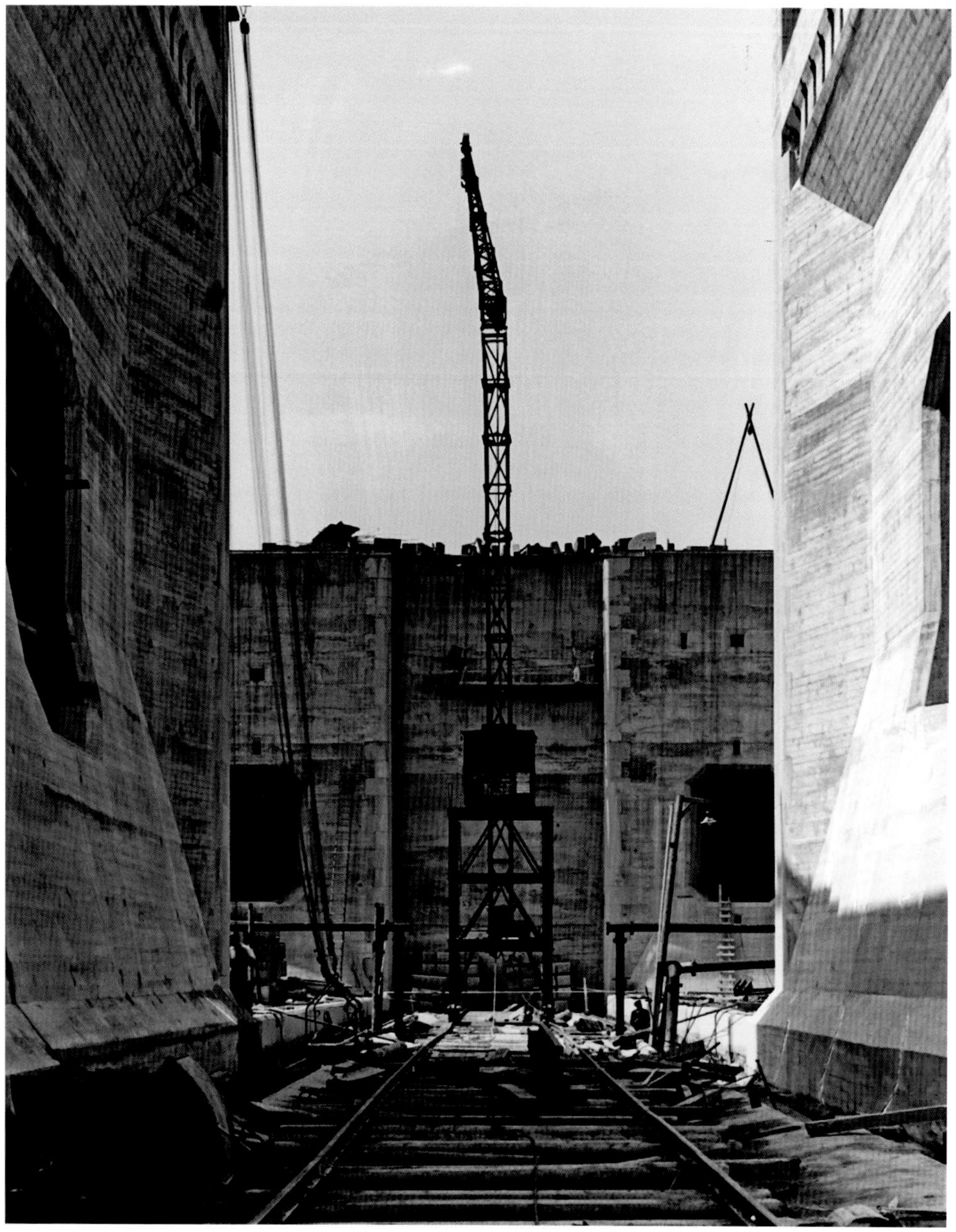

(above) Nord Schleuse Shipyards, Bremen. 1929.
(right) Blast Furnaces and Cooling Towers of Steelworks near Dortmund. 1929.

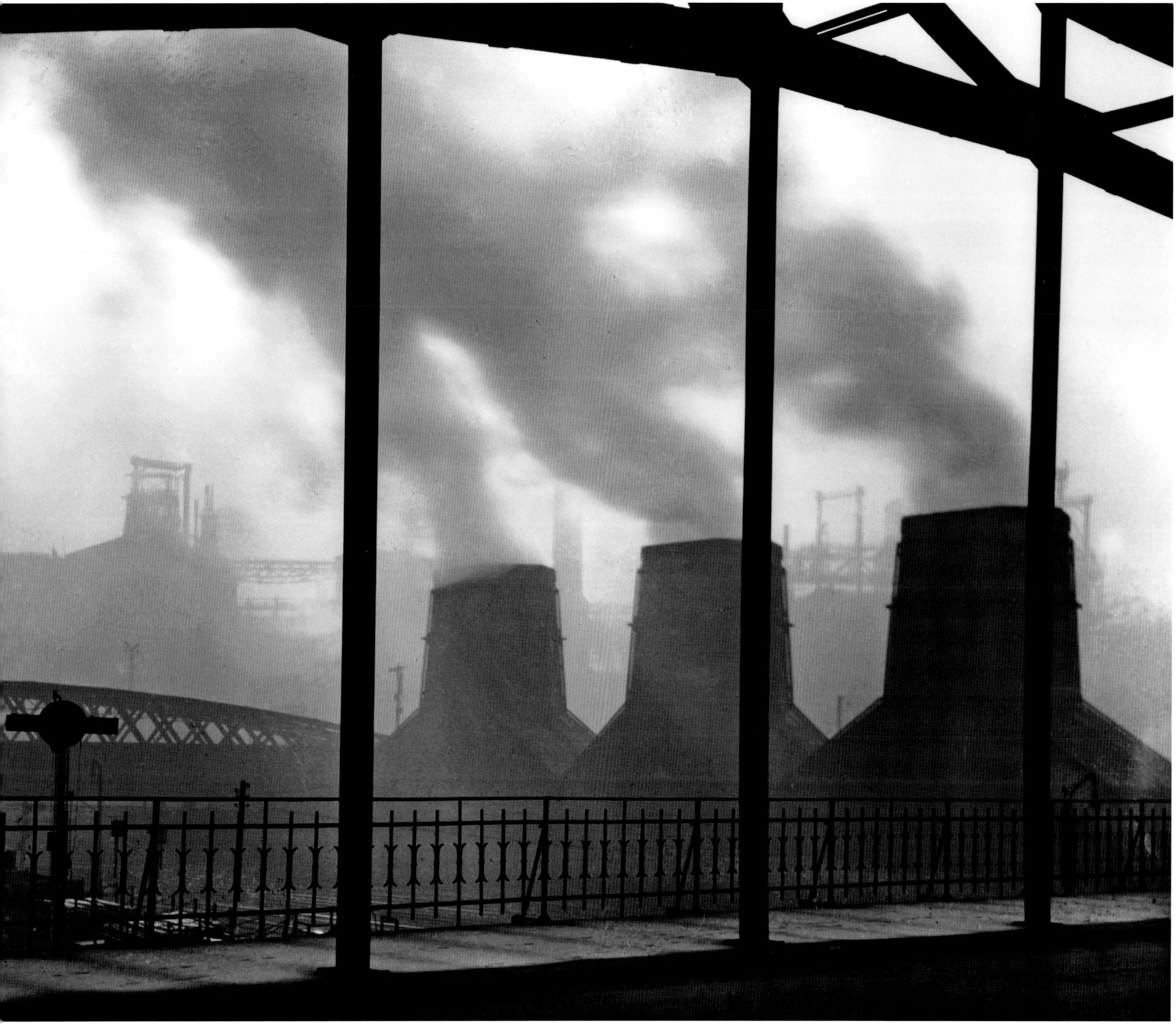

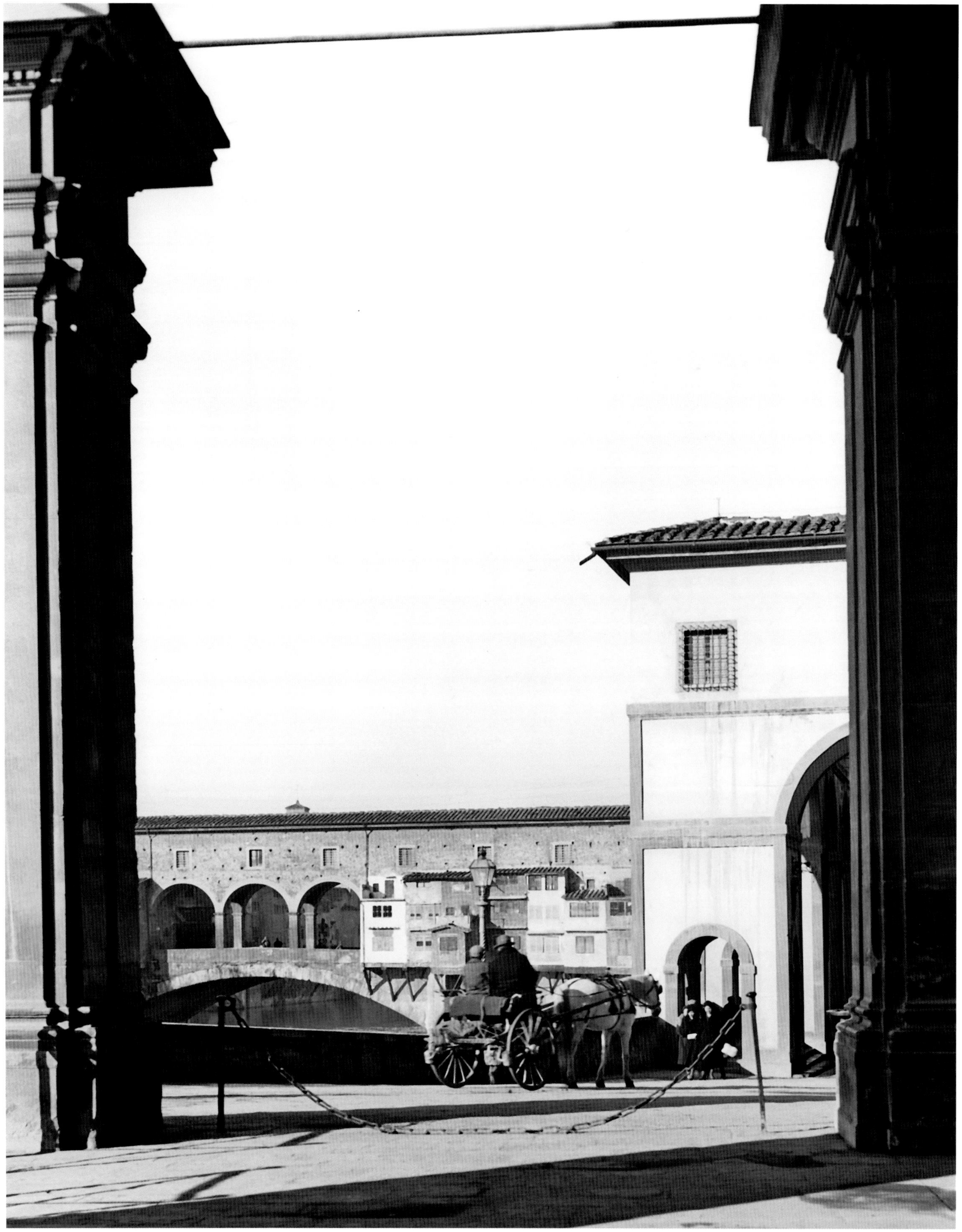

Ponte Vecchio with Horse Cart, Florence, Italy. 1931.

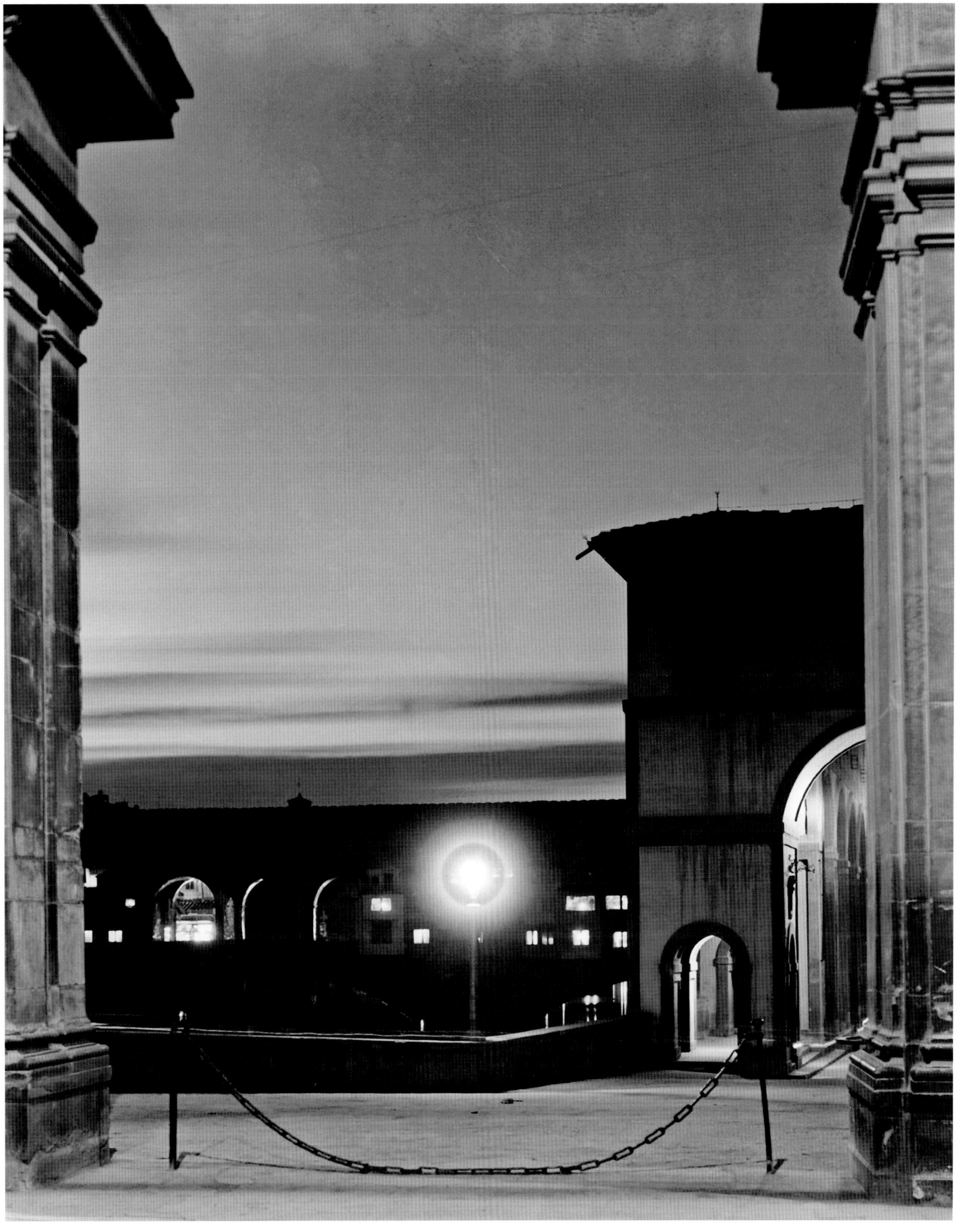

Ponte Vecchio at Night, Florence, Italy. 1931.

Cathedral Steps in the Rain, Siena, Italy. 1931.

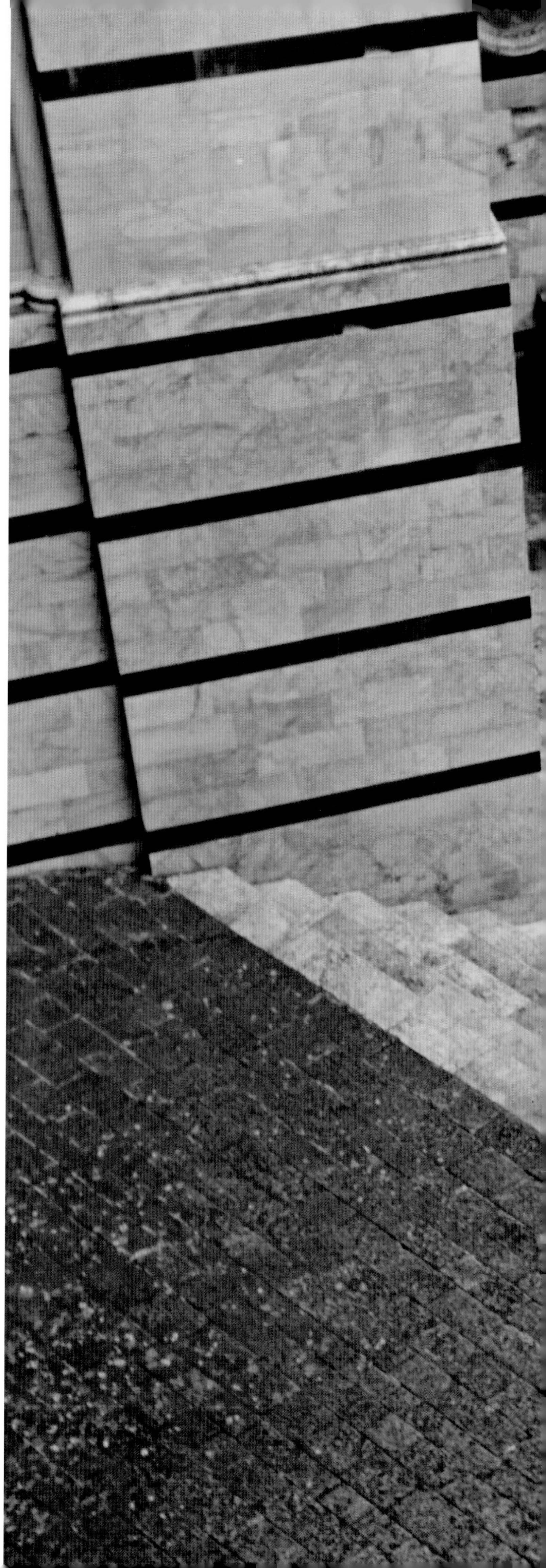

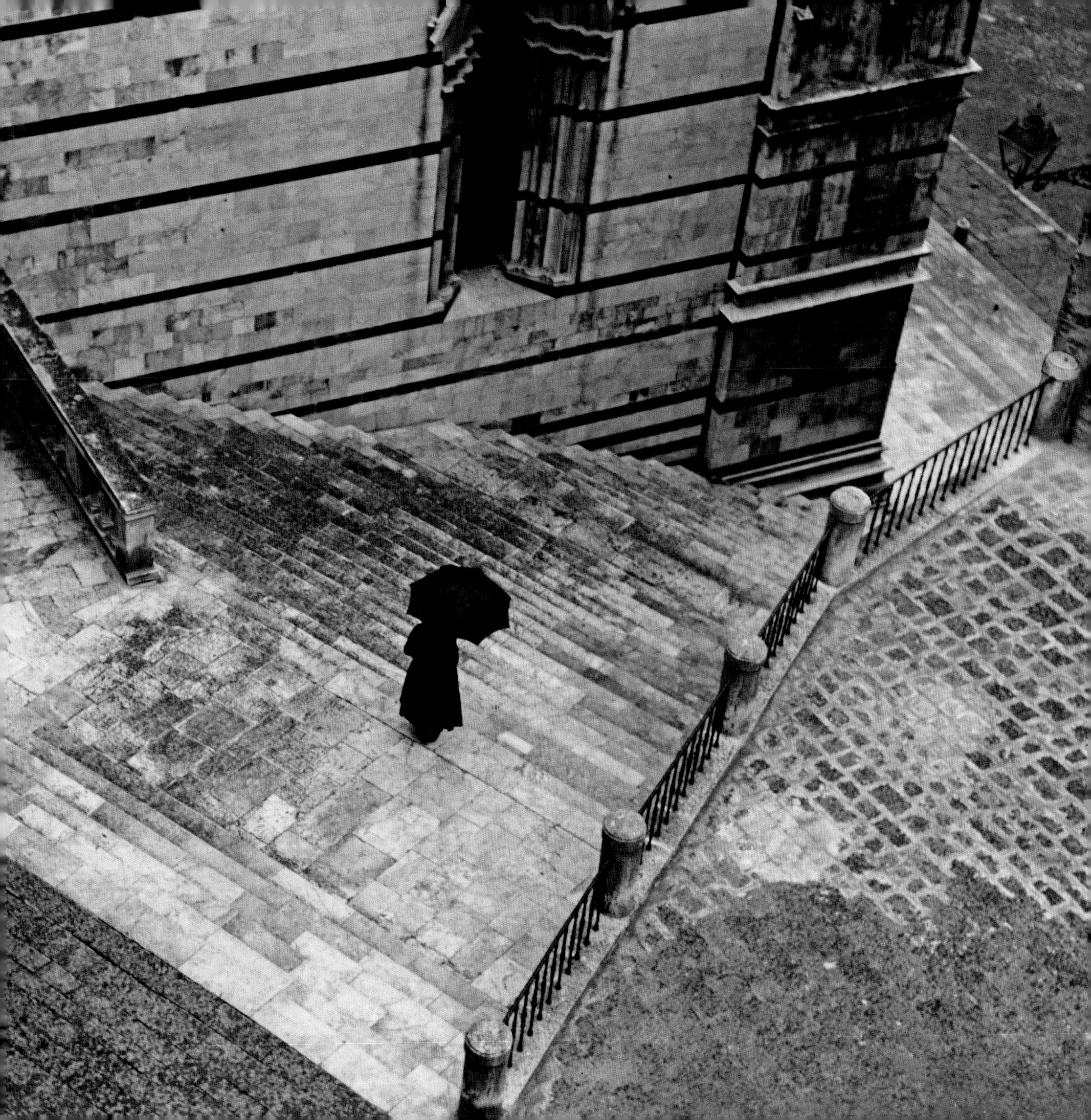

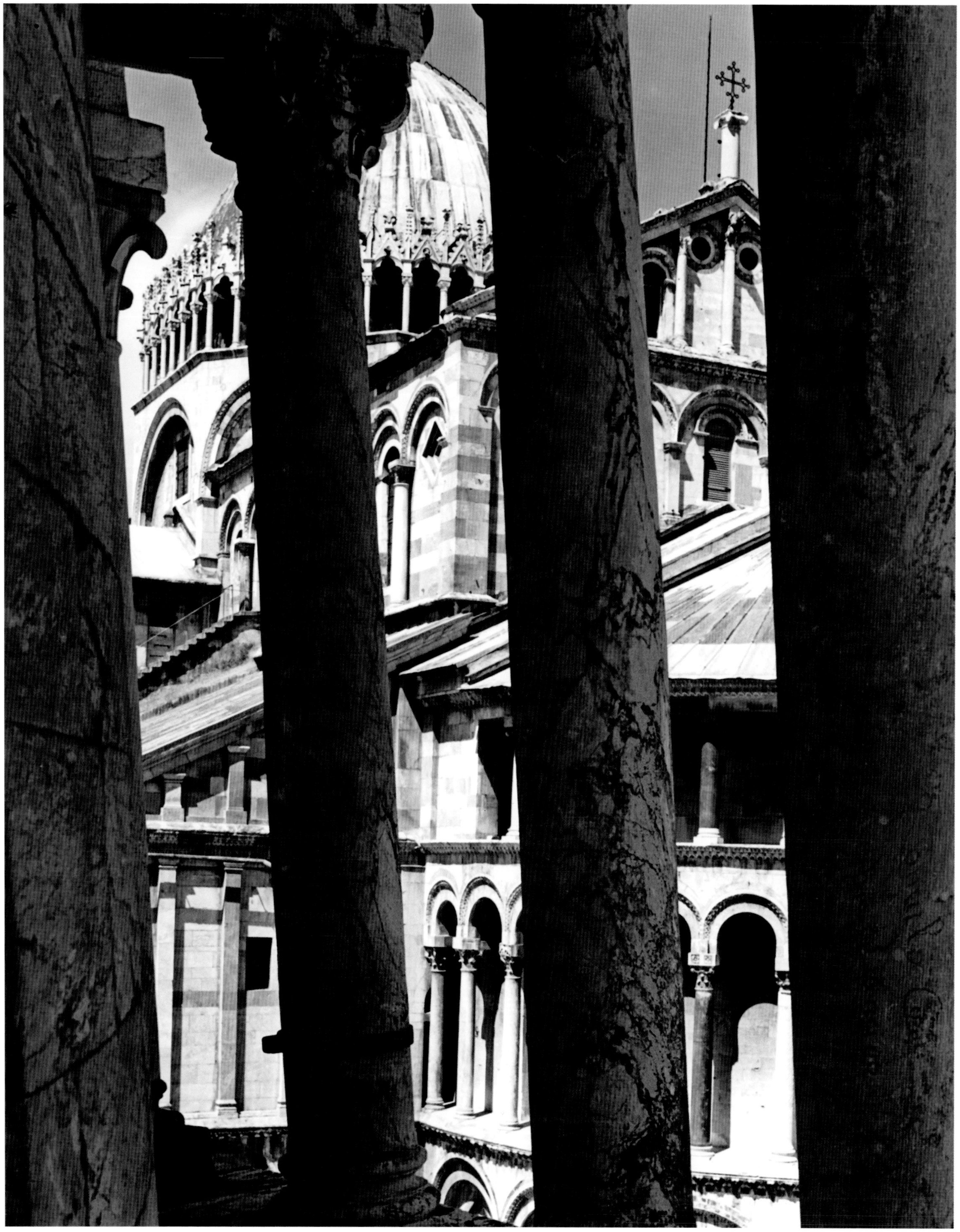

View from Leaning Tower of Pisa, Italy. 1931.

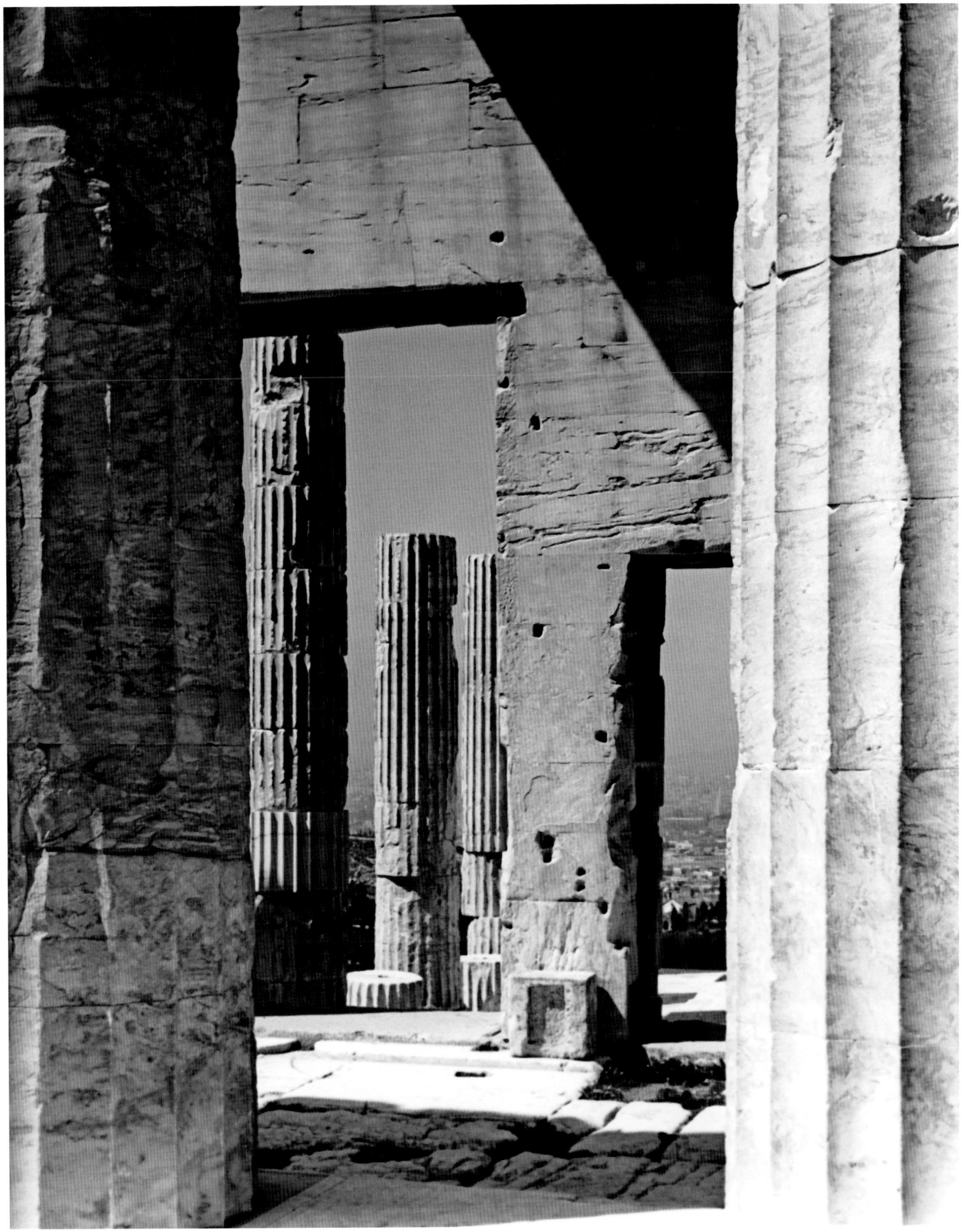

Acropolis: The Parthenon, Athens. 1930.

Pyramid of Cheops, Egypt. 1930.

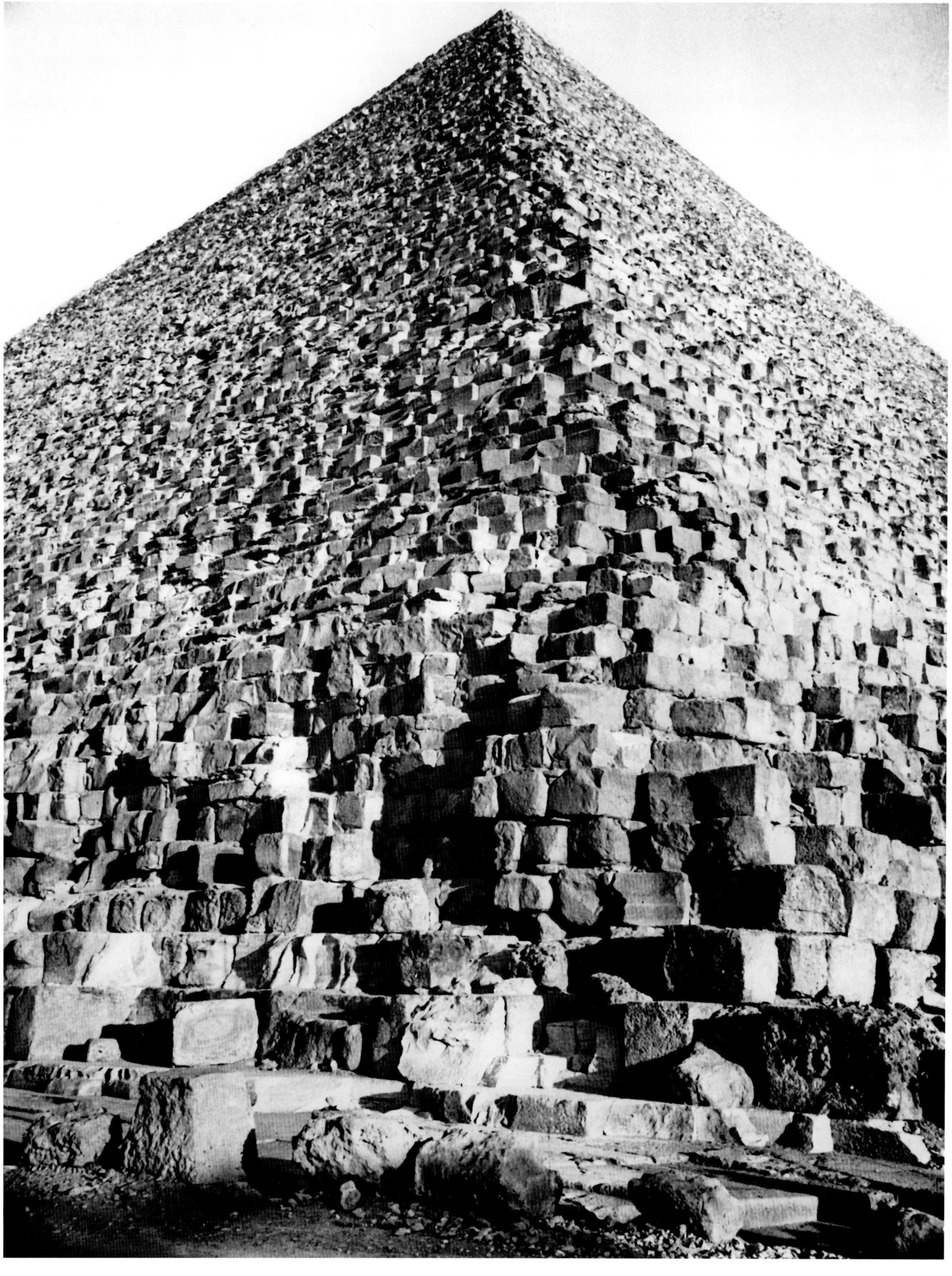

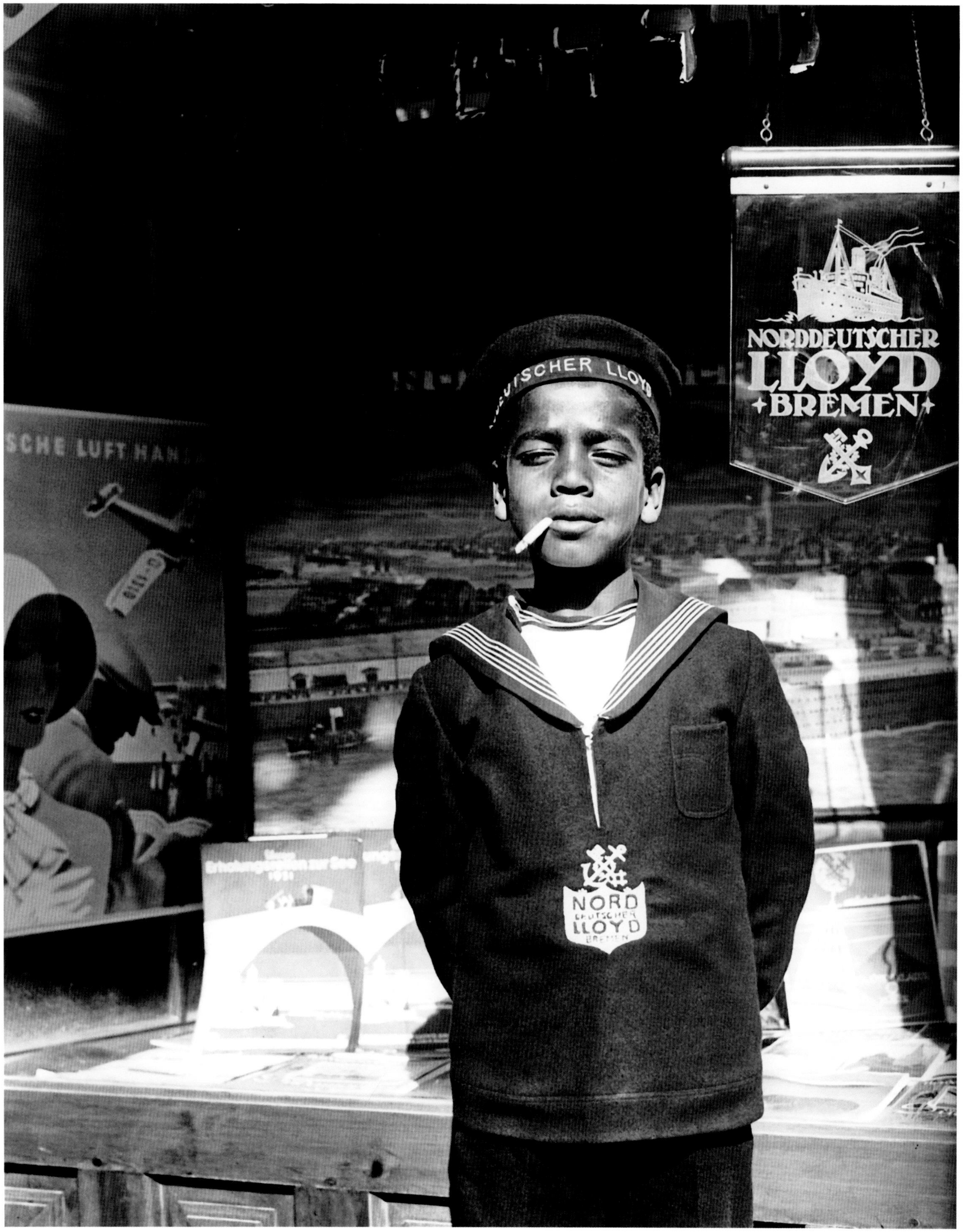
NORDDEUTSCHER
LLOYD
BREMEN
NORD
DEUTSCHER
LLOYD

Cabin Boy for the North German
Lloyd Line, Jerusalem, 1930

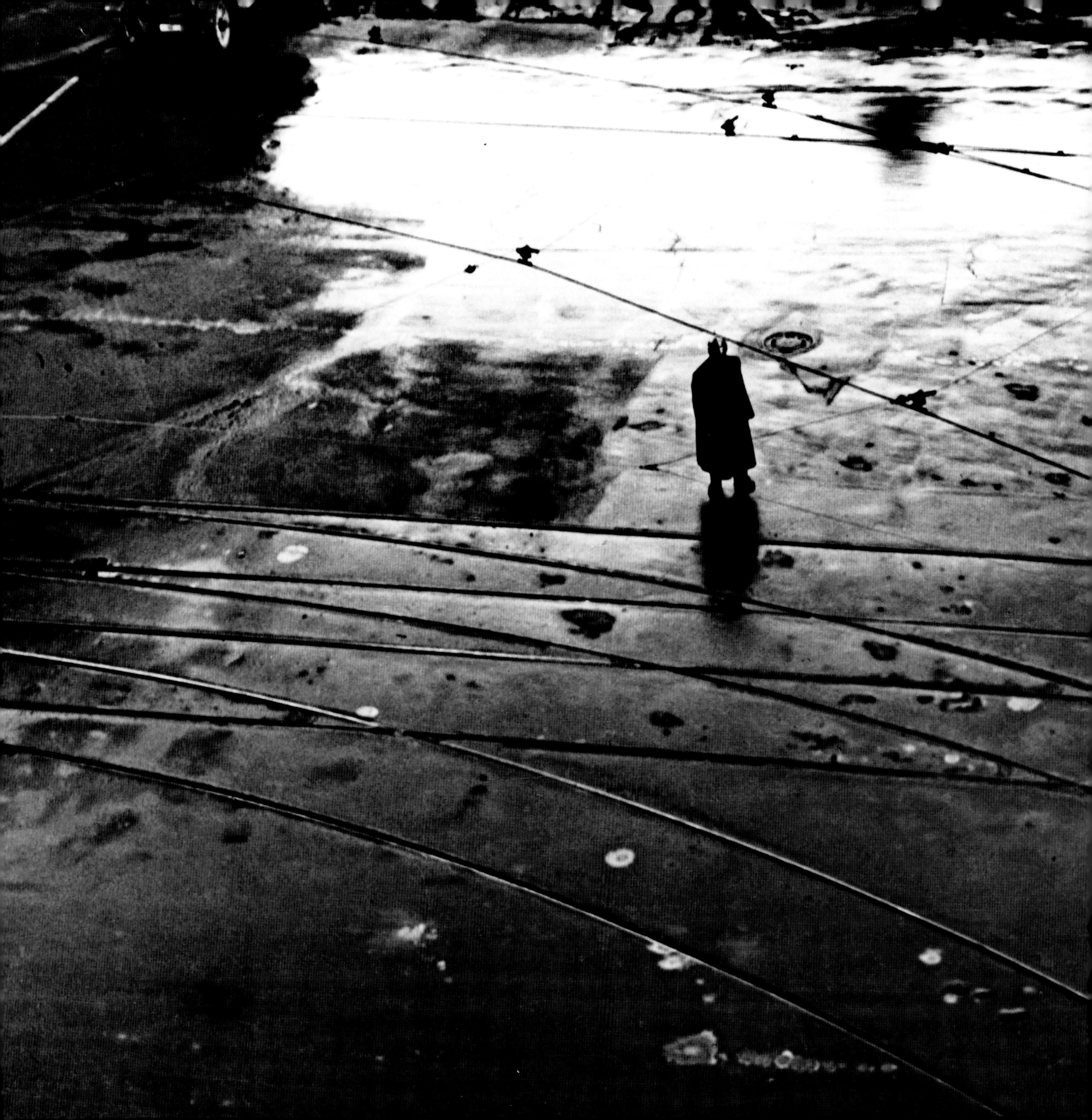

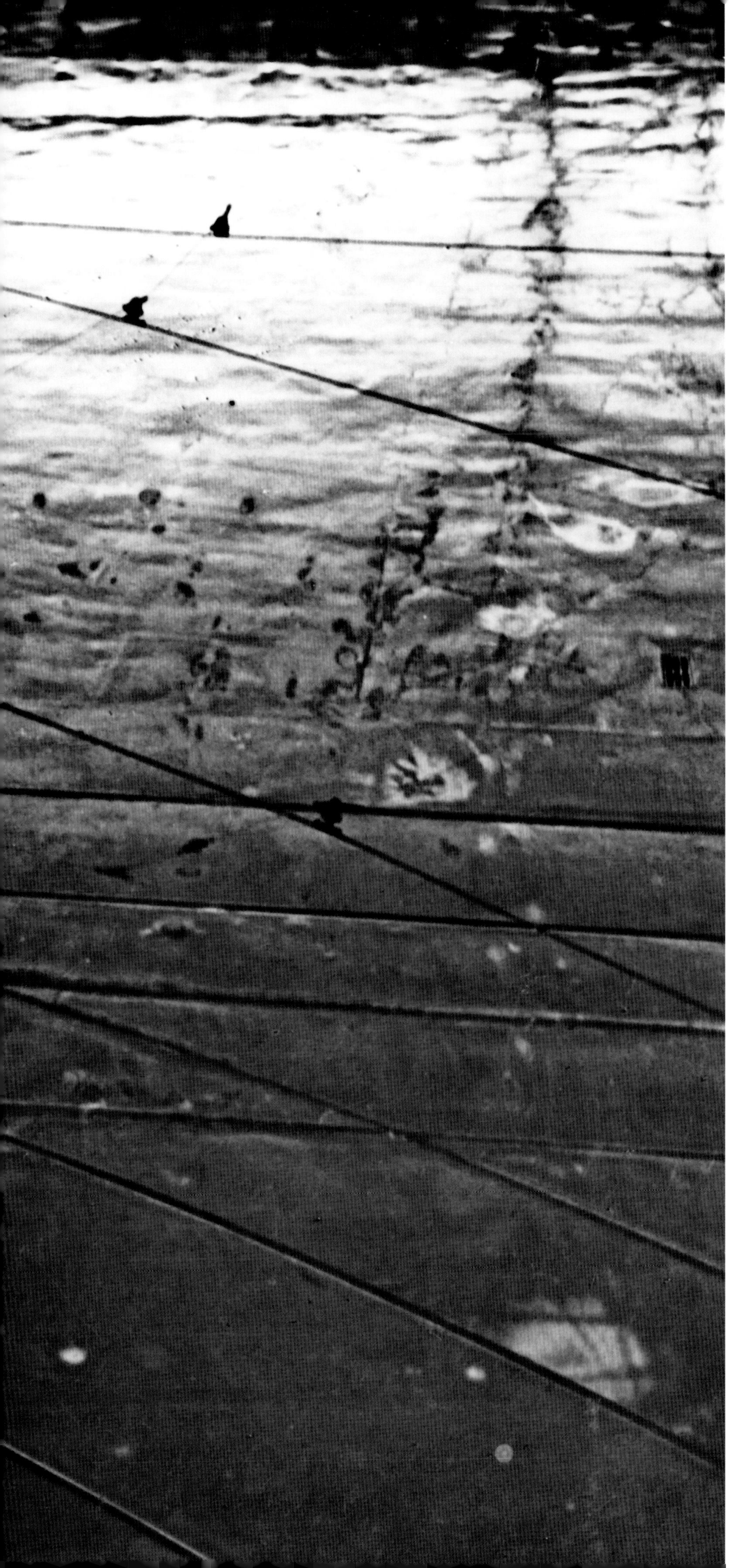

Policeman in the Rain,
Odeons-Platz, Munich. 1930.

Nazi Parade, Heidelberg. ca. 1936.

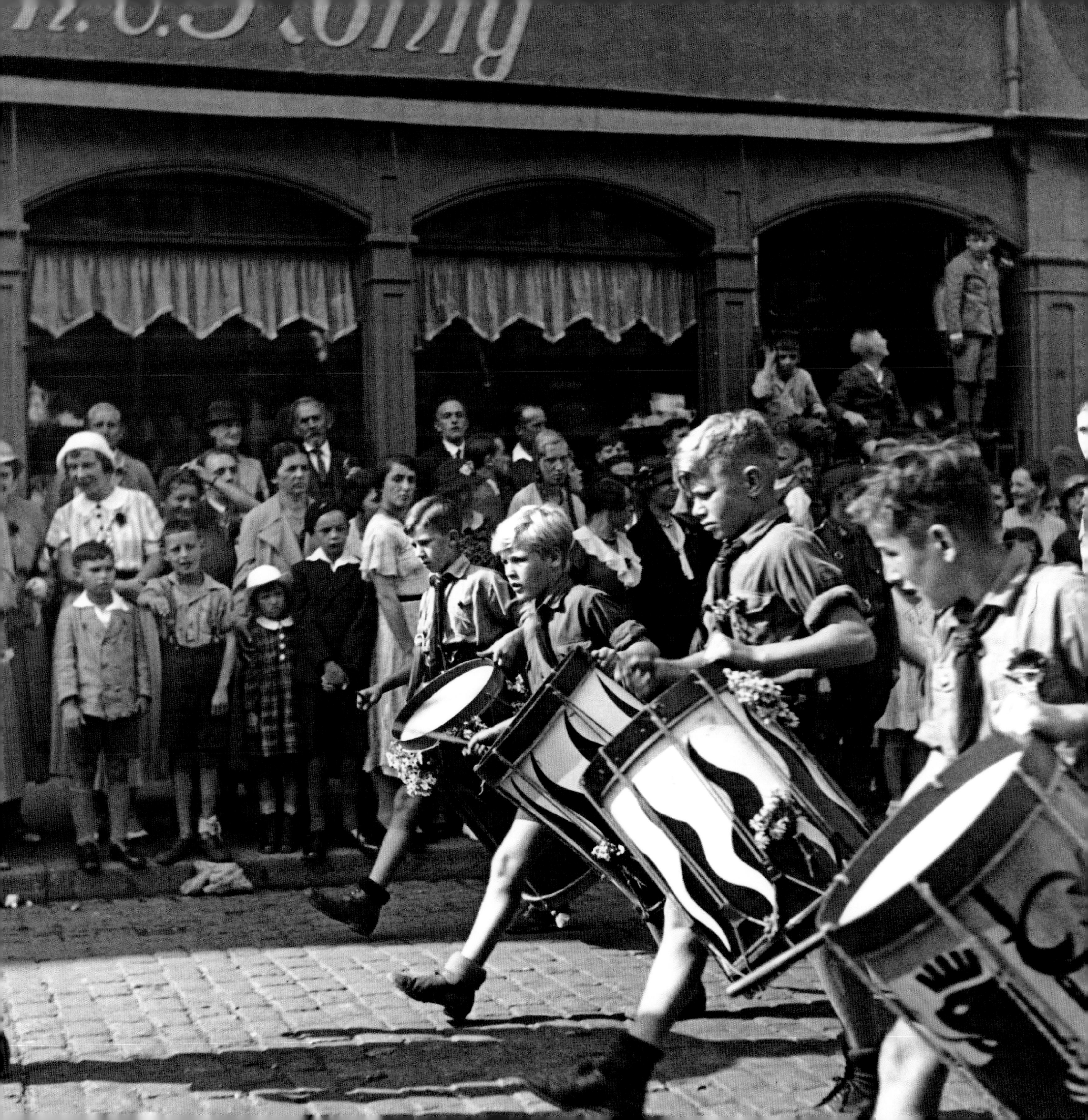

Everything has its beauty,
but not everyone sees it.

CONFUCIUS

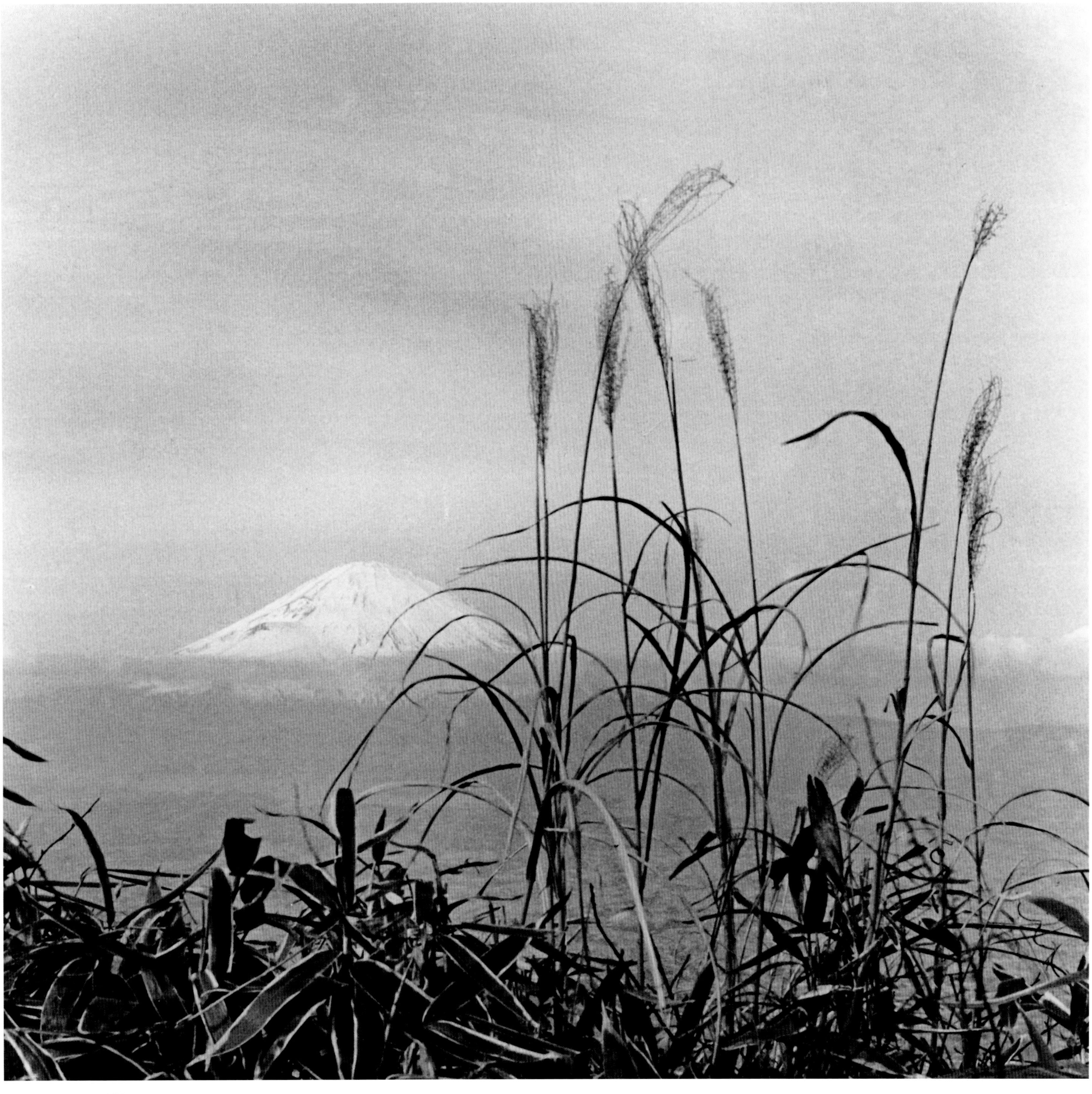

Fujiyama, Japan. 1936.

Hindu Mother and Child, India. 1934.

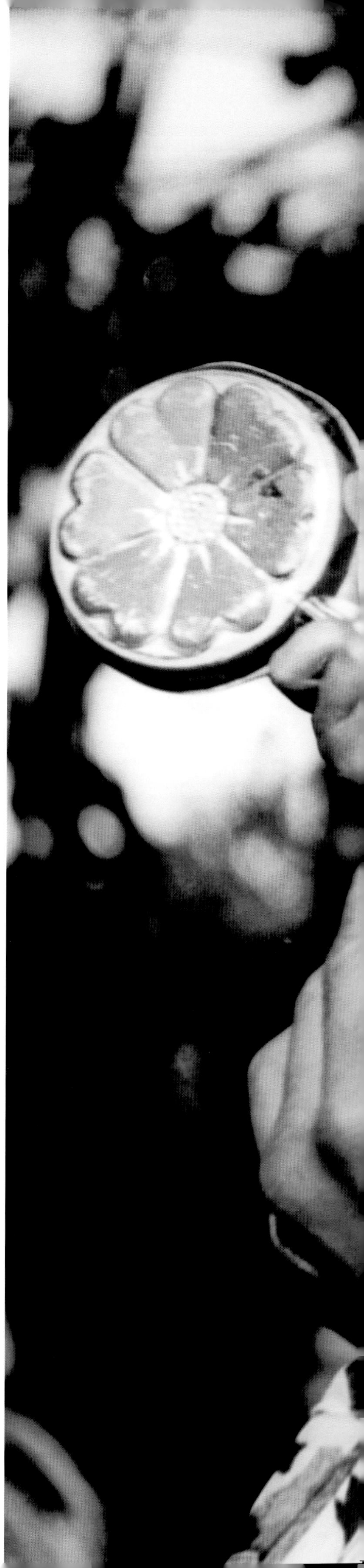

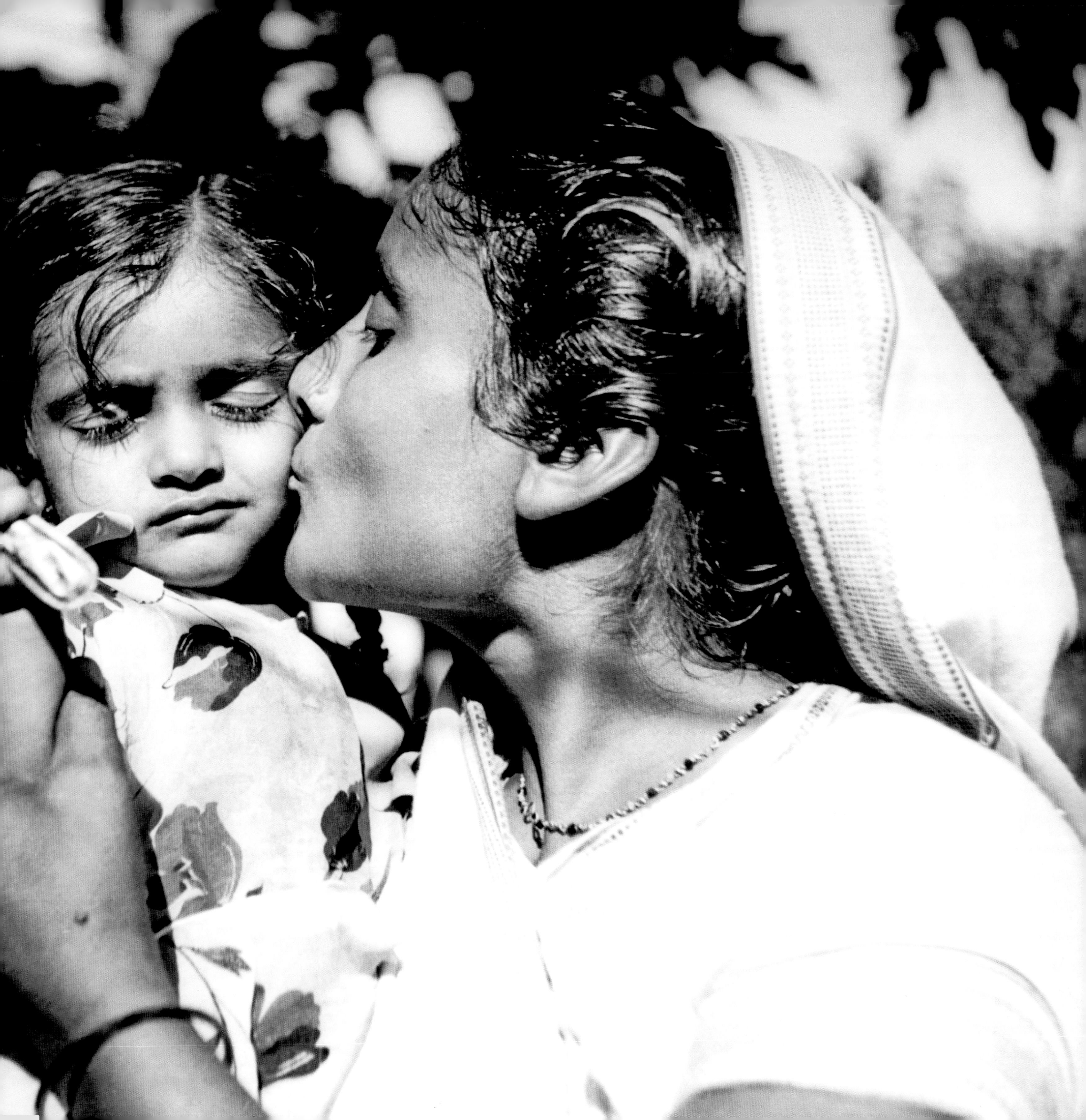

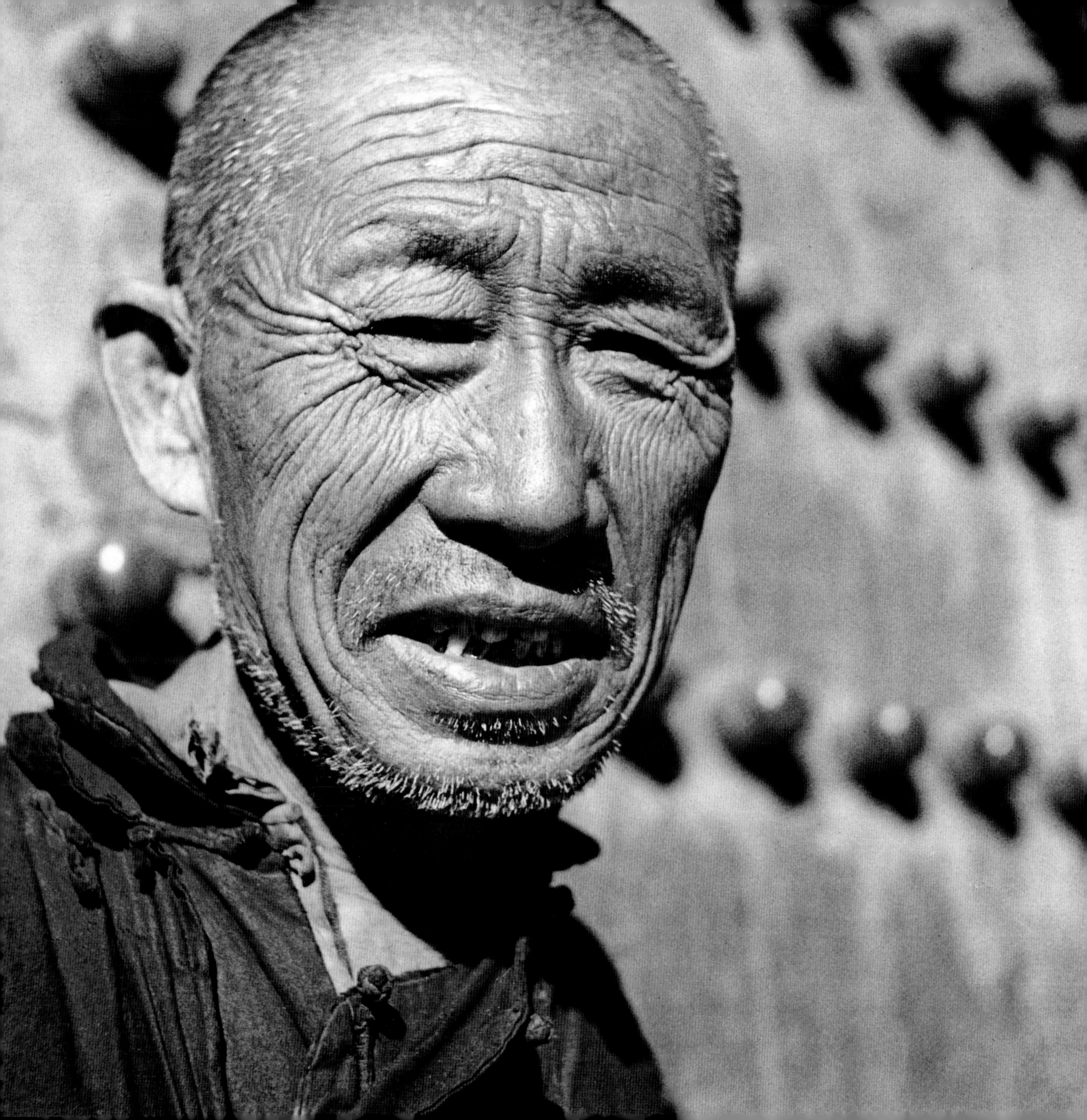

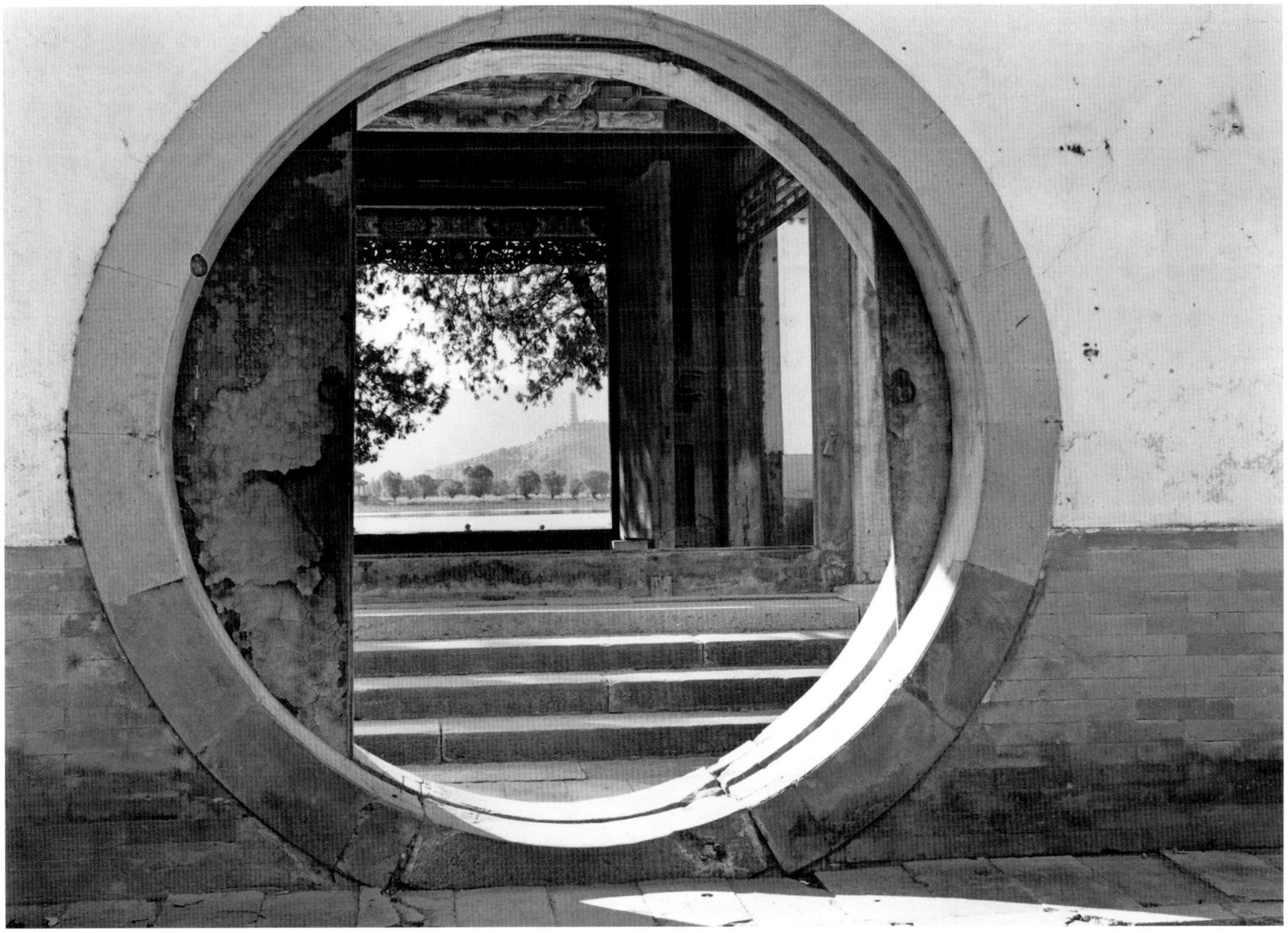

(left) Monastery Gatekeeper, Peking, China. 1935.
(above) Moongate in the Summer Palace near Peking, China. 1935.

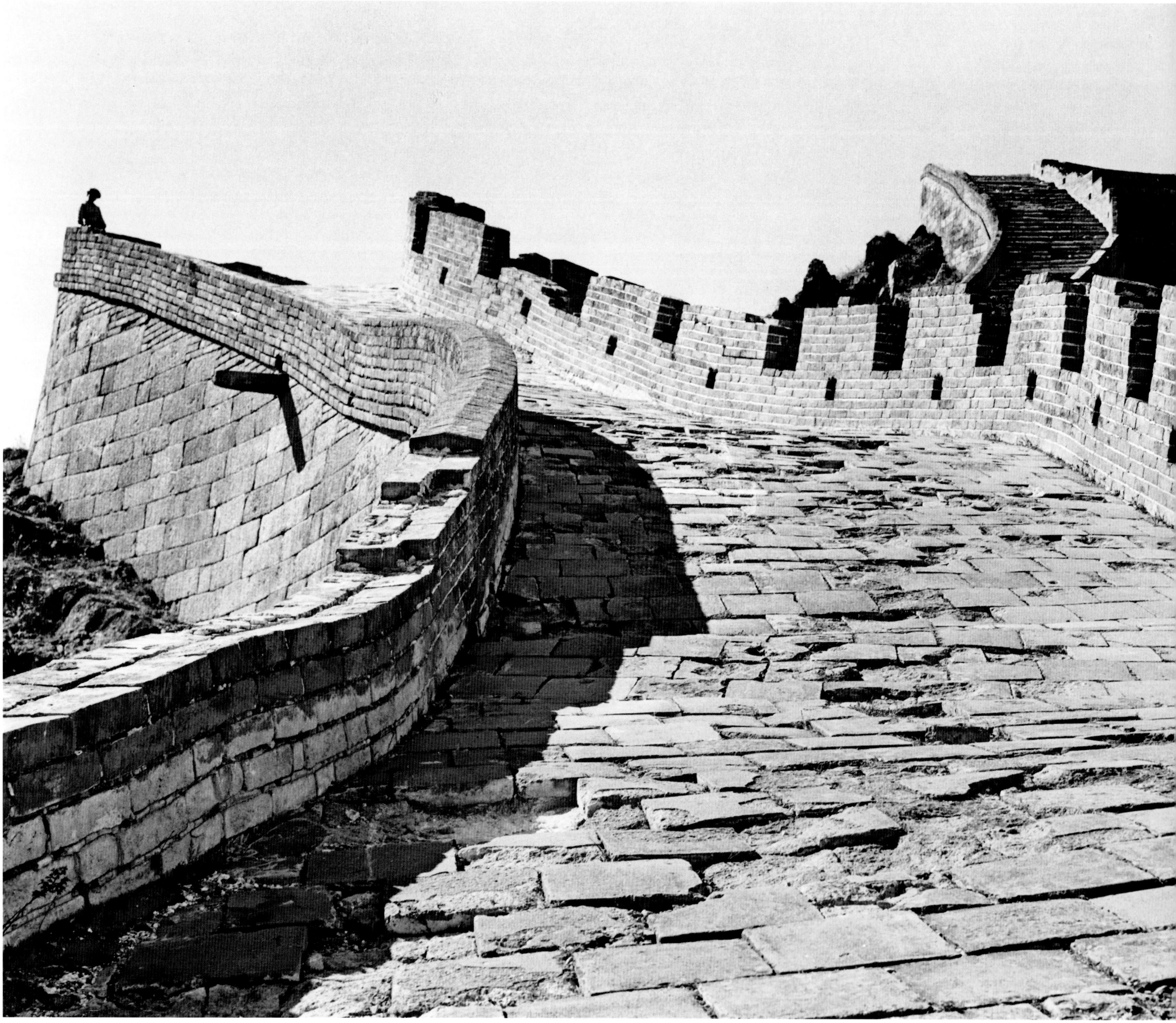

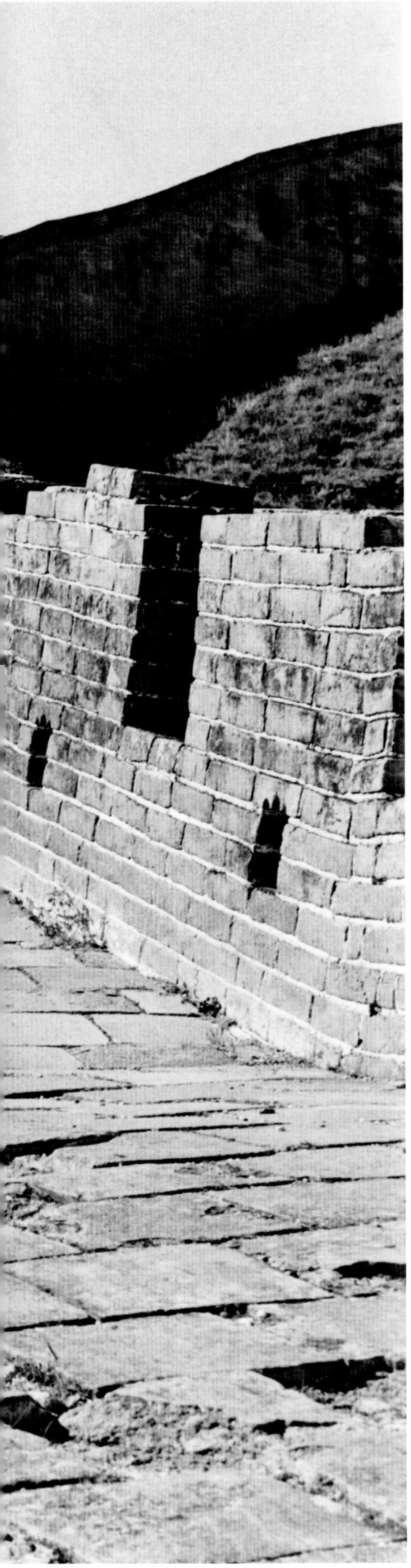

The Great Wall, China. 1935.

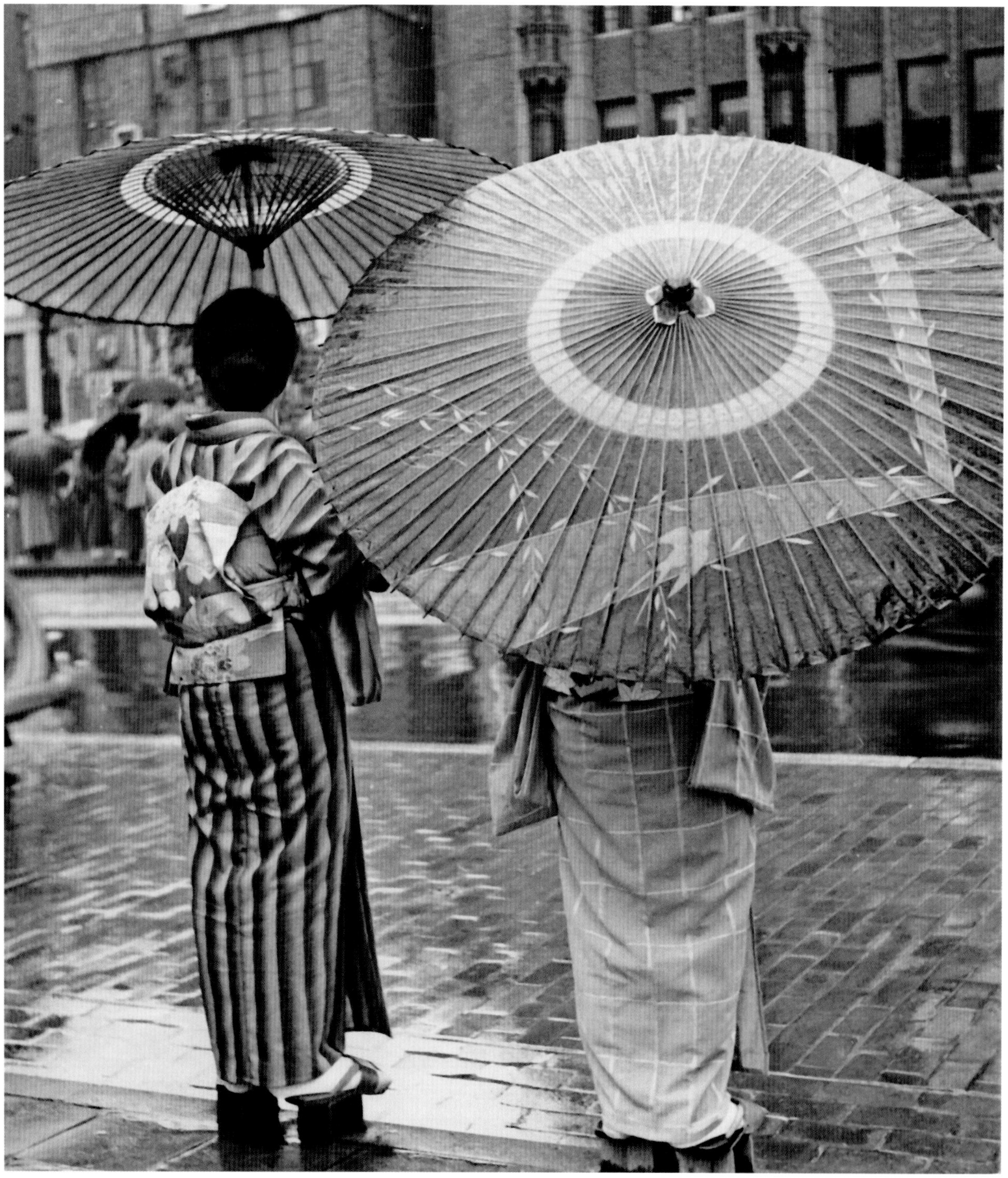

(above) Rainy Day in Tokyo, Japan. 1936.
(right) Rebel in the Making: Schoolboys Exercising, with One Eating an Apple, Tokyo, Japan. 1936.

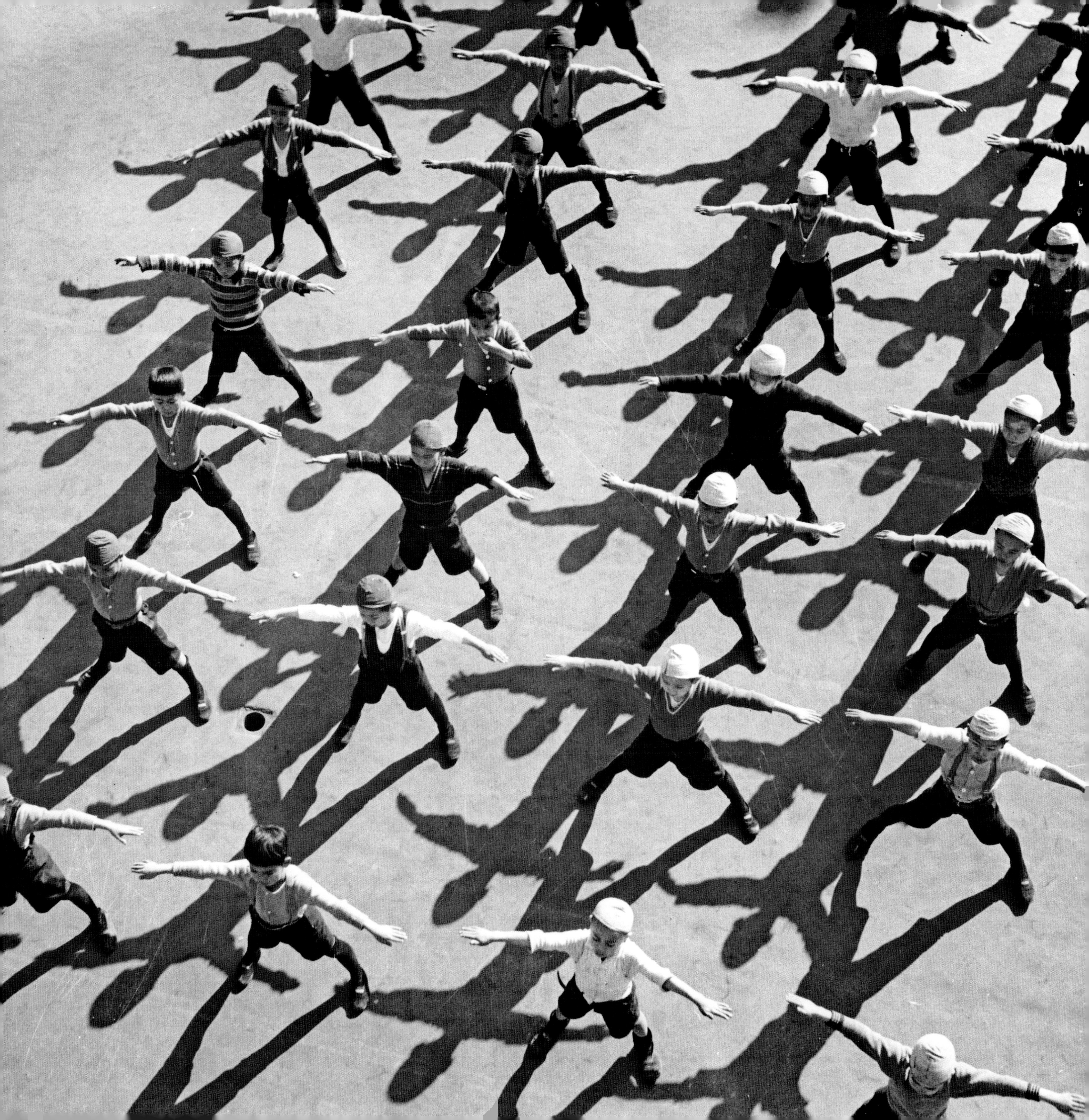

Beach near Colombo, Ceylon. 1934.

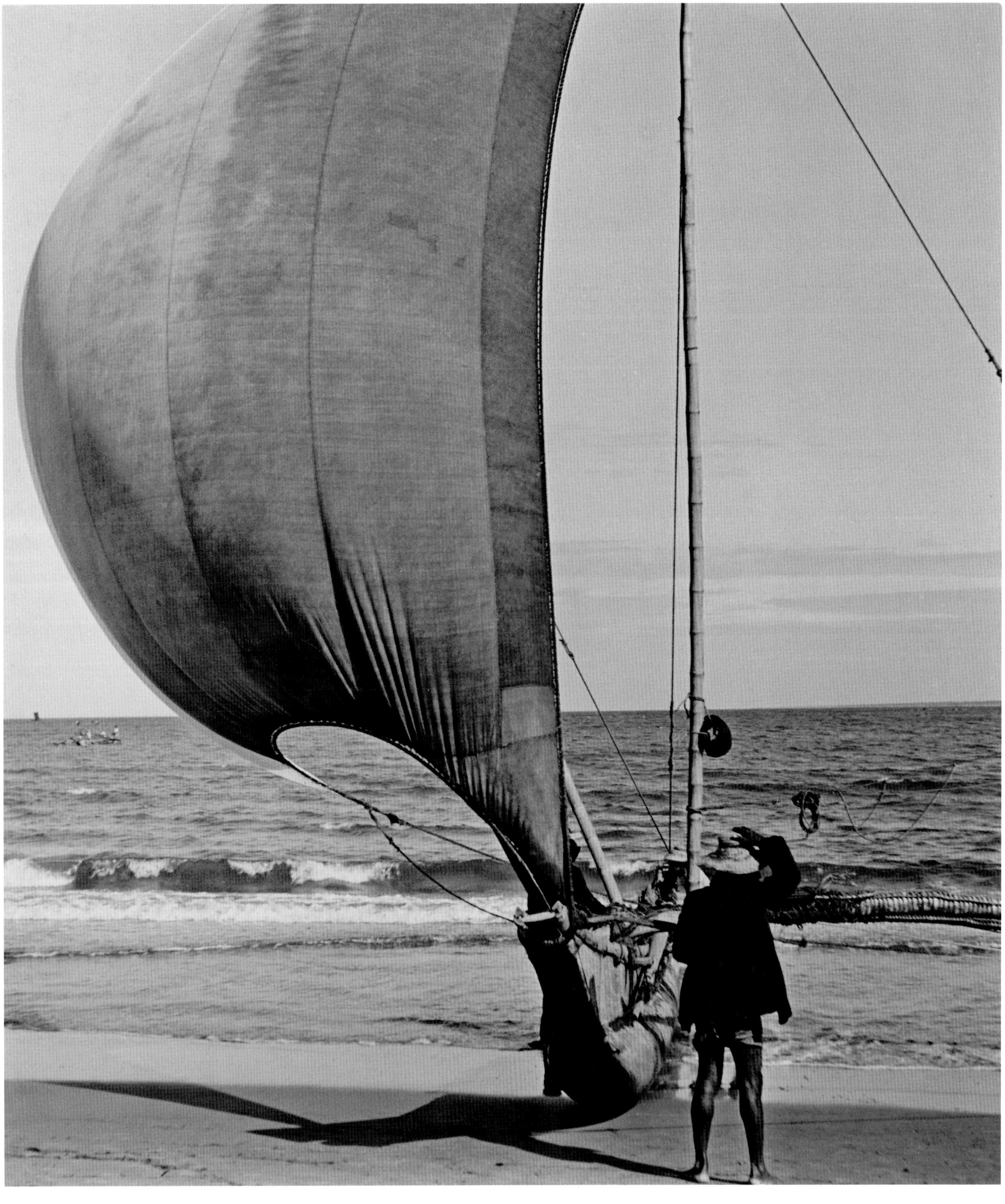

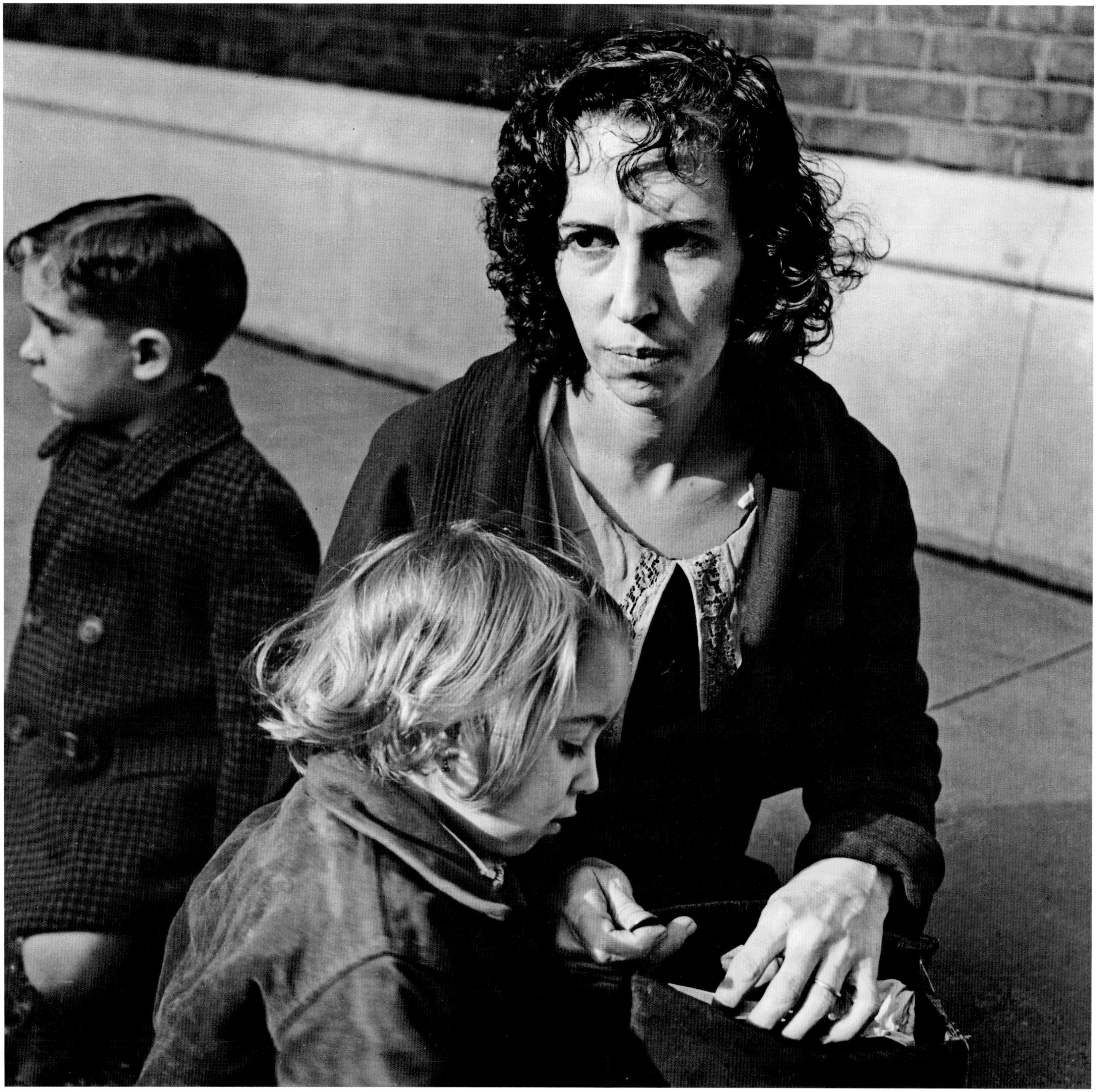

Mother and Children Living on the Streets of New York City. 1936.

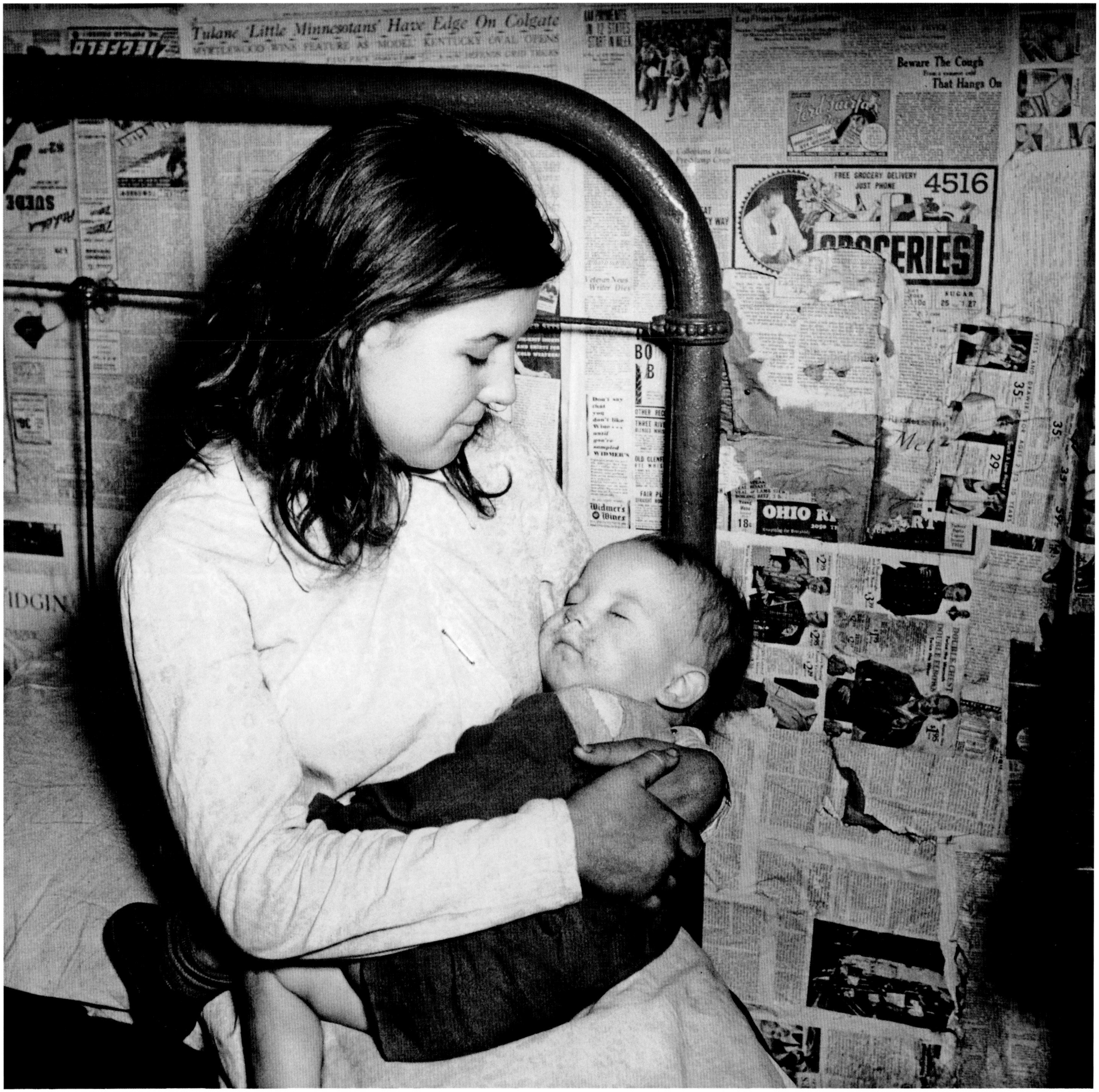

Miner's Wife and Baby, Logan, West Virginia. 1936.

Boy Seated on Church Steps,
Louisiana. 1937.

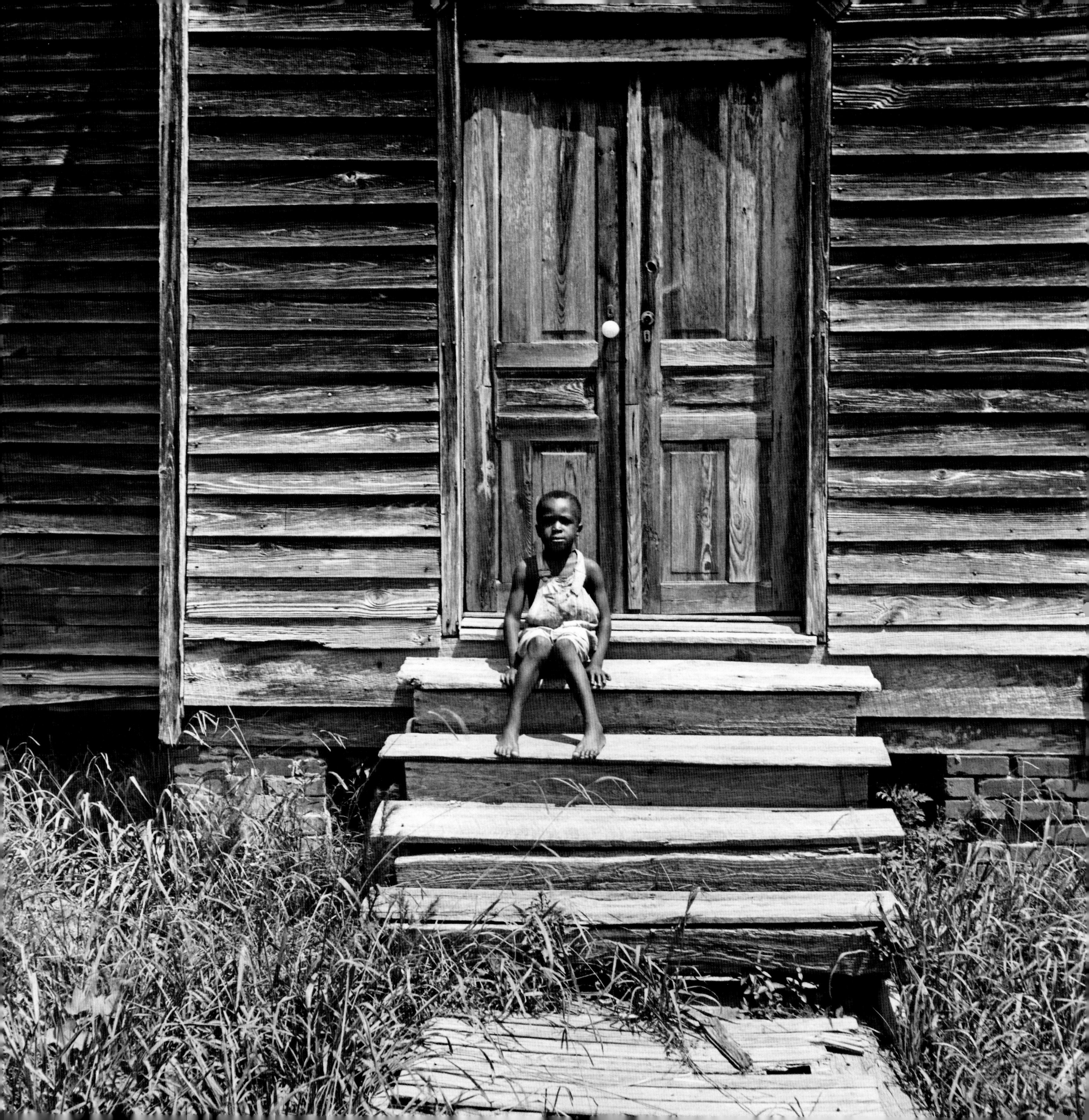

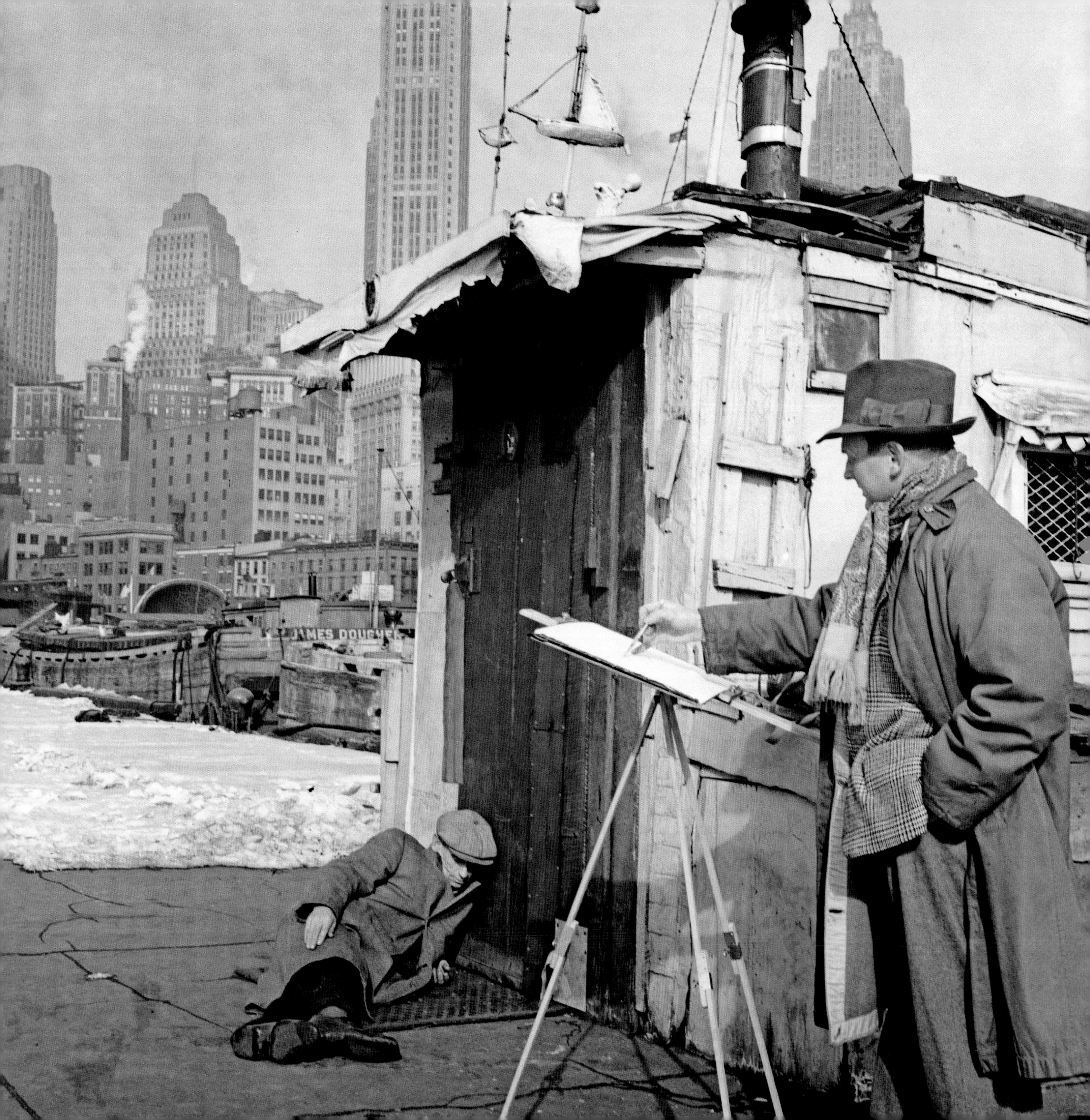

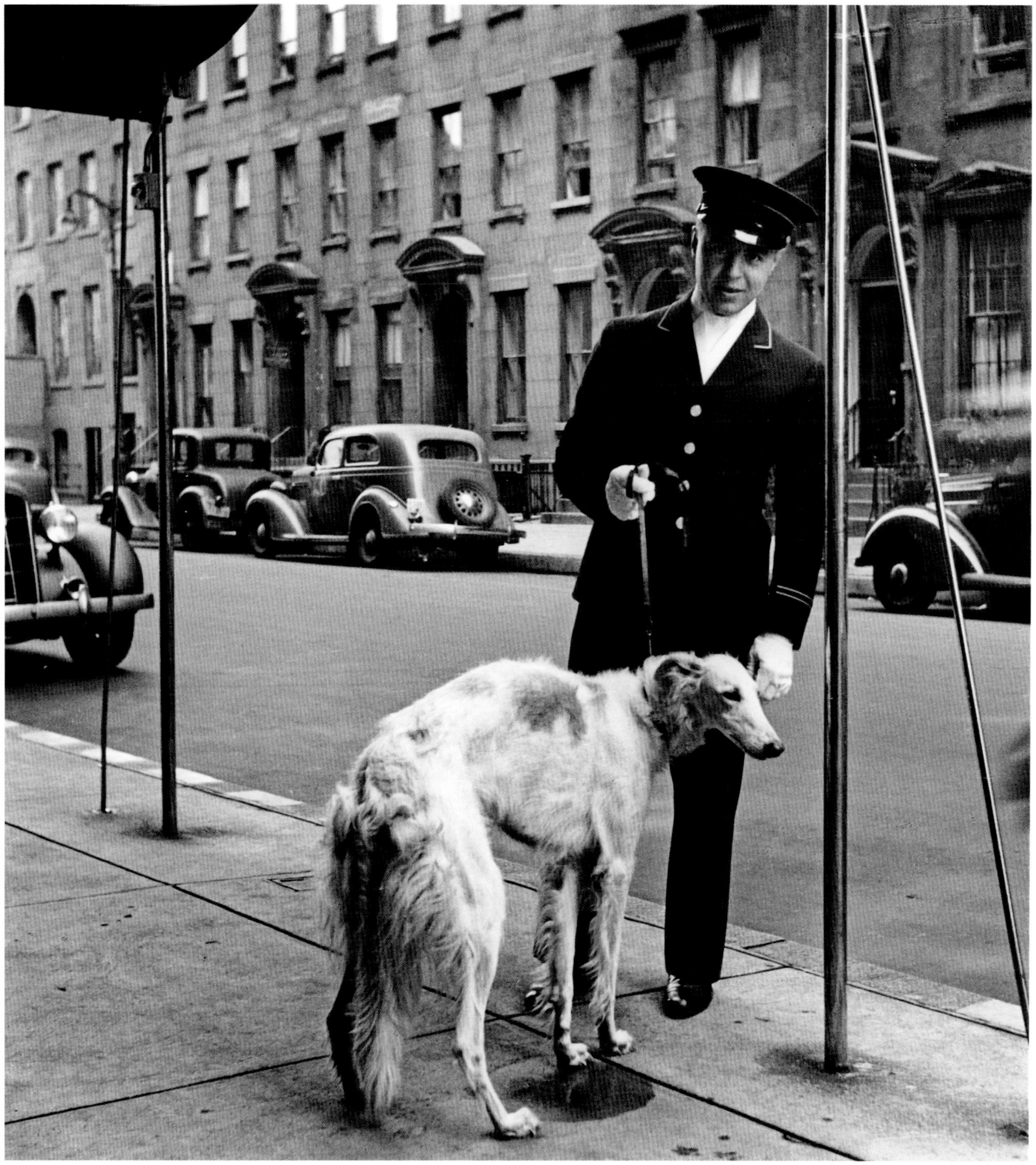

(left) Reginald Marsh Painting the Destitute on the Streets of New York City. 1938
(above) 52nd Street: Doorman with Dog, New York City. 1937.

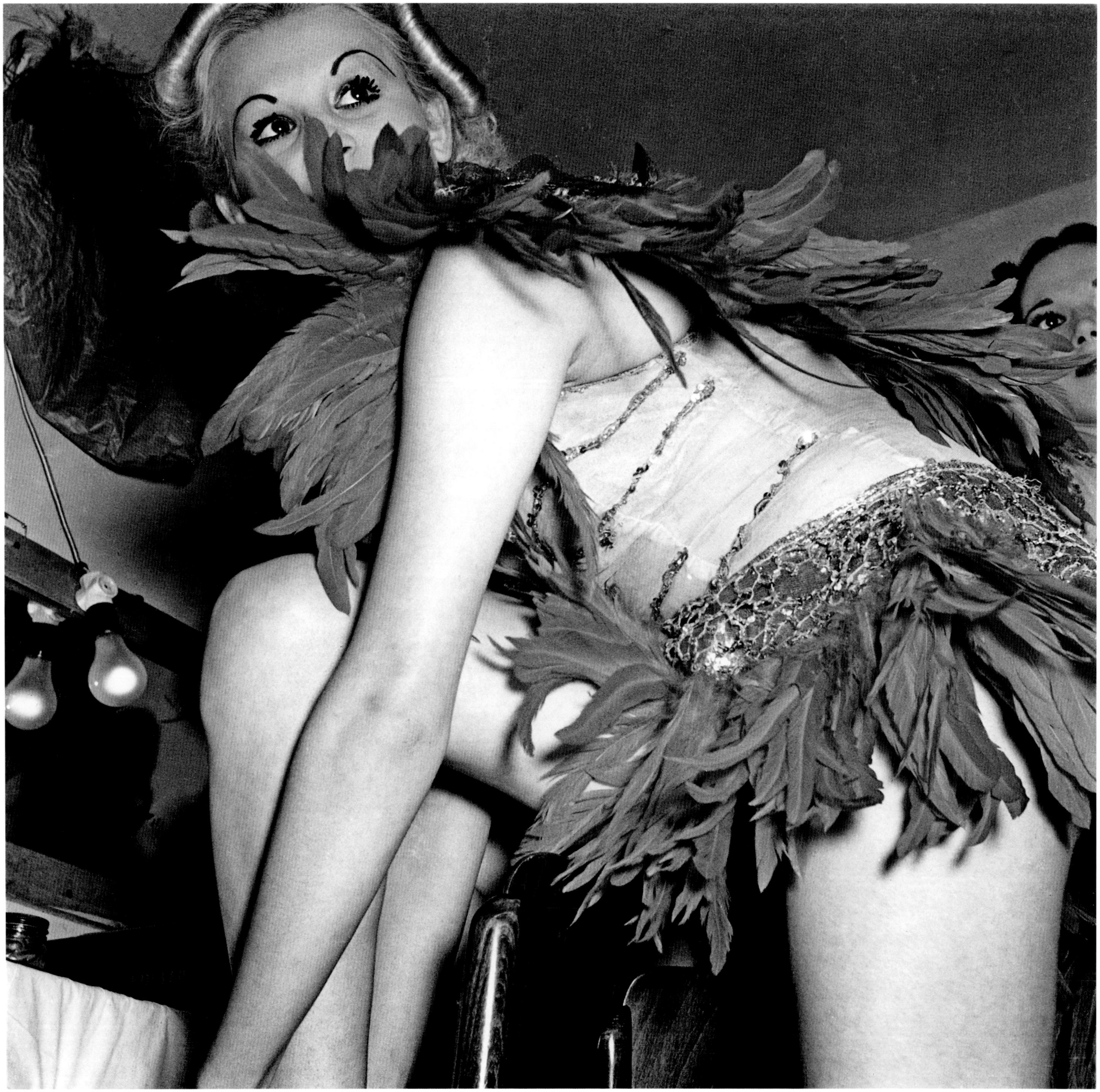

52nd Street: Chorus Girl in Night Club, New York City. 1937.

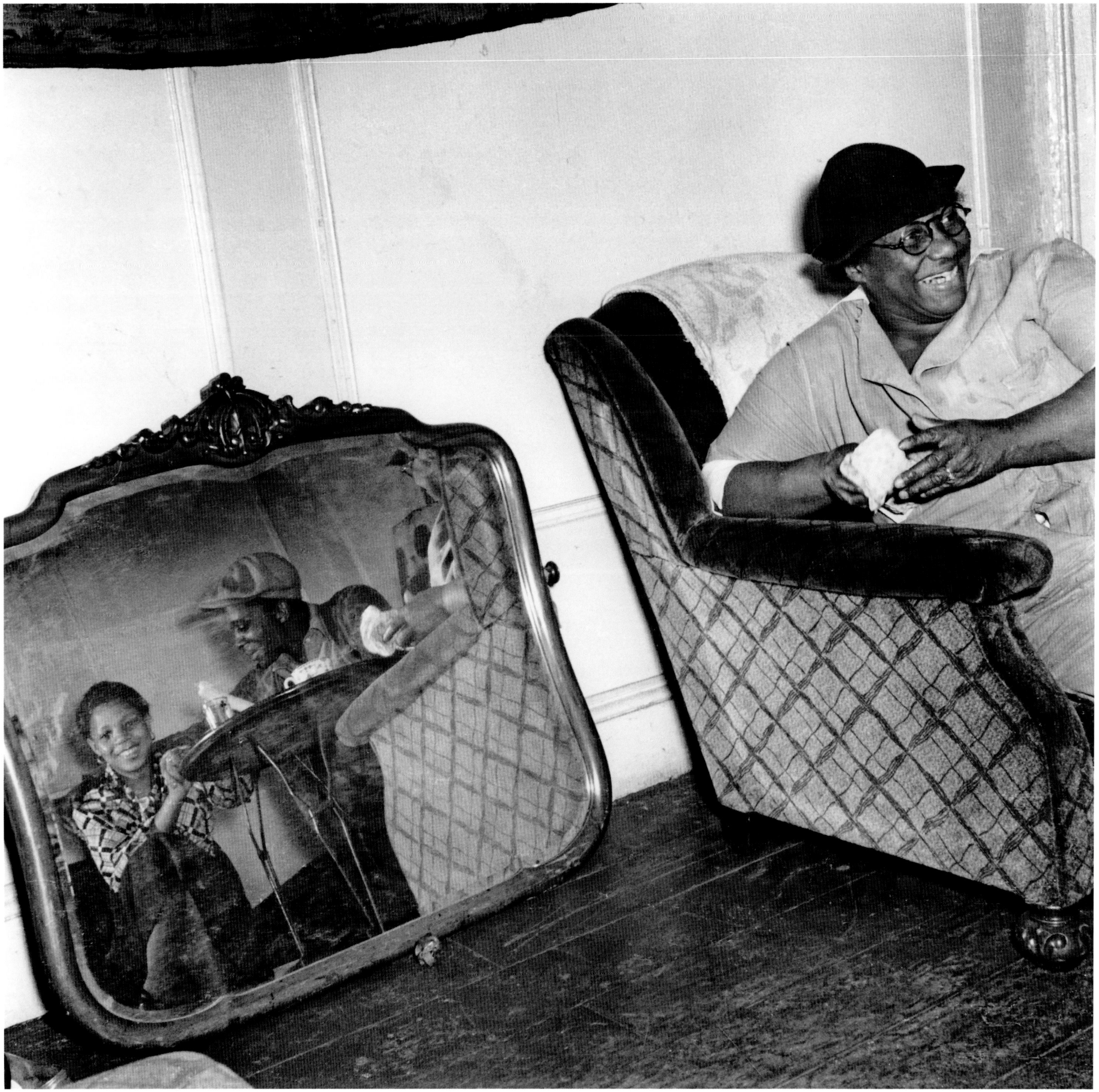

52nd Street: Tea Party, New York City. 1937.

There is a road from the eye to the heart that does not go through the intellect.

G.K. CHESTERTON

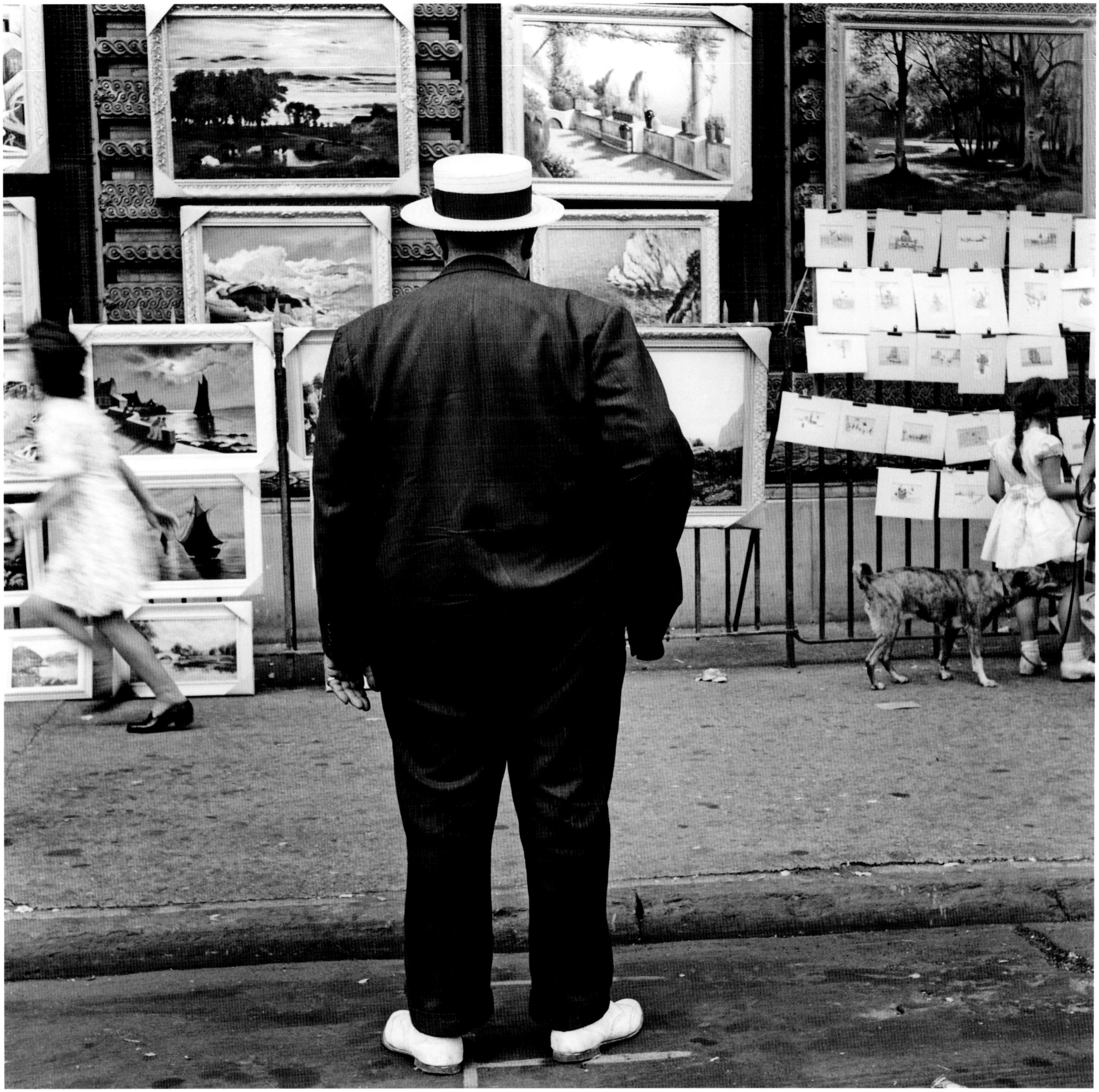

The Art Critic, Washington Square, New York City. 1947.

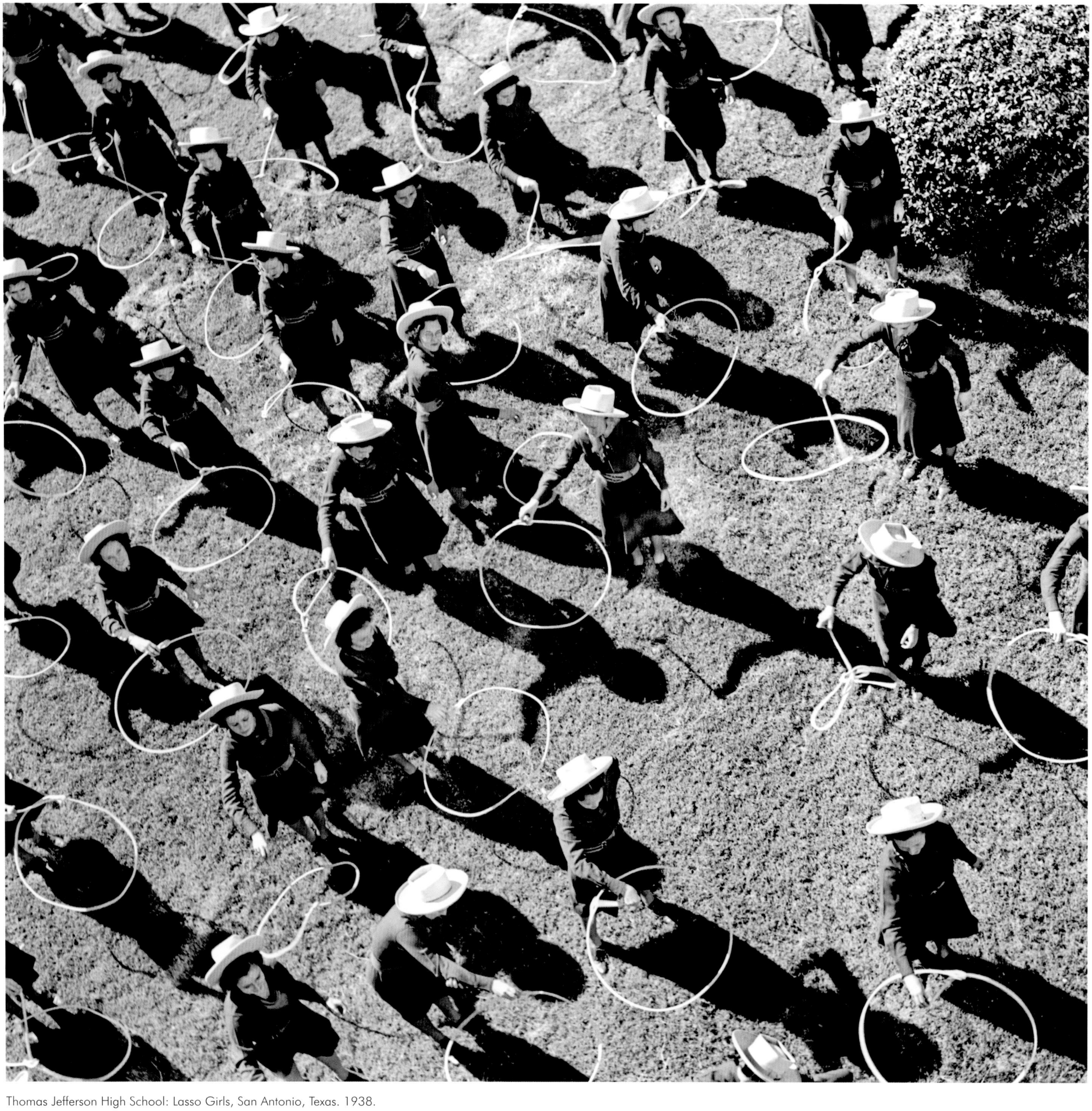

Thomas Jefferson High School: Lasso Girls, San Antonio, Texas. 1938.

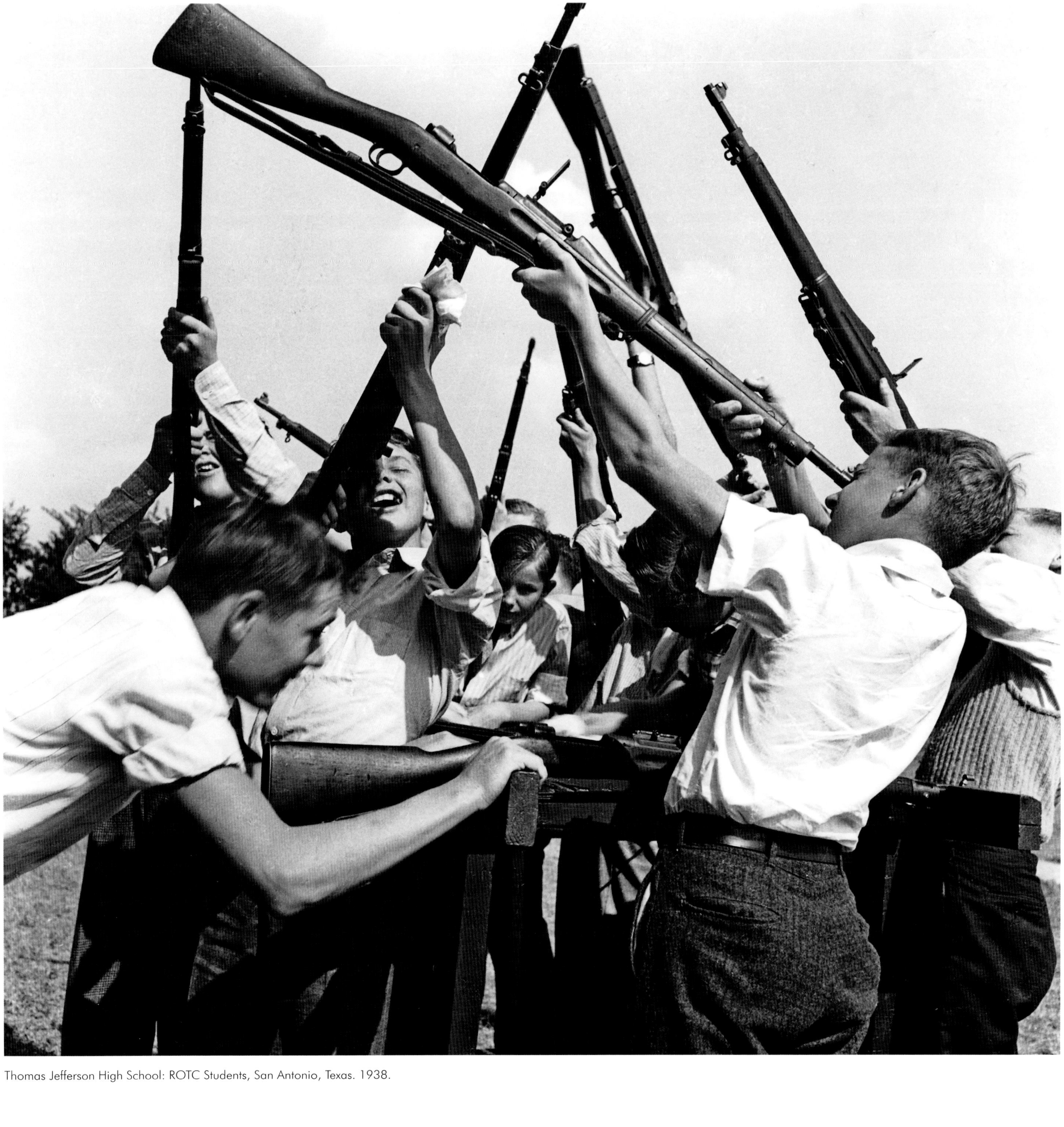

Thomas Jefferson High School: ROTC Students, San Antonio, Texas. 1938.

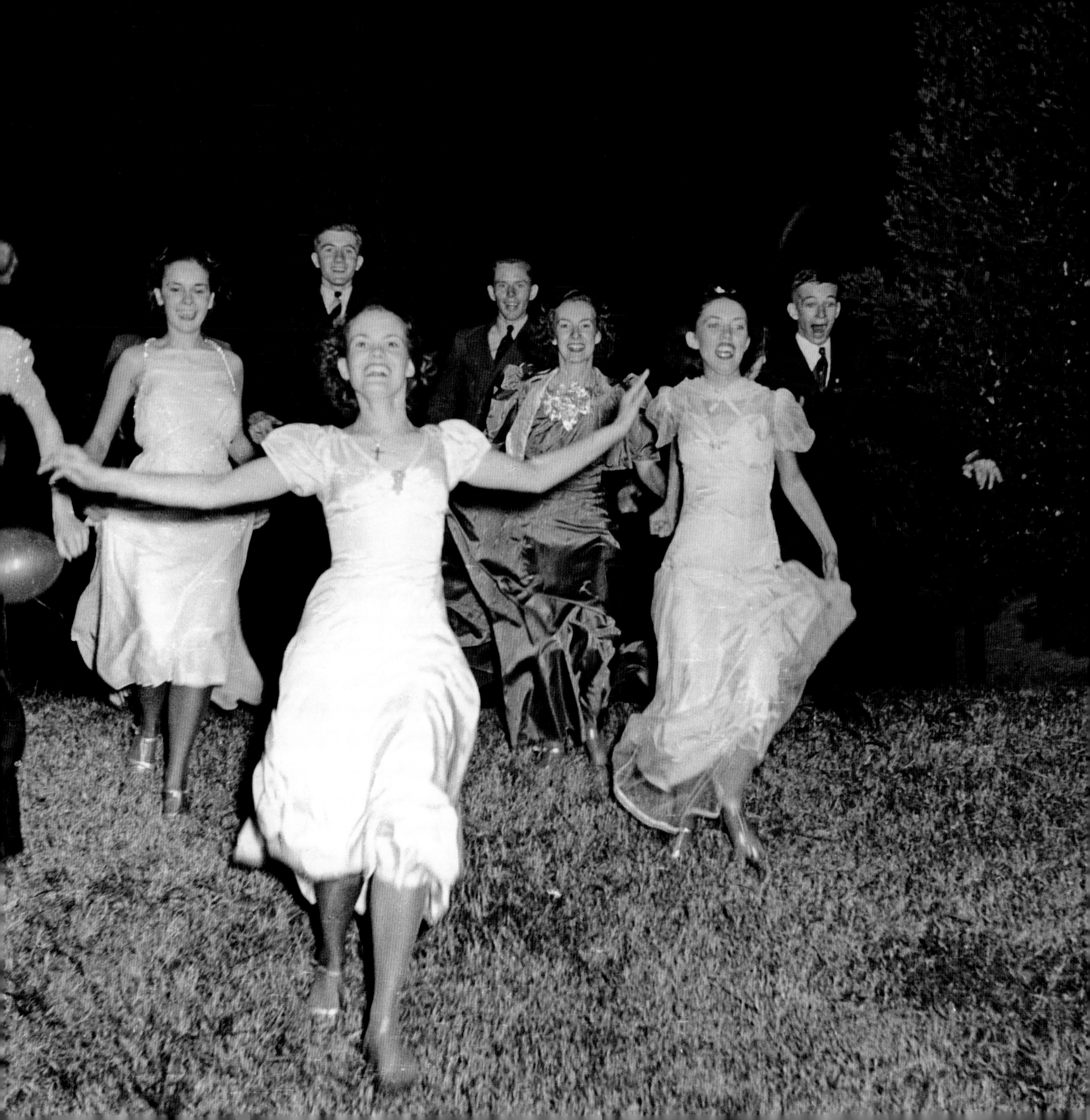

Thomas Jefferson High School:
Graduation Party,
San Antonio, Texas. 1938.

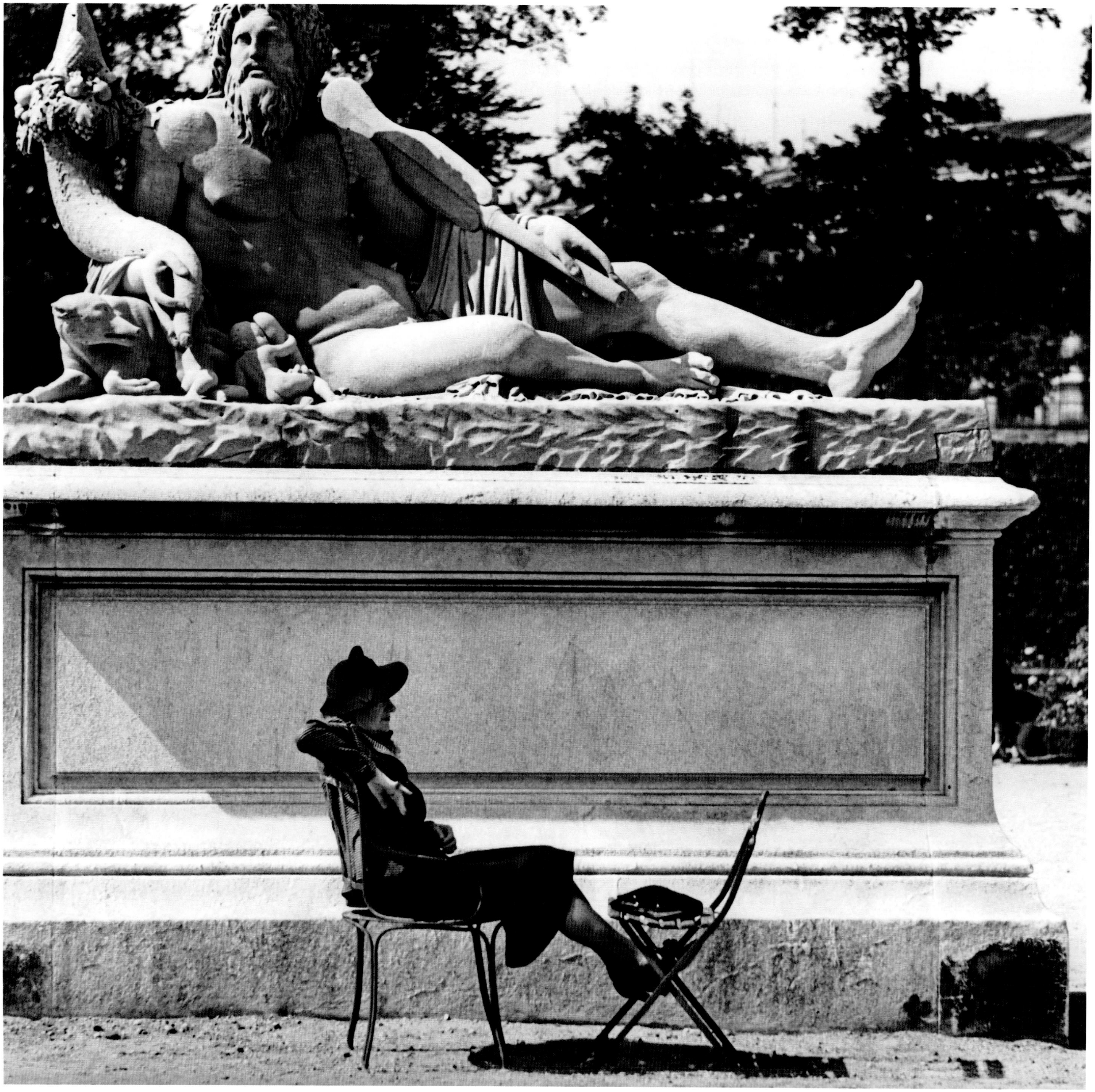

The Woman and the God, Paris, France. 1938.

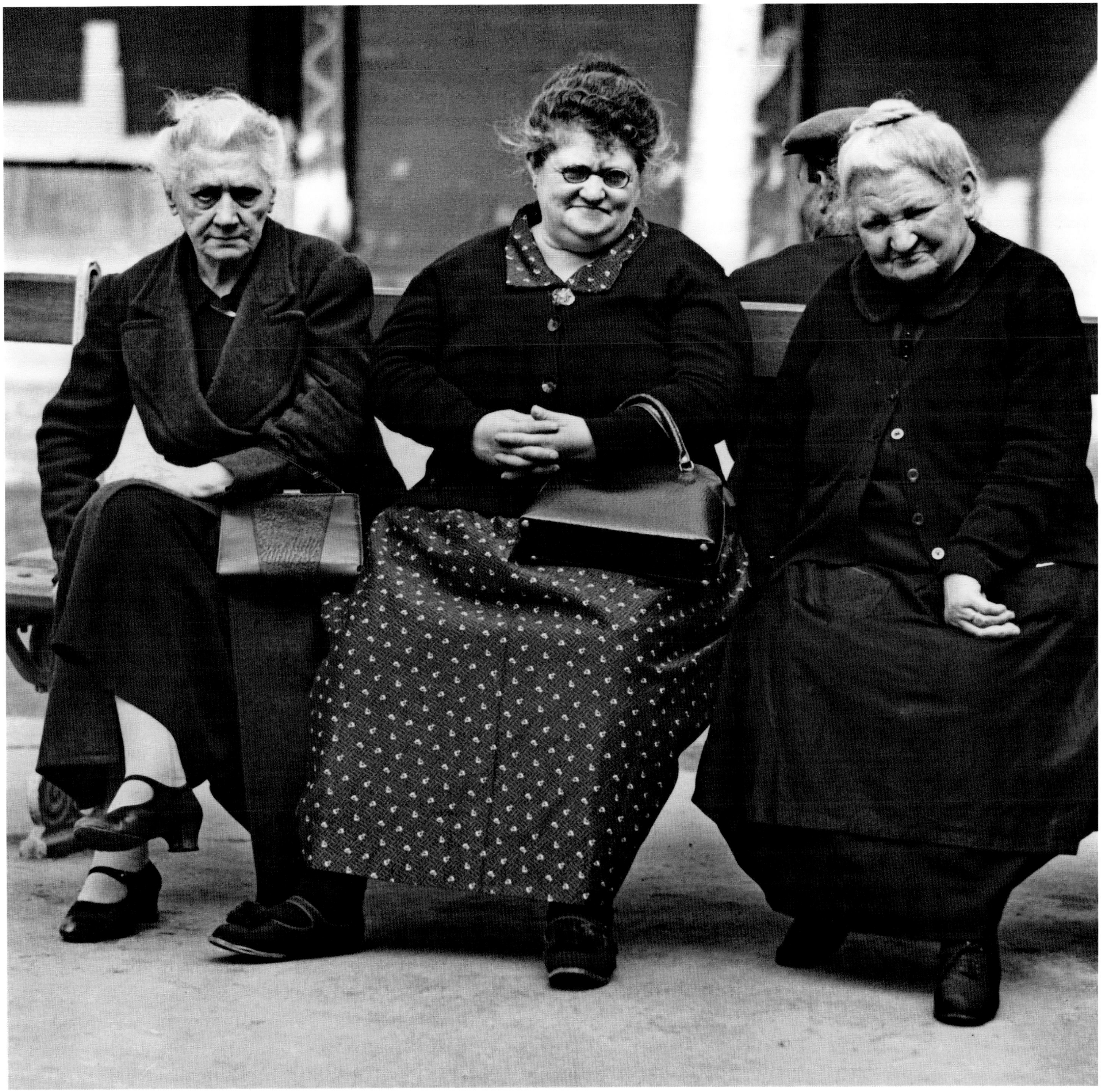

Housewives, Paris, France. 1938.

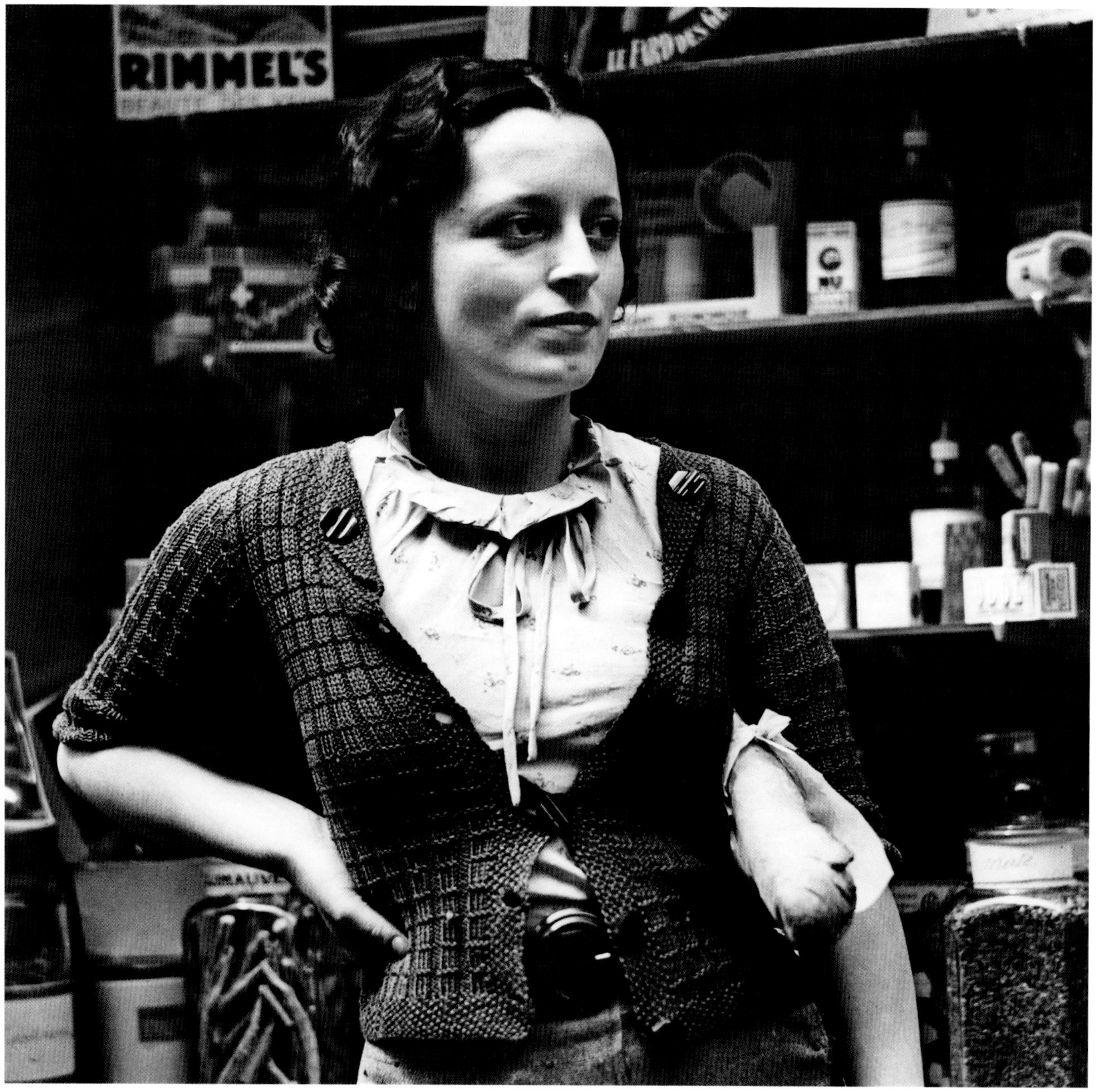

(above) Young Woman with Loaf of Bread, Paris, France. 1938.
(right) Café on the Bastille, Paris, France. 1938.

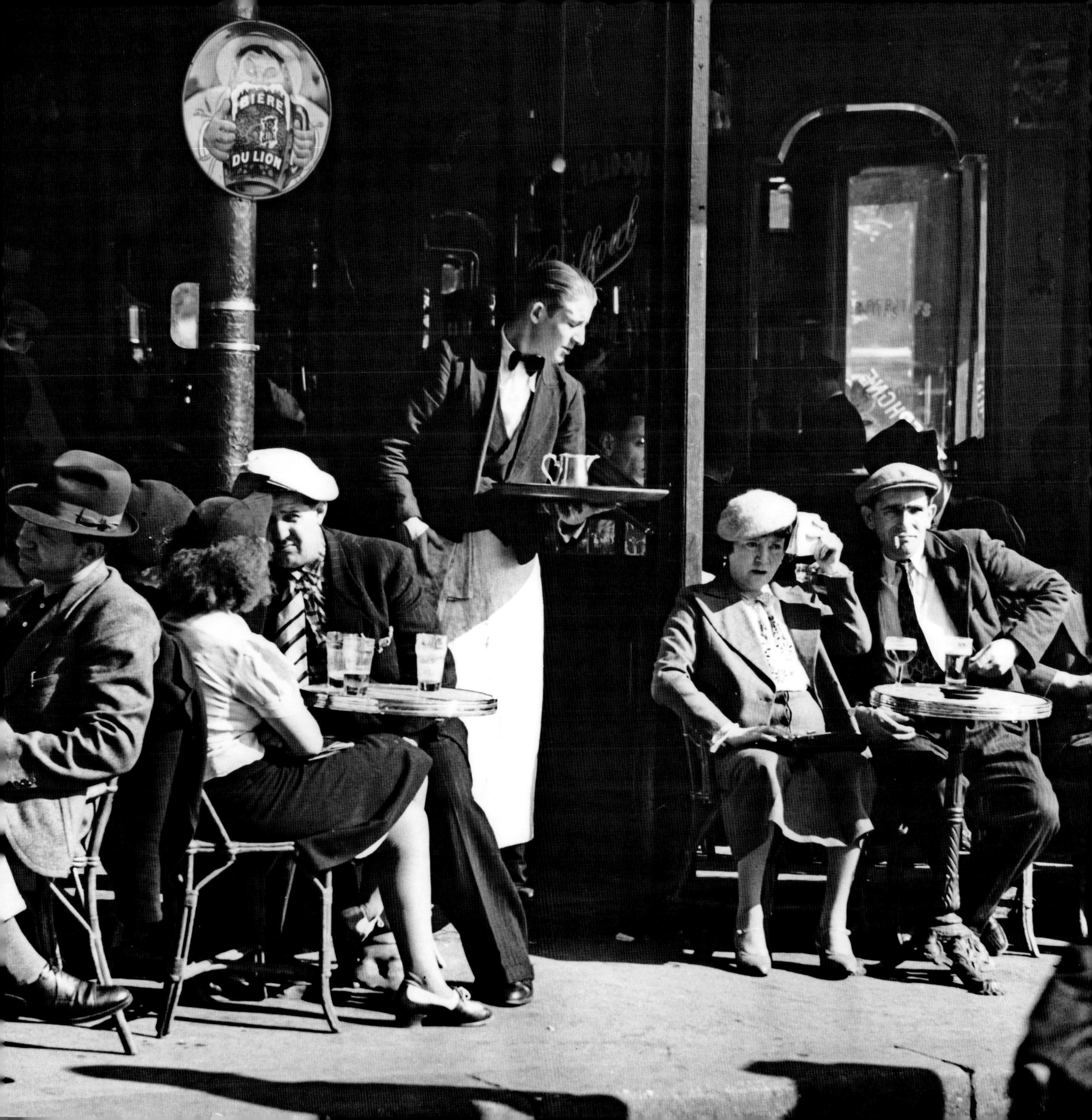
DU LION

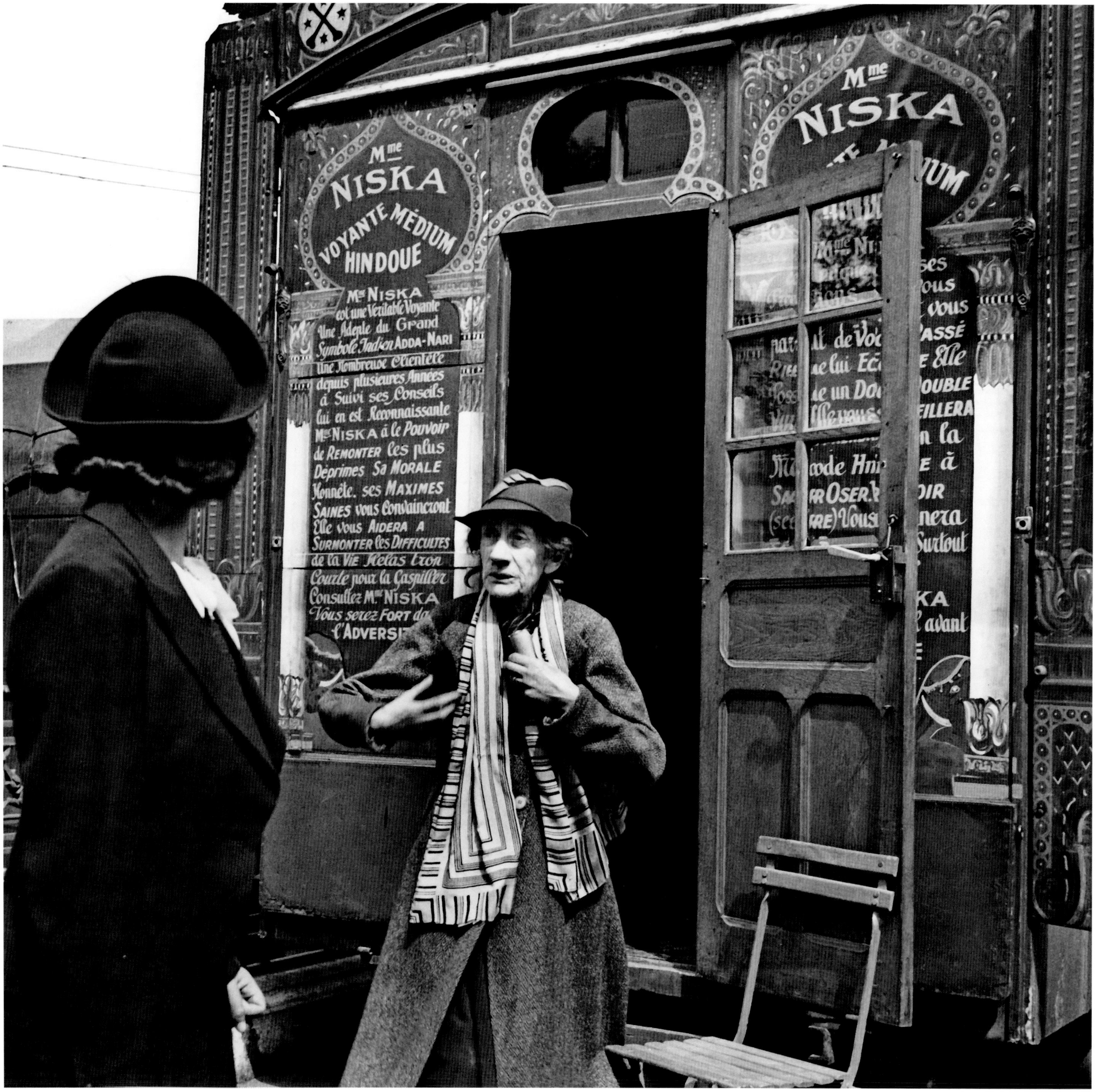

Mme. Niska, Paris, France. 1938.

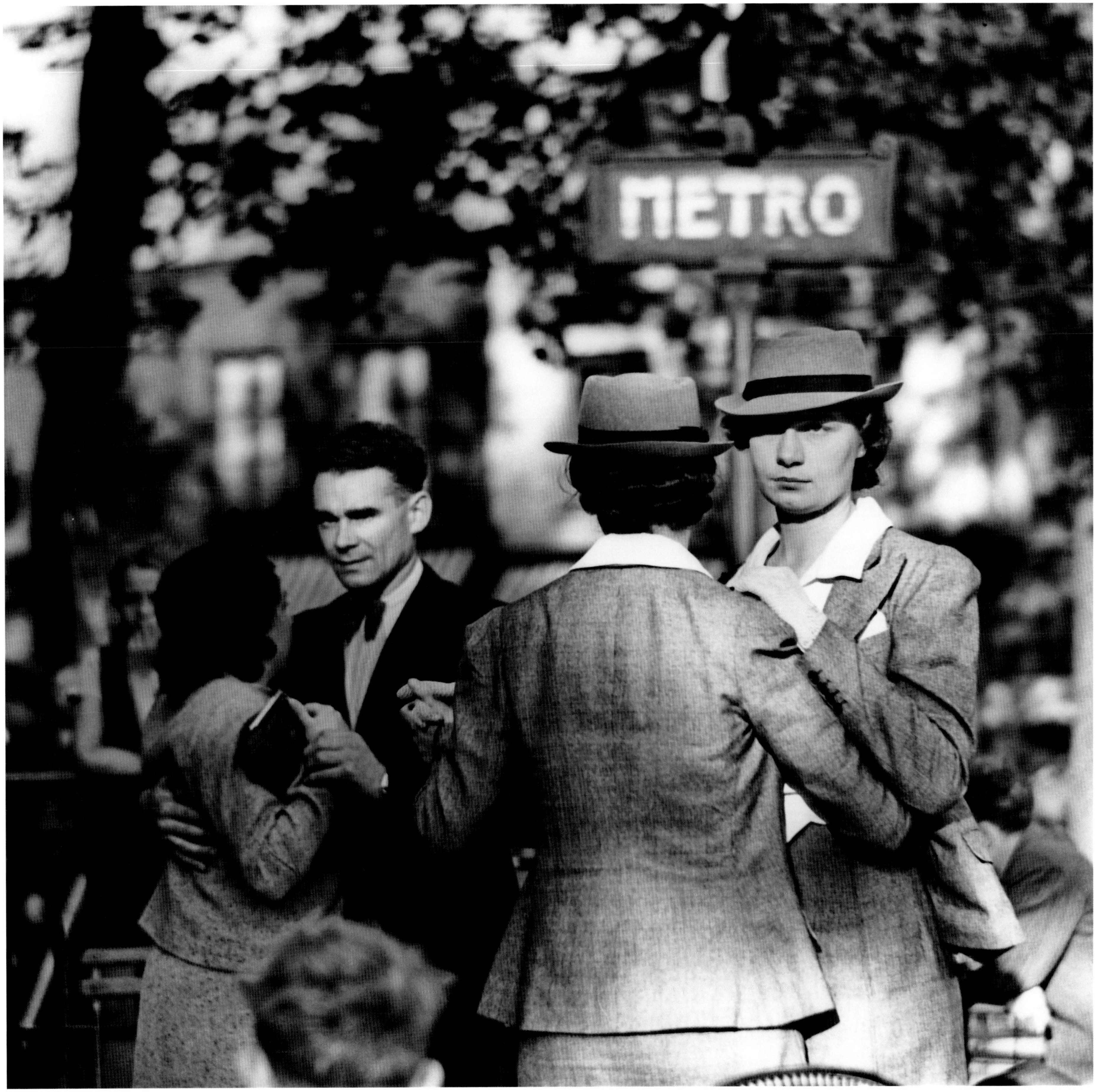

Dancers on Bastille Day, Paris, France. 1938.

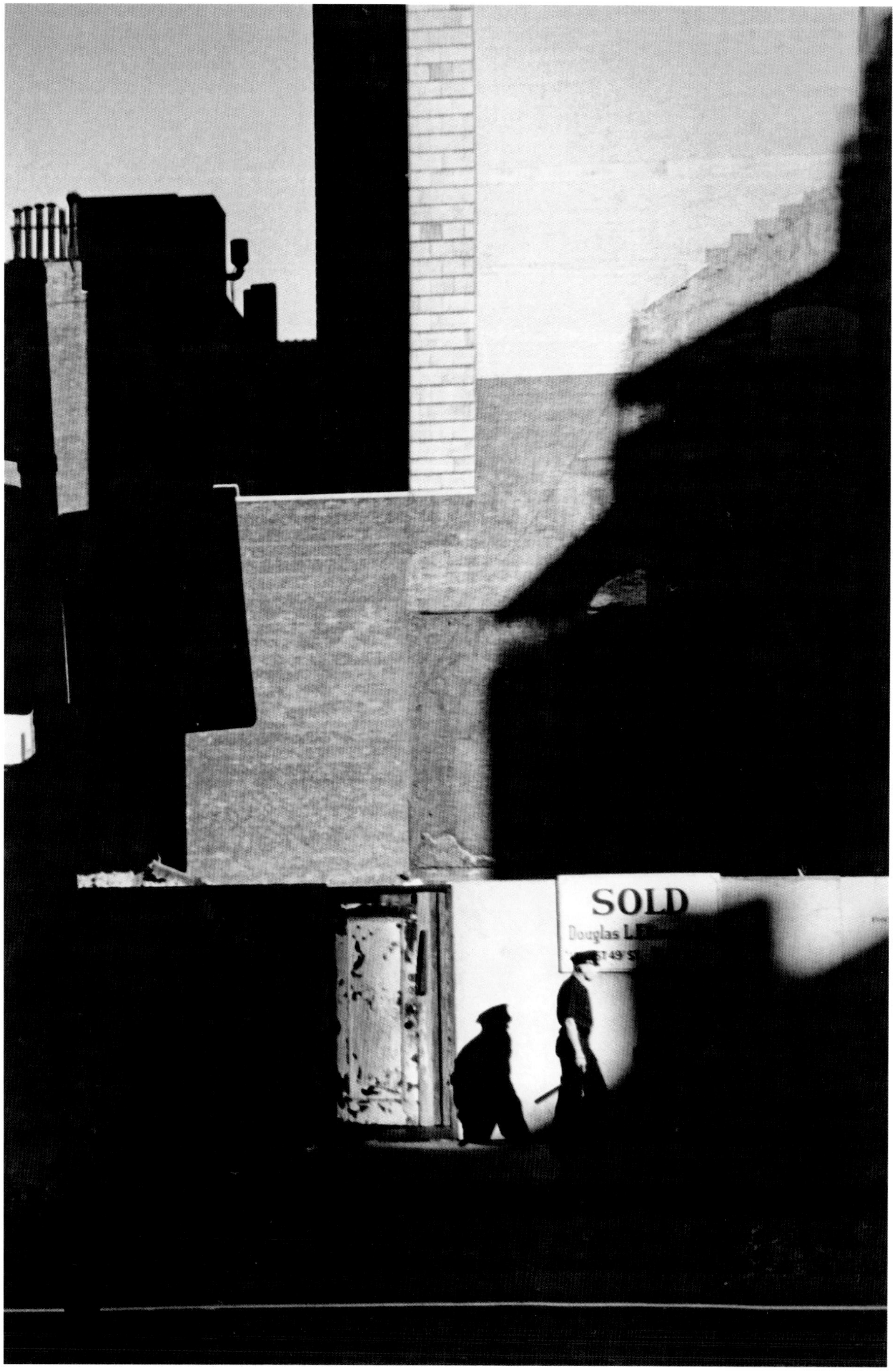
SOLD
Douglas

Madison Avenue,
New York City. ca. 1952.

American Legion Parade on Fifth Avenue, New York City. 1937.

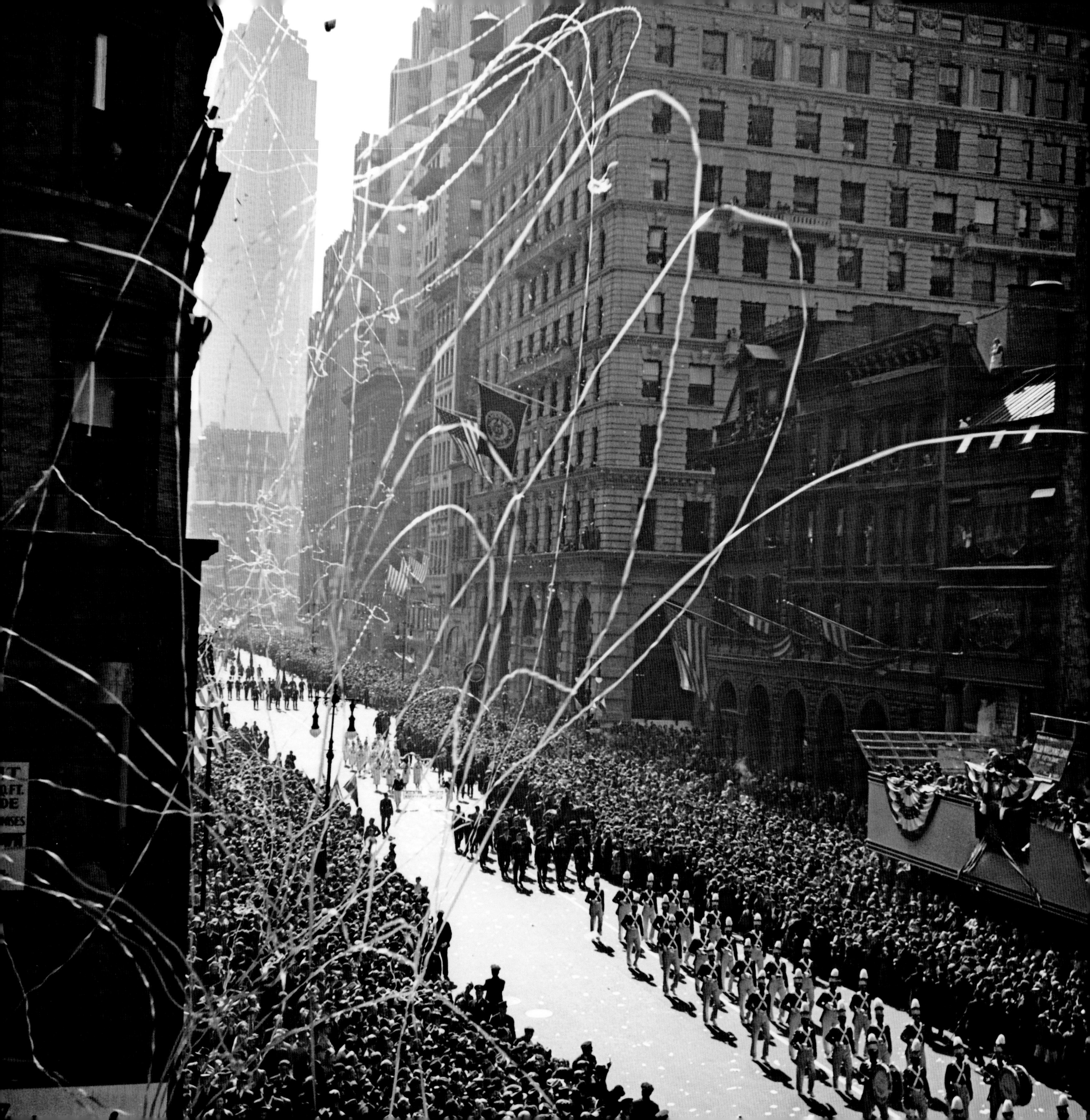

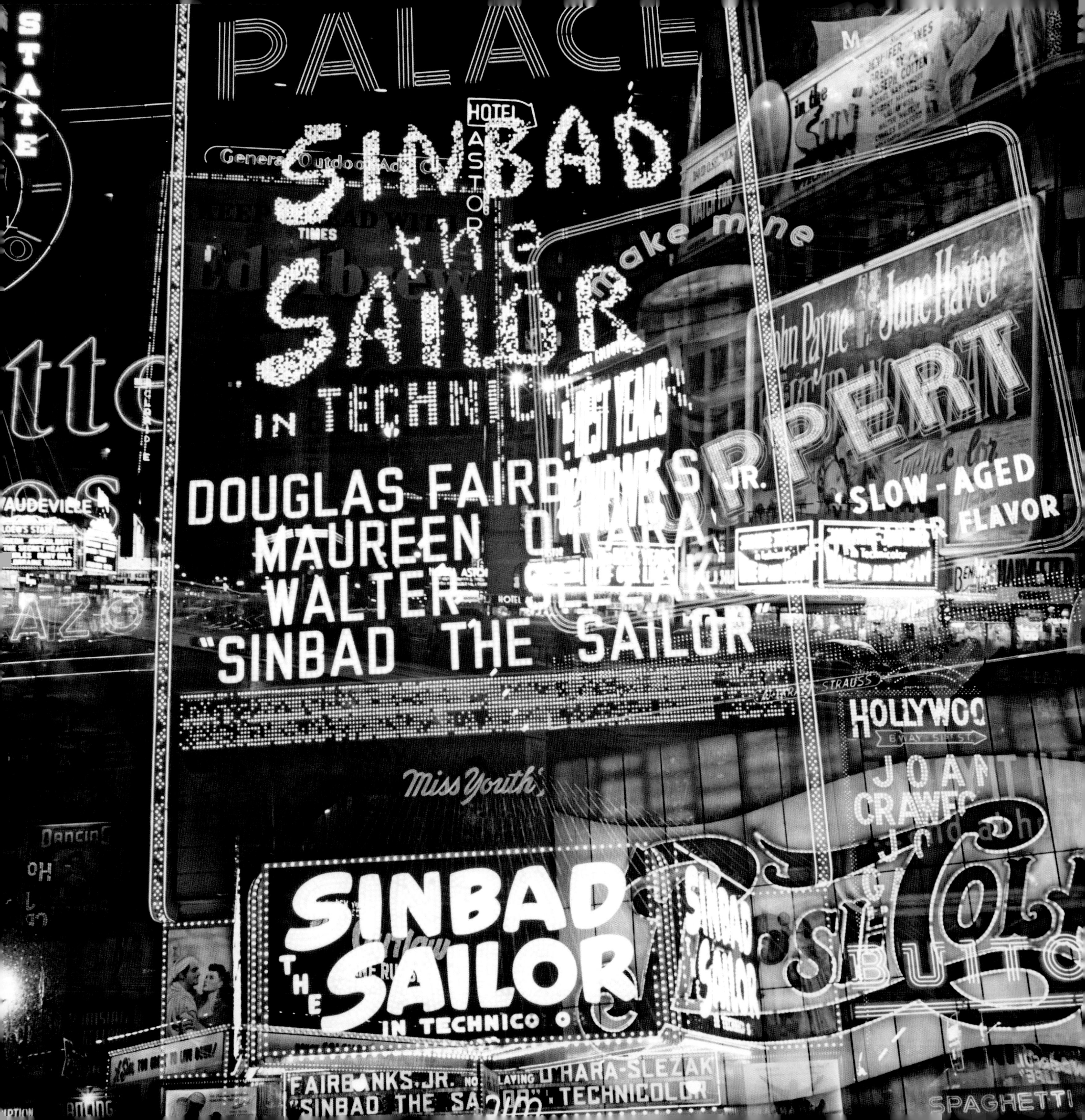
PALACE
STATE
HOTEL ASTOR
SINBAD THE SAILOR
IN TECHNIC
make mine
DOUGLAS FAIRBANKS JR.
MAUREEN O'HARA
WALTER SLEZAK
"SINBAD THE SAILOR"
SLOW-AGED
FLAVOR
VAUDEVILLE
STRAUSS
HOLLYWOO
B'WAY 51ST ST.
Miss Youth's
SINBAD THE SAILOR
IN TECHNICO
FAIRBANKS, JR.
O'HARA-SLEZAK
"SINBAD THE SA
TECHNICOLOR
SPAGHETTI

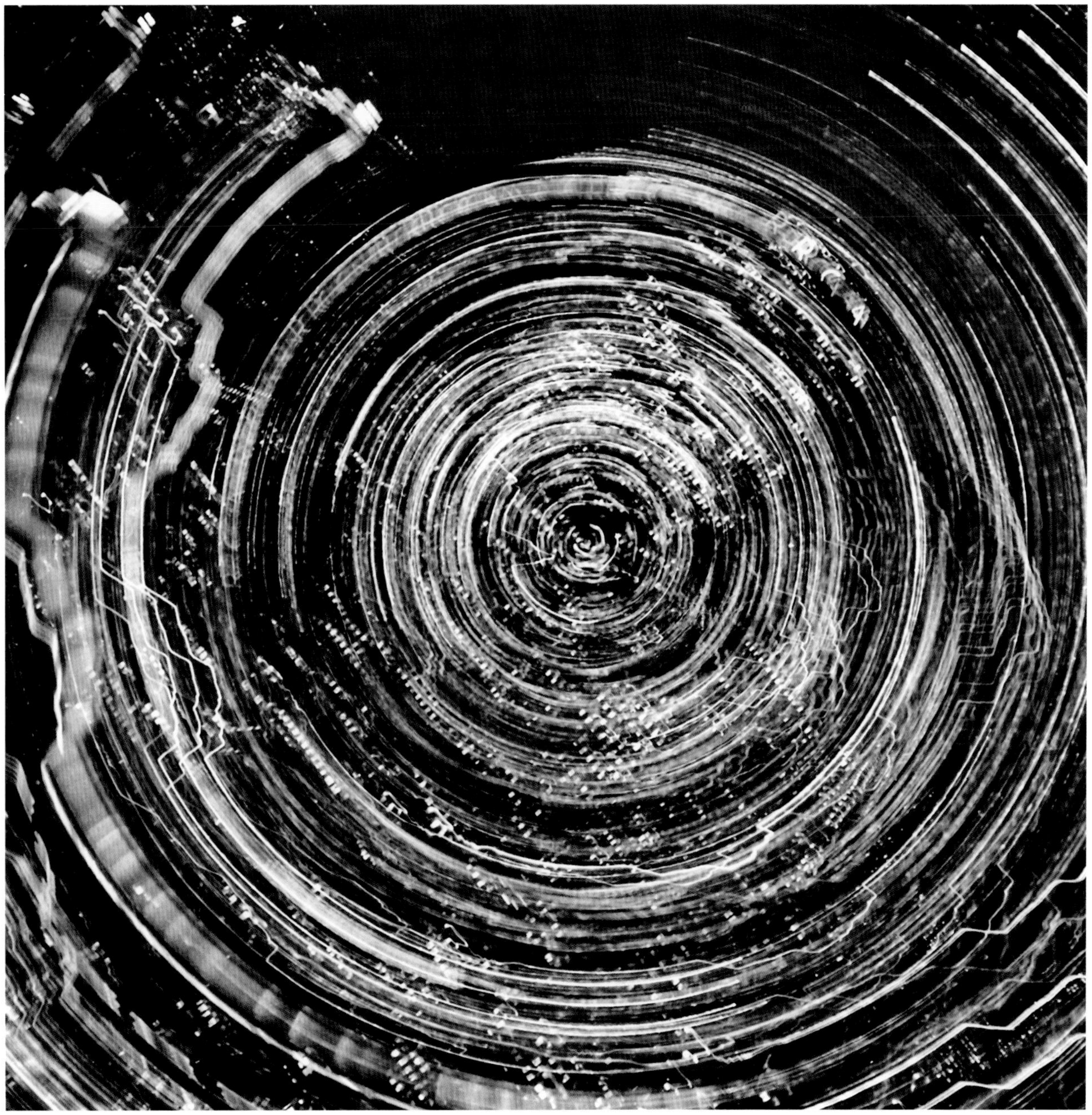

(left) Times Square at Night, New York City. ca. 1948.
(above) New York City at Night. 1945.

Father at the Brooklyn Bridge, Sunday Morning, Lower East Side, New York City. 1947.

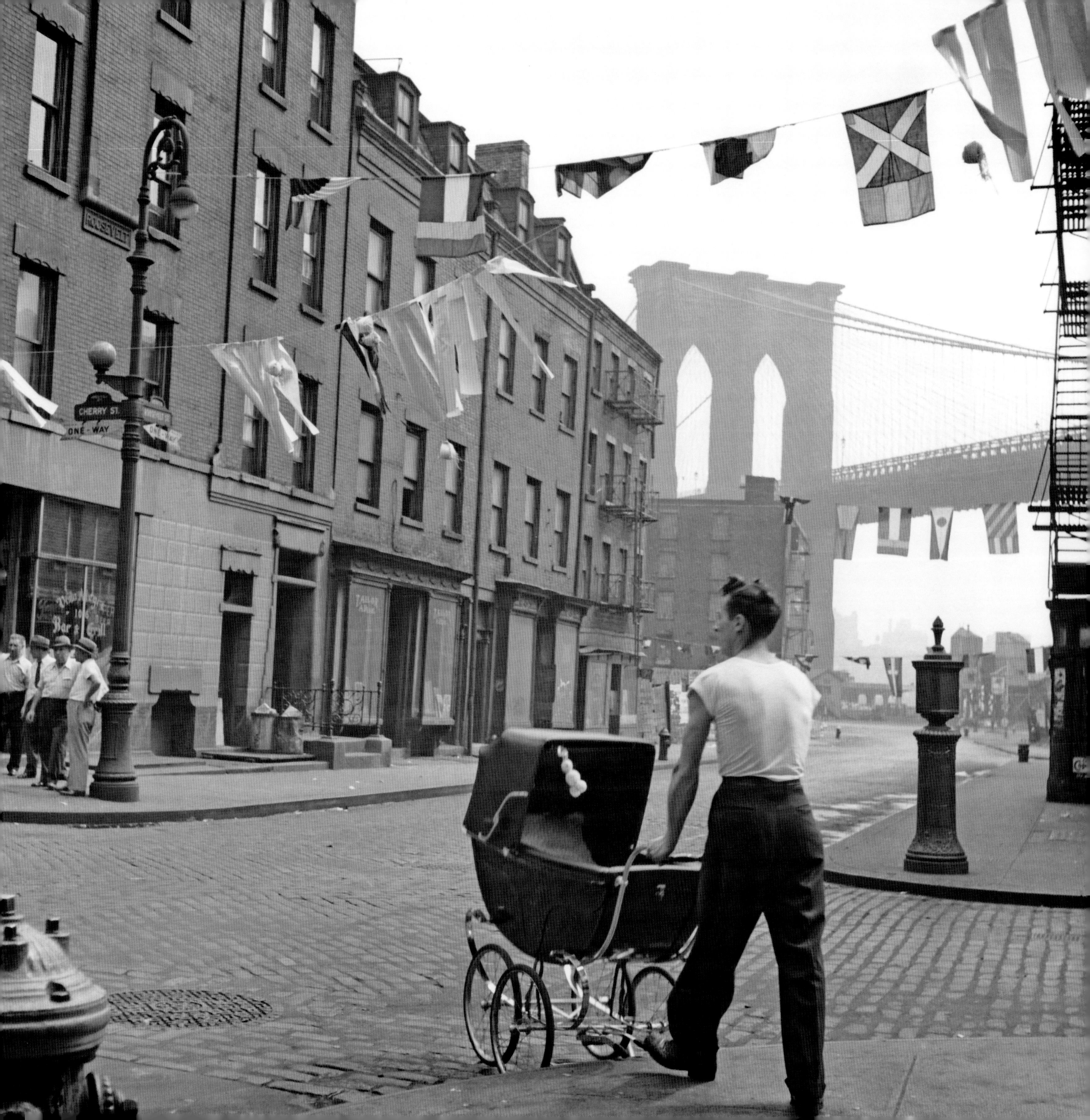
ROOSEVELT
CHERRY ST.
ONE-WAY

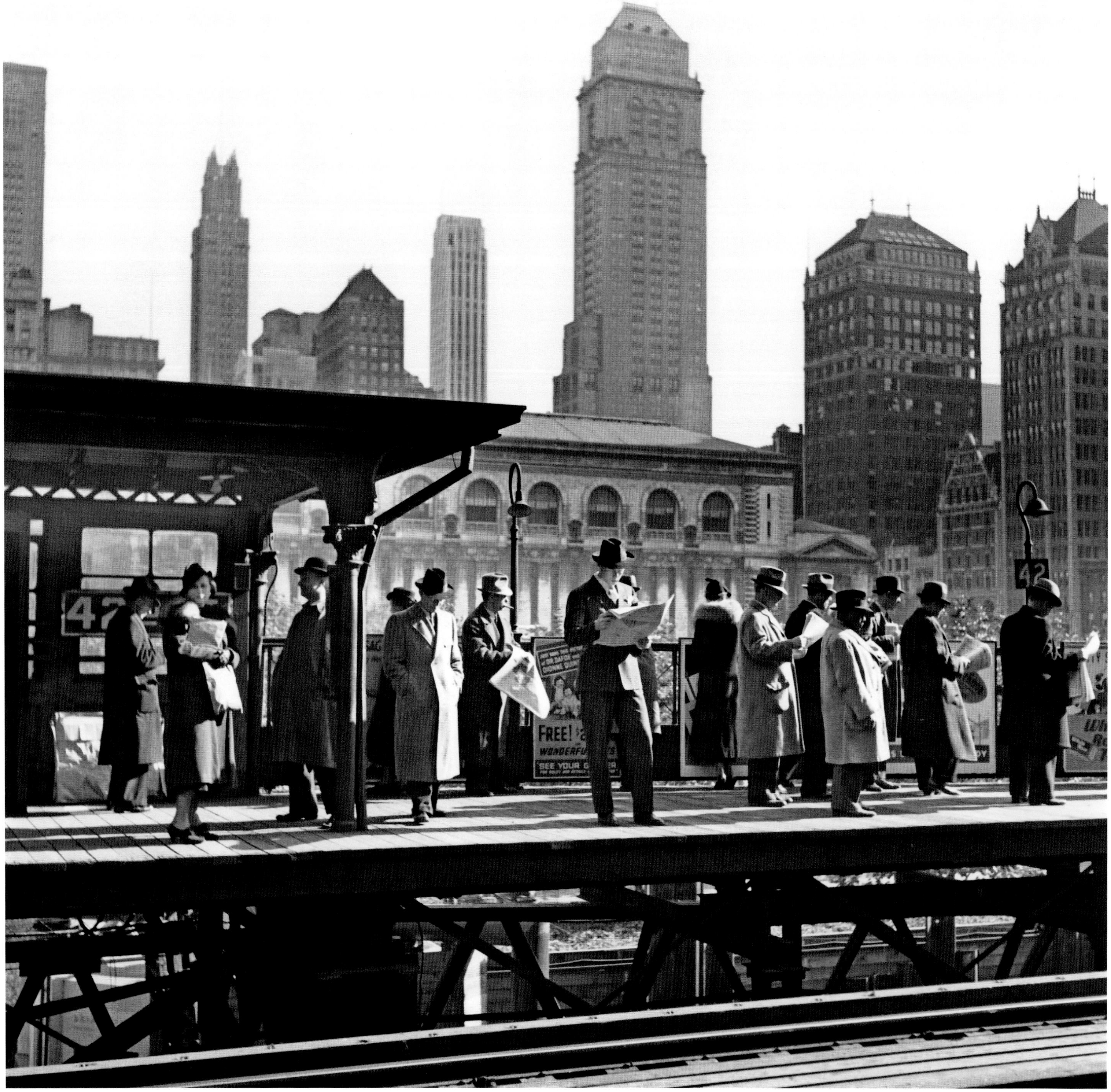

Elevated Train Station at 6th Avenue and 42nd Street, New York City. ca. 1945.

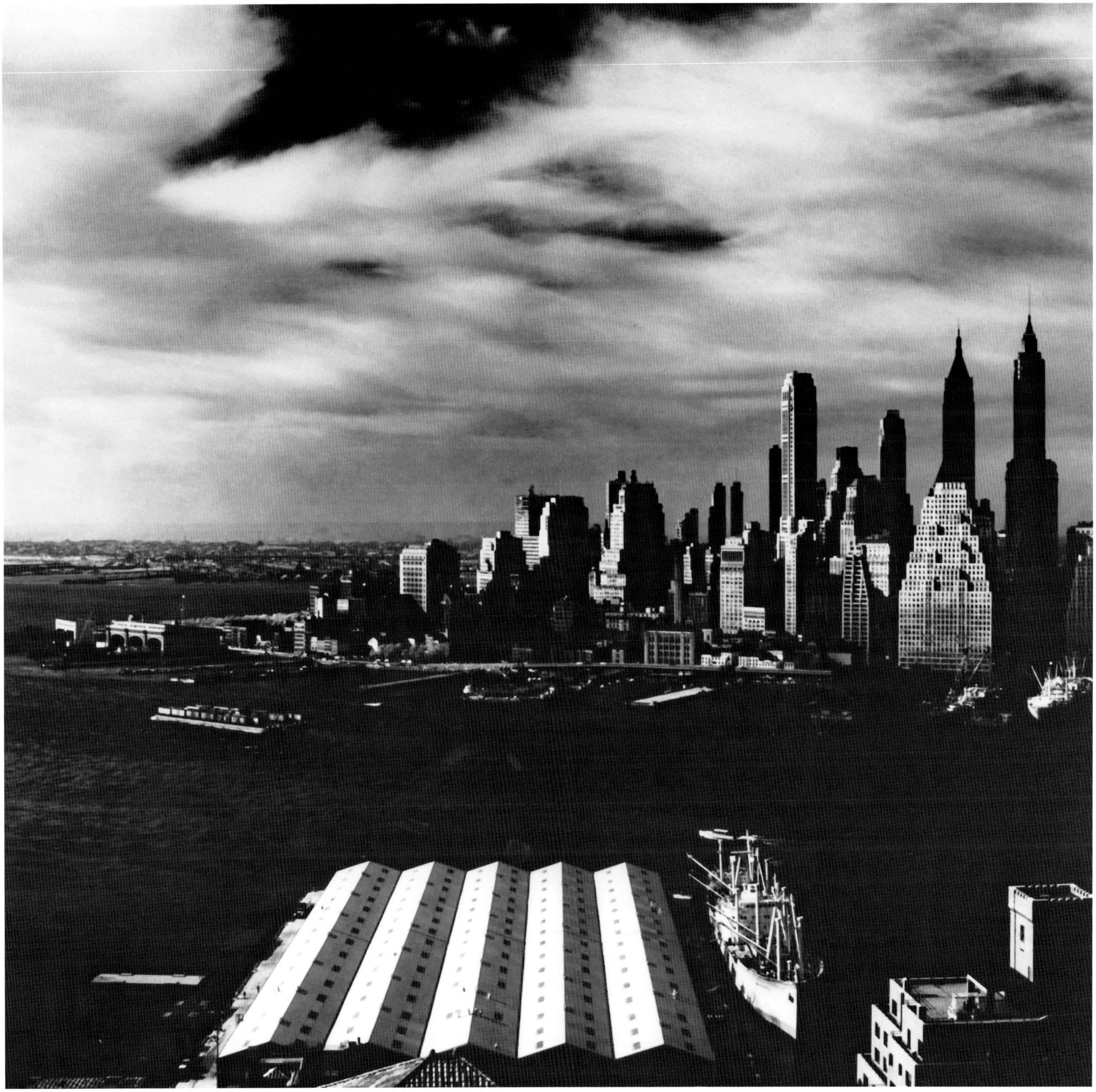

Lower Manhattan Seen from Brooklyn, New York City. 1950.

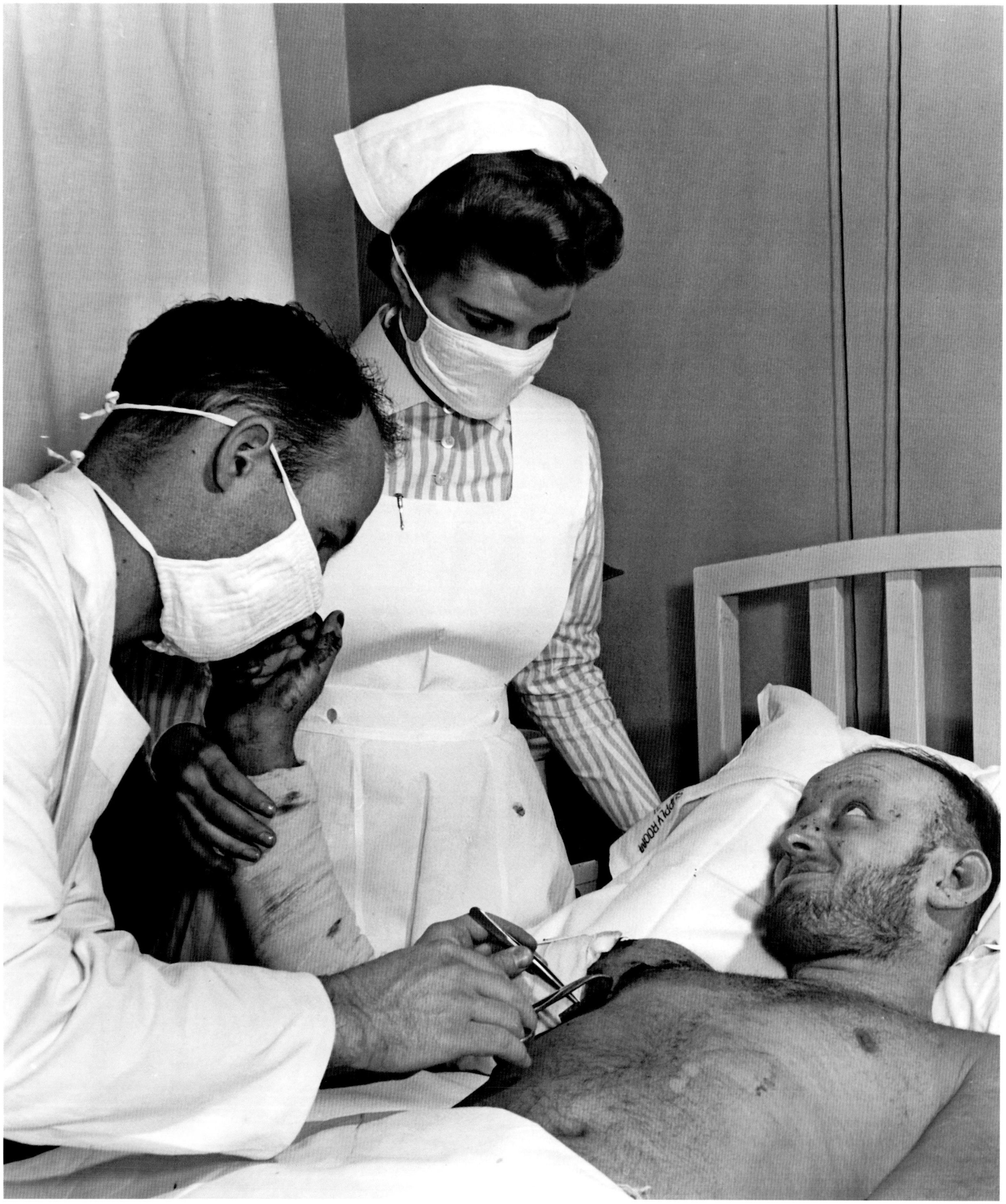

OWI: Nurse Assisting Doctor with
Wounded Sailor, New York City. ca. 1944.

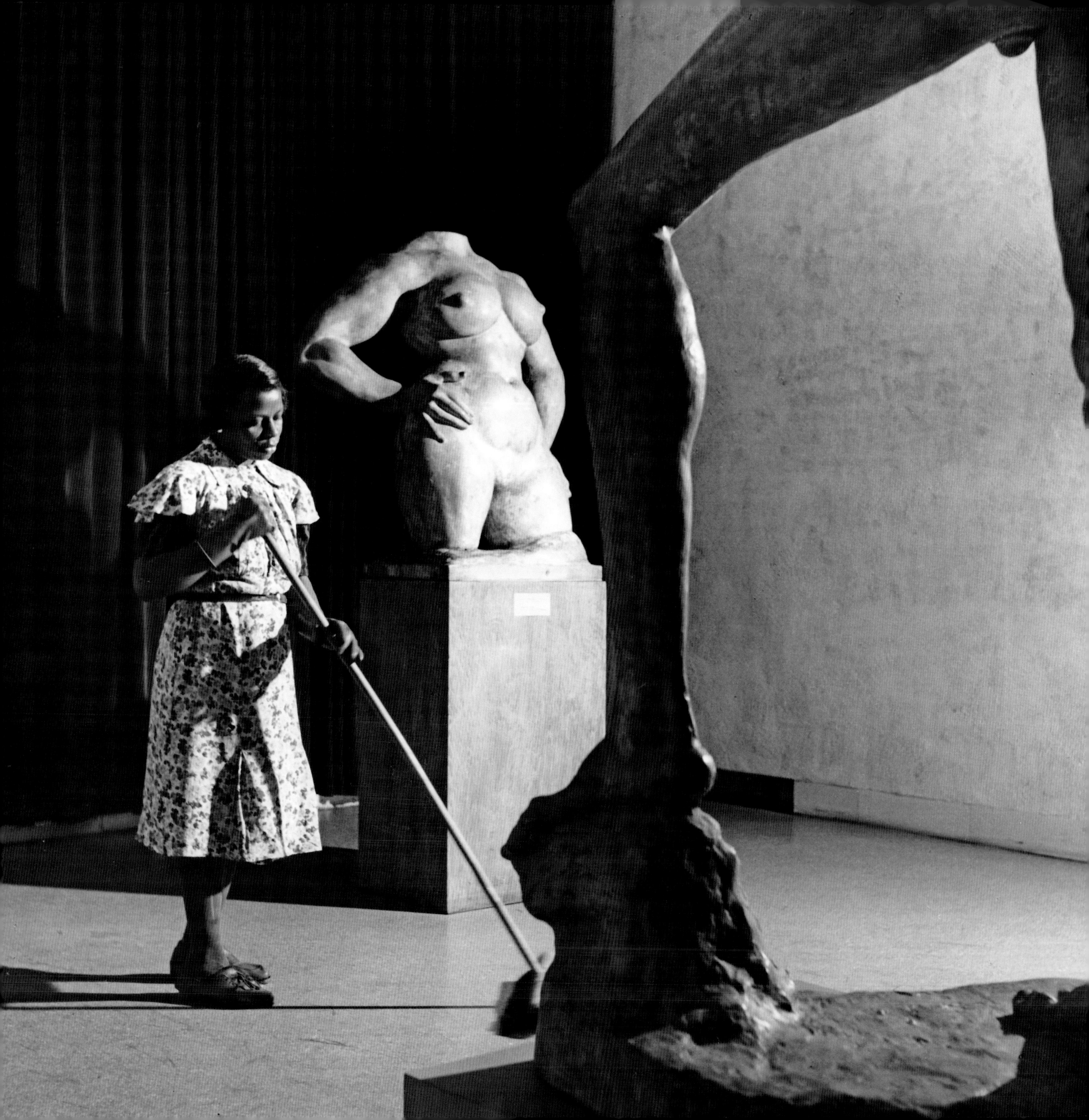

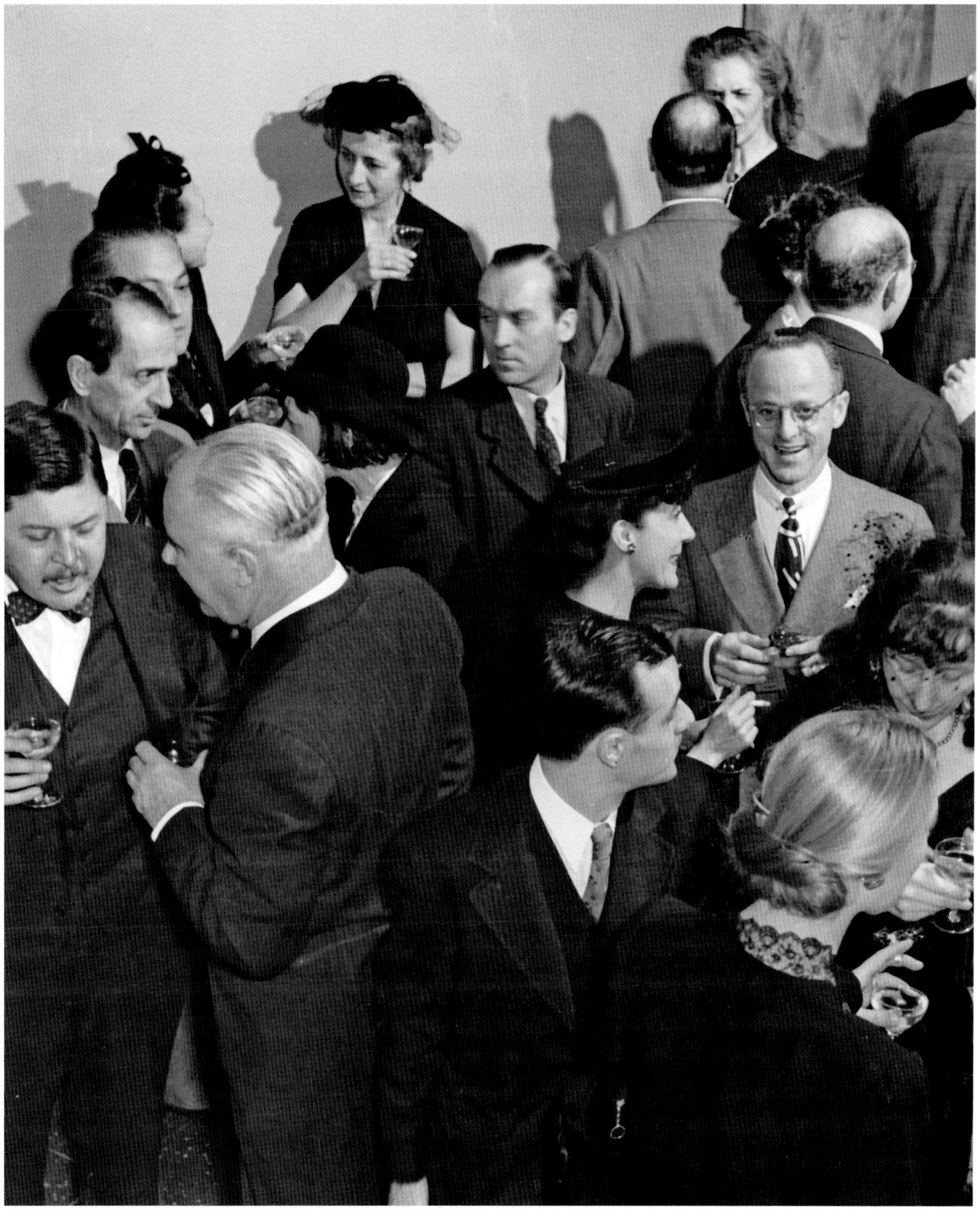

(left) Cleaning Lady in Museum of Modern Art, New York City. 1948.
(above) Opening Night of New Exhibition at Museum of Modern Art, New York City. ca. 1948.

For Saving Men: Street Preacher,
New York City. ca. 1946.

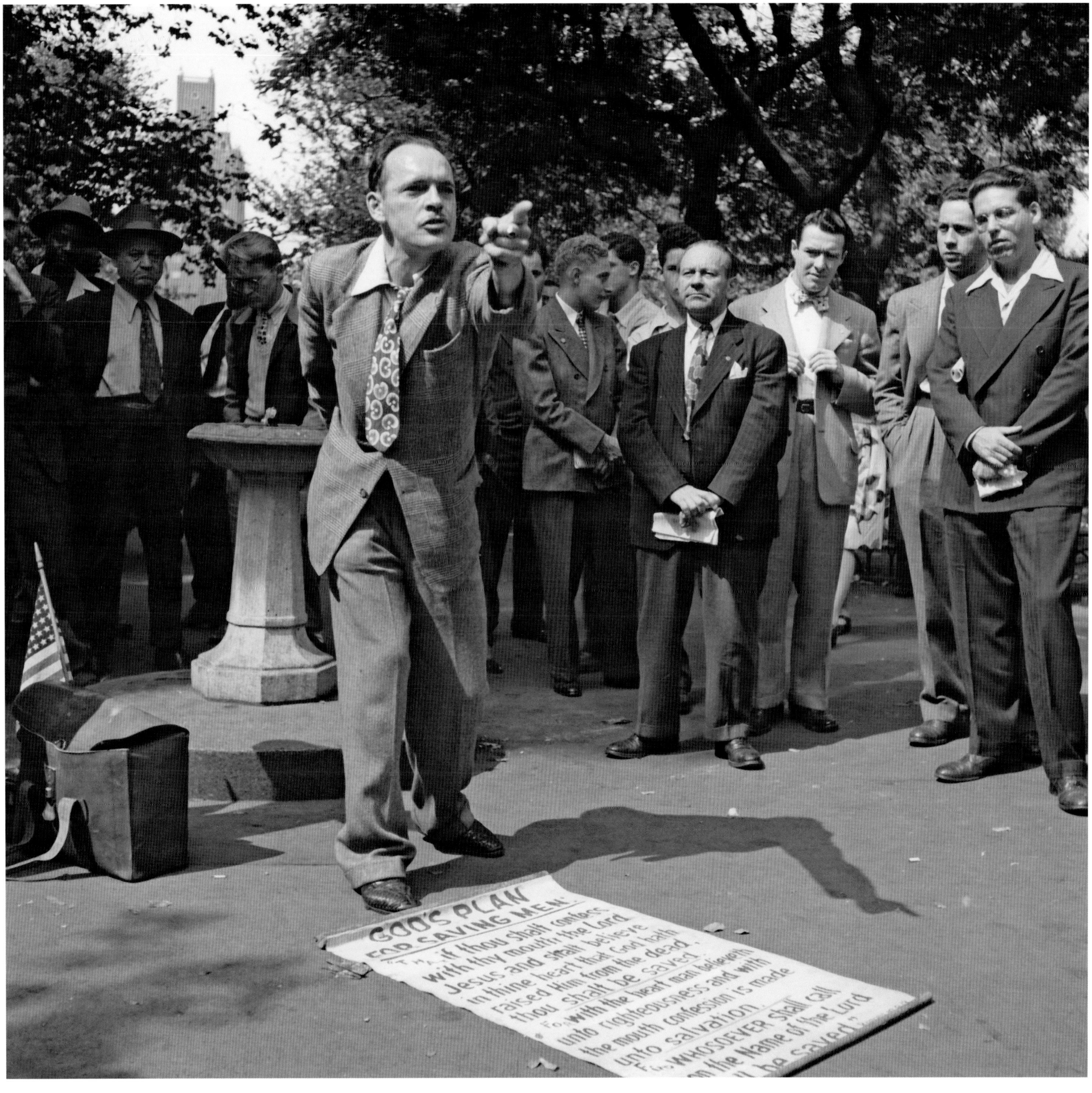
GOD'S PLAN
FOR SAVING MEN:
if thou shalt confess
with thy mouth the Lord
Jesus and shalt believe
in thine heart that God hath
raised Him from the dead
thou shalt be saved
with the heart man believeth
unto righteousness and with
the mouth confession is made
unto salvation.
WHOSOEVER shall call
the Name of the Lord
be saved."

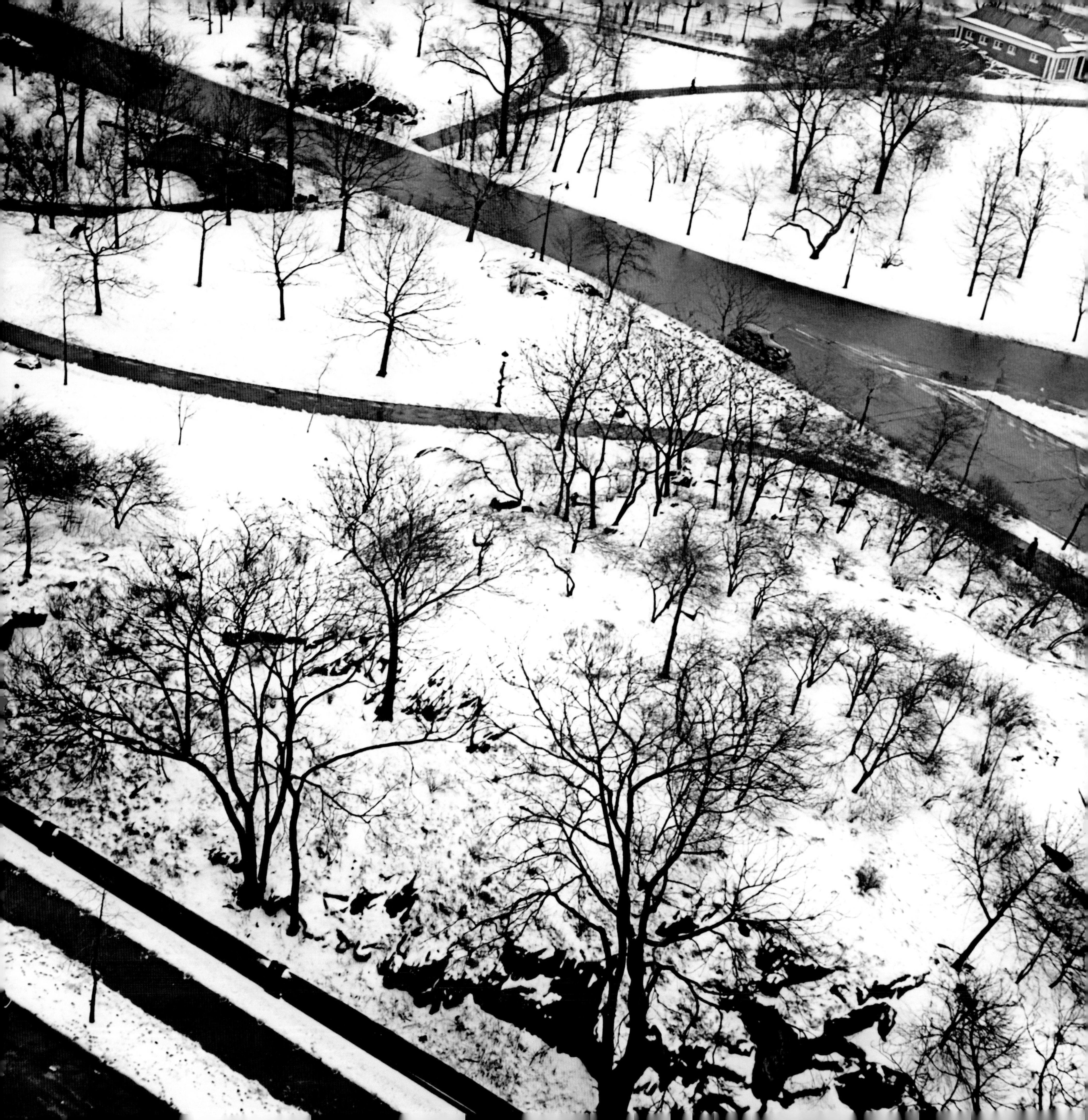

Central Park South in the Winter,
New York City. 1950.

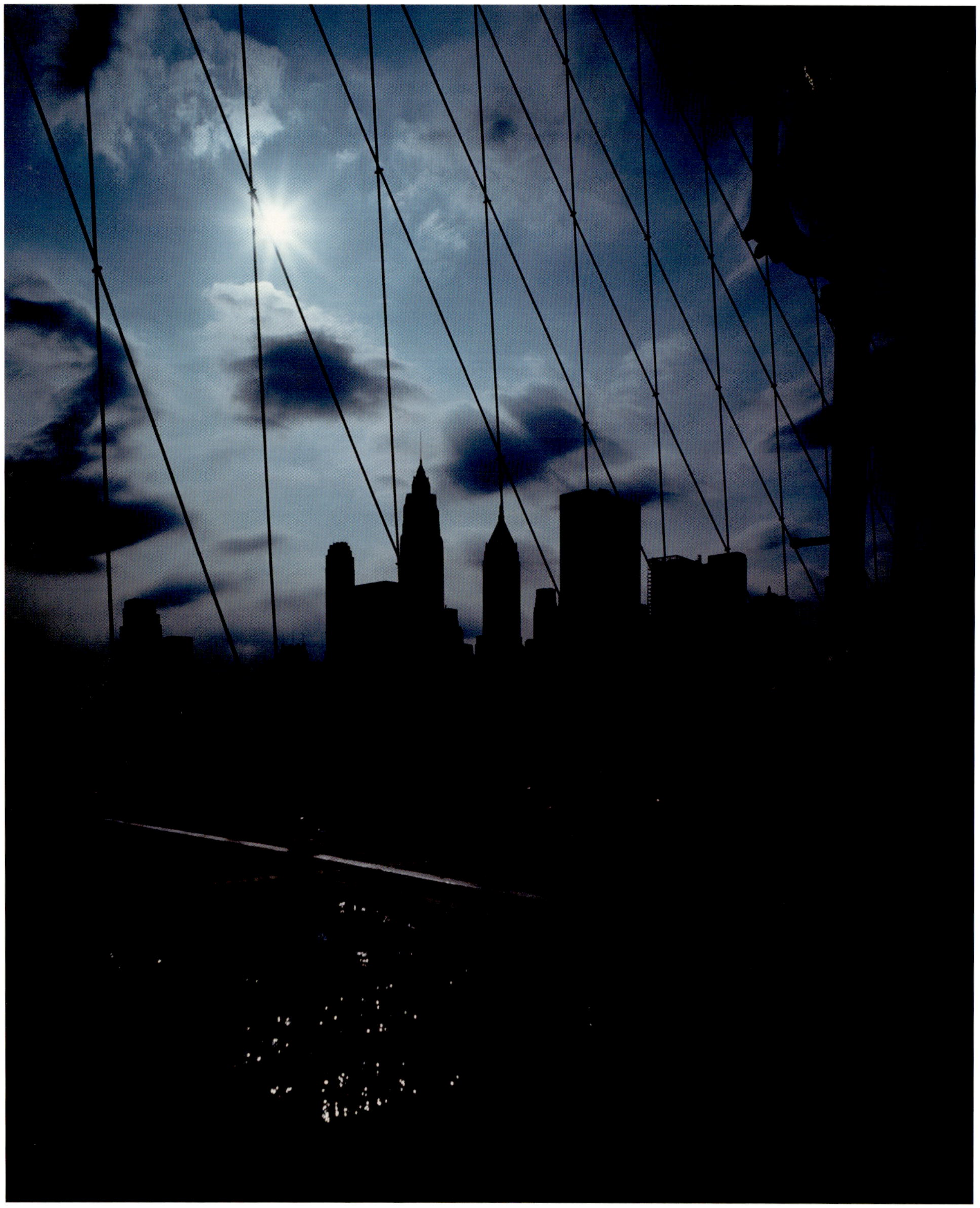

(above) Lower Manhattan from the Brooklyn Bridge, New York City. 1955.
(right) Sailor on the Brooklyn Bridge, New York City. 1950.

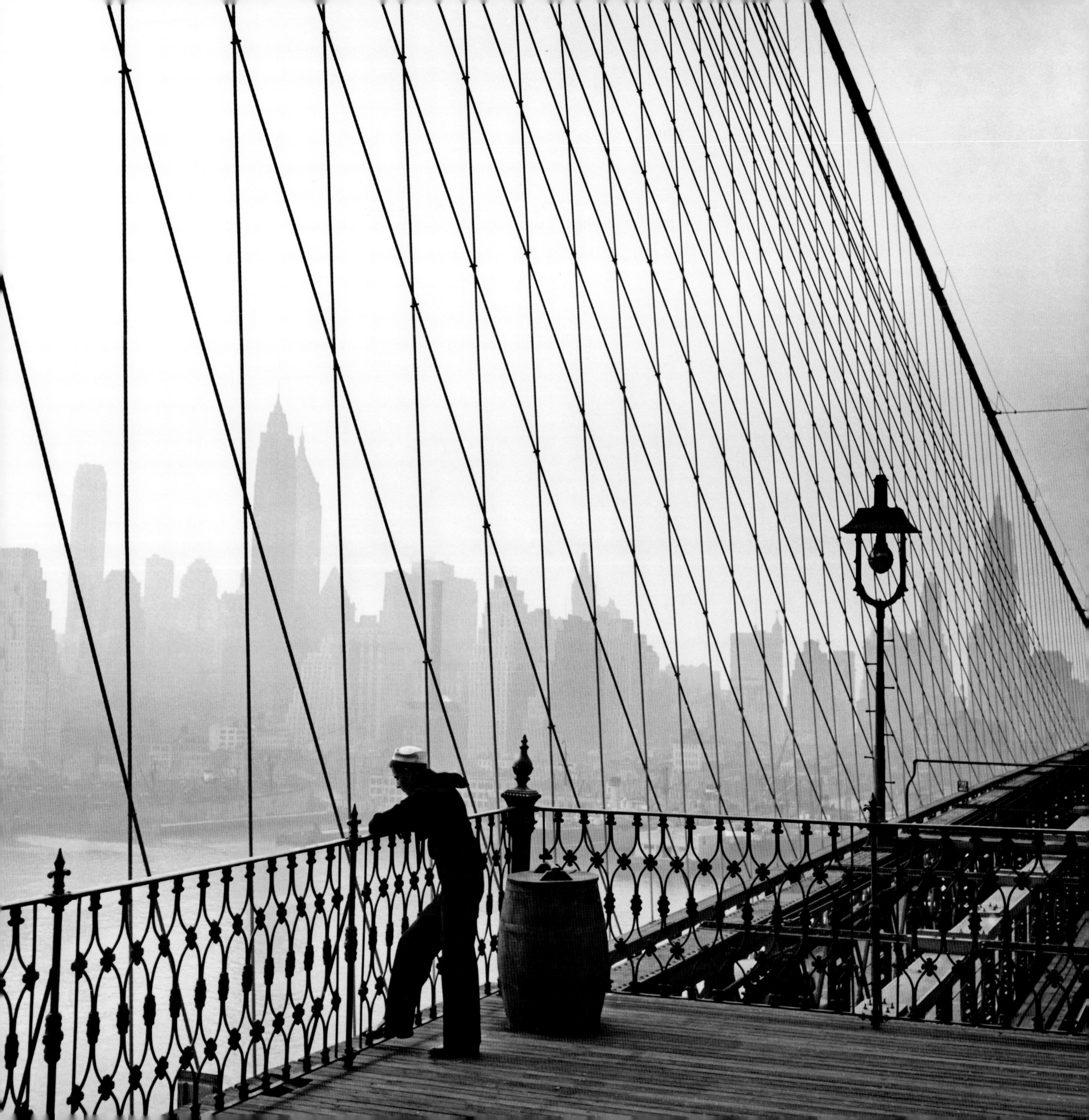

There is no
such thing as too
much beauty.

REX STOUT

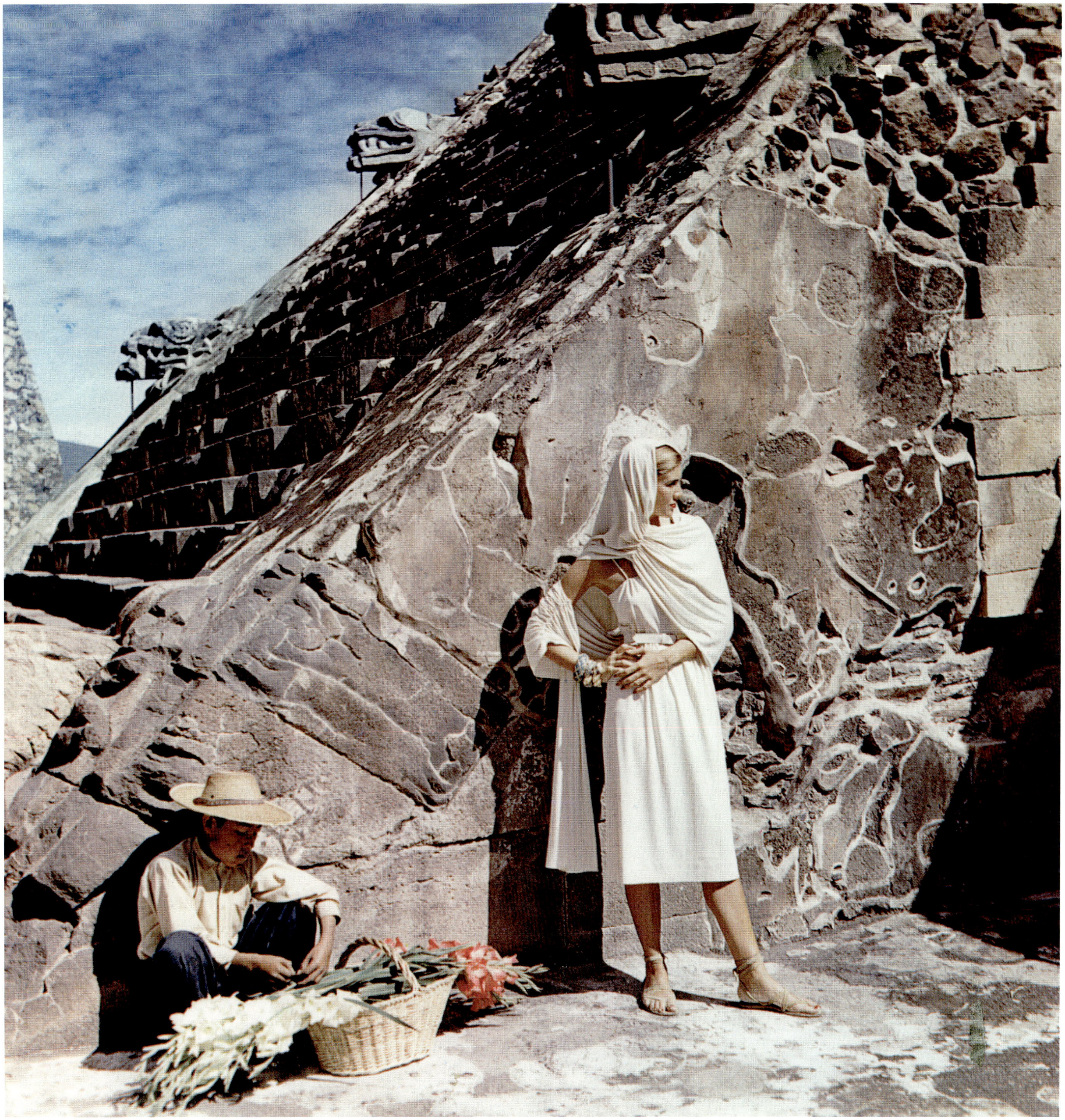

Fashion Model with Flower Vendor at the Pyramid of the Sun, Teotihuacan, Mexico. 1945.

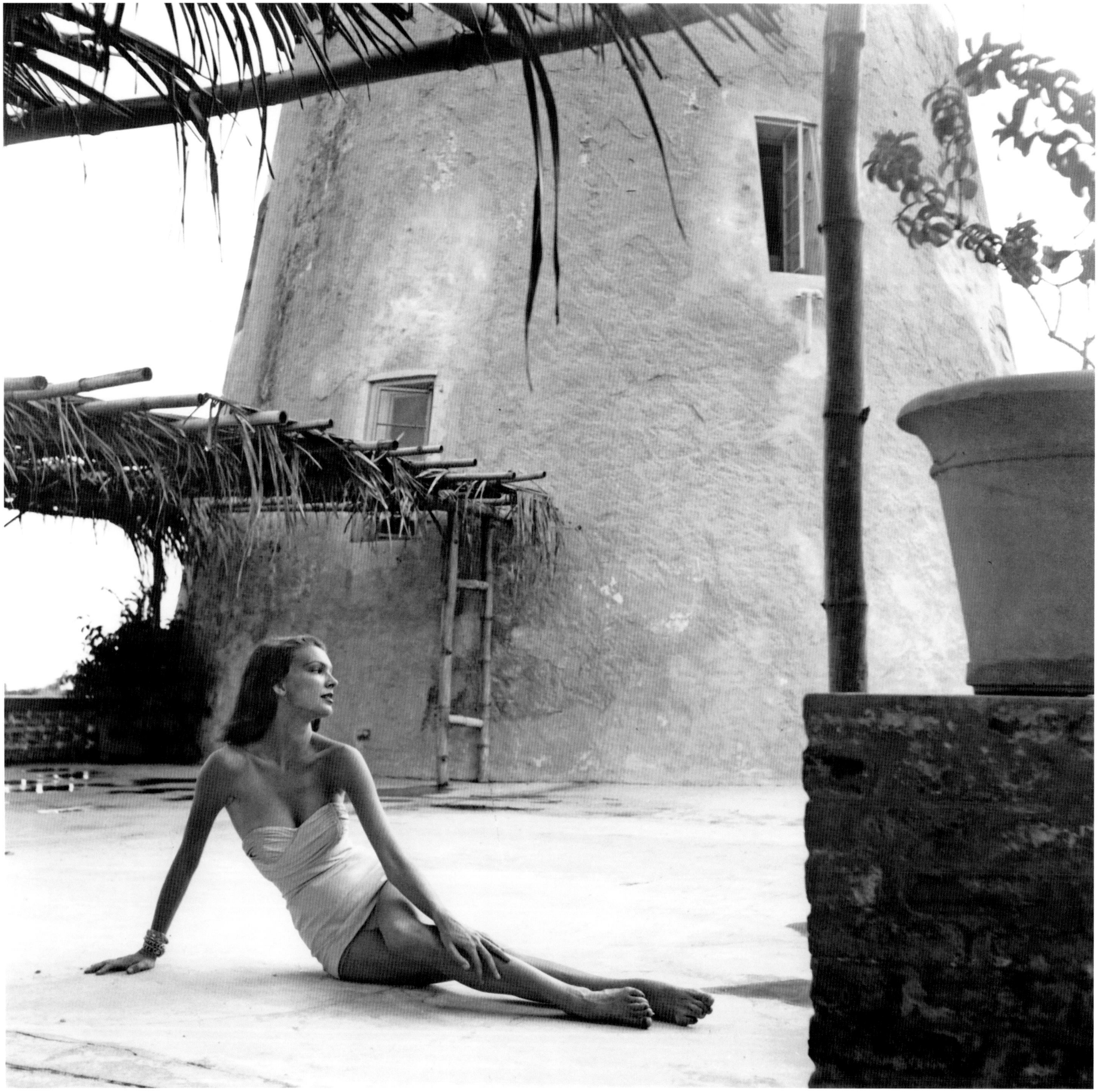

Model Catherine Cassidy at the Old Sugar Mill, St. Croix, Virgin Islands. 1948.

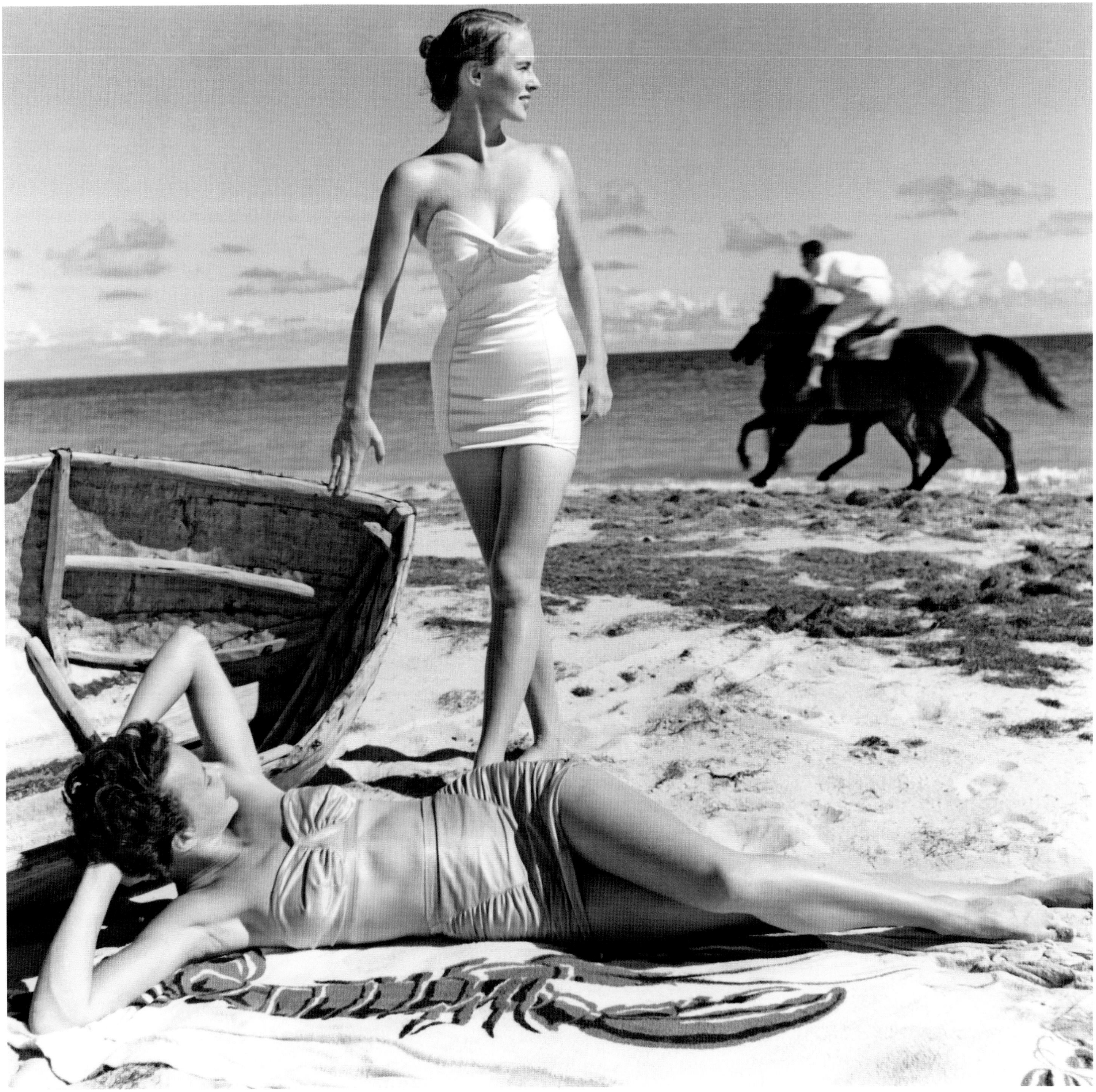

On the Beach, Fredericksted, St. Croix, Virgin Islands. 1948.

Jeannie Patchett, Fashion Model,
New York City. ca. 1952.

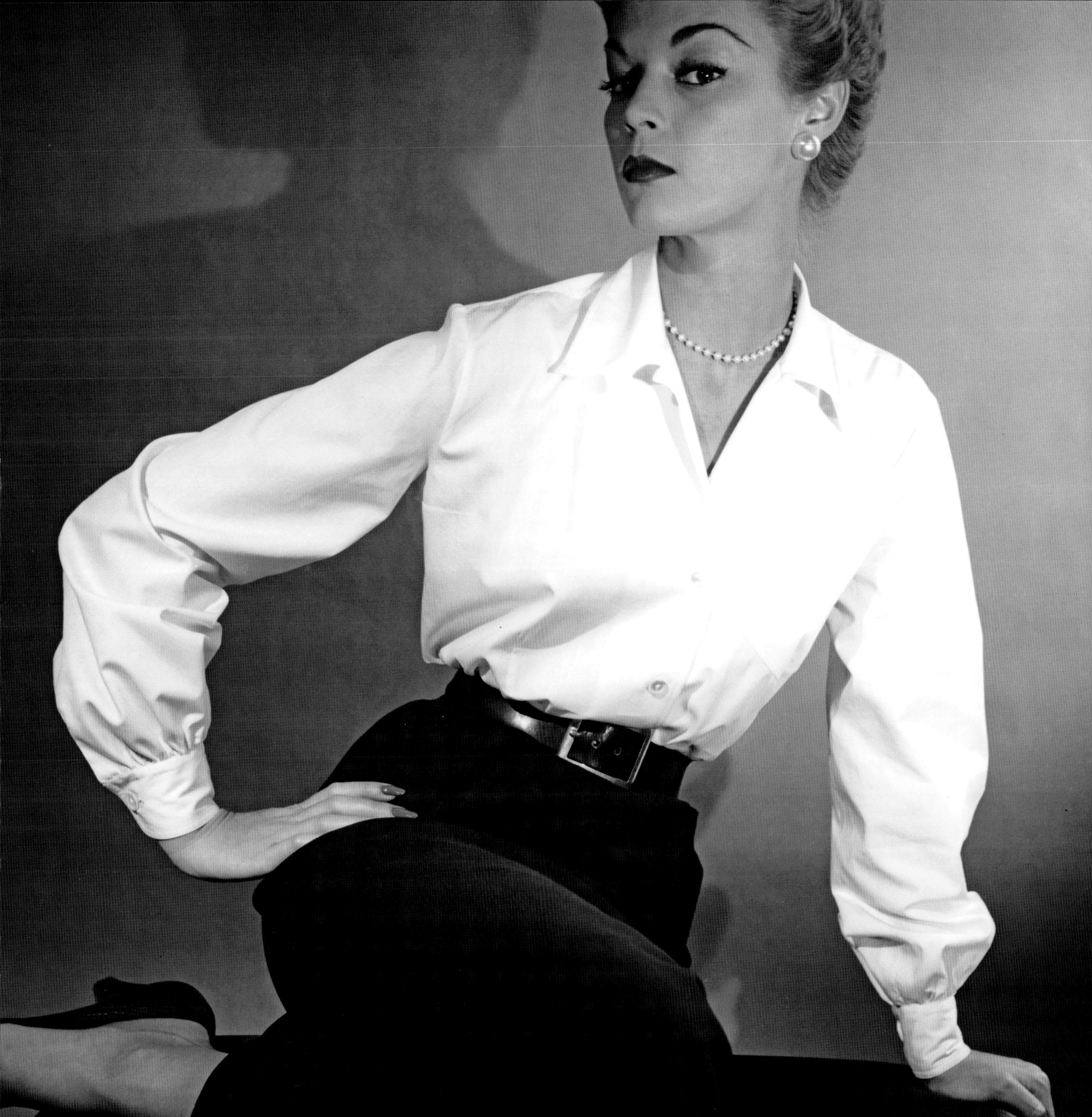

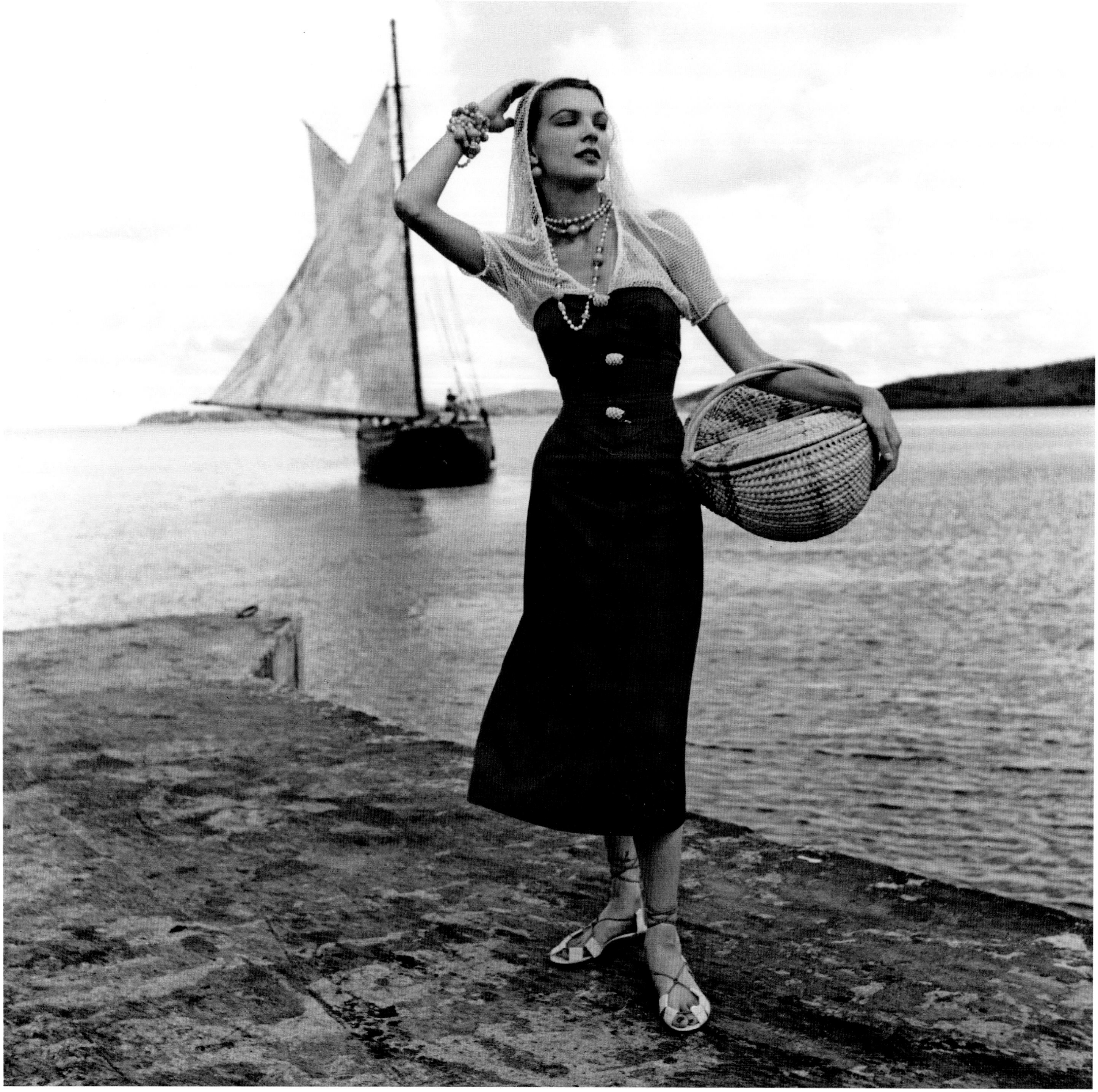

Model Catherine Cassidy with Caribbean Schooner Leaving the Harbor, Christiansted, St. Croix, Virgin Islands. 1948.

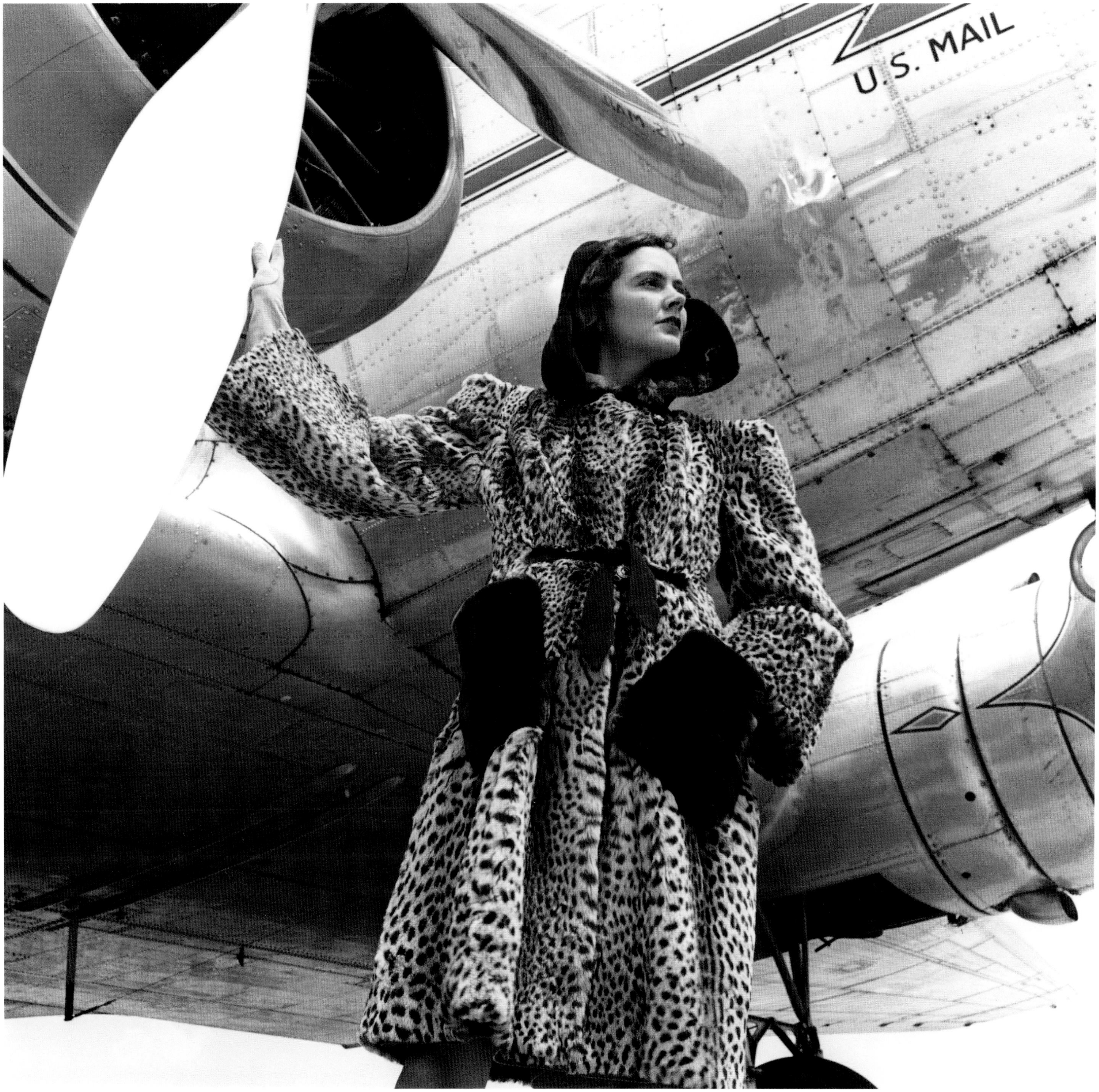

Model in Leopard Coat at LaGuardia Airport, New York City. 1947.

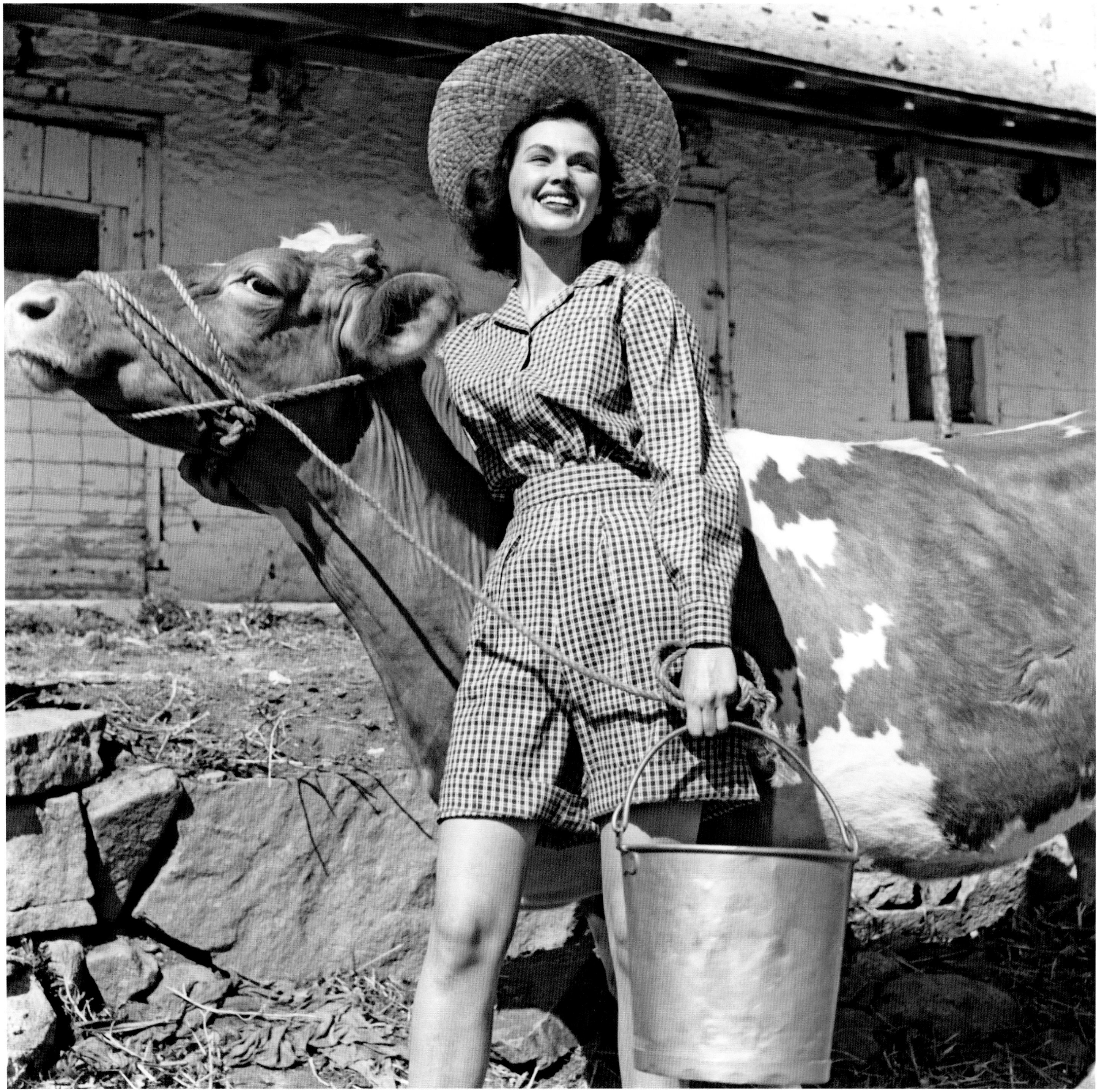

Fashion for the Farm by Mary Lewis, New York. 1945.

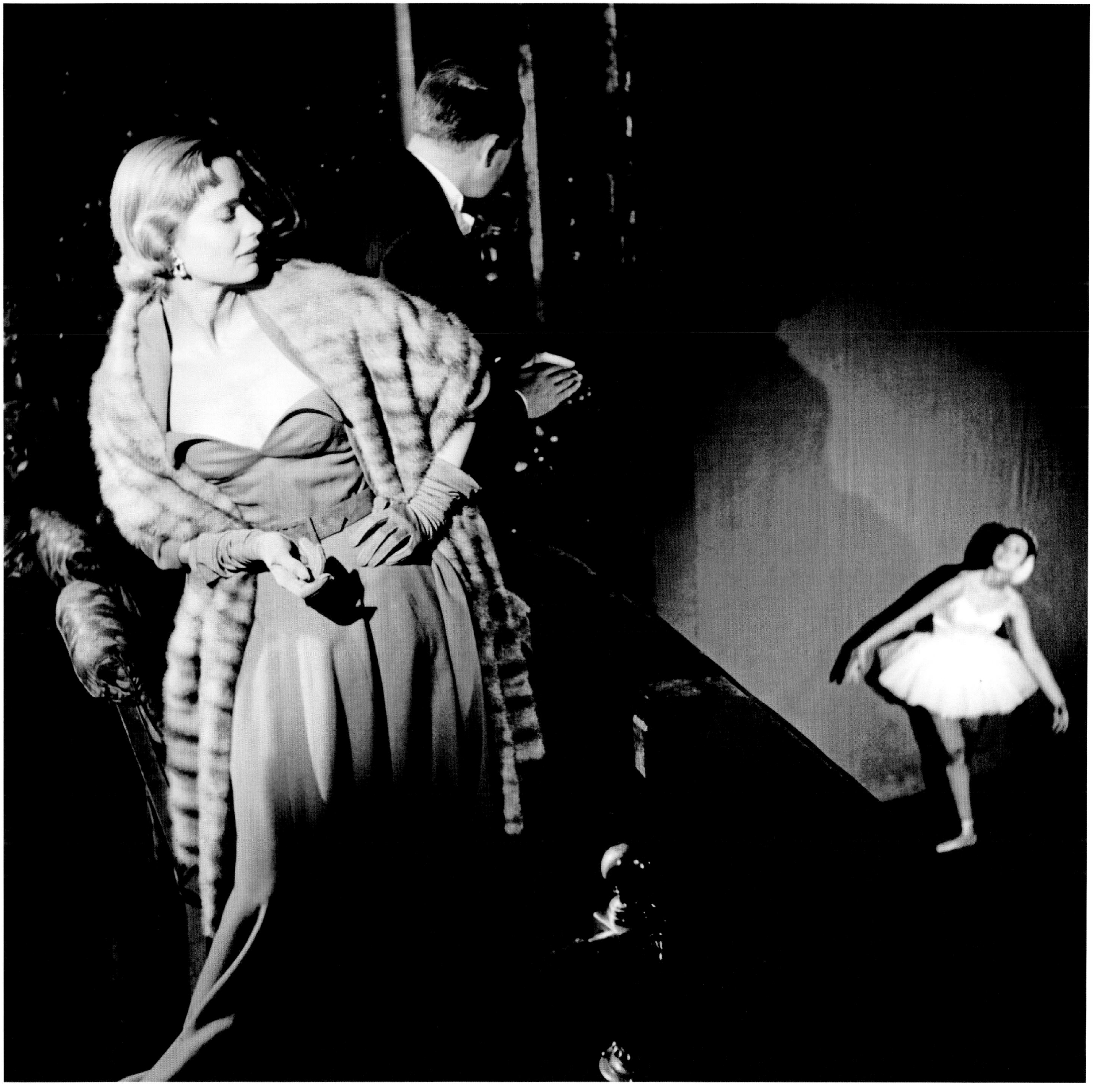
Gala Evening at the Met, New York City. ca. 1950.

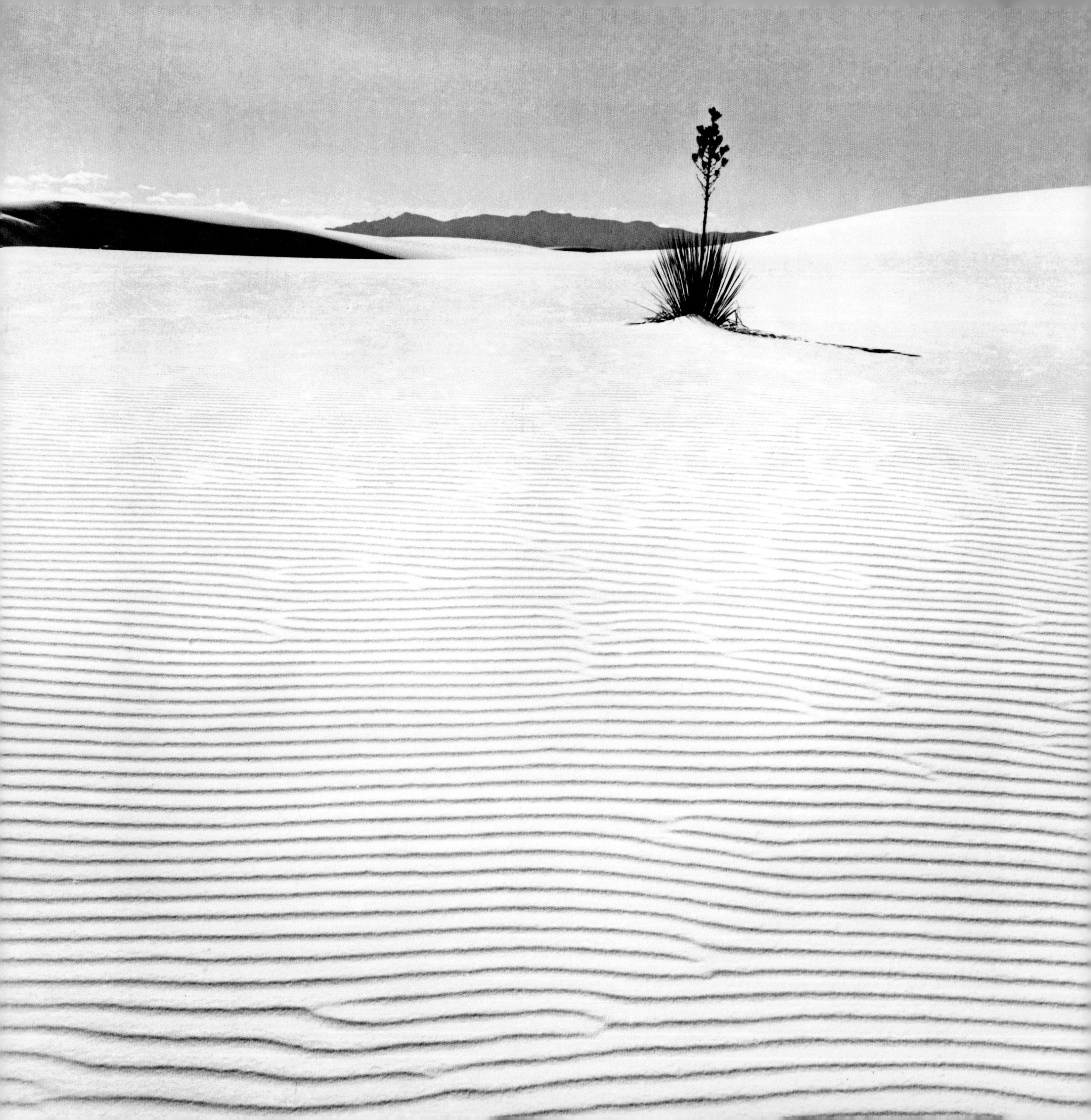

Freedom: Yucca Plant,
New Mexico. ca. 1943.

Cowboys and Oil Derrick, Texas. 1949.

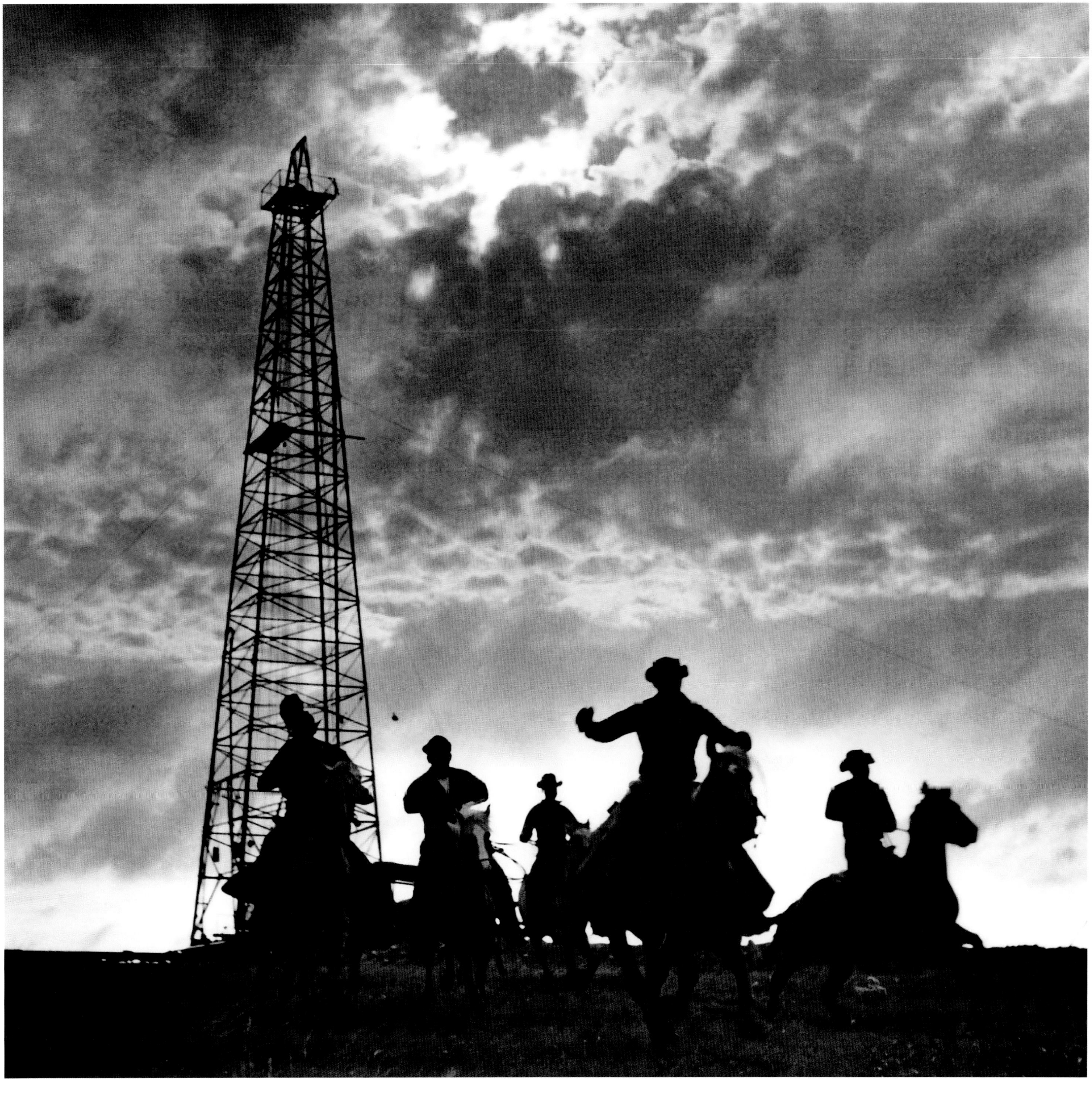

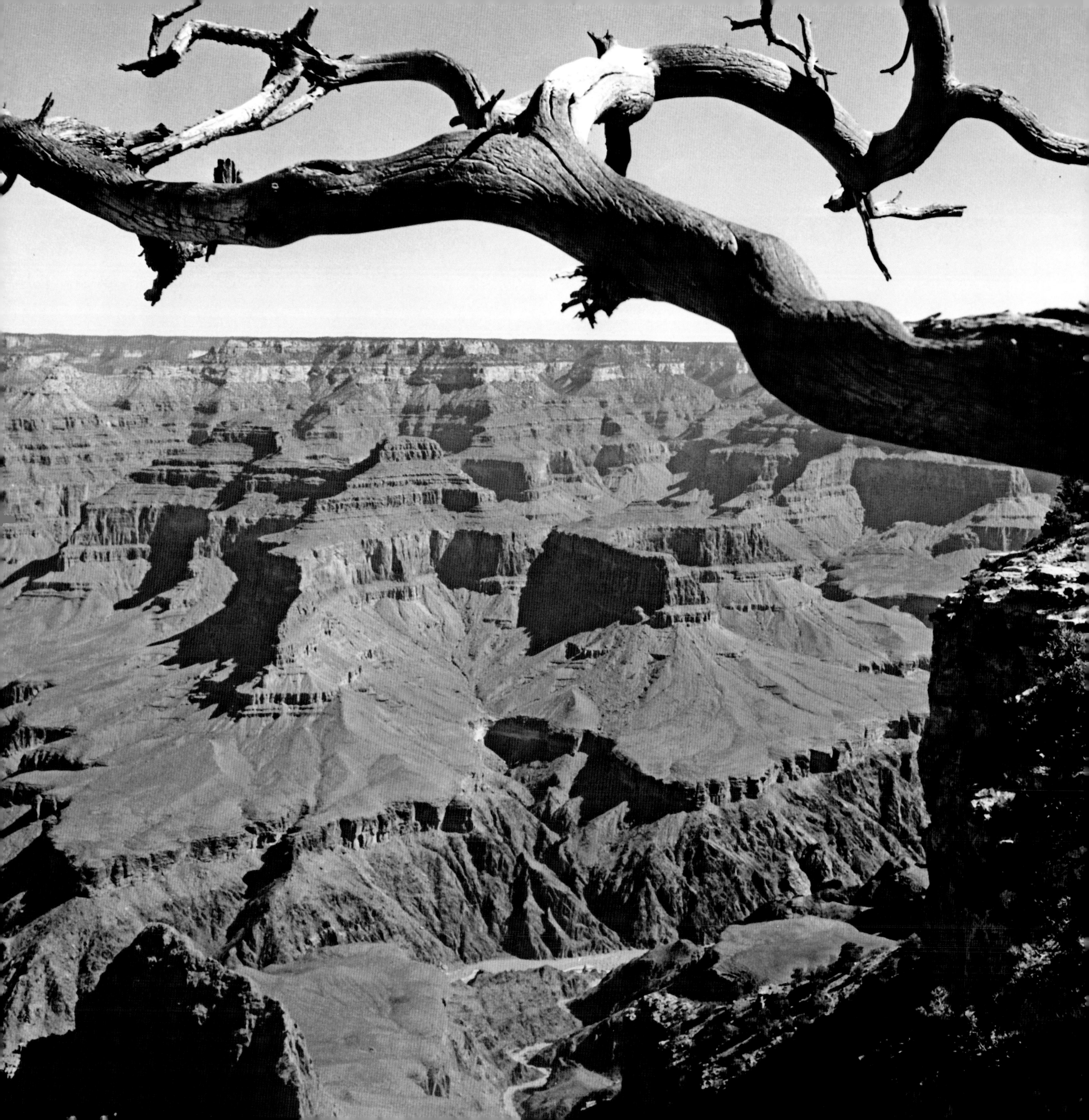

Grand Canyon, Arizona. 1941.

Wyoming Ranch. 1940.

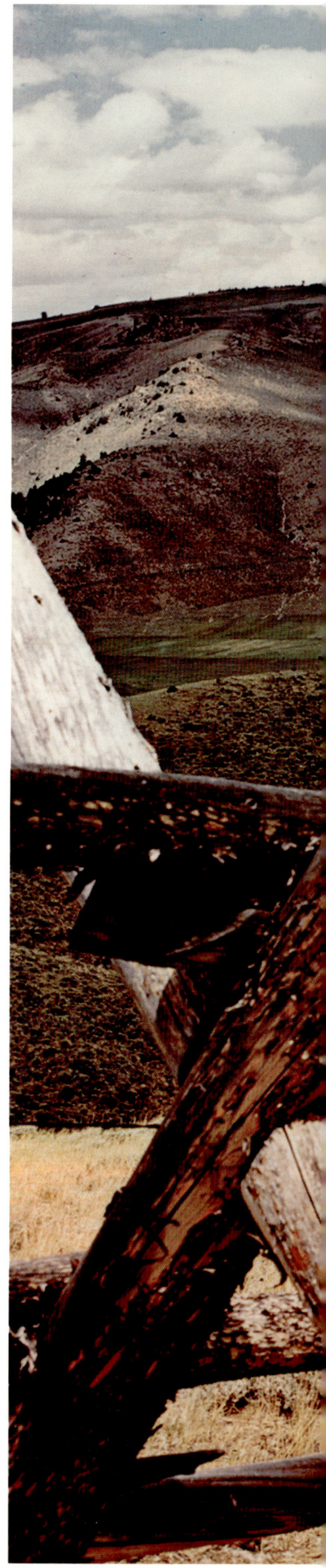

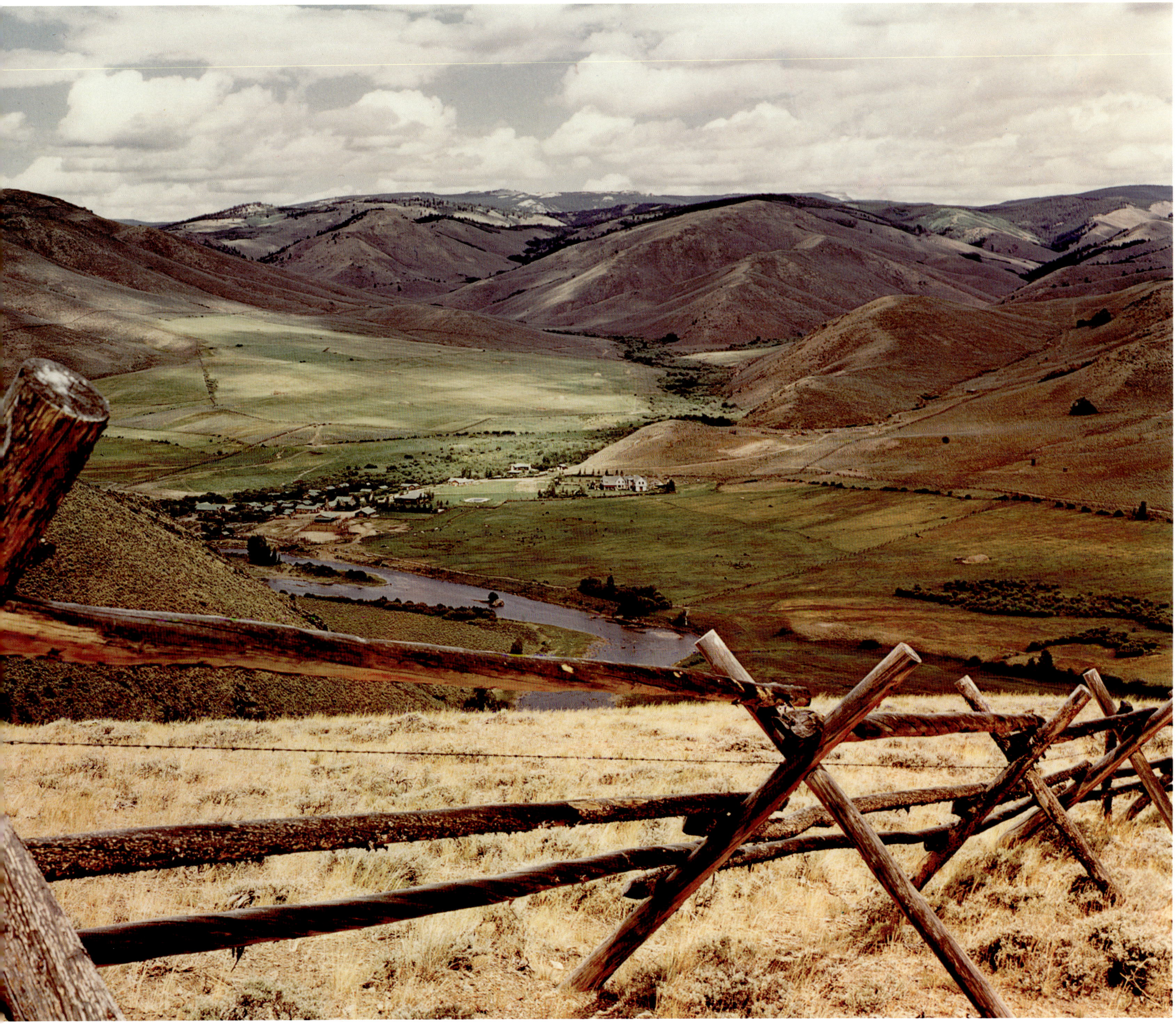

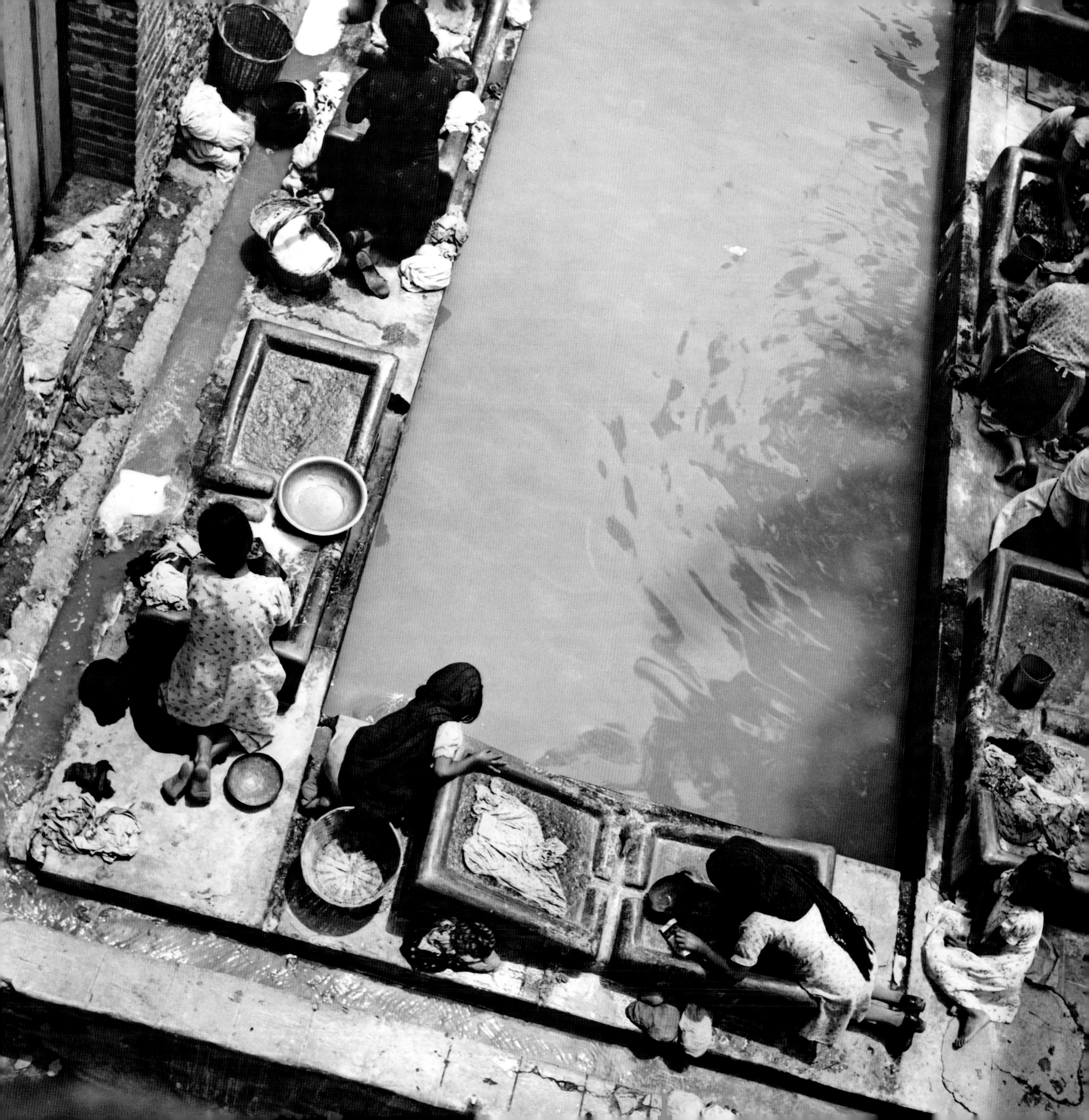

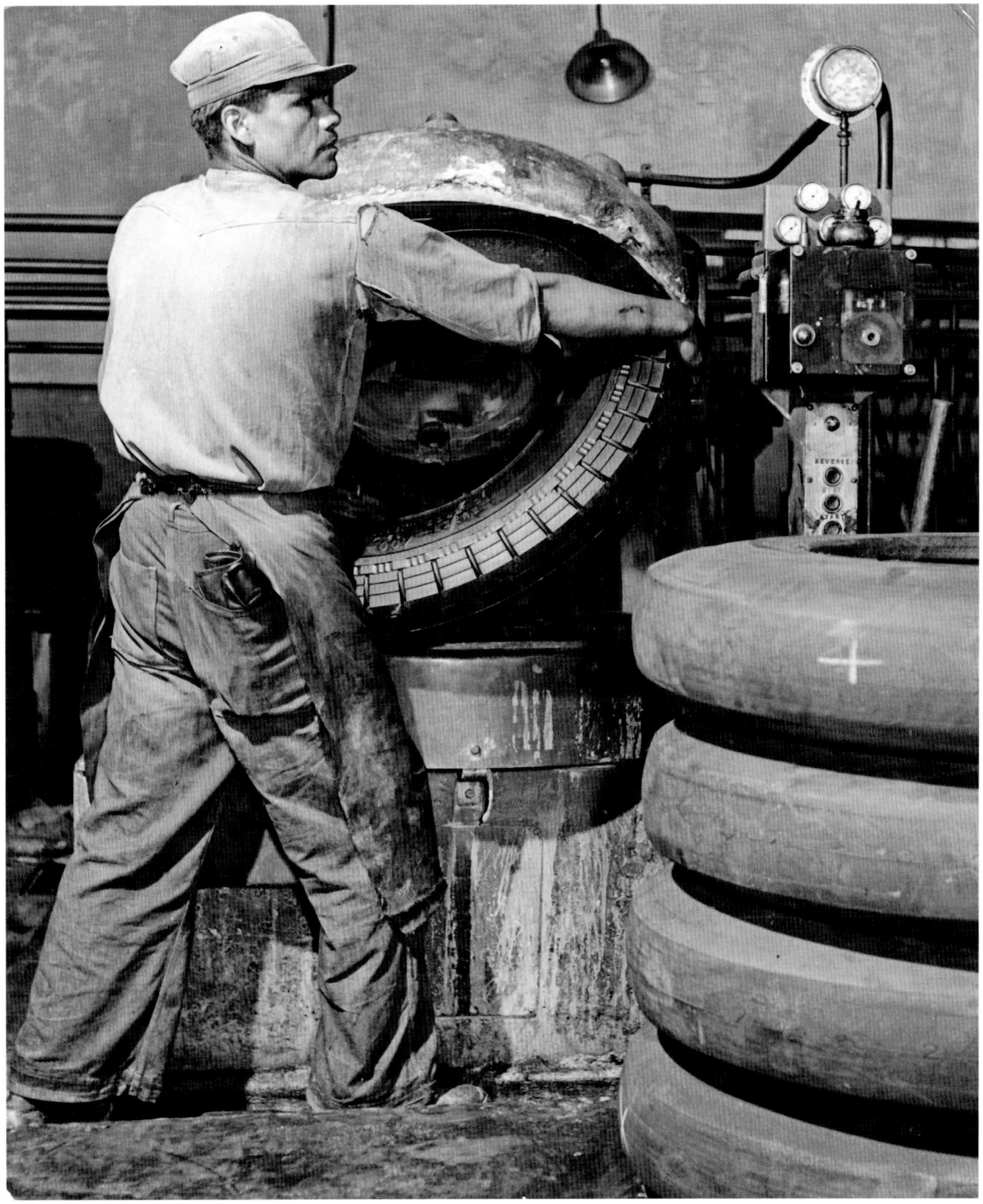

(left) Women Washing, Taxco, Mexico. 1943.
(above) Factory Worker, Mexico. 1943.

Hospital, Mexico. 1943.

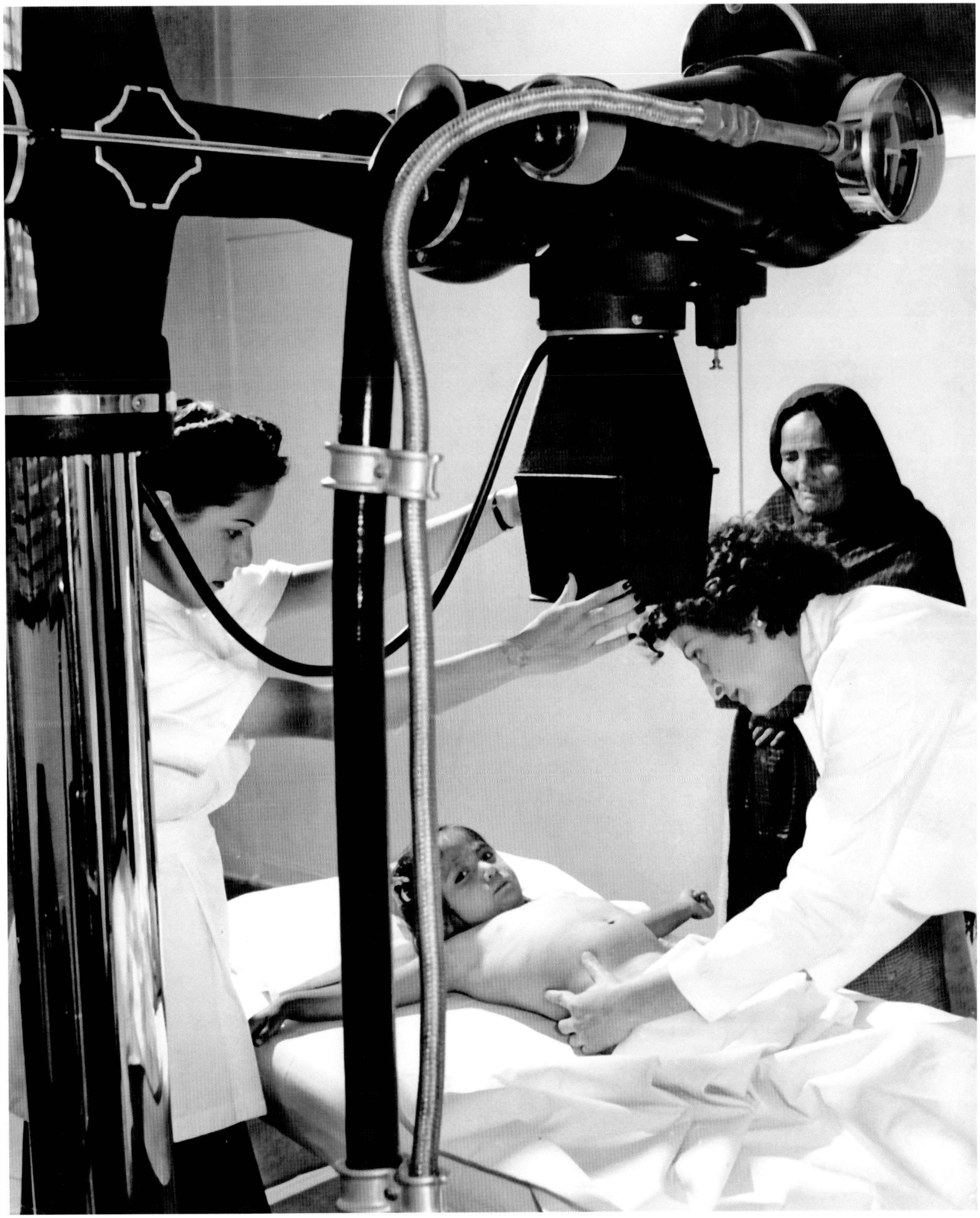

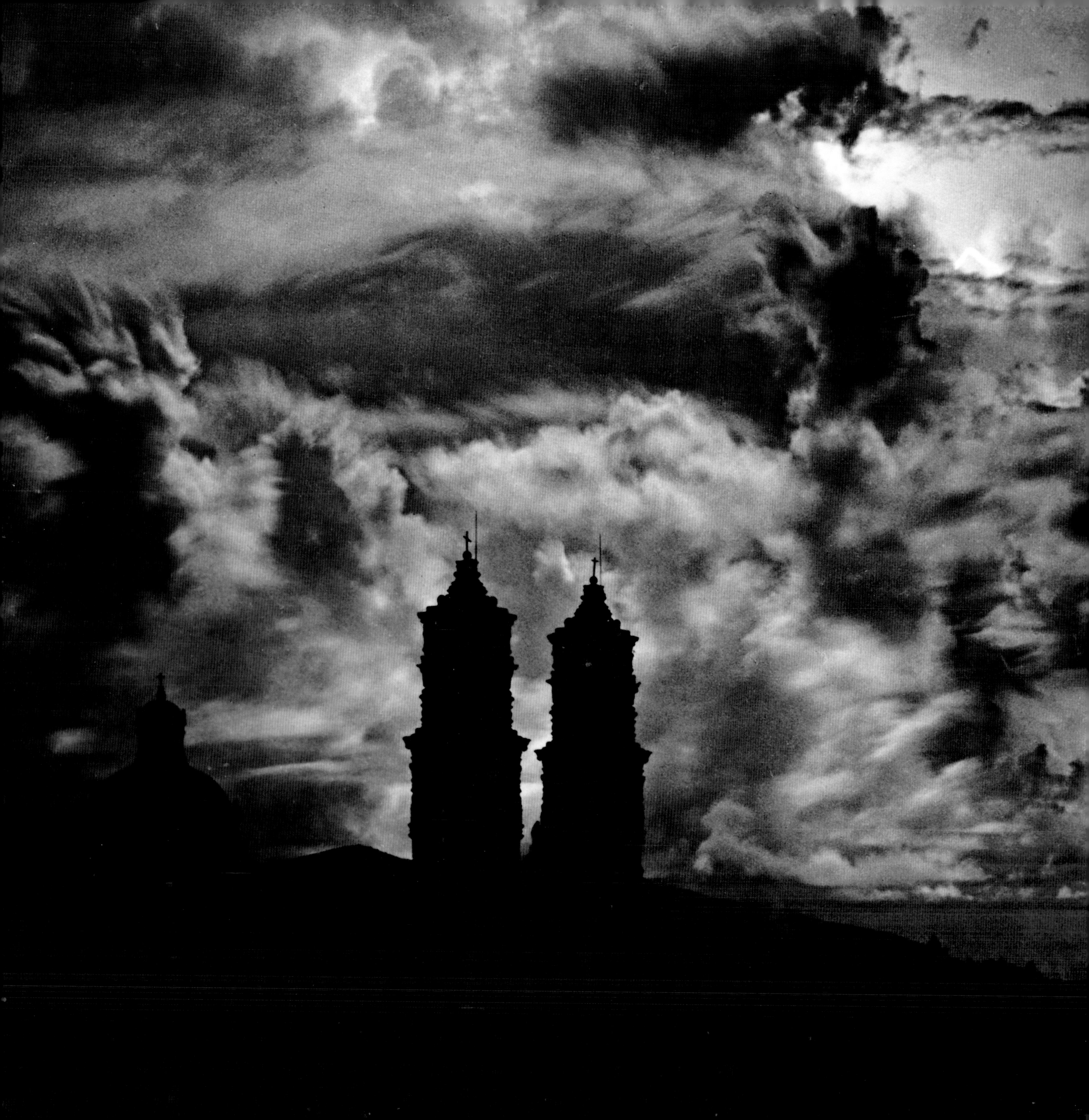

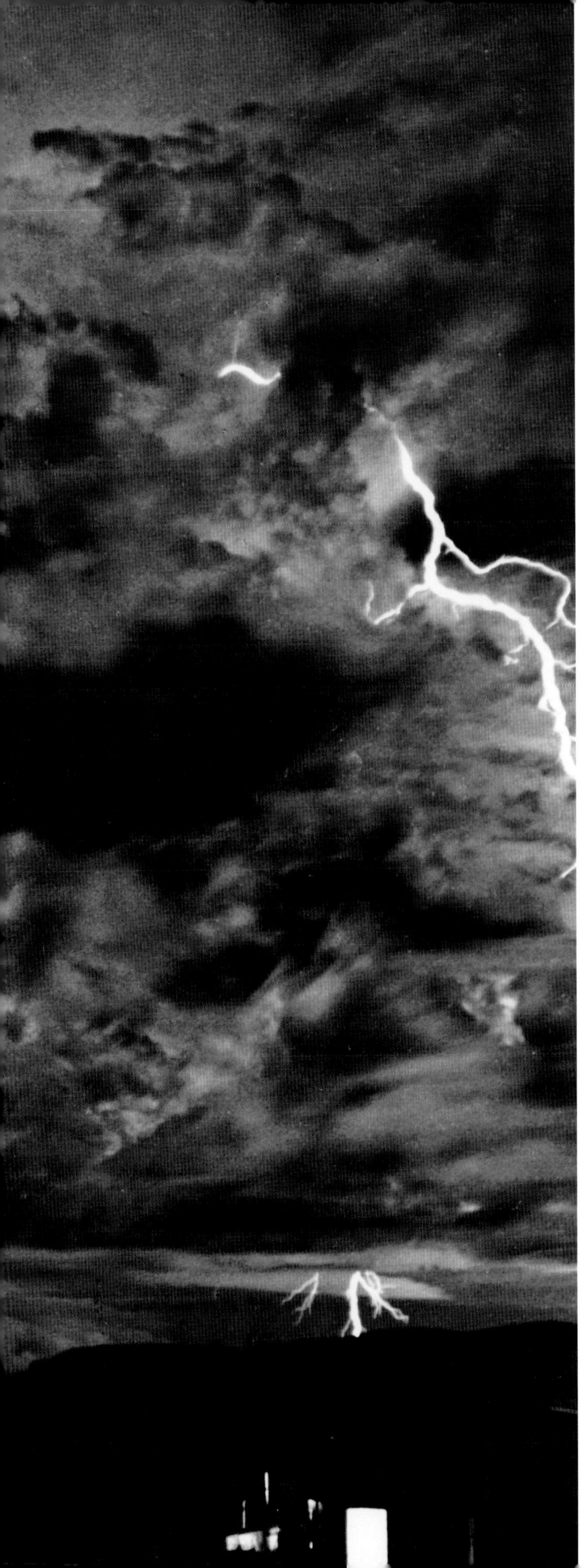

Storm over Taxco, Mexico. 1943.

The Diver, Mexico. 1945.

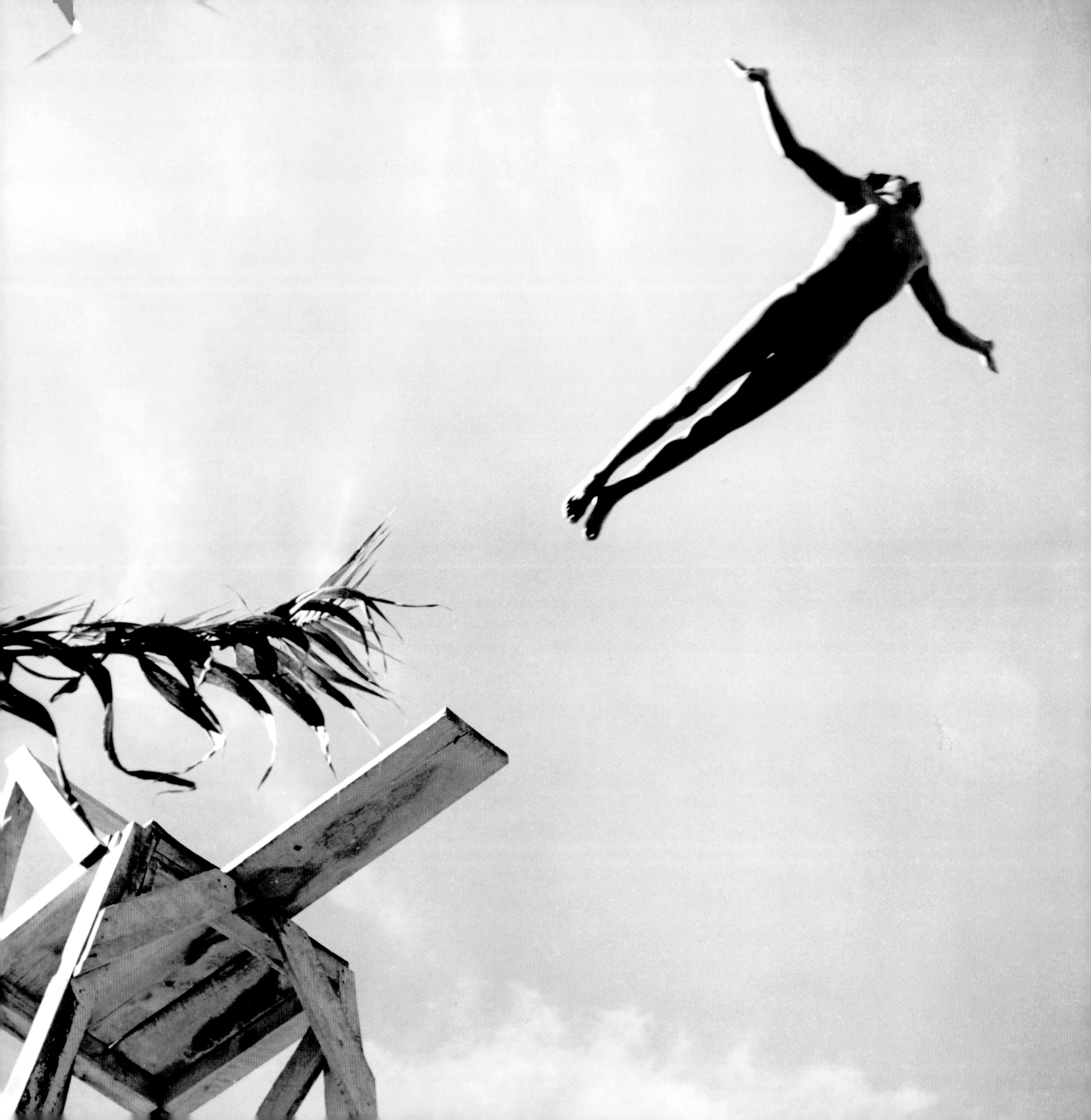

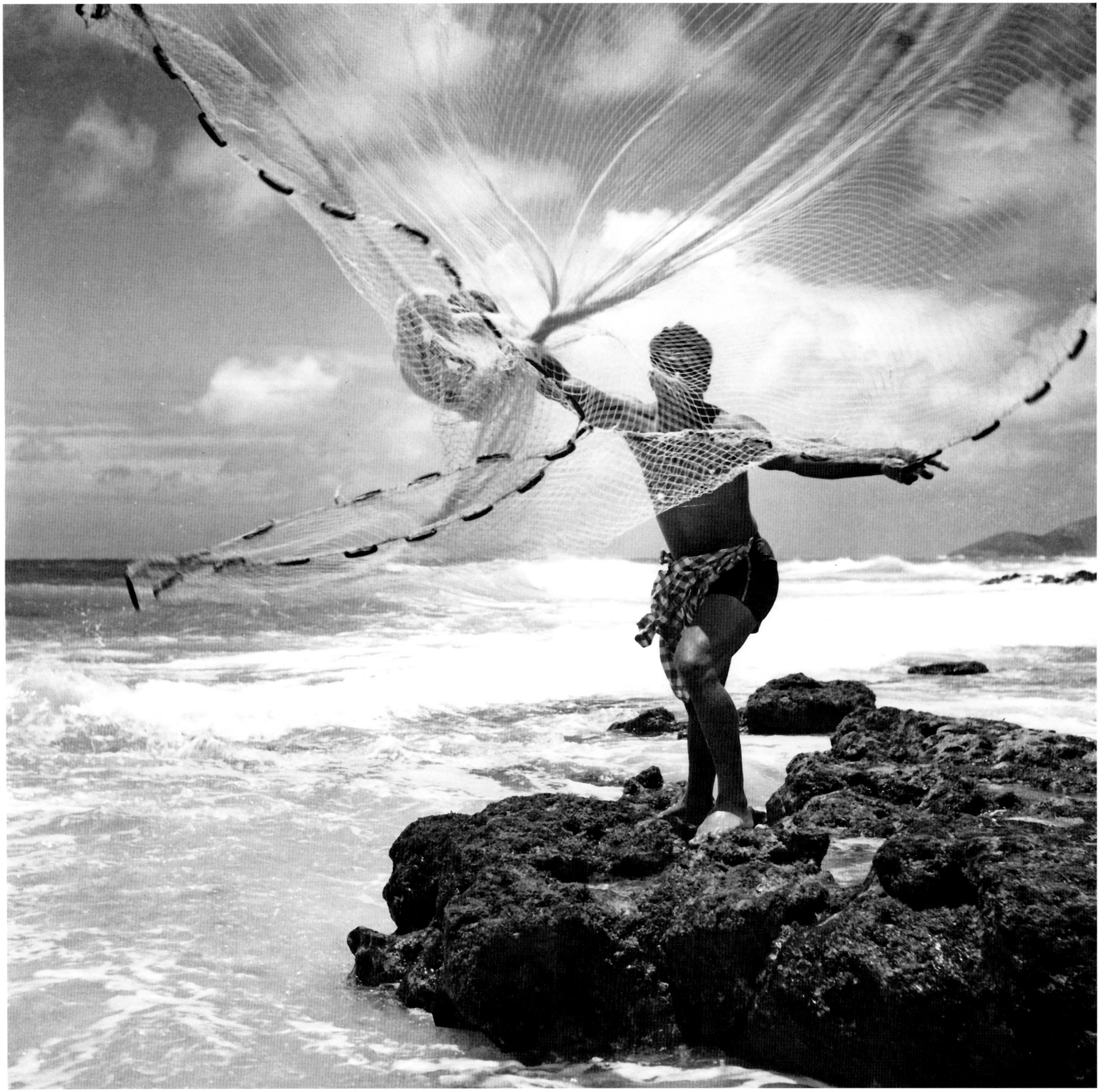

Hawaiian Net Caster, Hawaii. 1947.

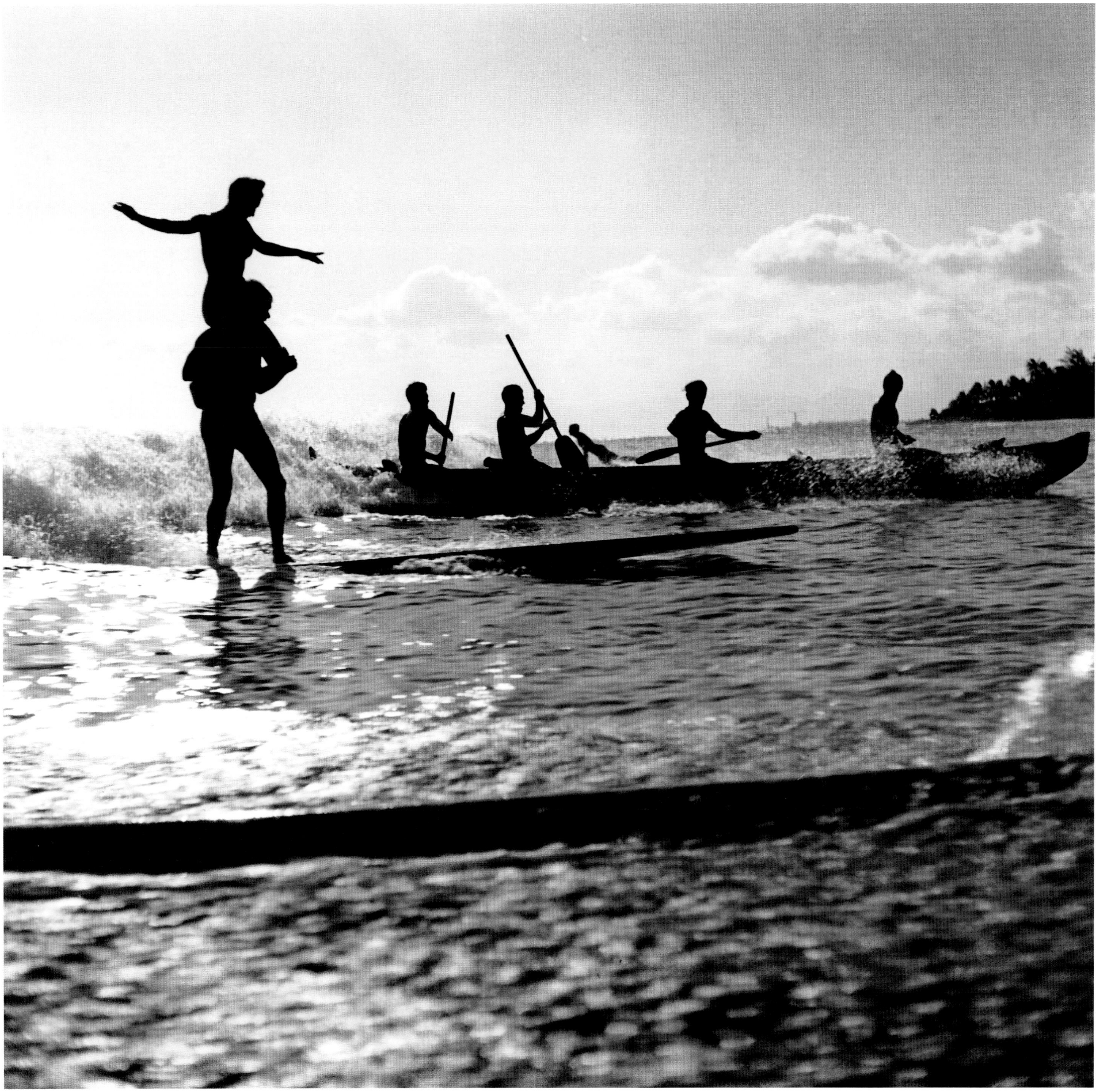

Riding the Waves off Waikiki, Hawaii. 1948.

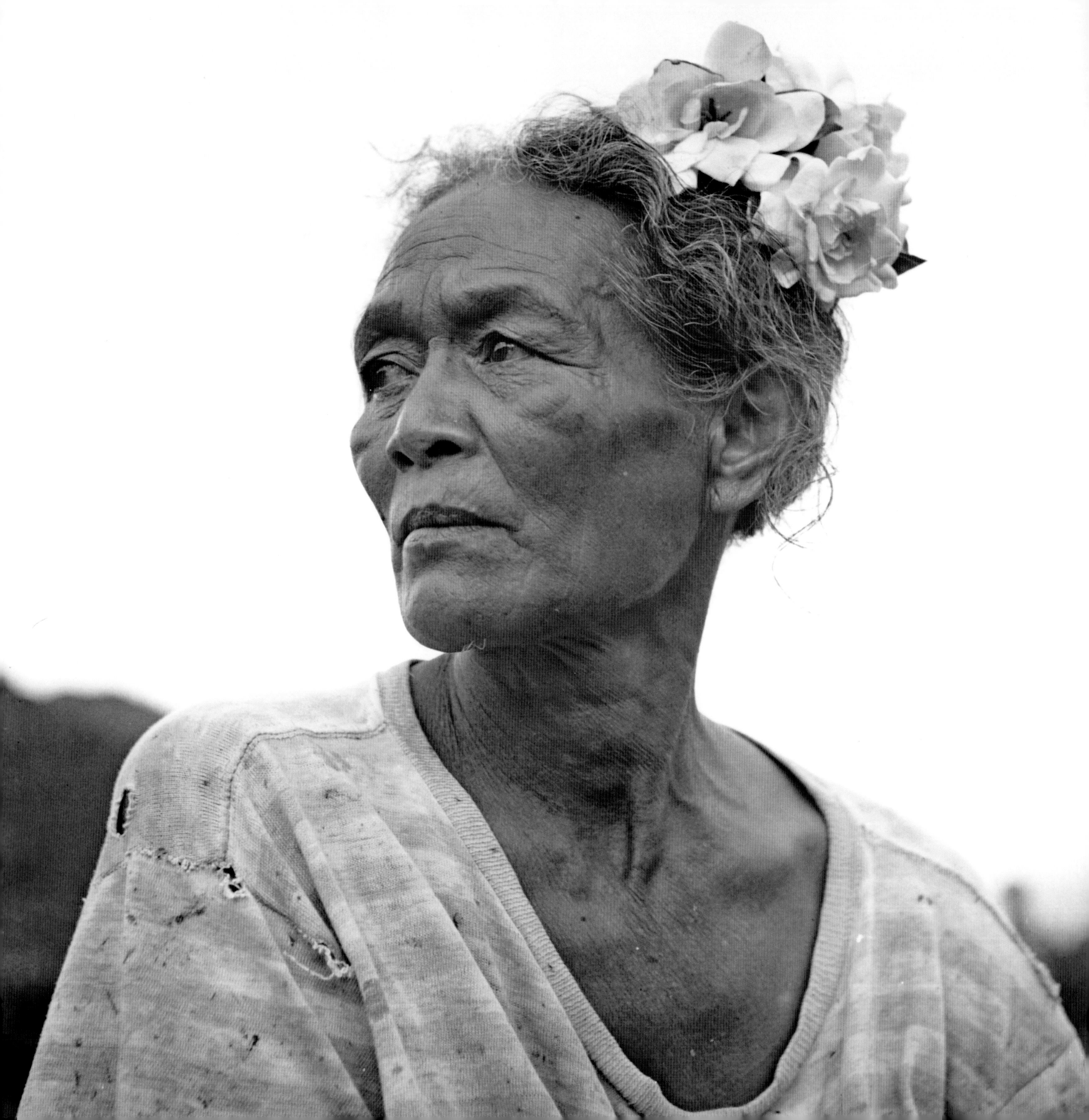

Old Woman from Kauai, Hawaii. 1948.

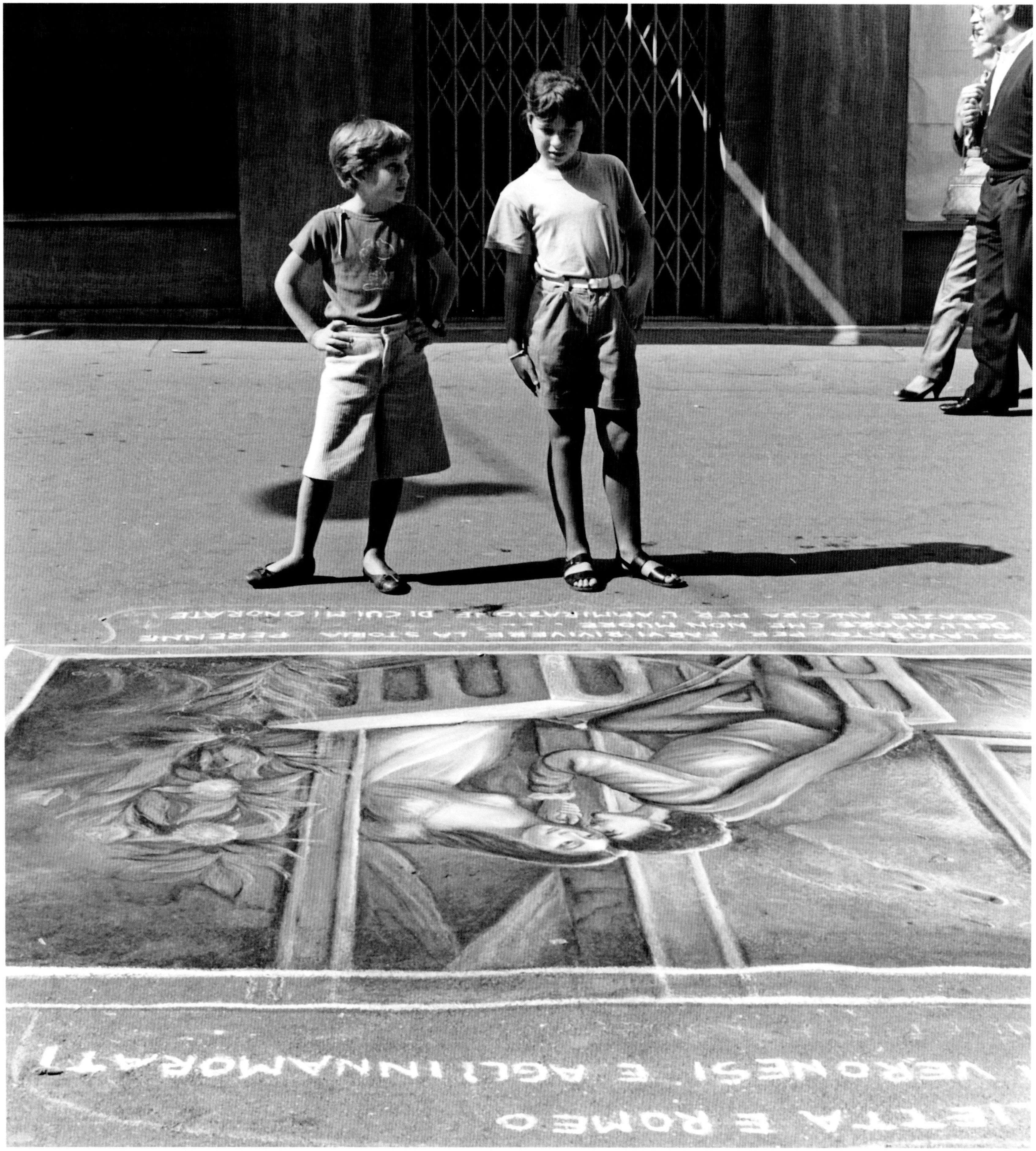
VERONESI E AGLI INNAMORATI
E ROMEO

Romeo and Julietta, Verona, Italy. 1984.

Stonehenge, Great Britain. 1960.

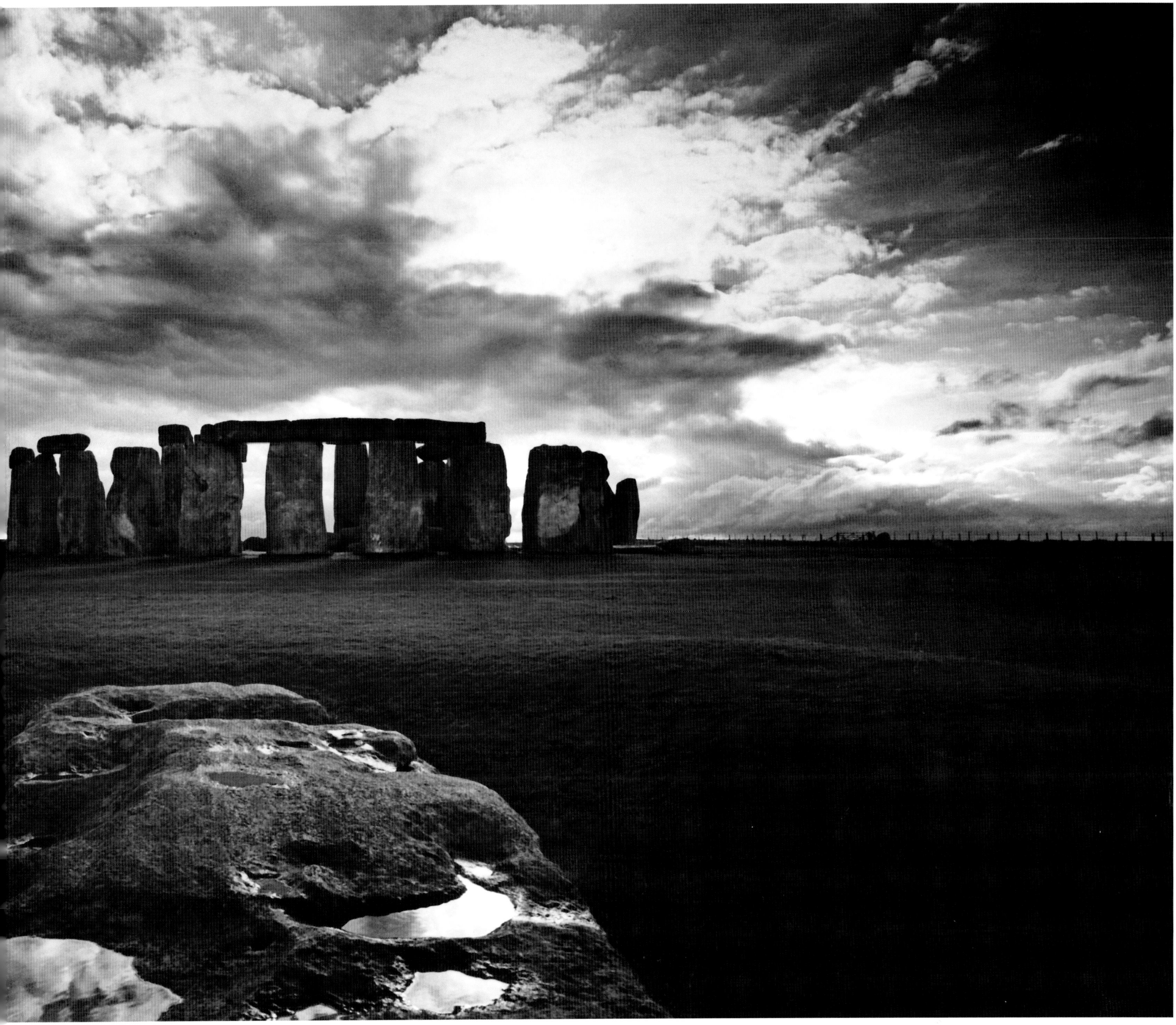

Hamlet's Castle, Elsinor, Reflected
in Its Moat, Denmark. 1961.

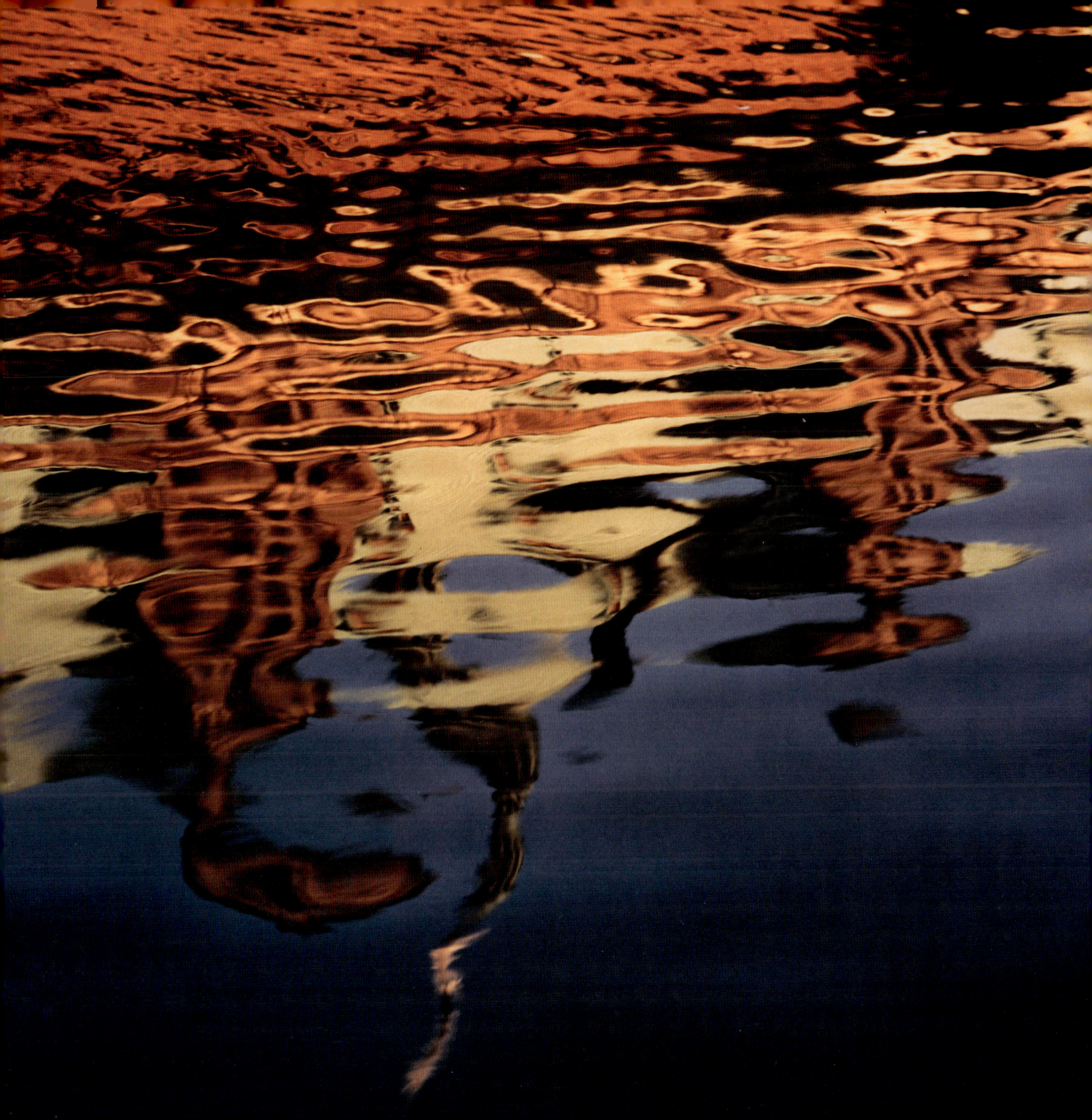

I can never feel certain of any truth, but from a clear perception of its beauty.

JOHN KEATS

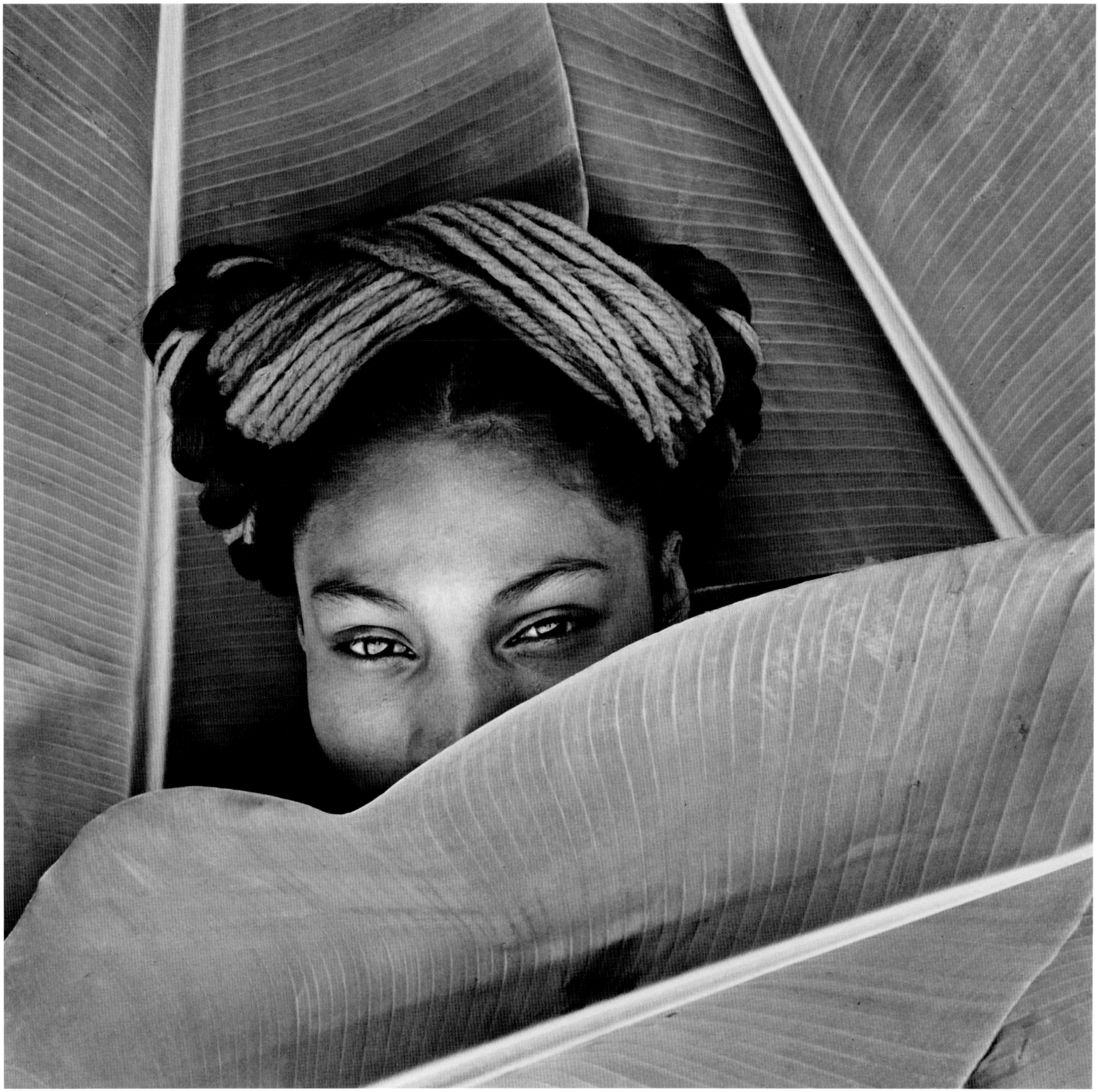

Nieves, Mexico. 1943.

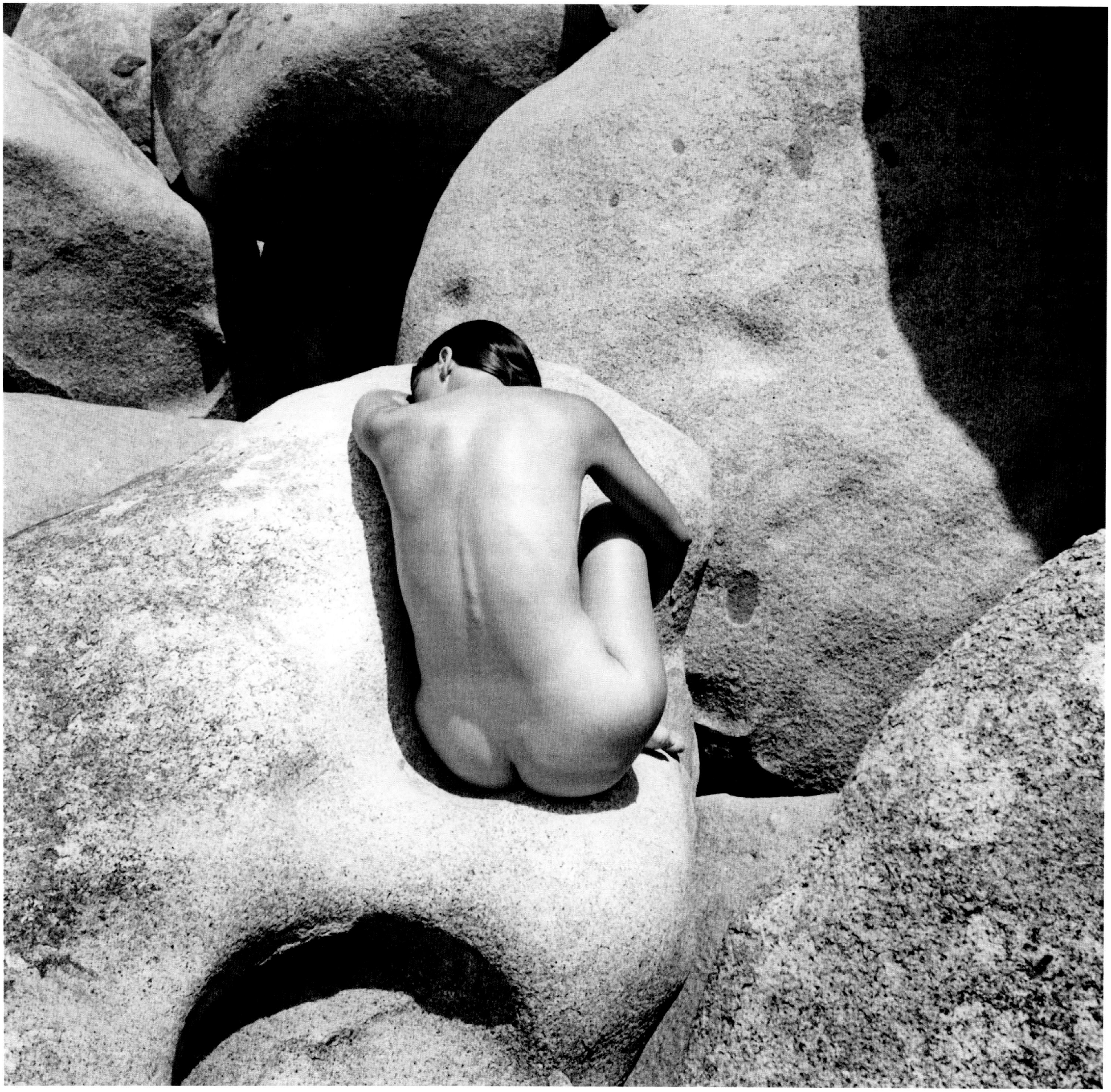

Nude, Virgin Gorda,
Virgin Islands. 1953.

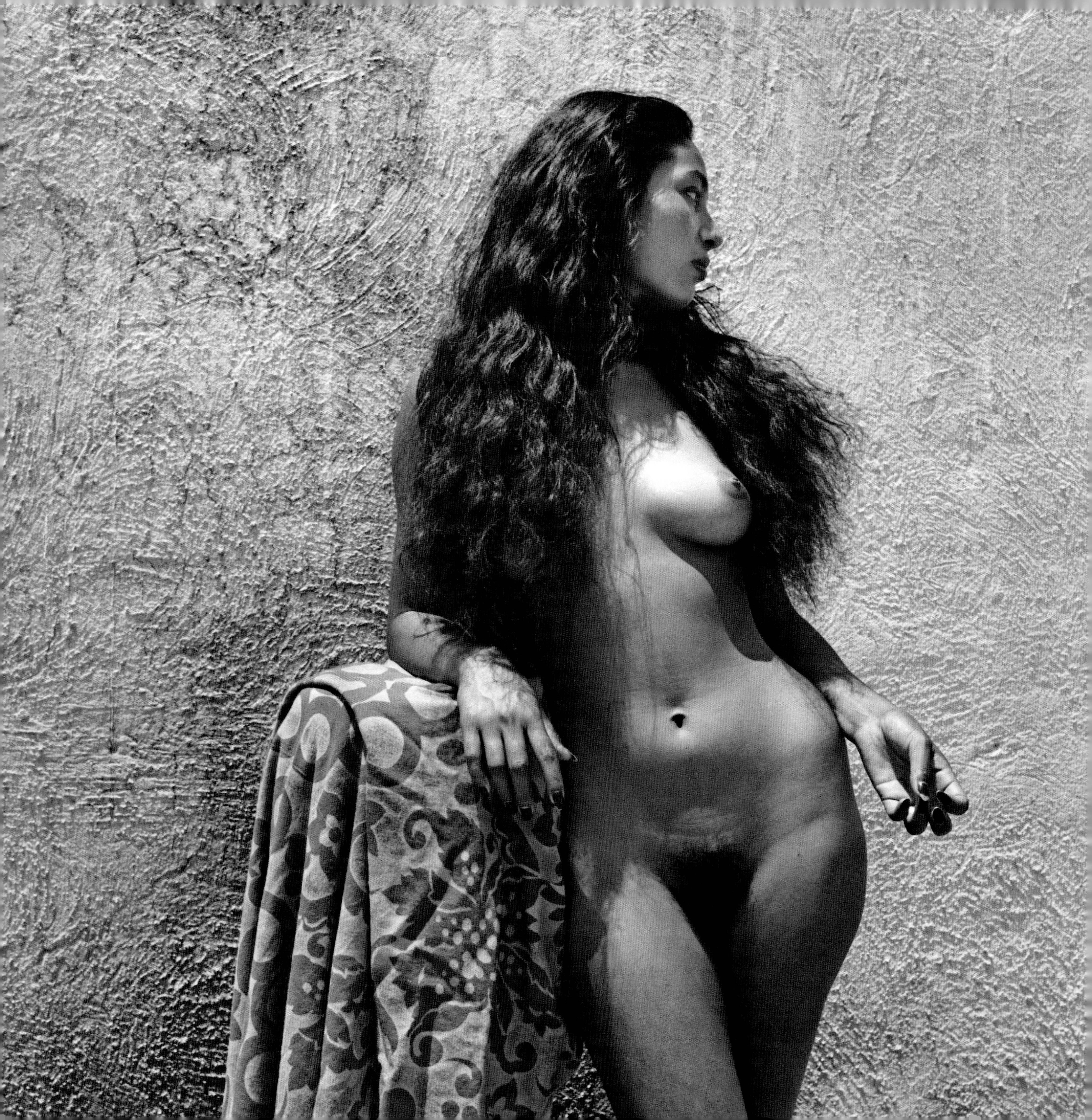

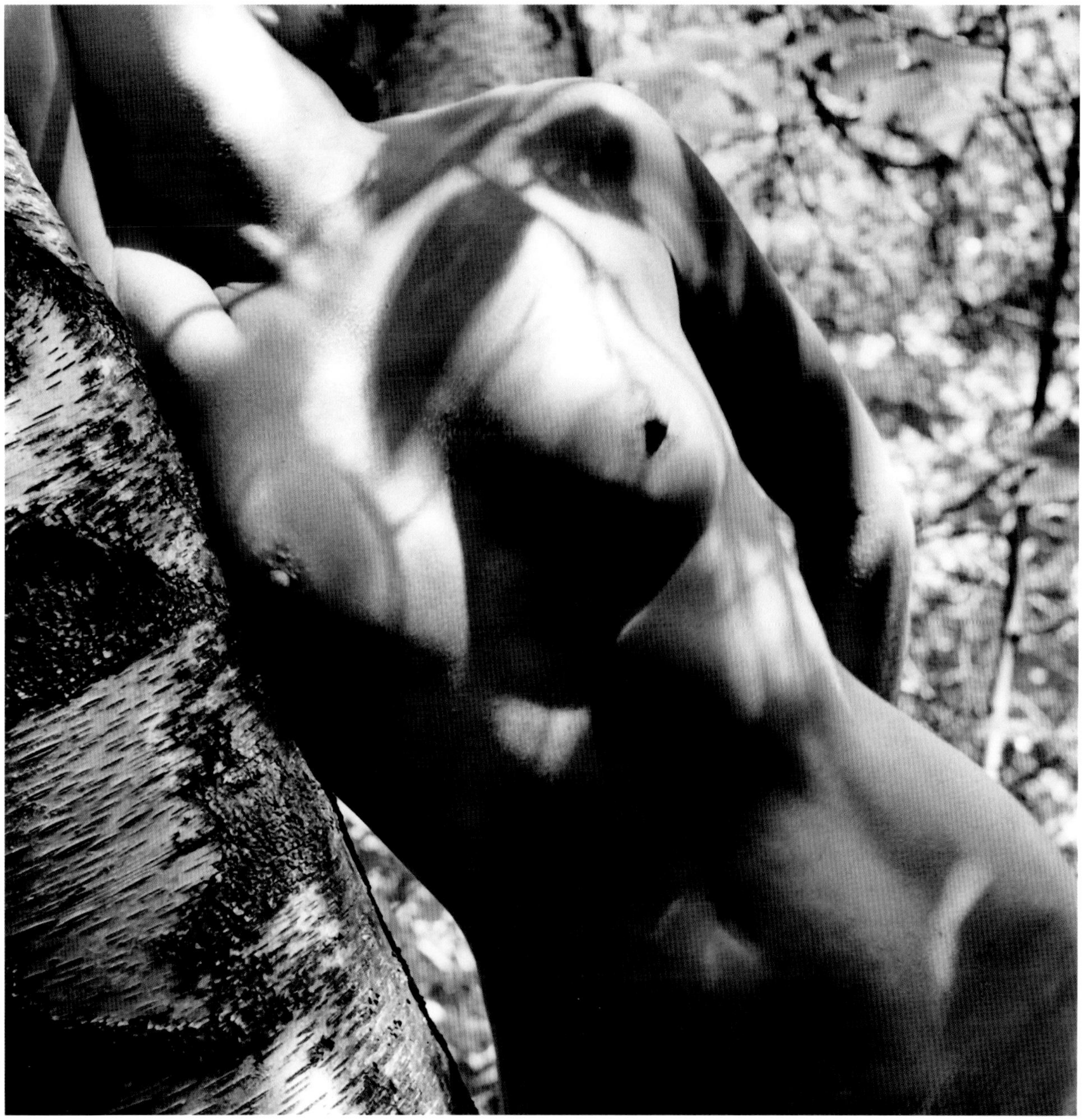

(left) Nieves Nude, Mexico. 1943.
(above) Forest Nude, New York. 1942.

Surf Nude: Maguerite Laughing, Montauk Beach, Long Island, New York. 1953.

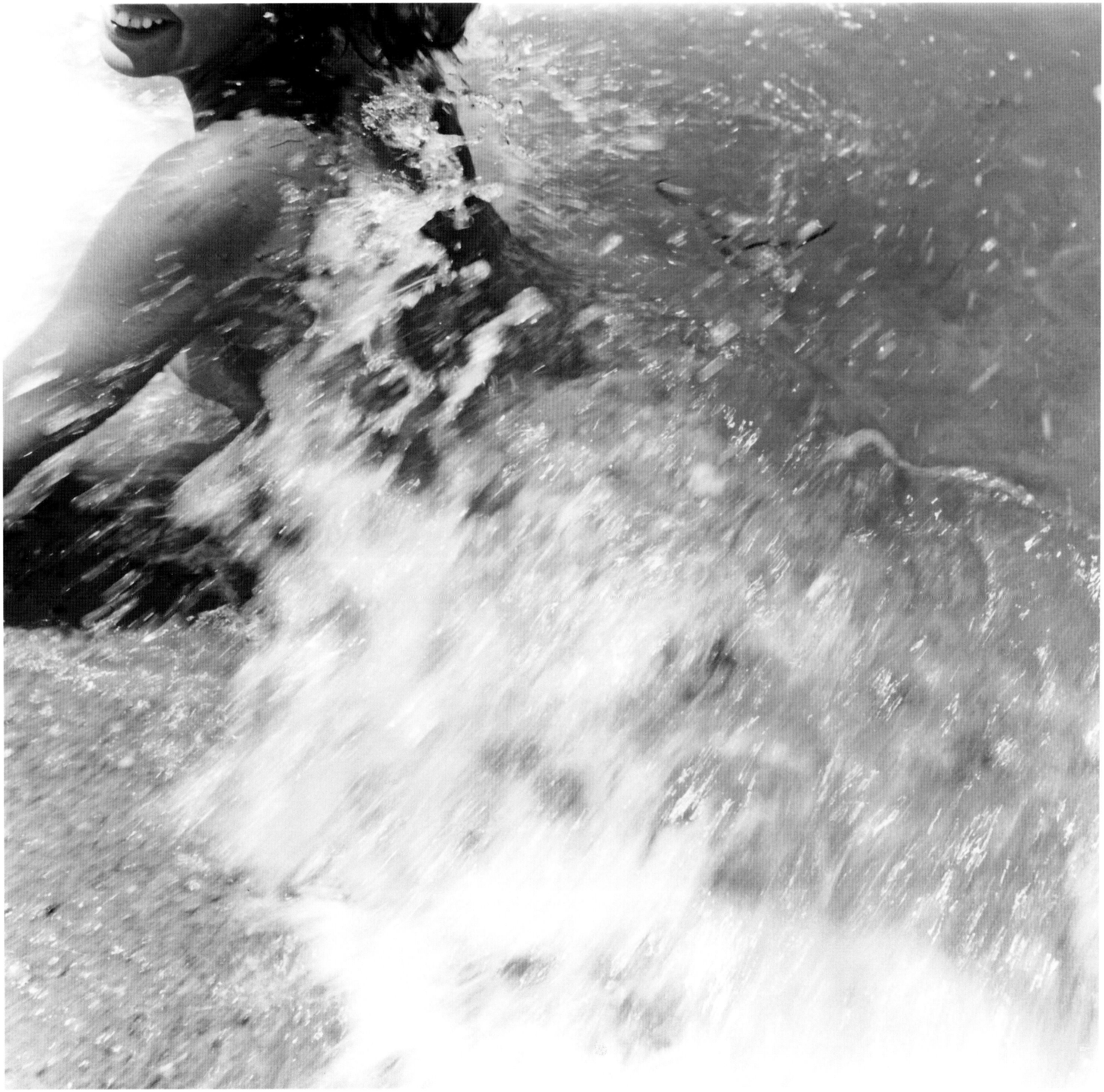

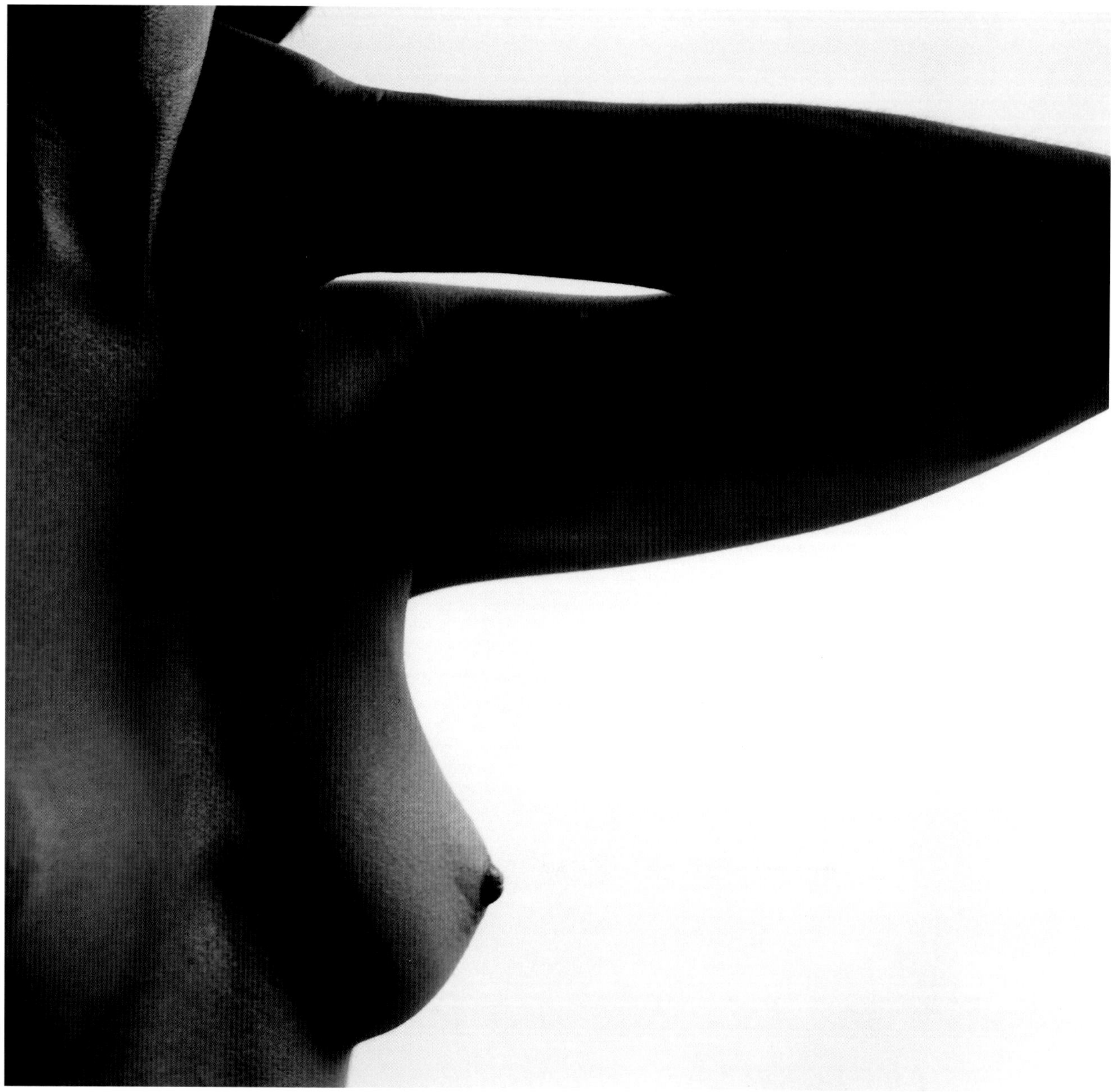

(above) Nude Study: Arm and Breast, New York City. 1953.
(right) Beach Nude: Marguerite with Driftwood, Montauk Beach, Long Island, New York. 1954.

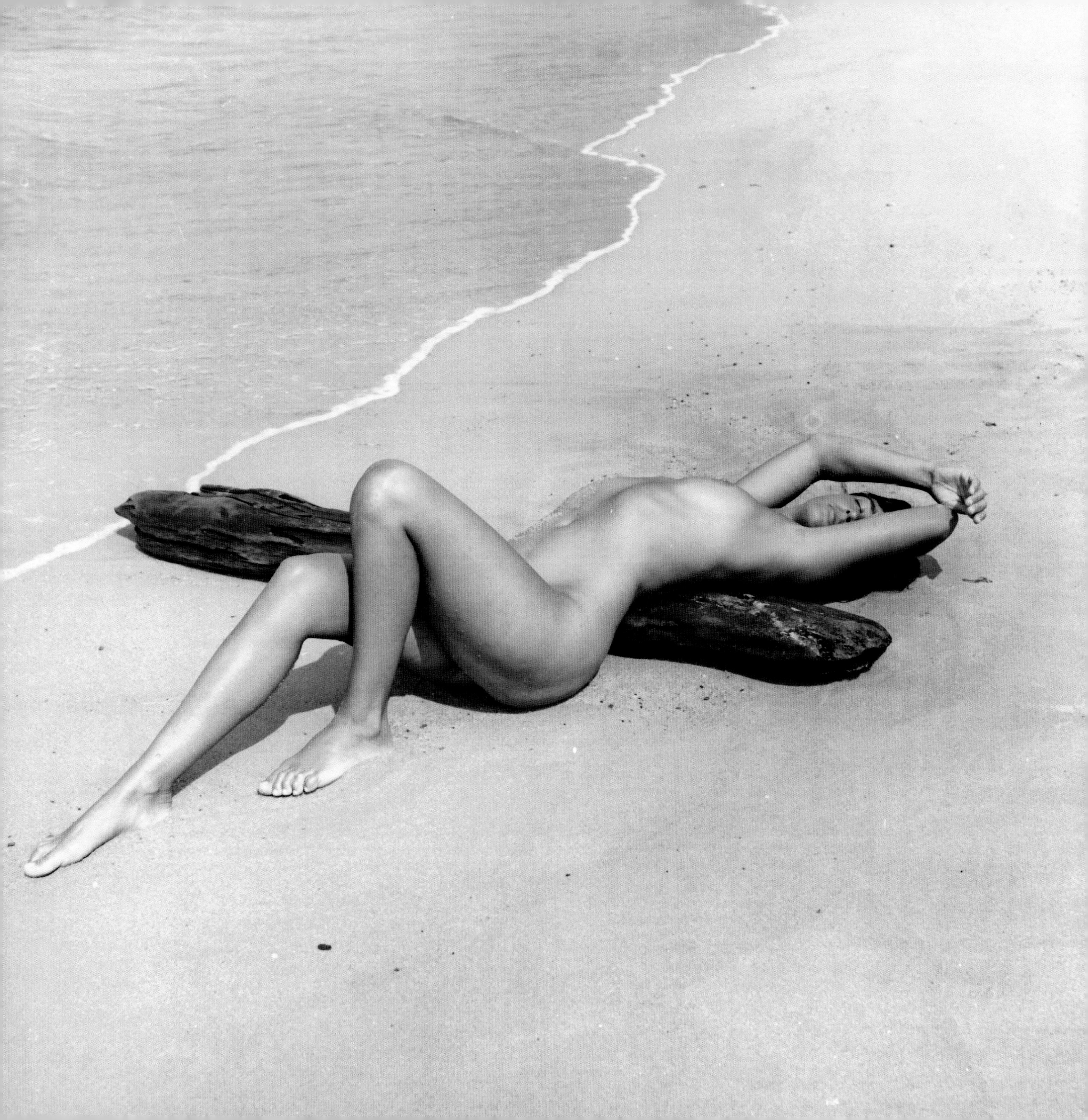

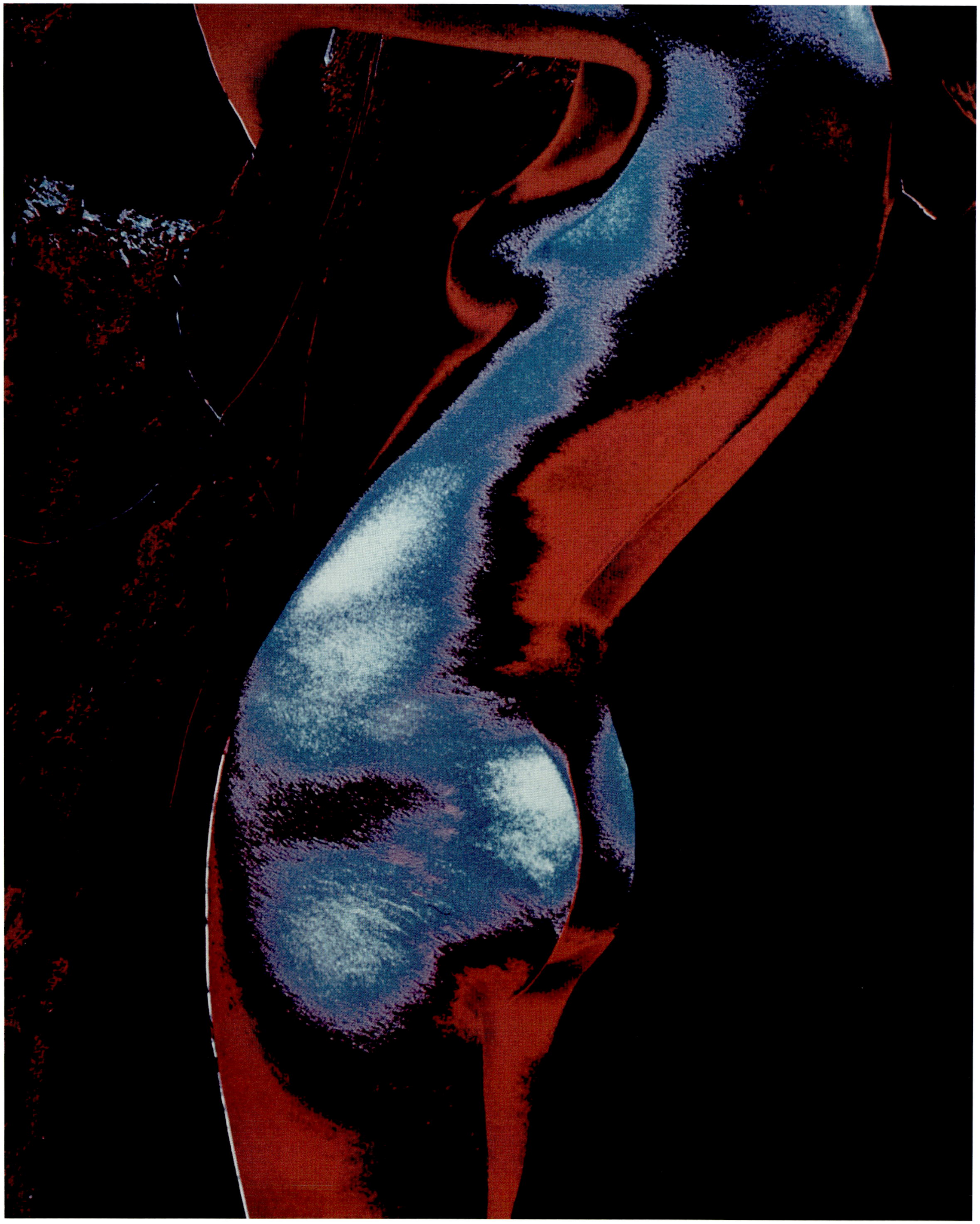

Many-Colored Torso,
St. Croix, Virgin Islands. 1982.

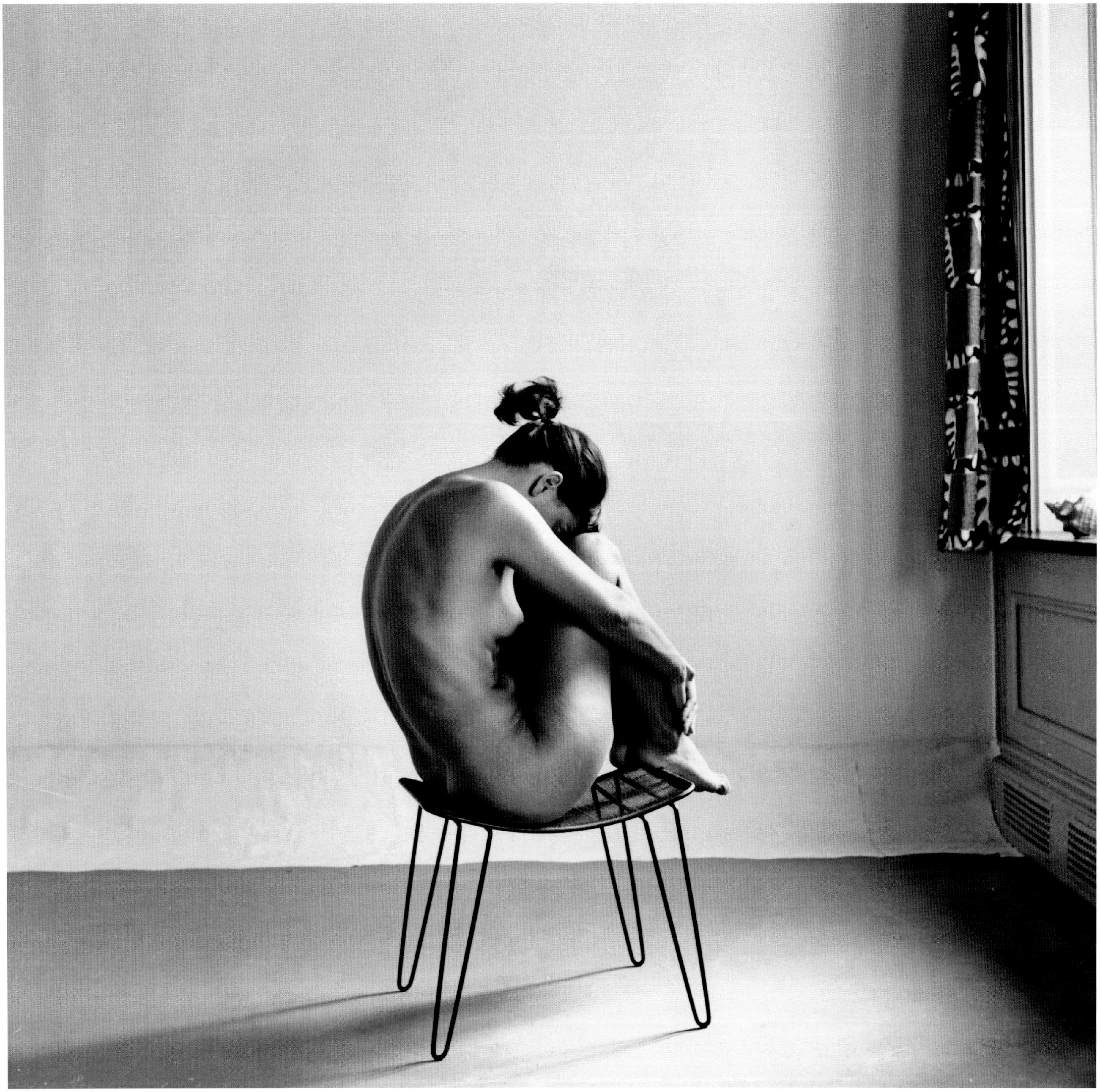

Nude in Wire Chair, New York City. 1954.

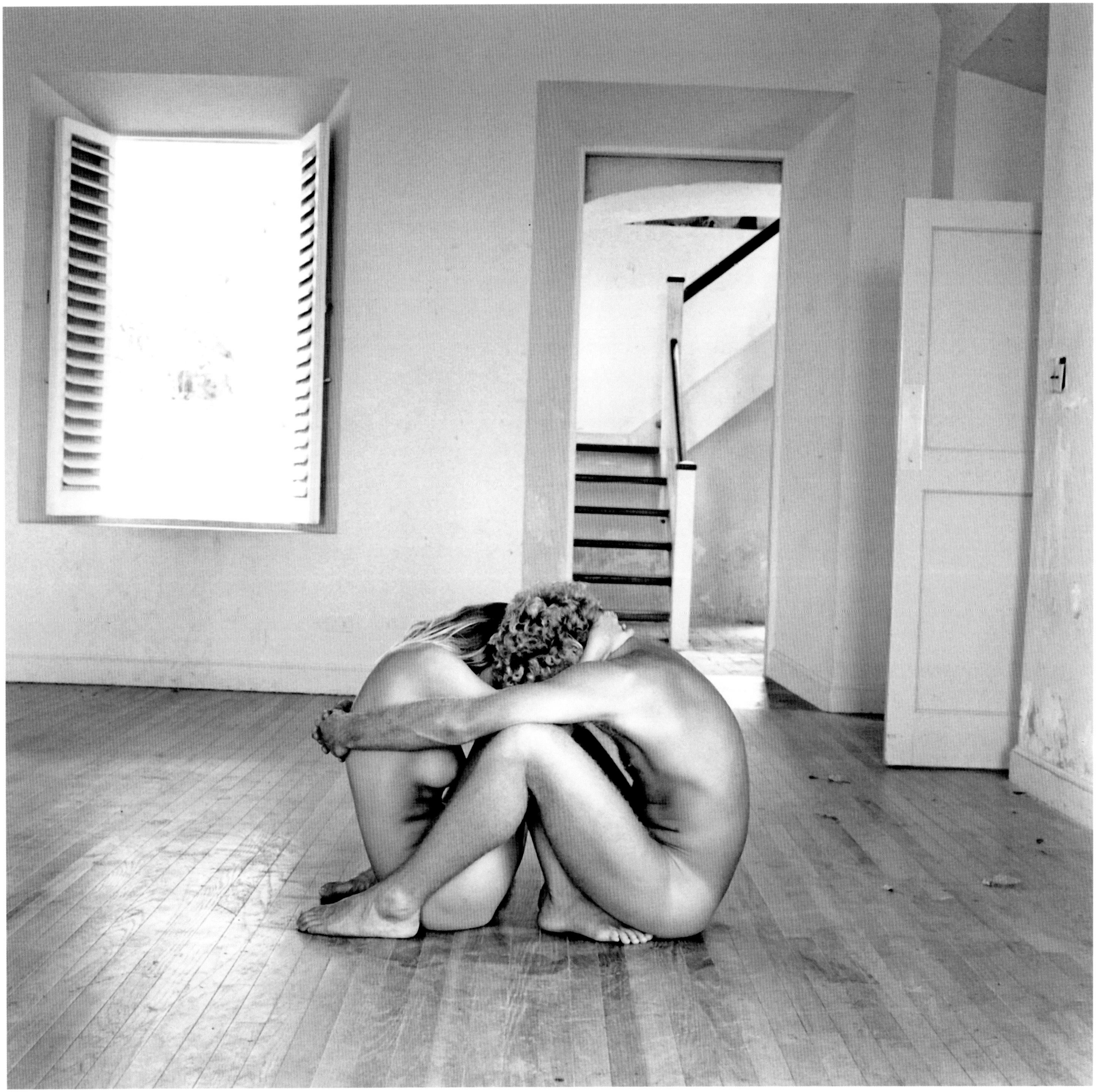

The Story of Life: The Couple, St. Croix, Virgin Islands. ca. 1976.

The Story of Life: Underwater Nude,
St. Croix, Virgin Islands. ca. 1975.

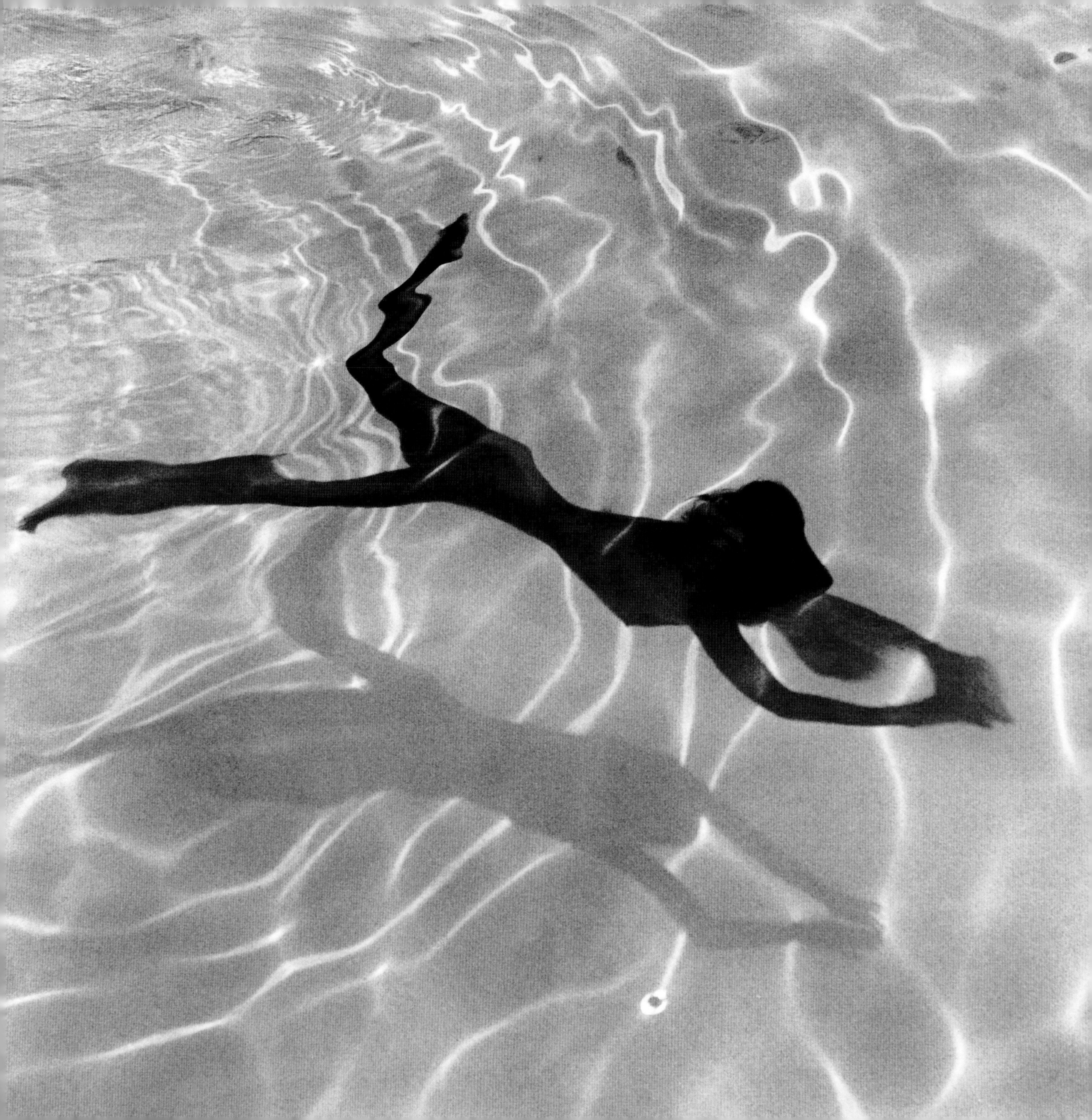

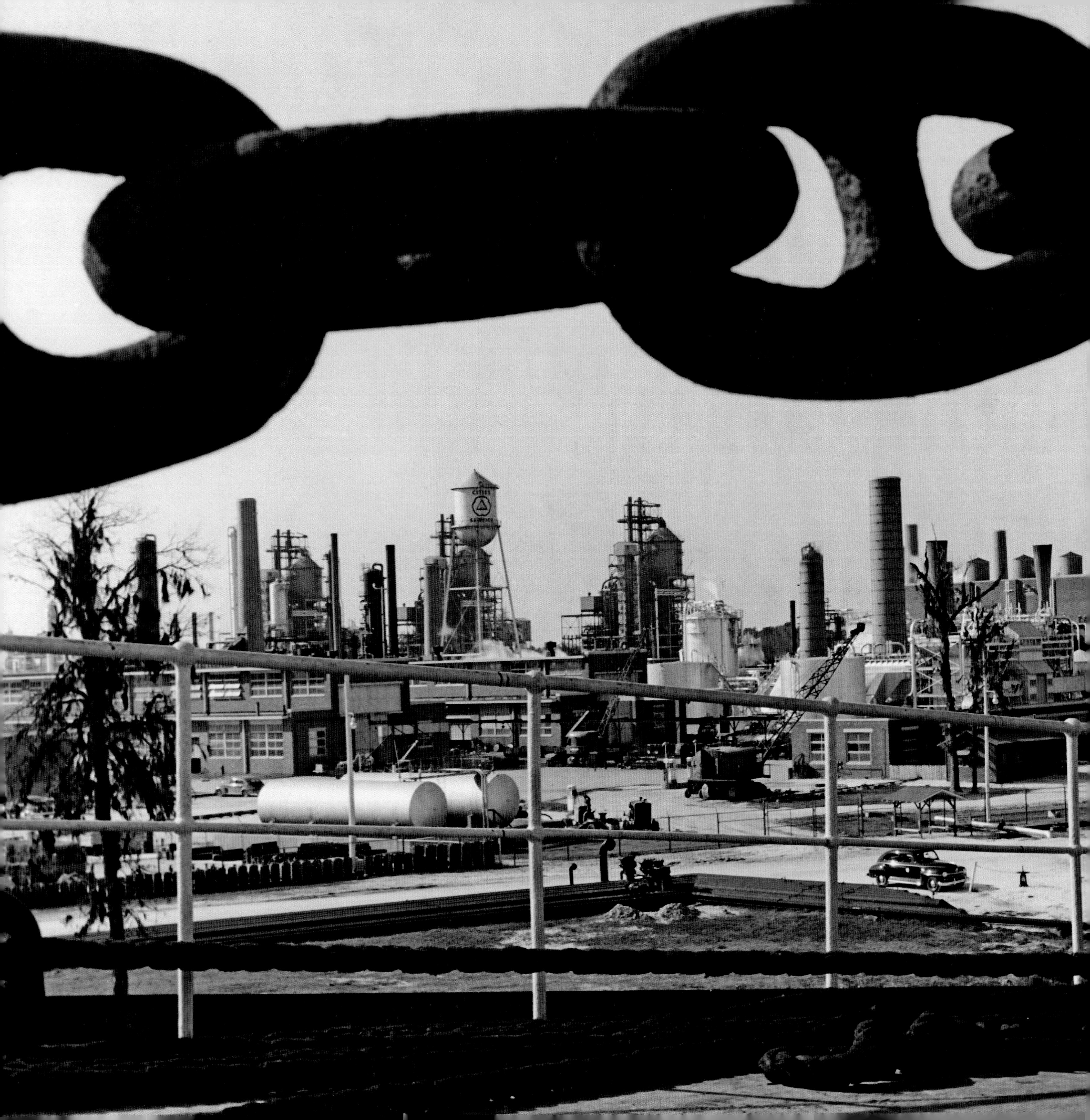
CITIES

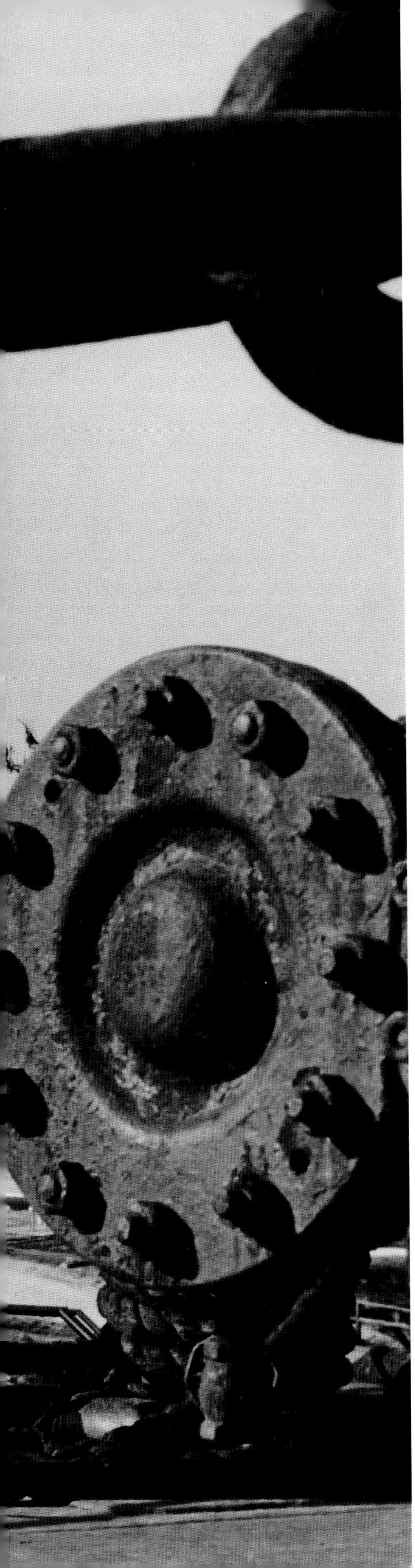

Tanker Chain and Oil Refinery,
Lake Charles, Louisiana. ca. 1952.

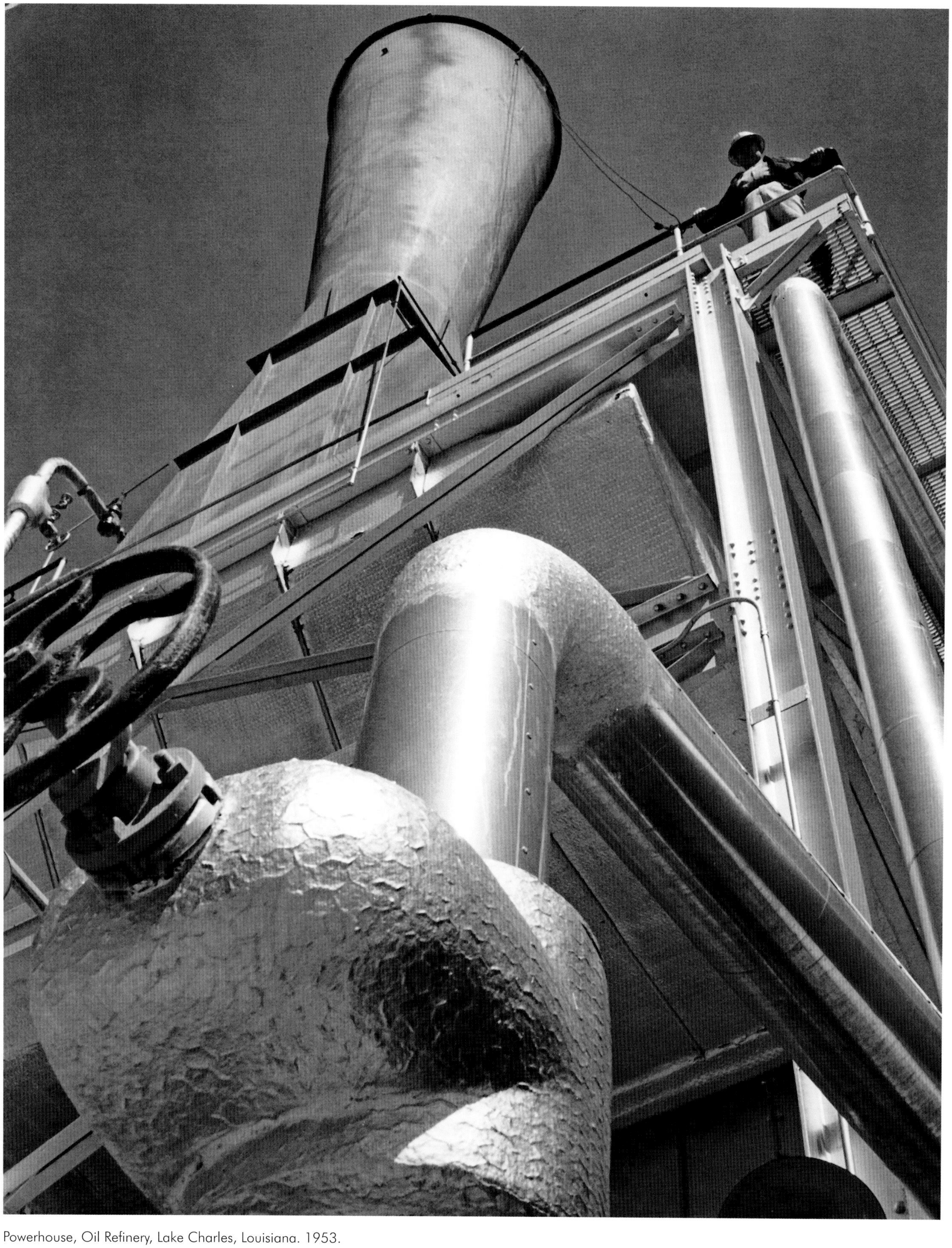

Powerhouse, Oil Refinery, Lake Charles, Louisiana. 1953.

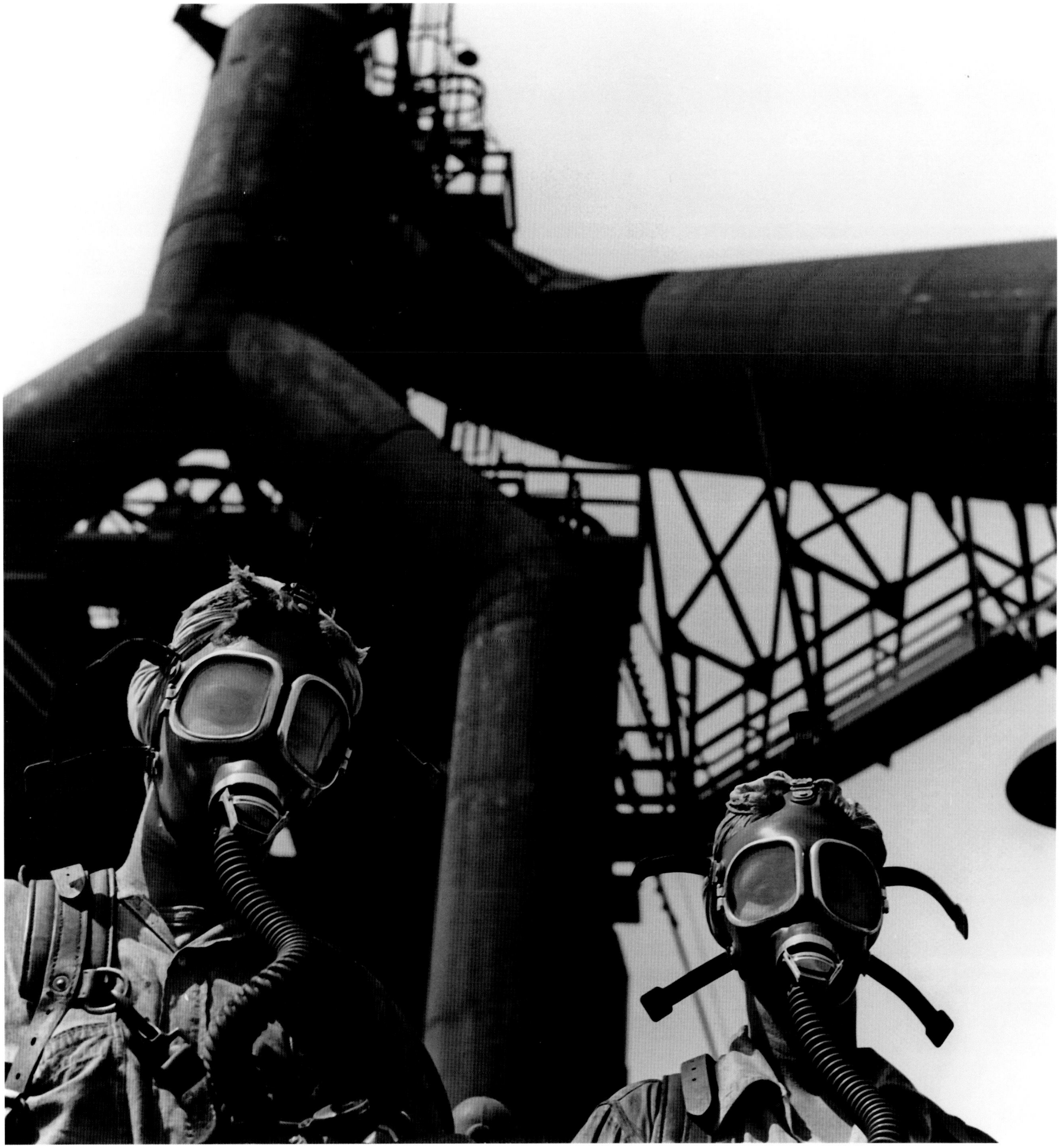

Top Women, Blast Furnace, U.S. Steel Plant, Gary, Indiana. ca. 1950.

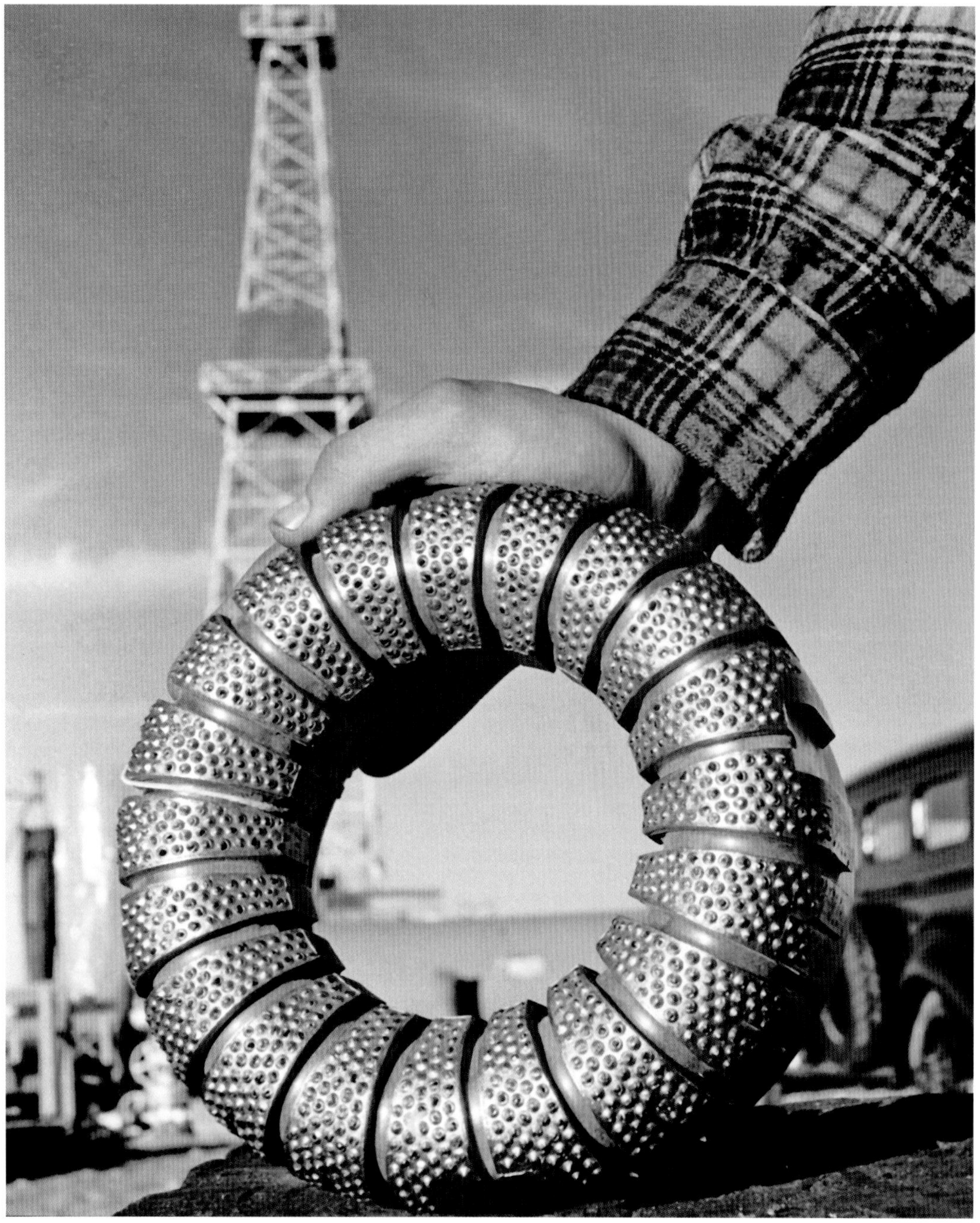

(above) Diamond Drill Bit for Cutting Cores, Cities Service Oil Field, Texas. ca. 1952.
(right) Oil Exploration: Seismographic Explosion in the Gulf of Mexico. 1954.

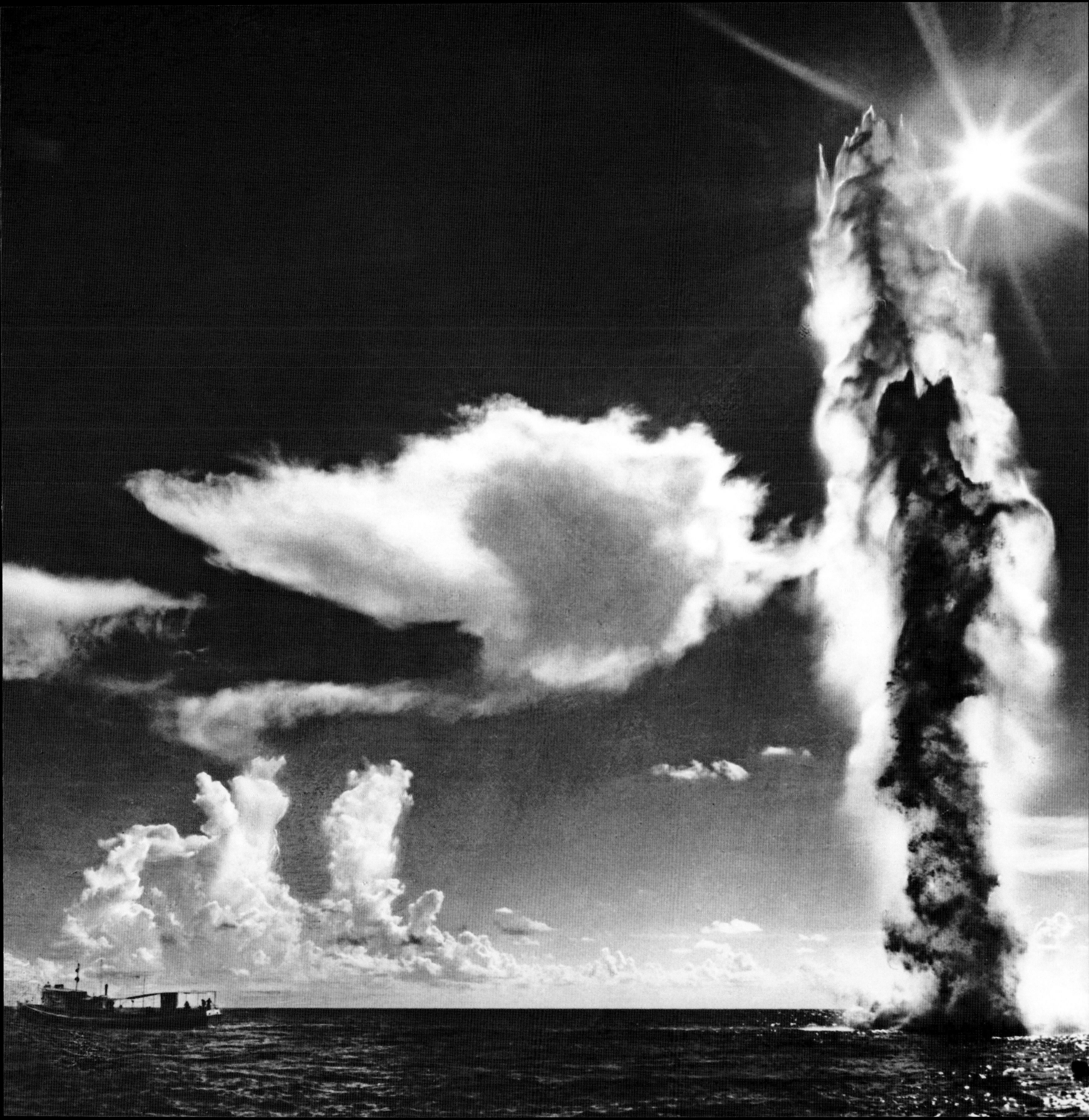

Cities Service Oil Refinery at Night,
Lake Charles, Louisiana. ca. 1953.

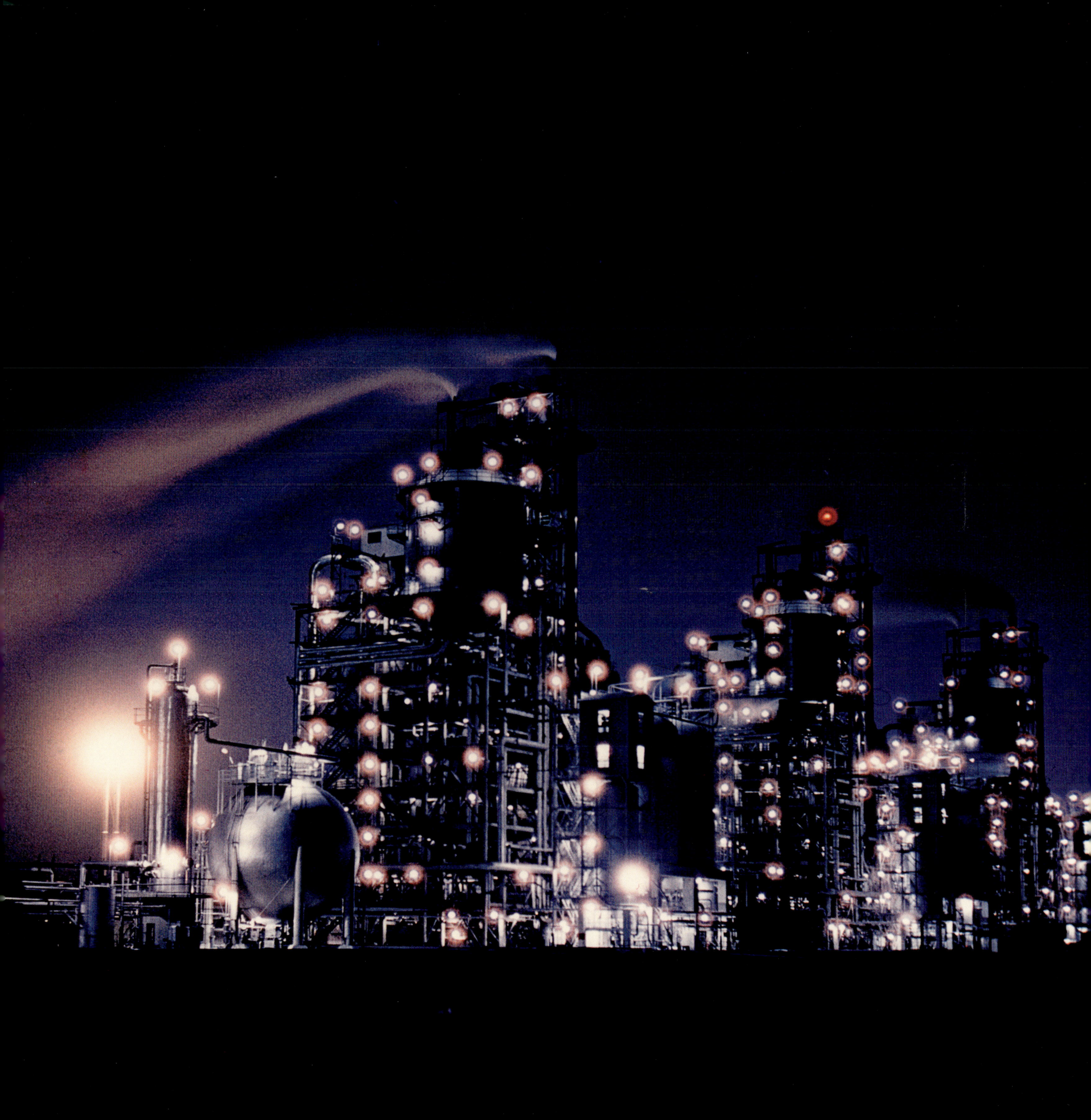

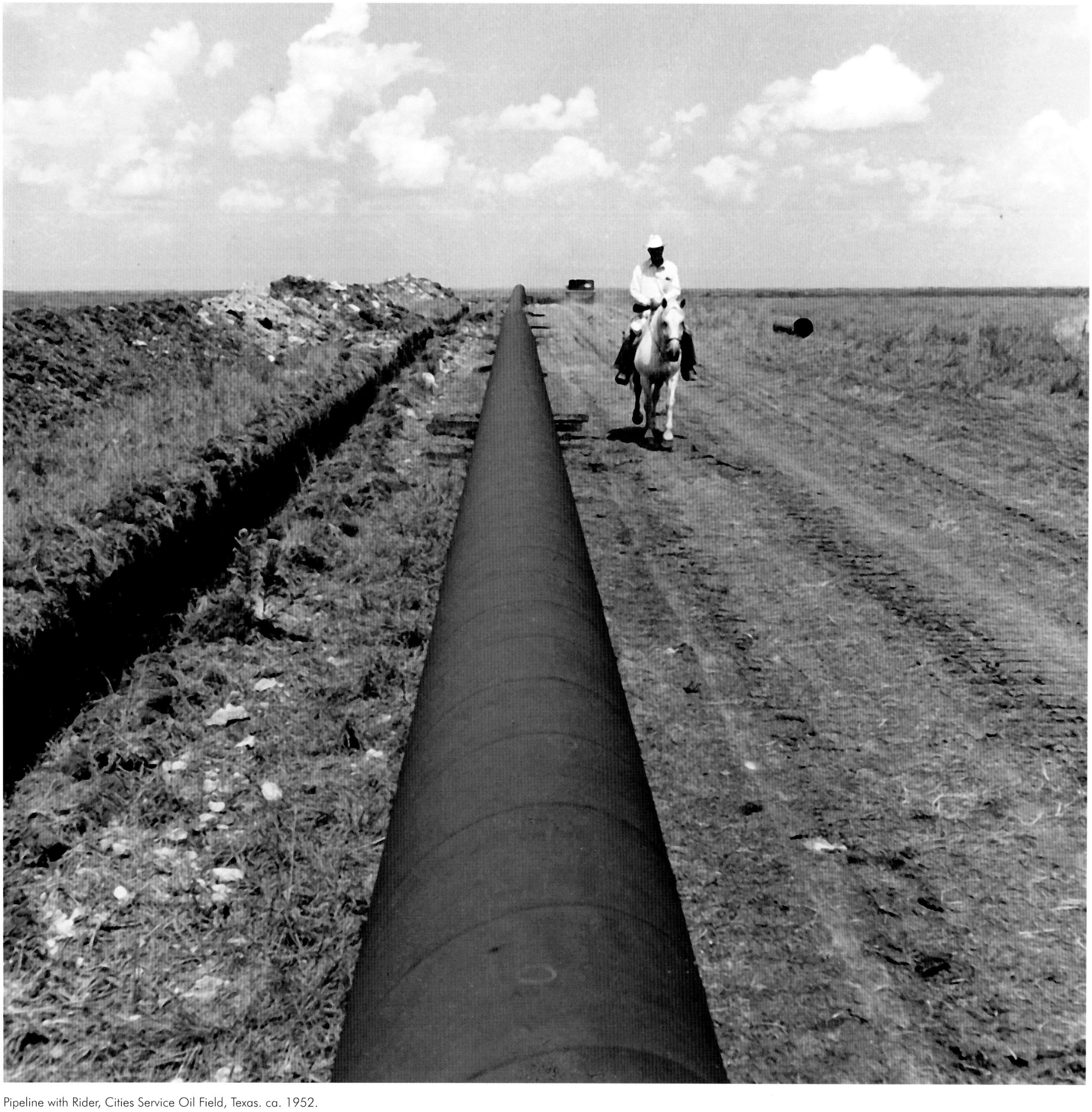

Pipeline with Rider, Cities Service Oil Field, Texas. ca. 1952.

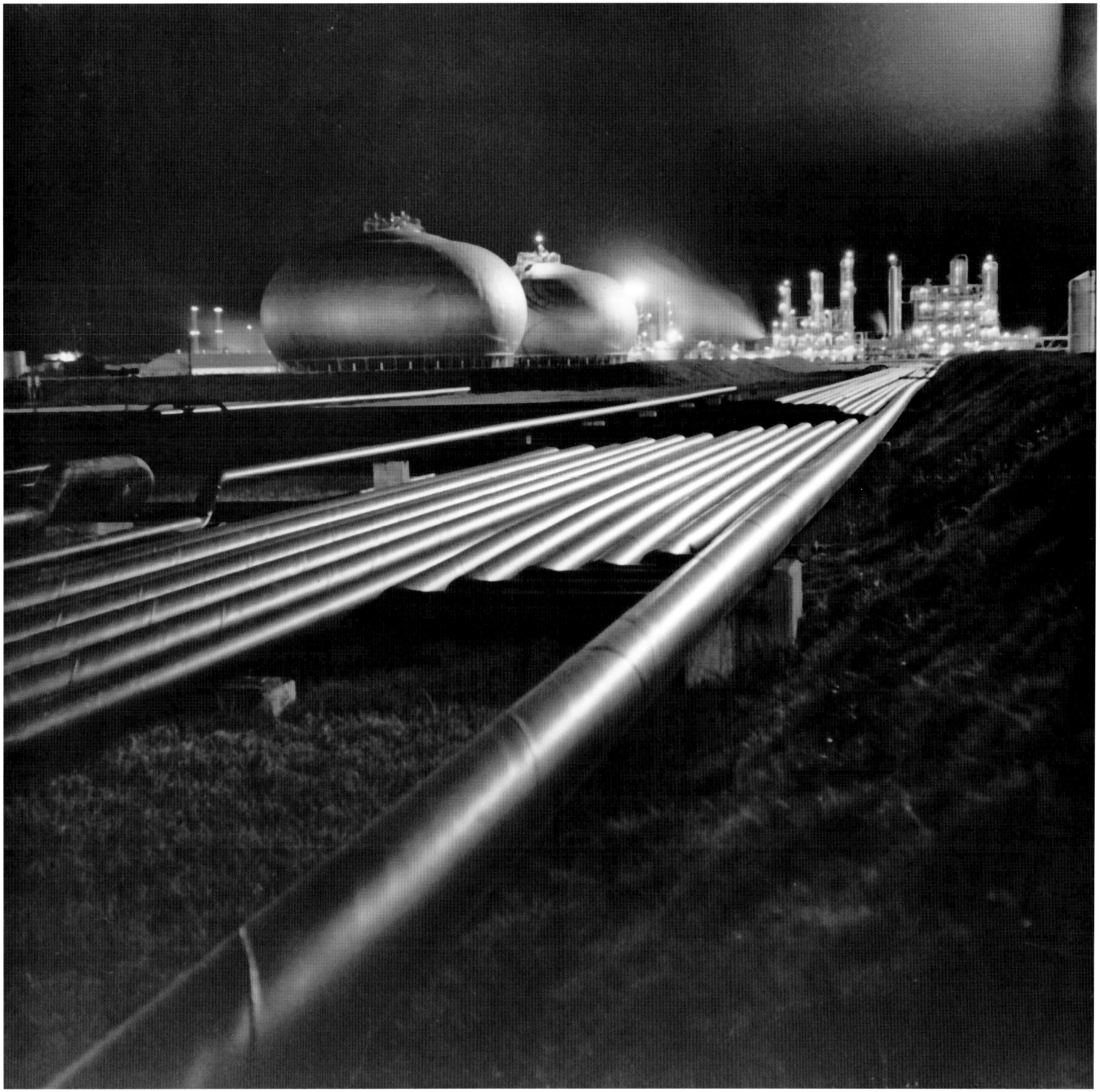

Tutwiler Refinery at Night, Lake Charles, Louisiana. 1949.

Though we travel the world over to find the beautiful, we must carry it with us or we find it not.

RALPH WALDO EMERSON

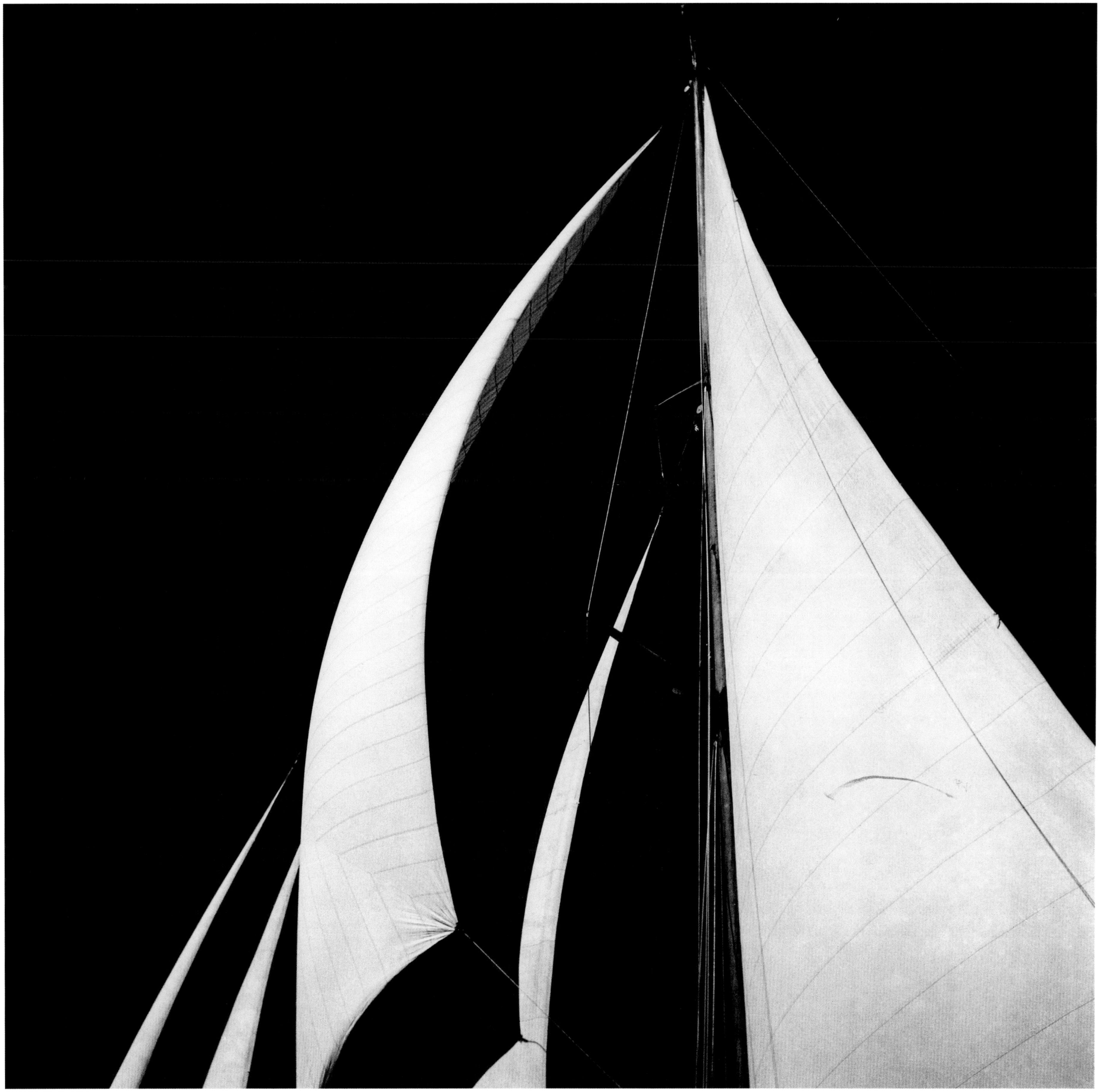

Sails of a Yacht in the Caribbean. 1955.

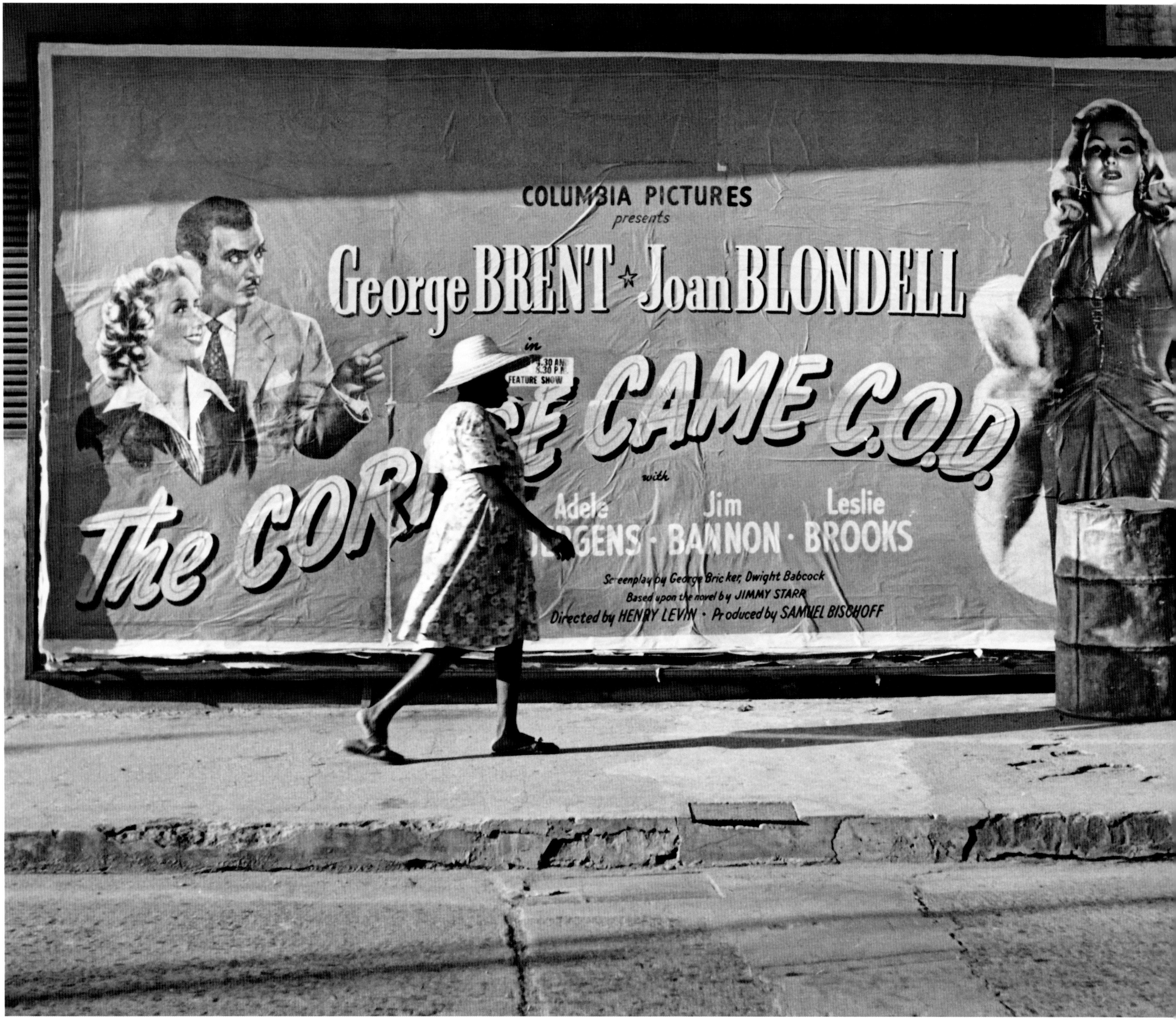
COLUMBIA PICTURES
presents
George BRENT ☆ Joan BLONDELL
in
FEATURE SHOW
The COR
E CAME C.O.D.
with
Adele
Jim
BANNON
Leslie
BROOKS
Screenplay by George Bricker, Dwight Babcock
Based upon the novel by JIMMY STARR
Directed by HENRY LEVIN · Produced by SAMUEL BISCHOFF

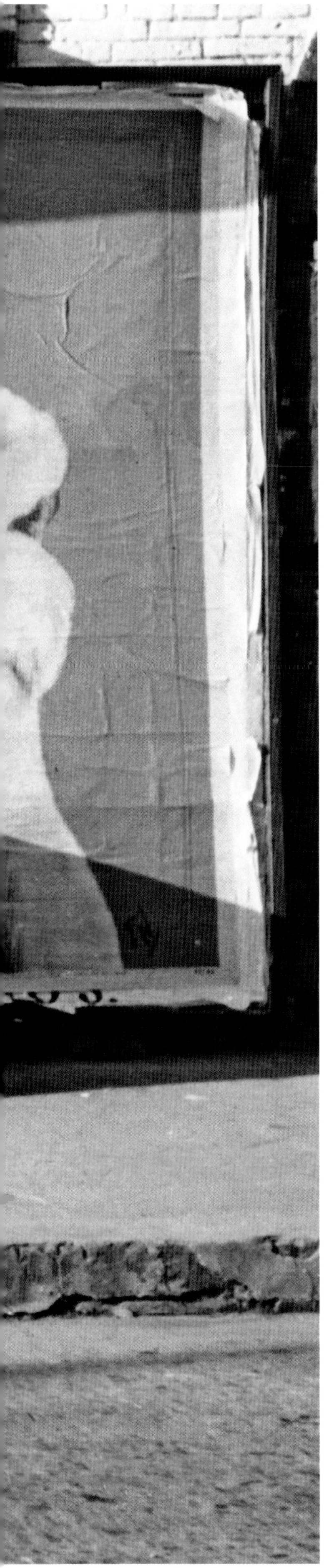

Main Street, Charlotte Amalie,
St. Thomas, Virgin Islands. 1947.

Women Waiting for Transportation on Tortola Wharf, St. Thomas, Virgin Islands. 1947.

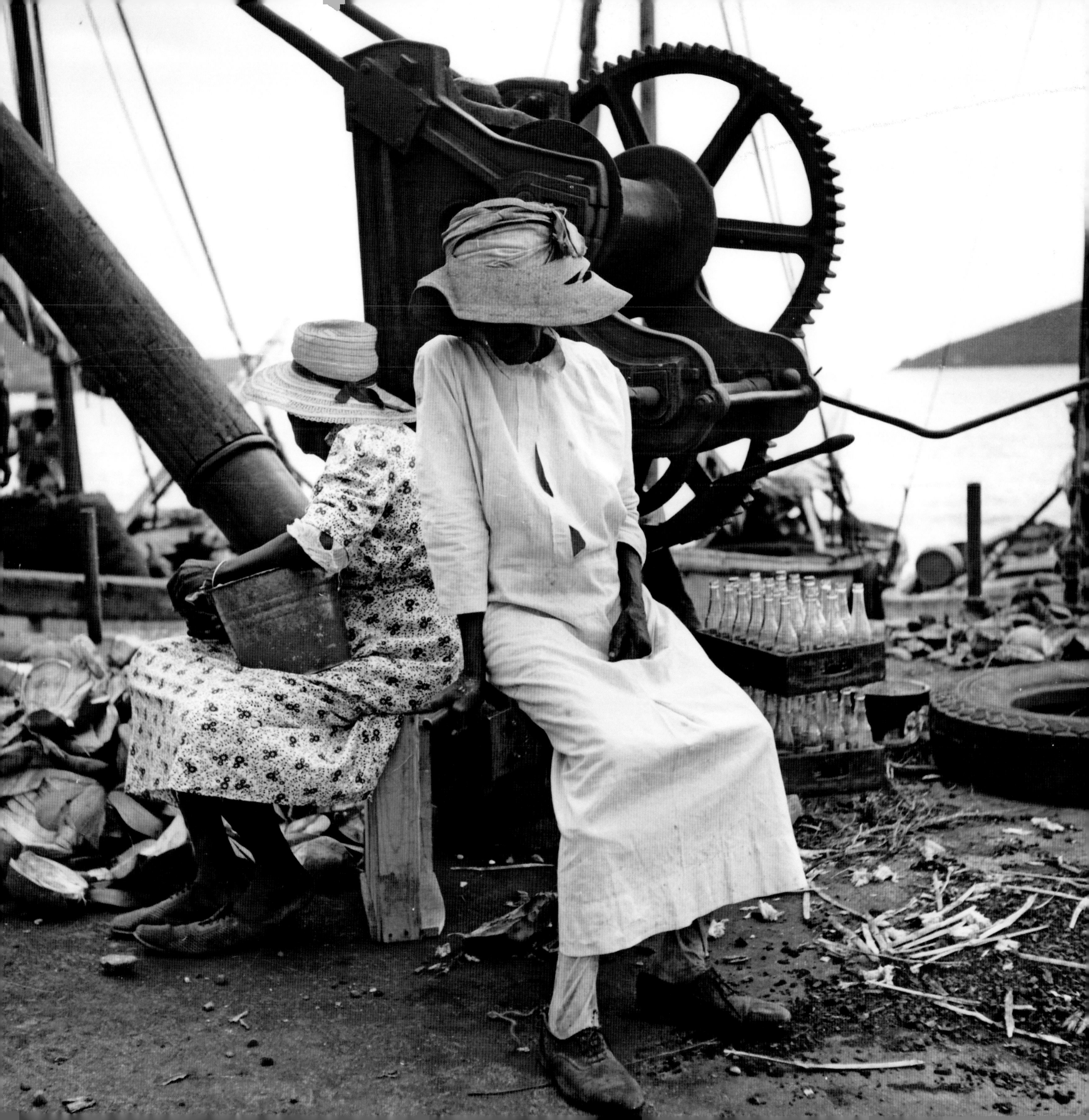

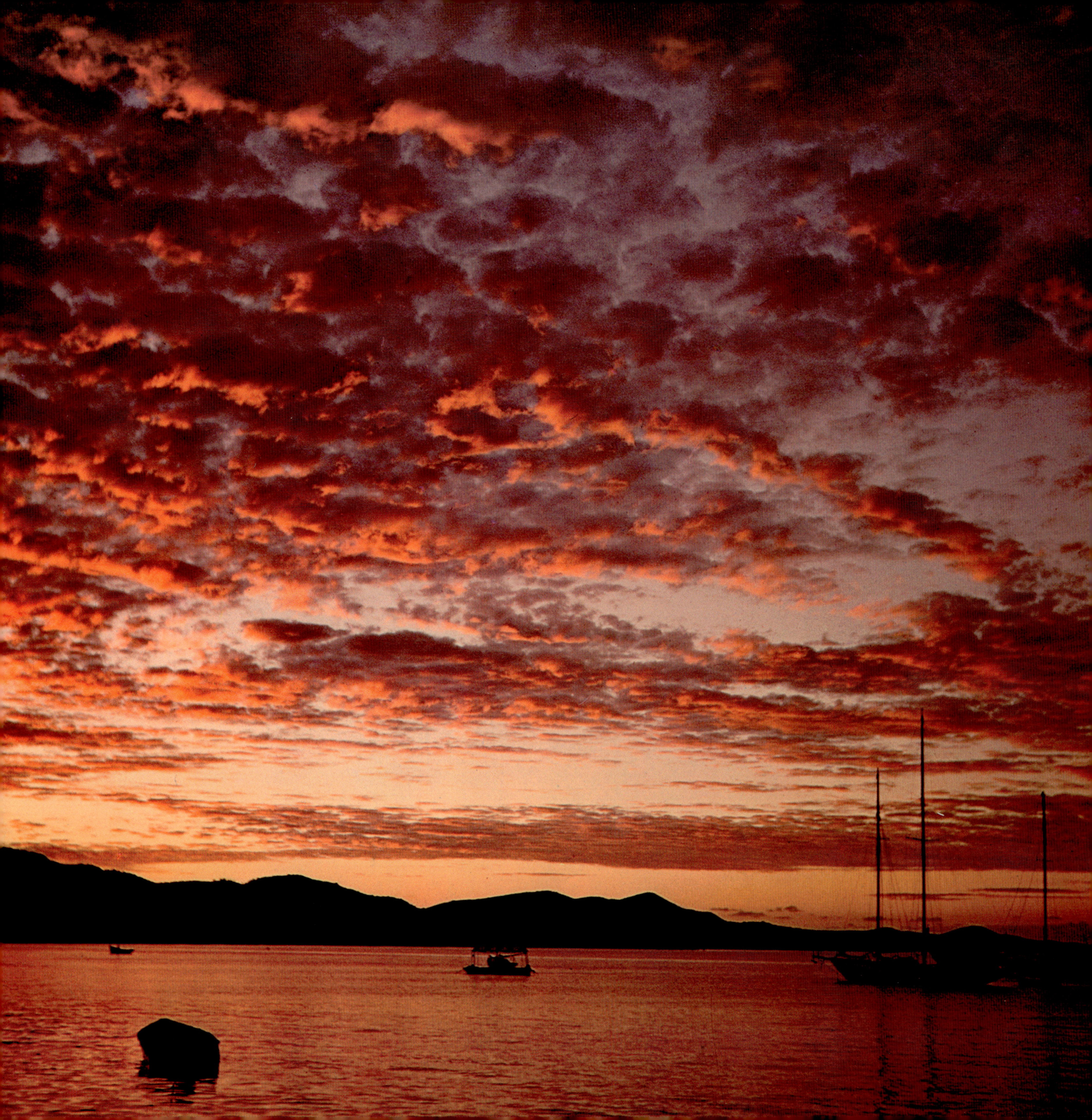

Sunset on Christiansted Harbor,
St. Croix, Virgin Islands. 1960.

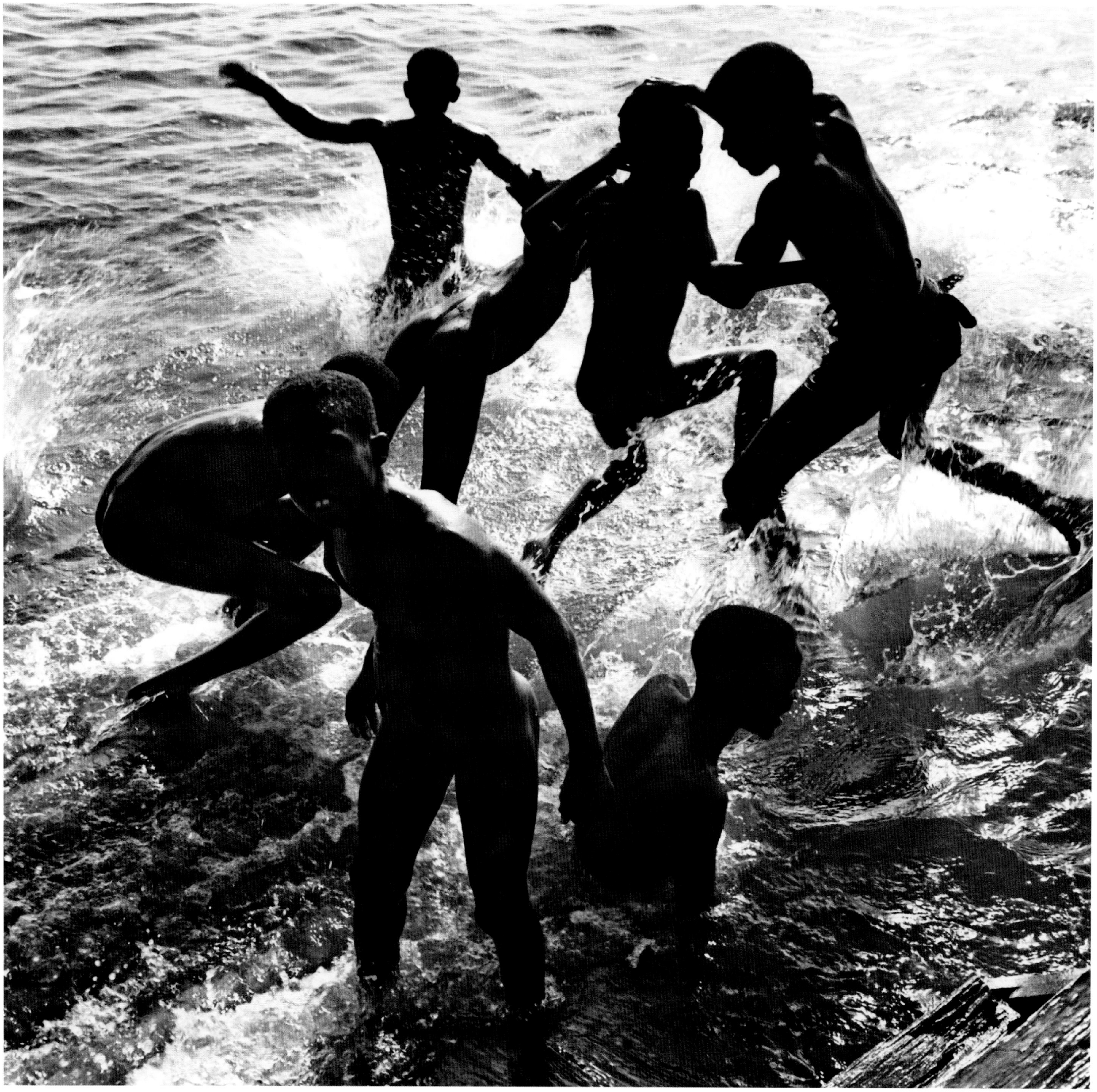

Boys Frolicking in the Water, St. Lucia. 1970.

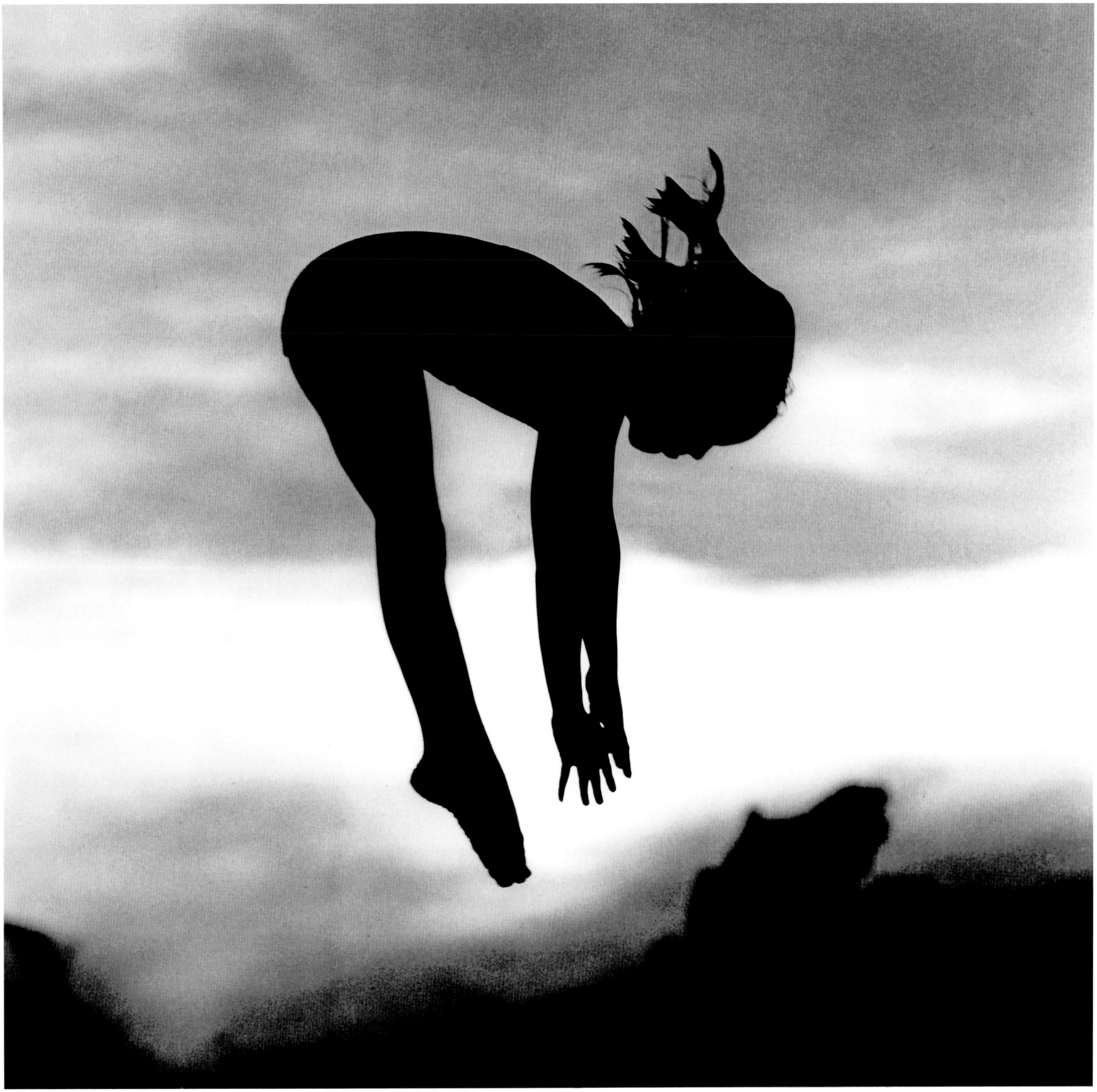

Jackknife Dive, Tina Henle, St. Croix, Virgin Islands. 1969.

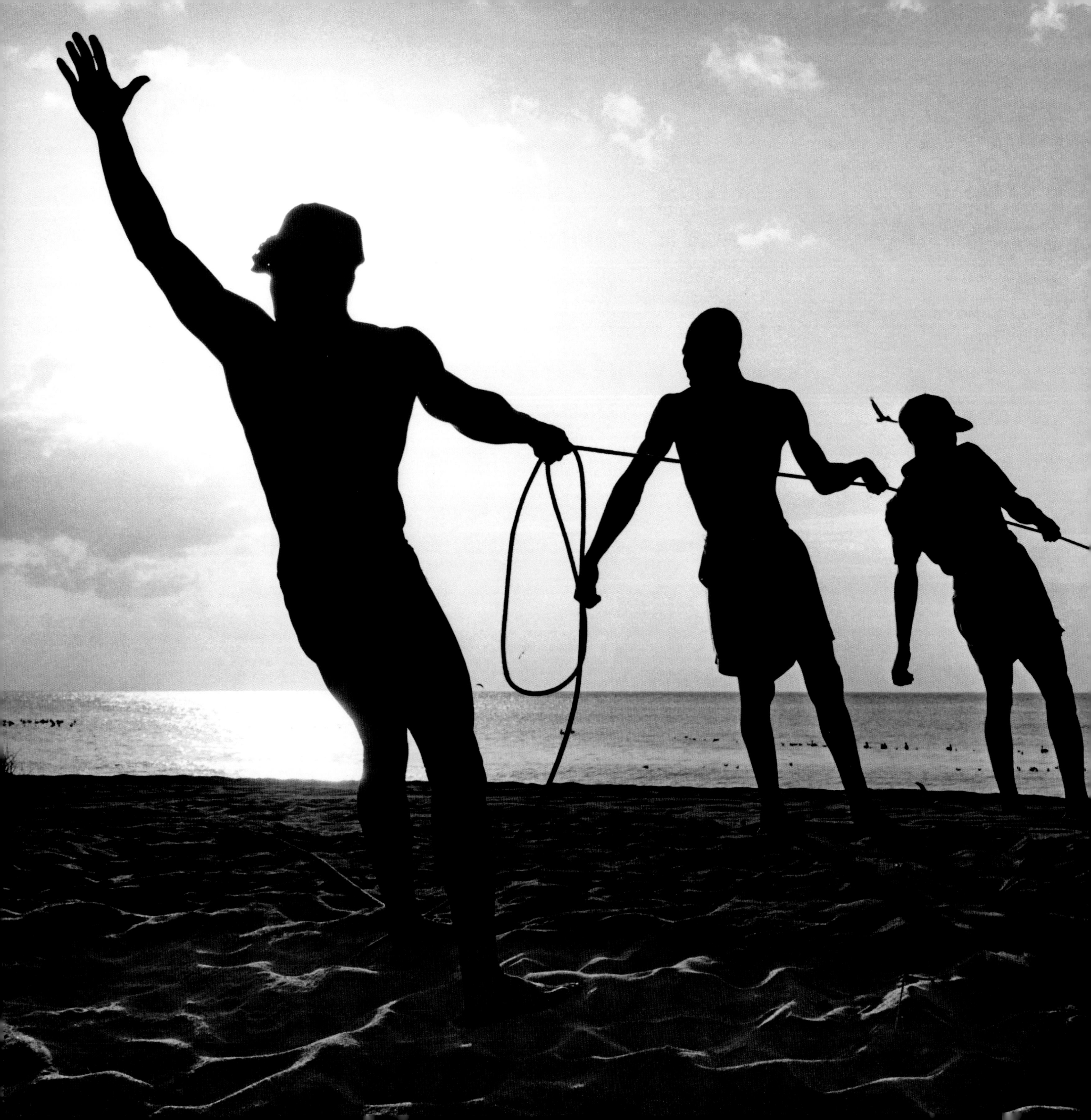

Fishermen on the Beach
Pulling in the Net, Tobago. 1959.

Hurricane in the Caribbean,
Tobago. 1960.

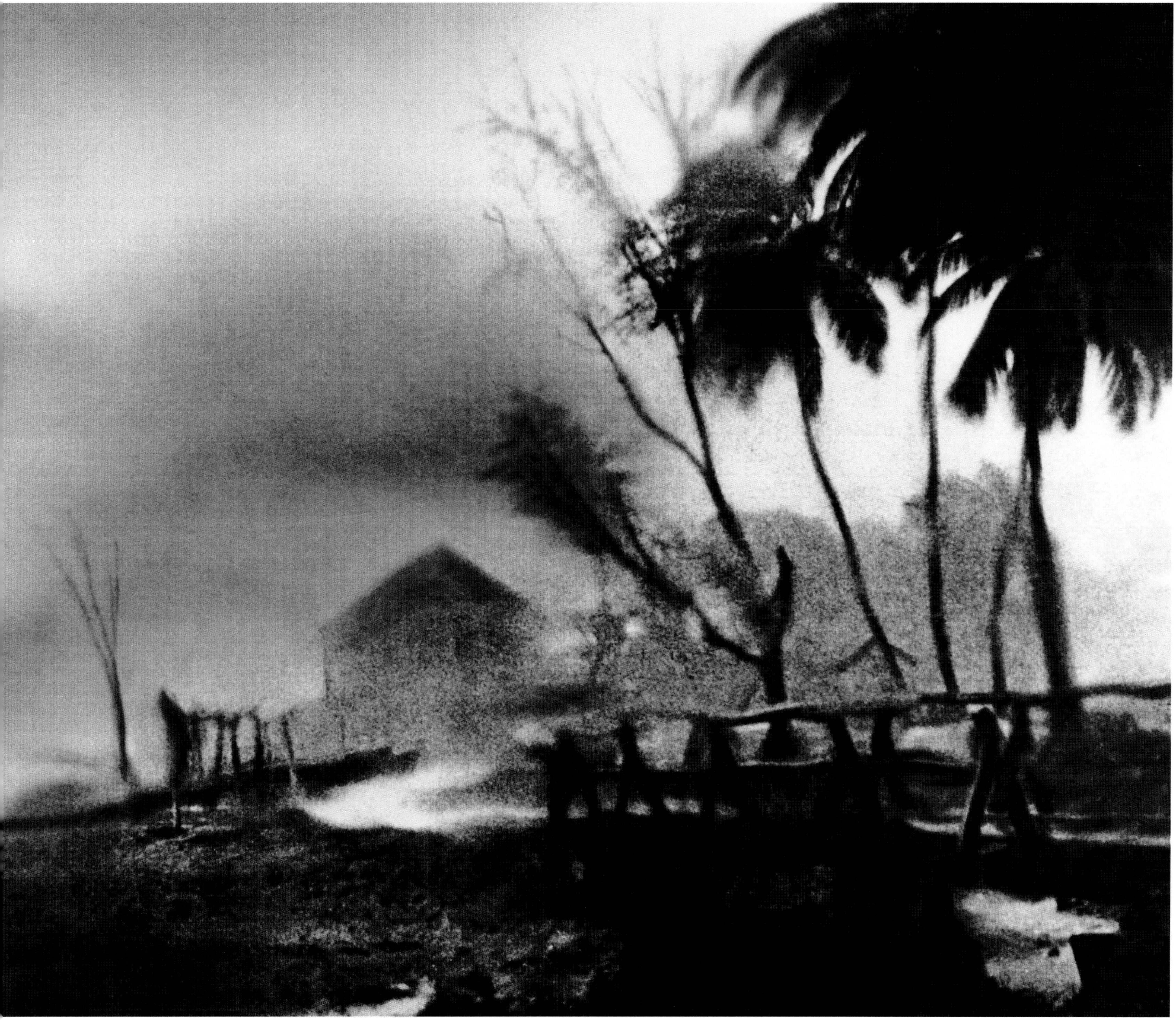

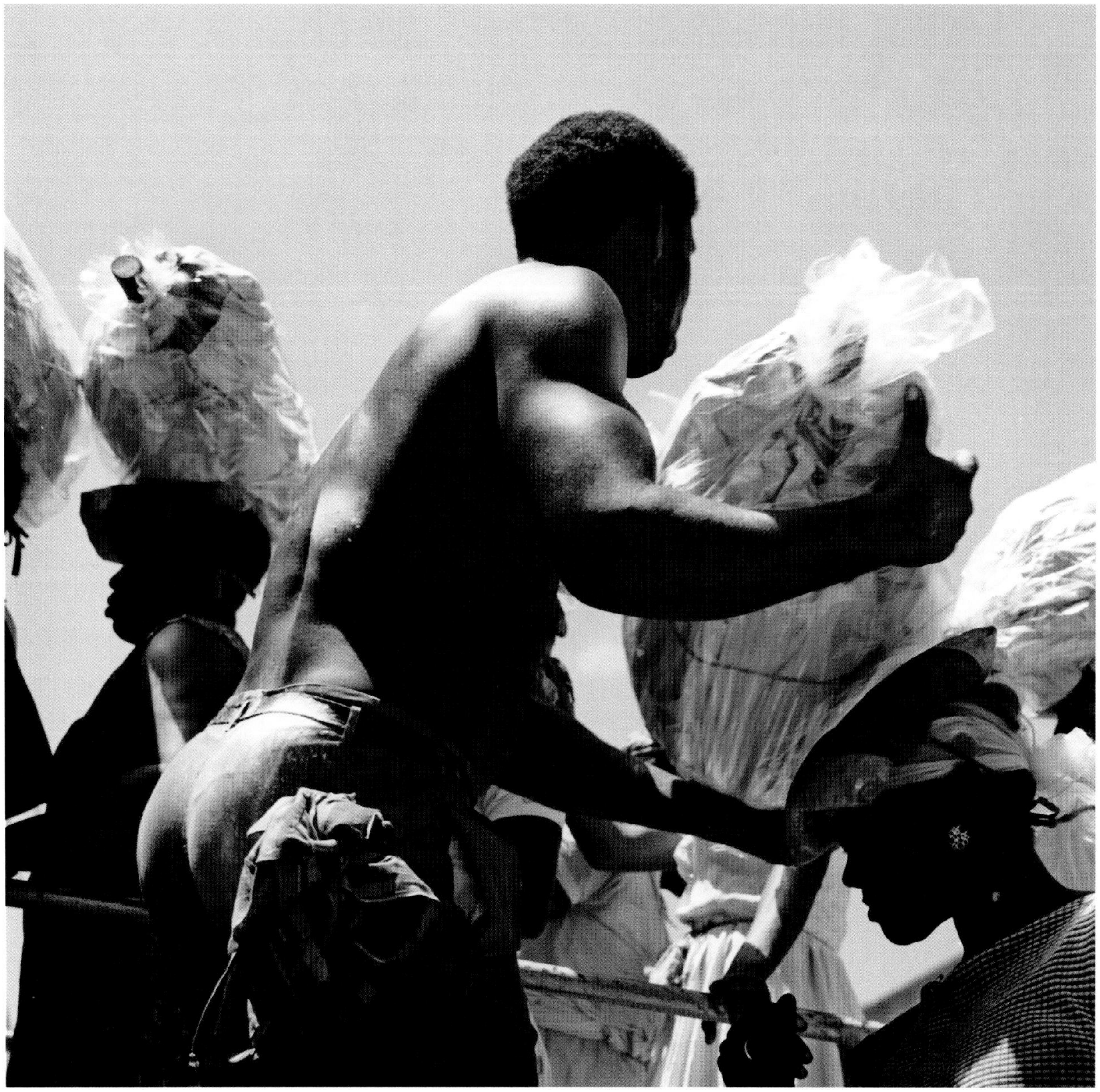

(above) Loading Bananas, St. Lucia. 1959.
(right) Schooner Viewed through the Rigging of *Baby Mack* from the Christiansted Docks, St. Croix, Virgin Islands. 1950.

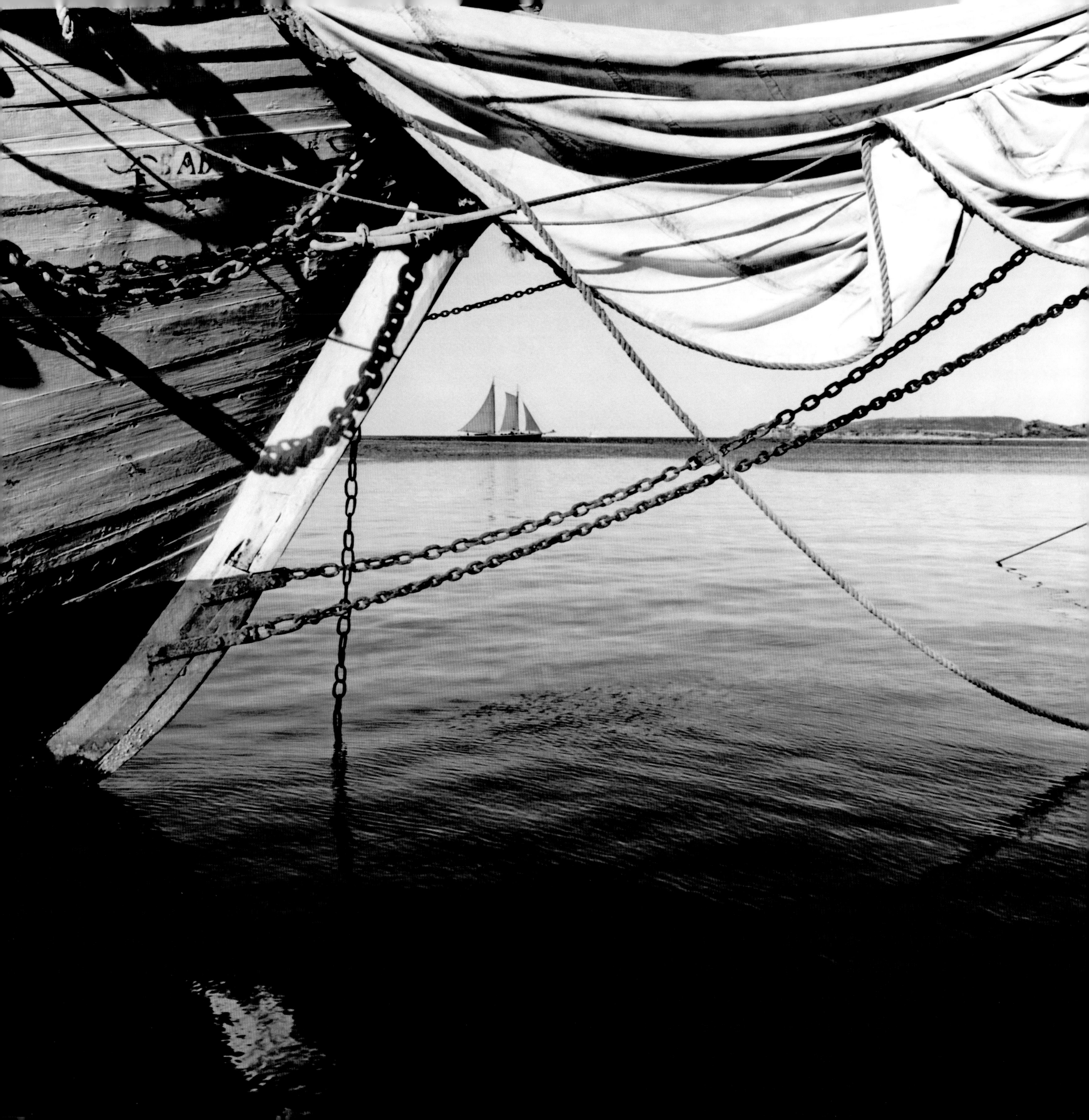

Hands of the Old Straw Weaver,
St. Croix, Virgin Islands. 1970.

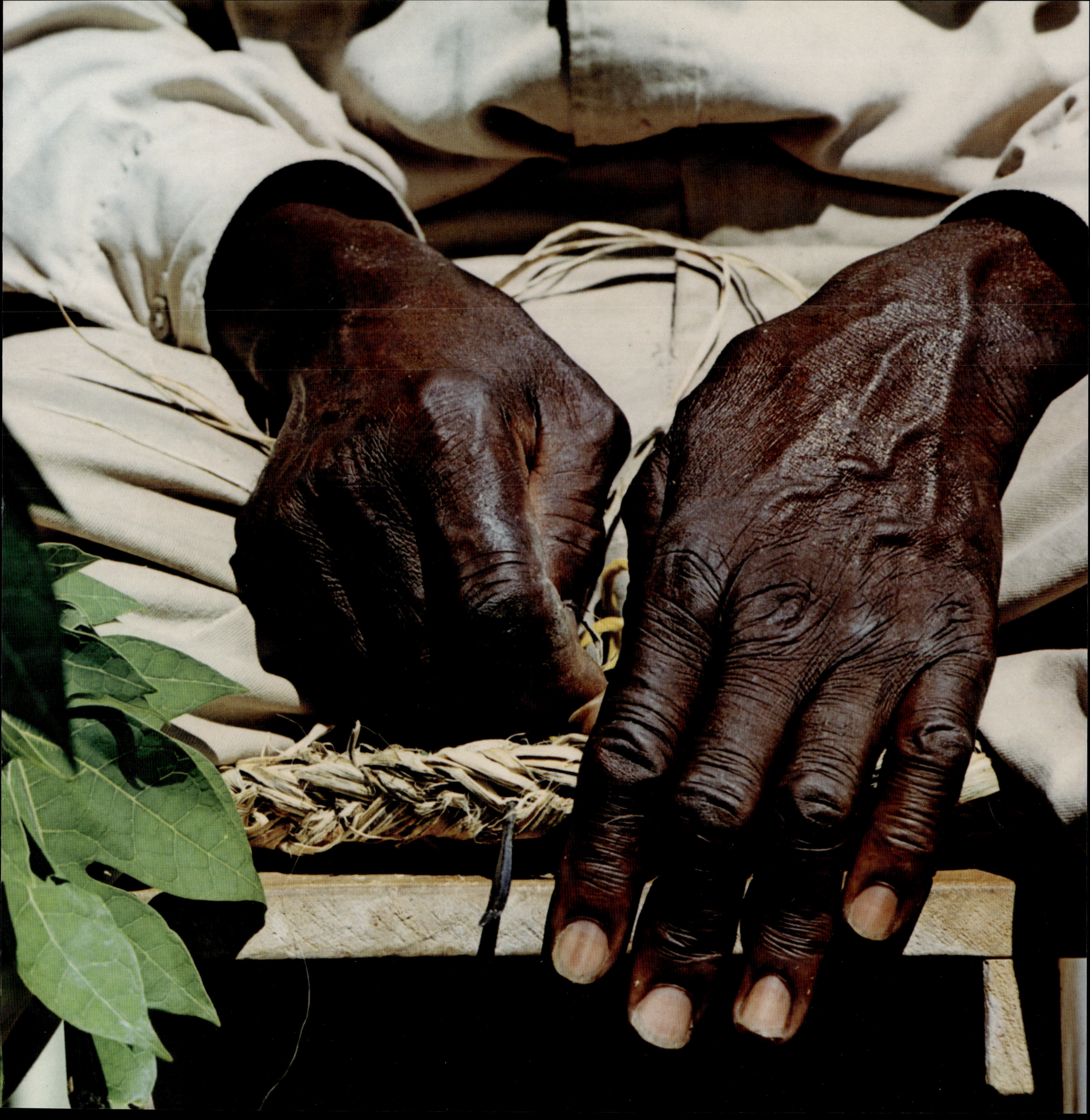

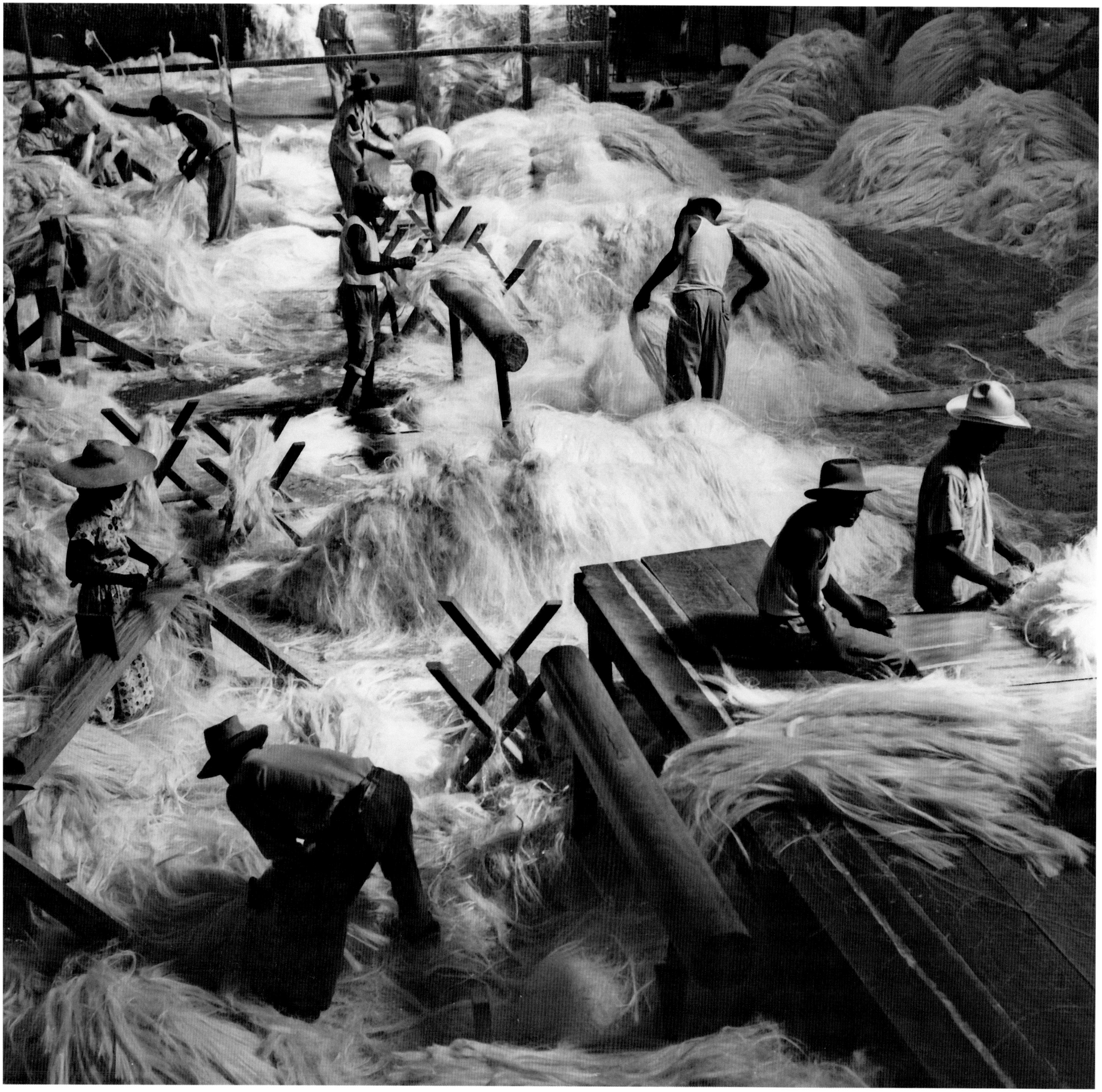

Sisal Factory, Haiti. 1958.

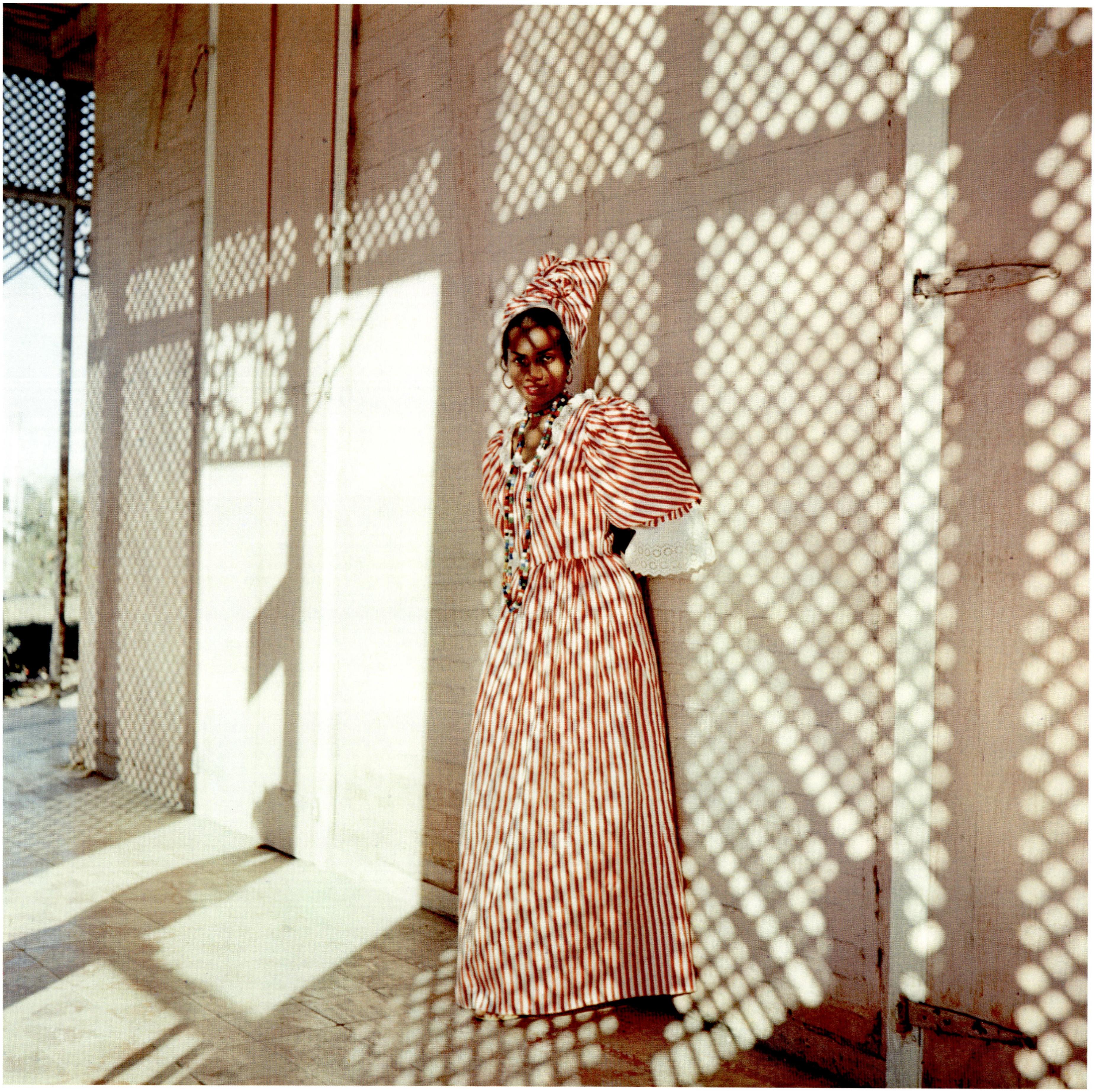

Haitian Beauty, Petionville, Haiti. 1959.

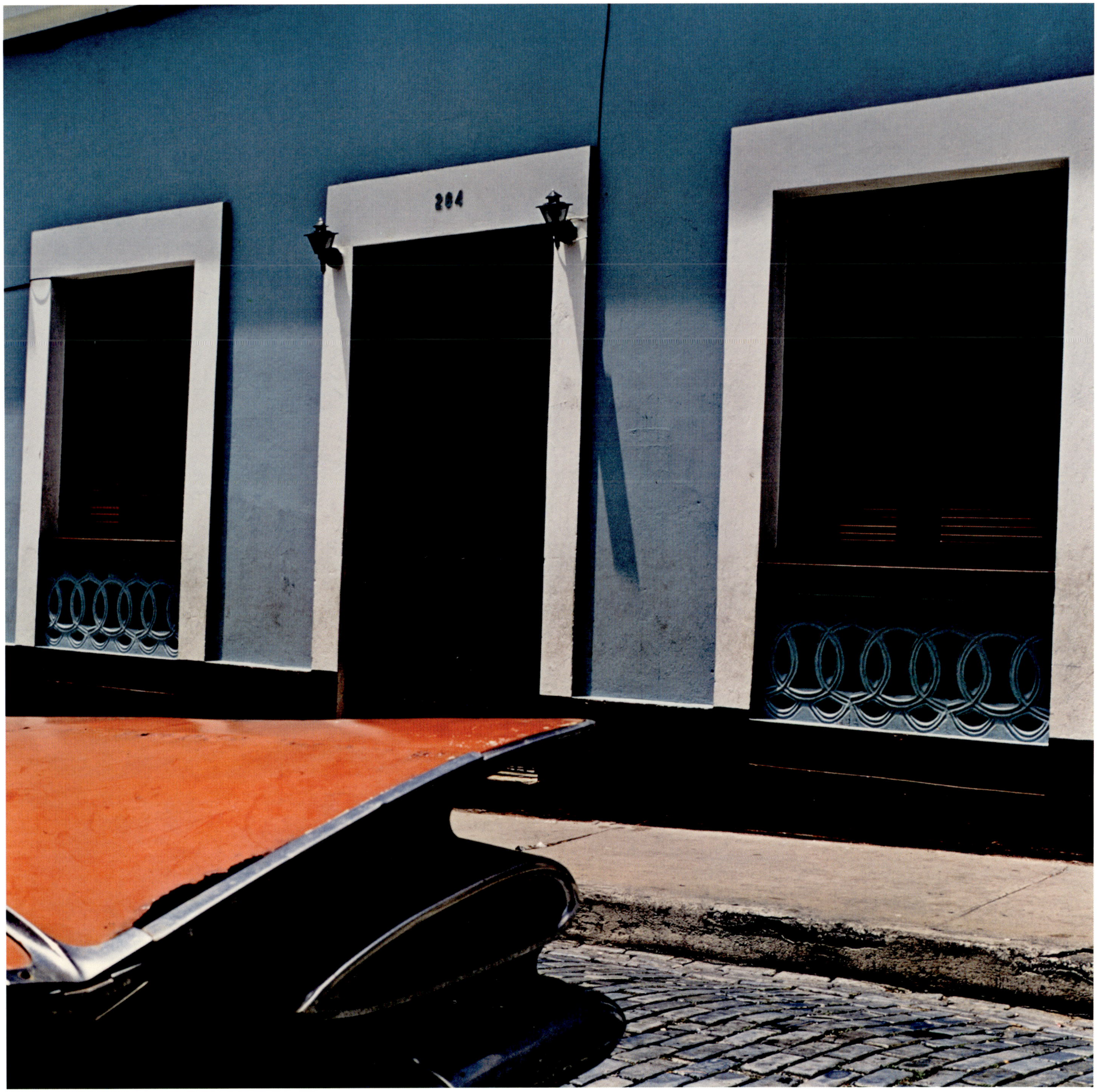

Street in Old San Juan, Puerto Rico. ca. 1971.

A Djuka Belle in Her Jungle Village, Surinam. 1959.

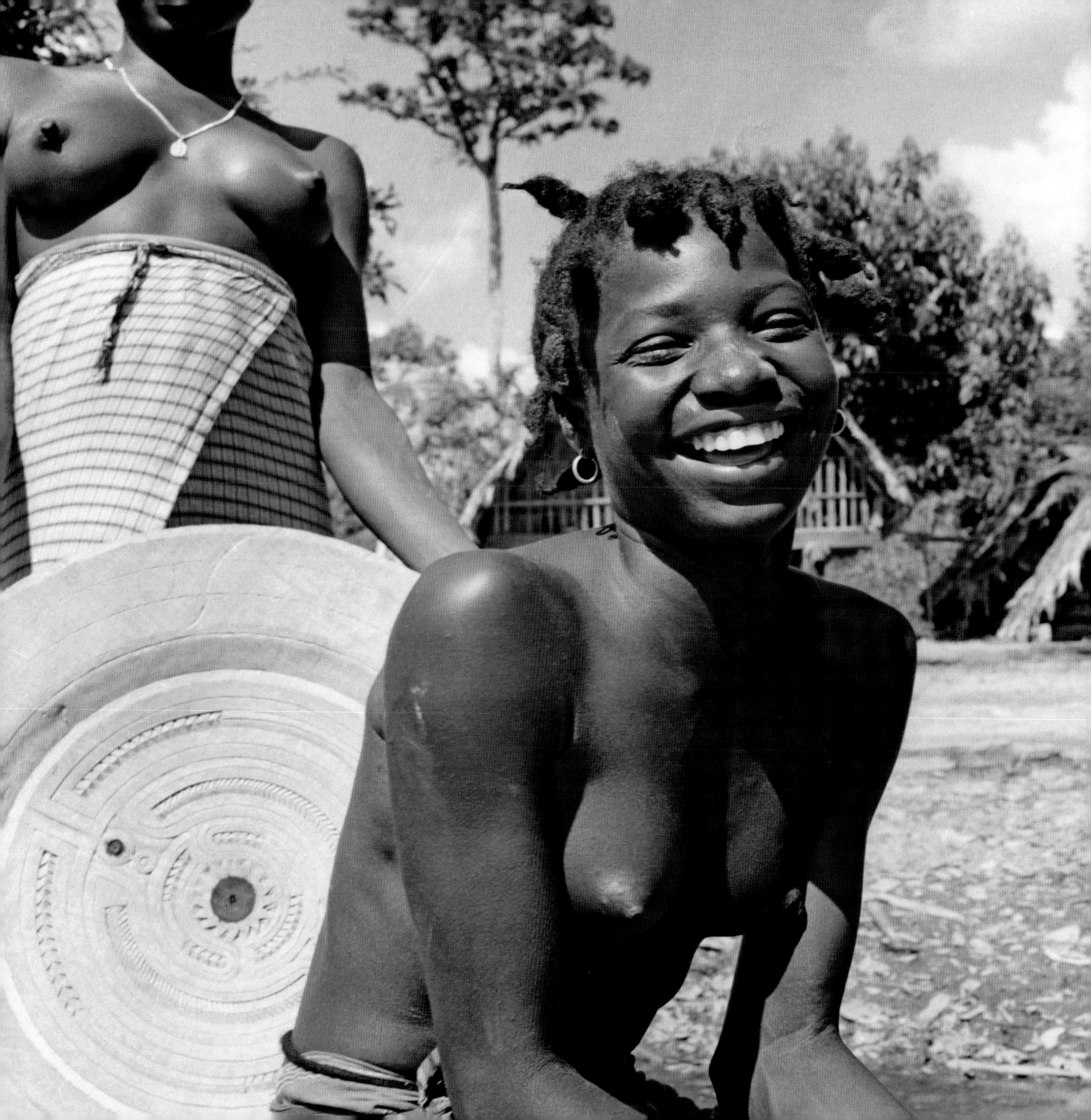

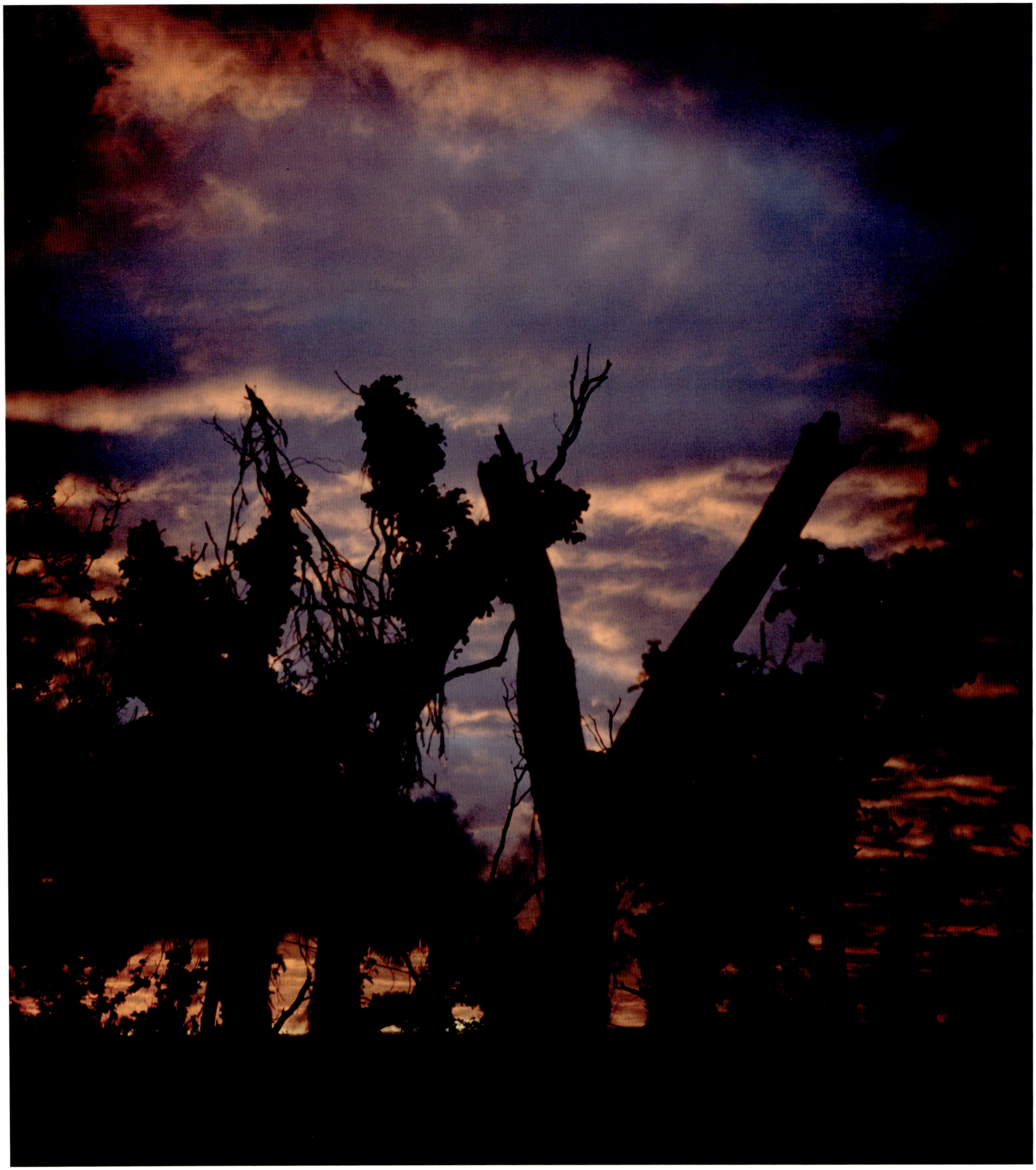

New Growth after Hurricane Hugo, Christiansted, St. Croix, Virgin Islands. 1989.

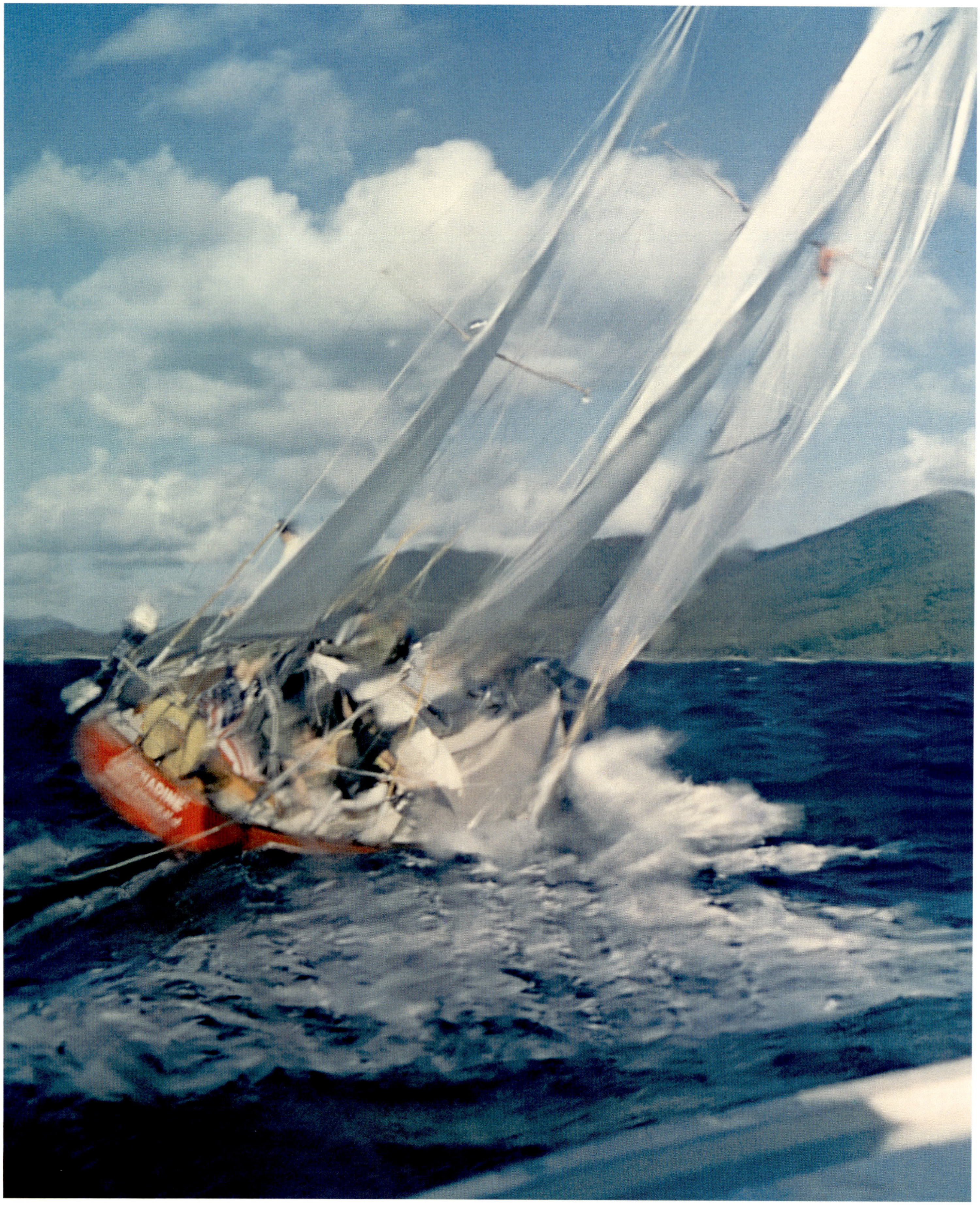

The *Grenadine* Racing off St. John, Virgin Islands. 1974.

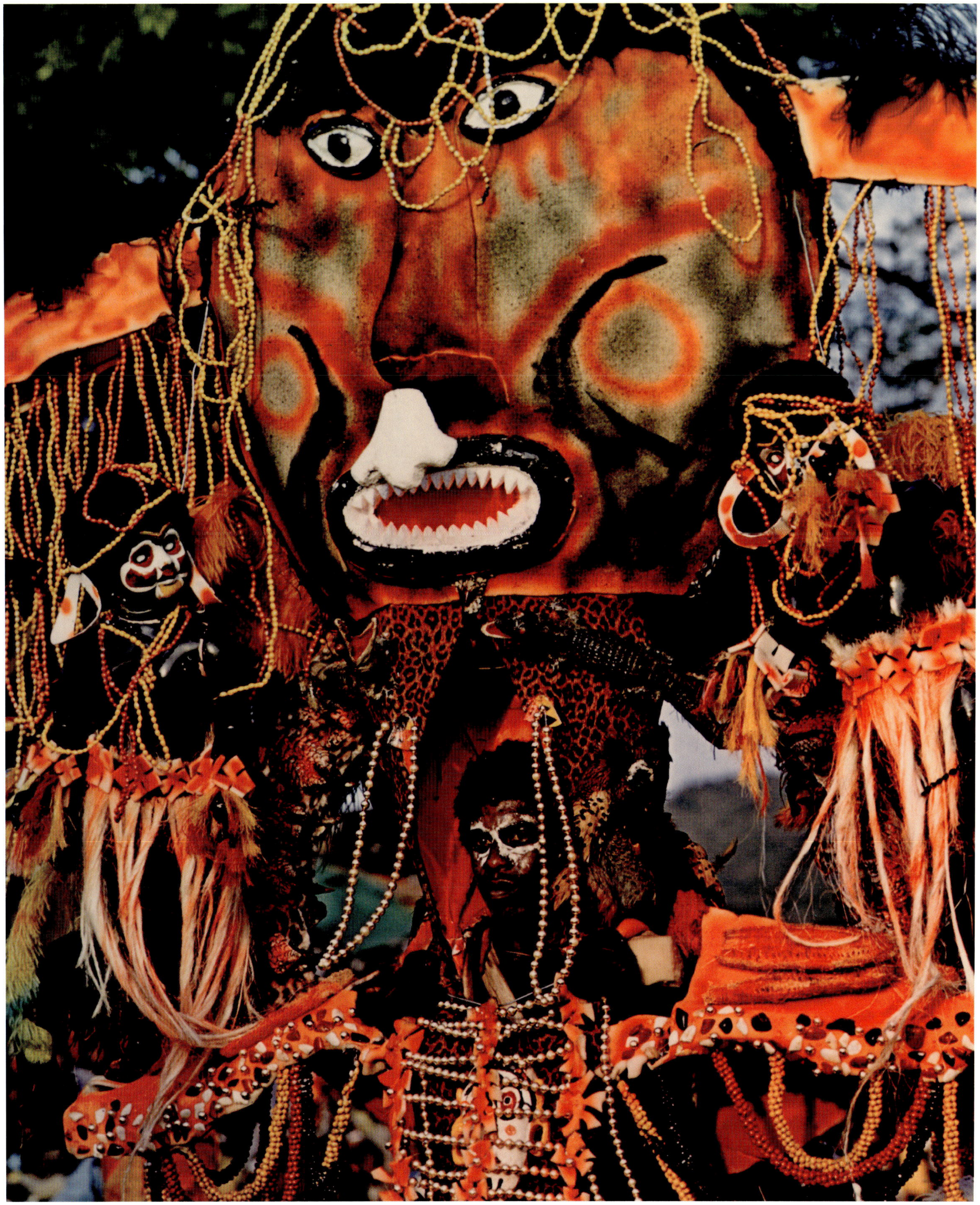

Masque *The Beauty of Africa* at Carnival, Trinidad. ca. 1960.

A morning glory
at my window satisfies
me more than the
metaphysics of books.

WALT WHITMAN

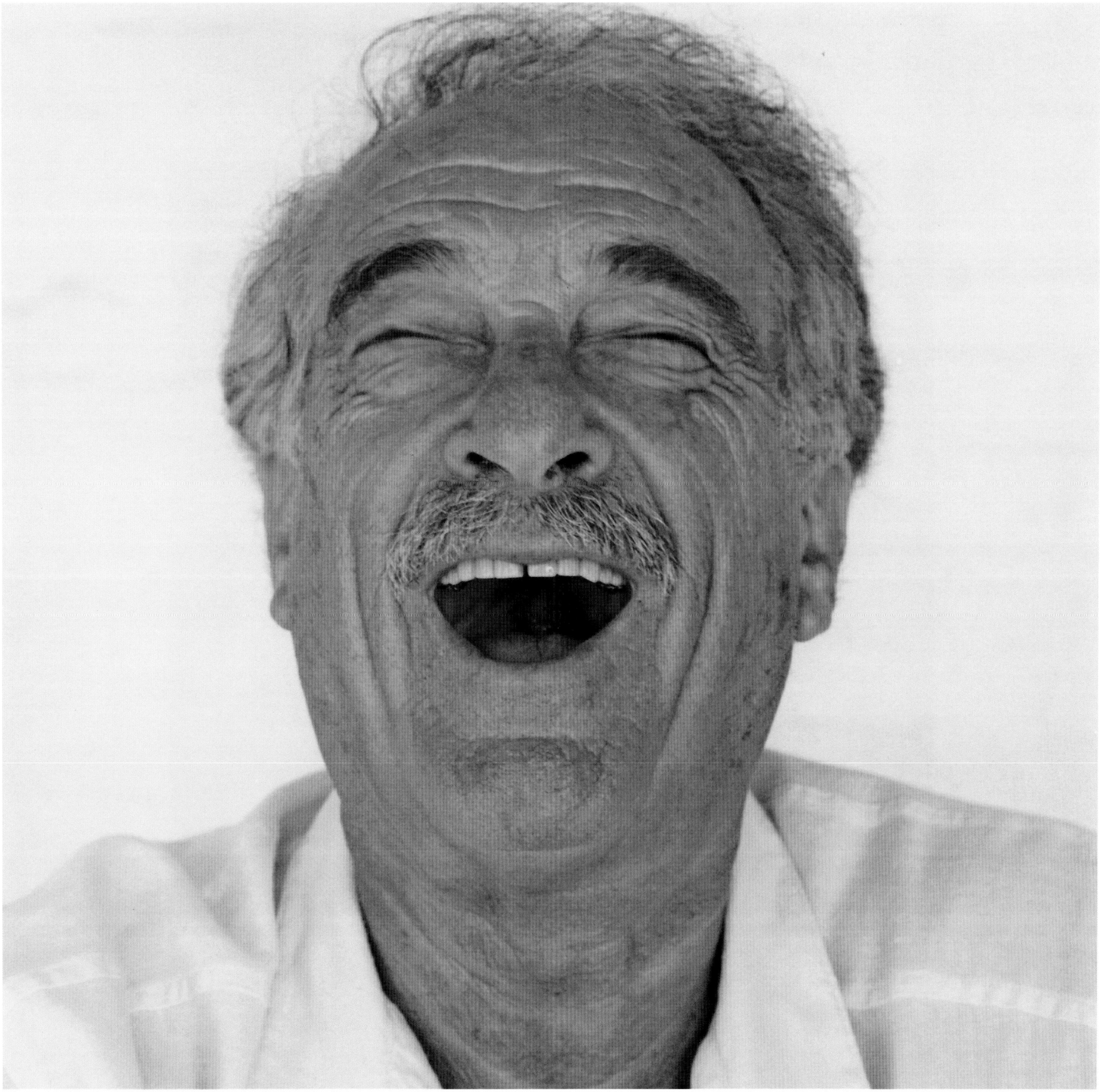

Victor Borge Laughing, St. Croix, Virgin Islands. 1984.

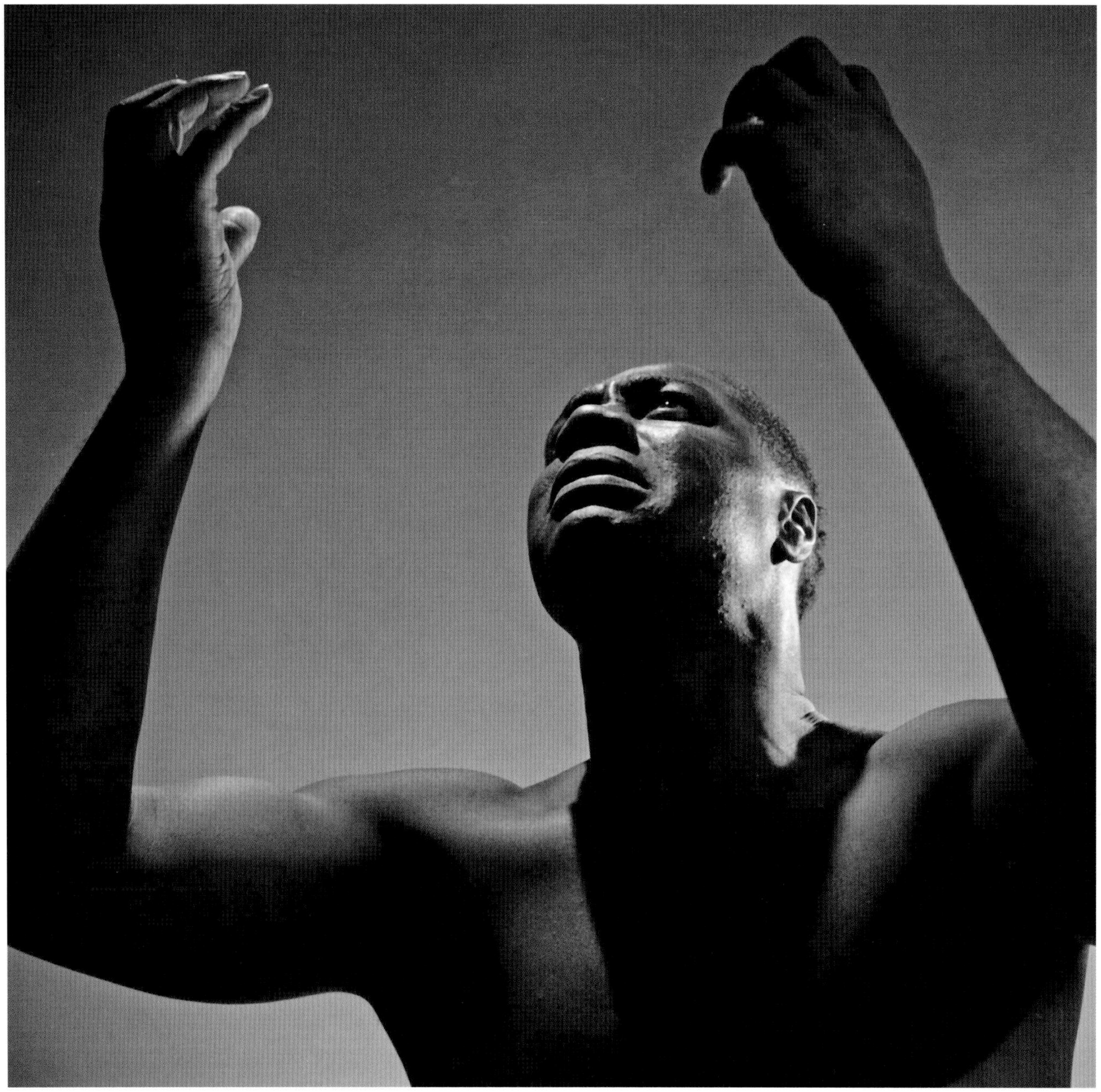

(above) Canada Lee in *Native Son,* New York City. ca. 1941.
(right) Marian Anderson Rehearsing on Her Farm, New York. 1946.

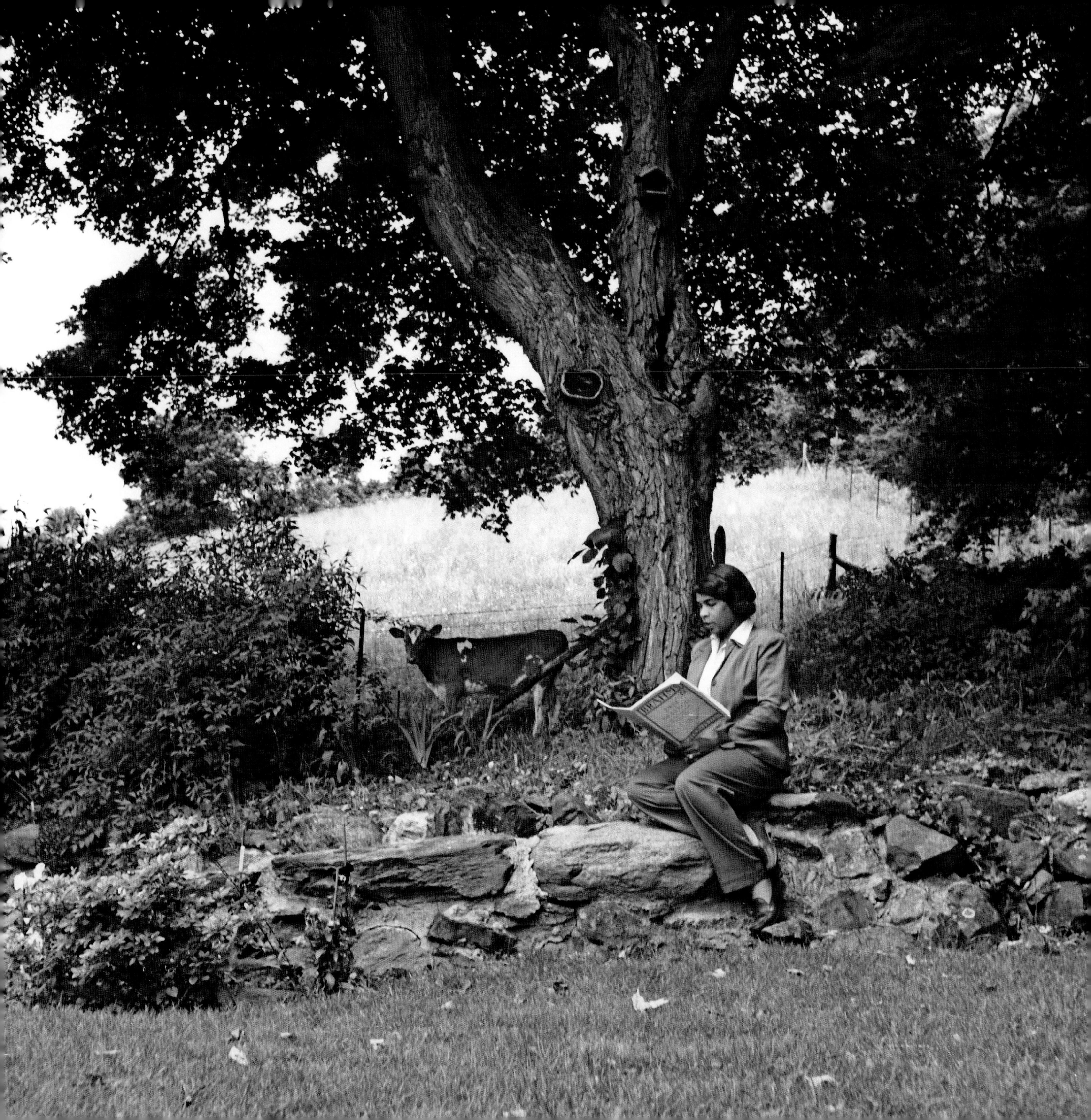

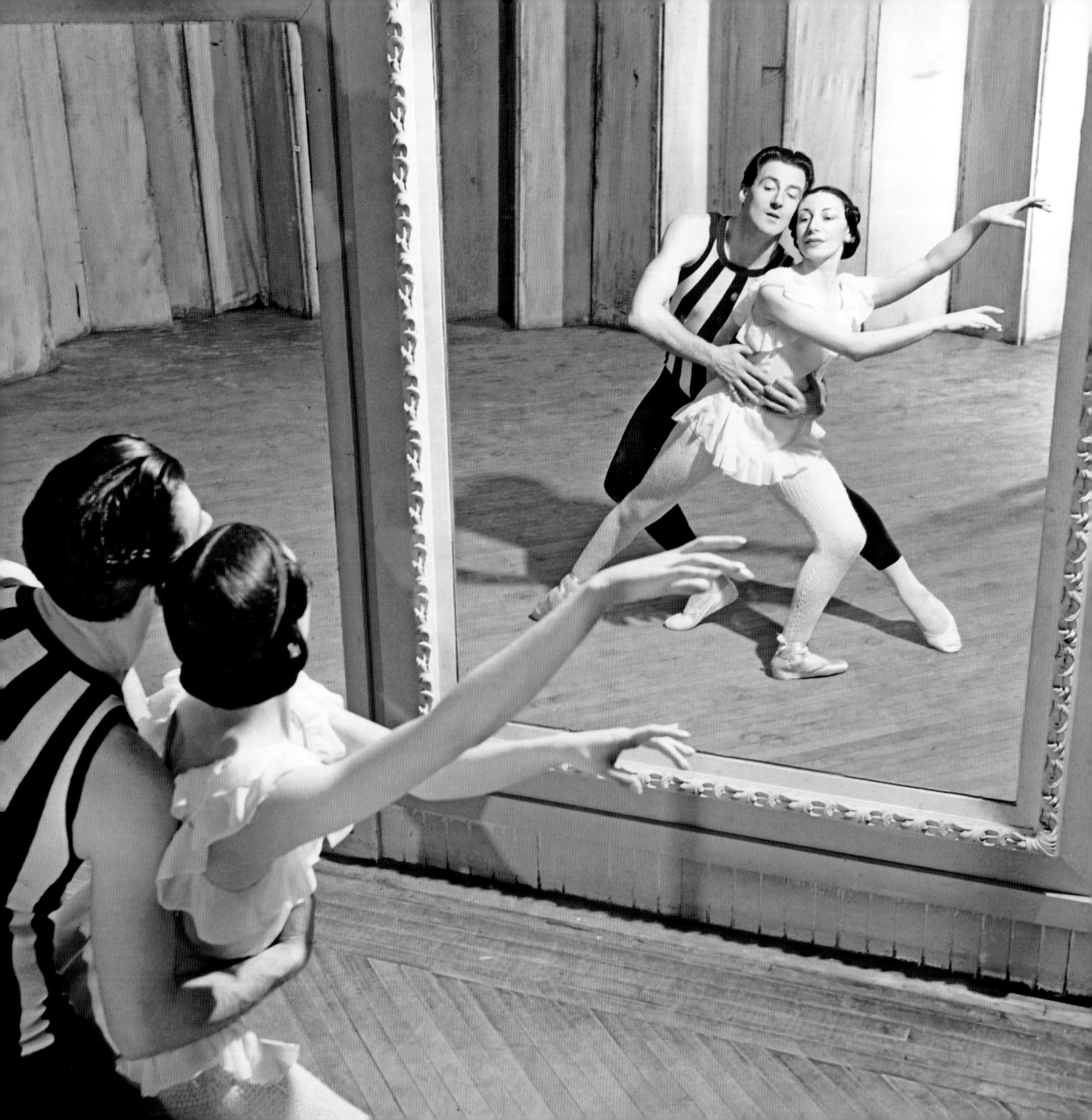

Dolin and Markova of Ballet Russe,
New York City. 1939.

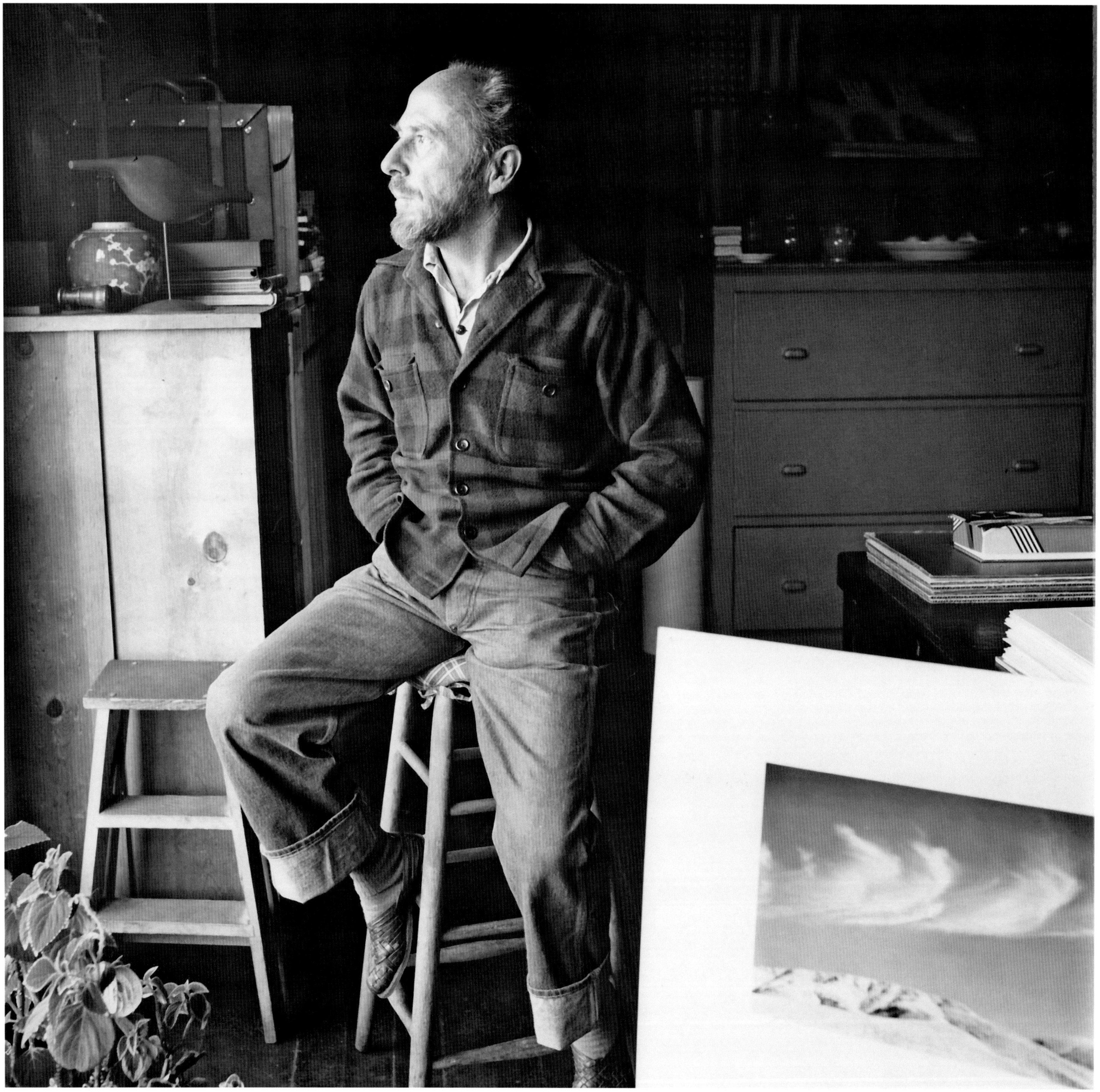

Edward Weston at Wild Cat Hill, Point Lobos, California. 1942.

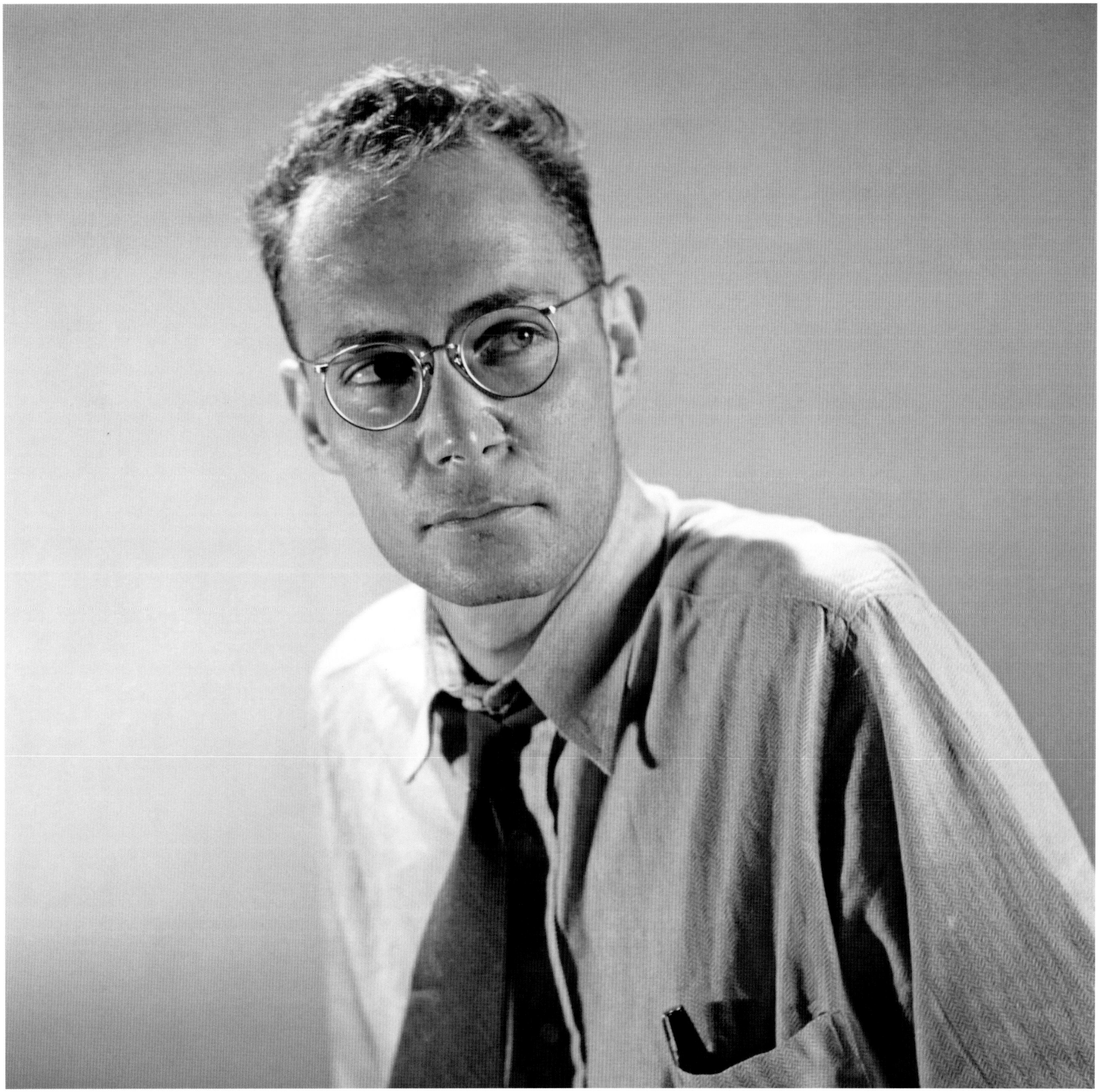

W. Eugene Smith at the 538 Fifth Avenue Studio, New York City. ca. 1940.

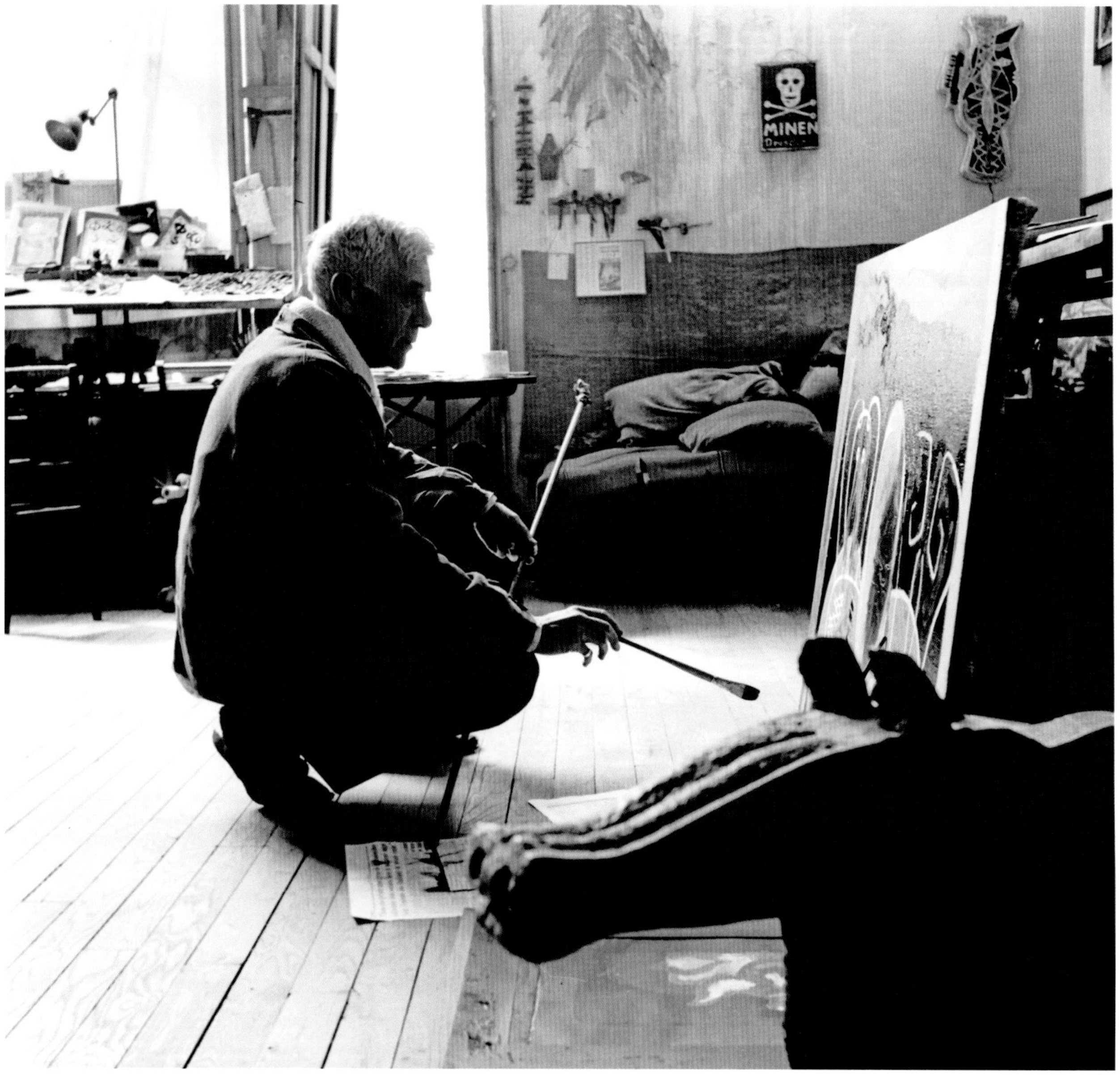

(above) Georges Braque Painting in His Studio, Paris, France. 1950.
(right) Geoffrey Holder at His Painting Exhibition, New York City. ca. 1965.

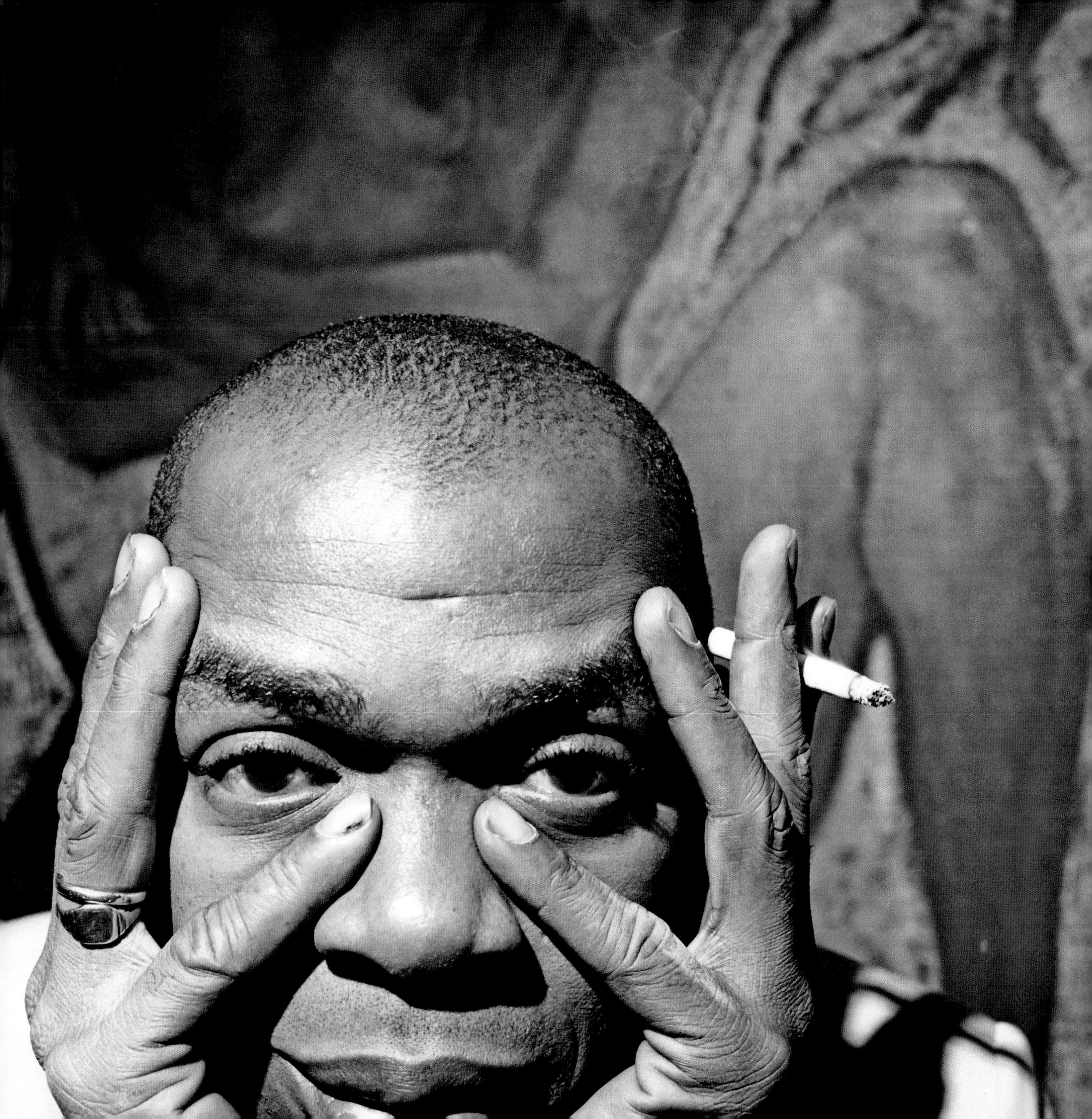

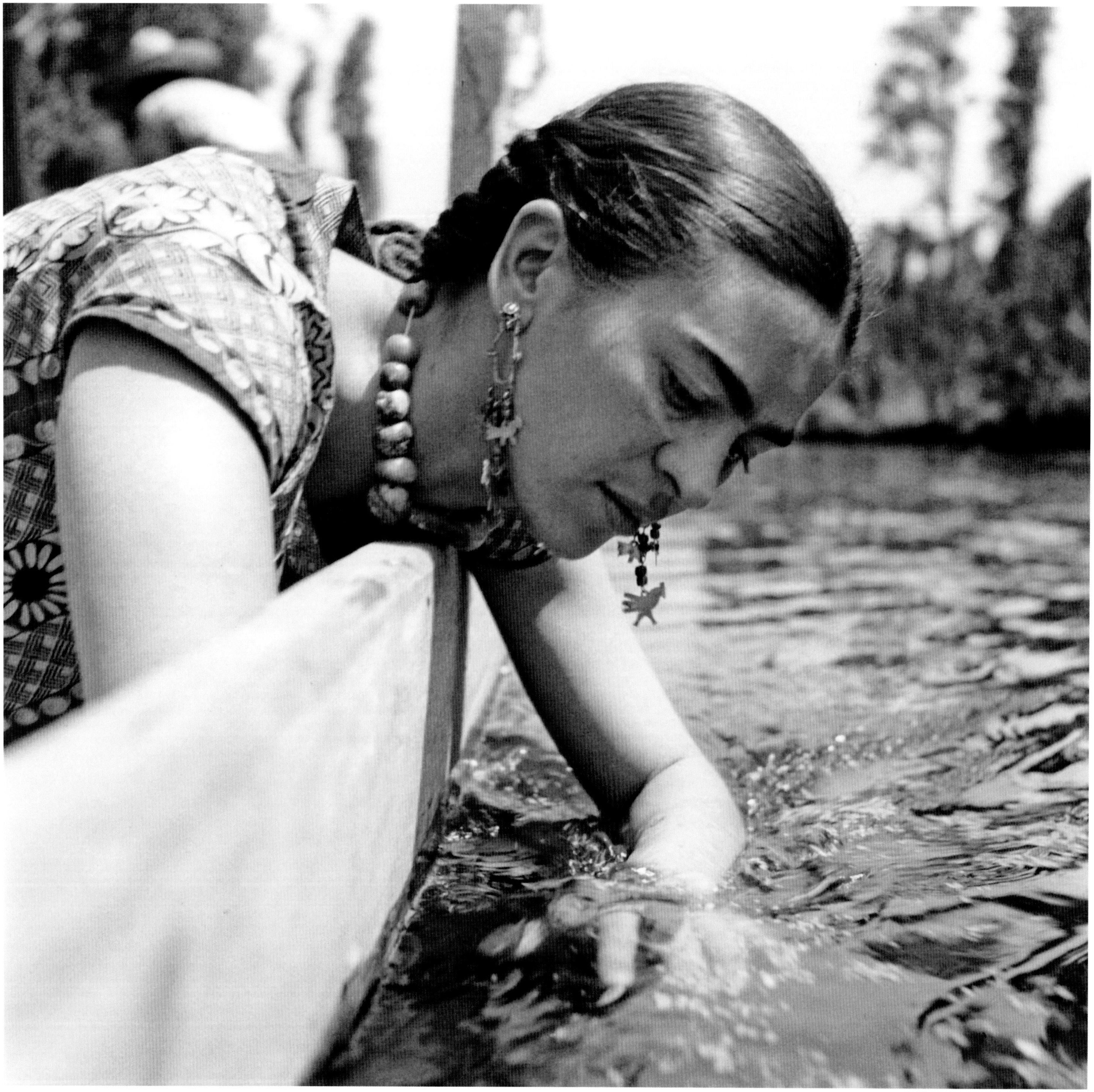

Frida Kahlo at Xochimilco, Mexico. 1937.

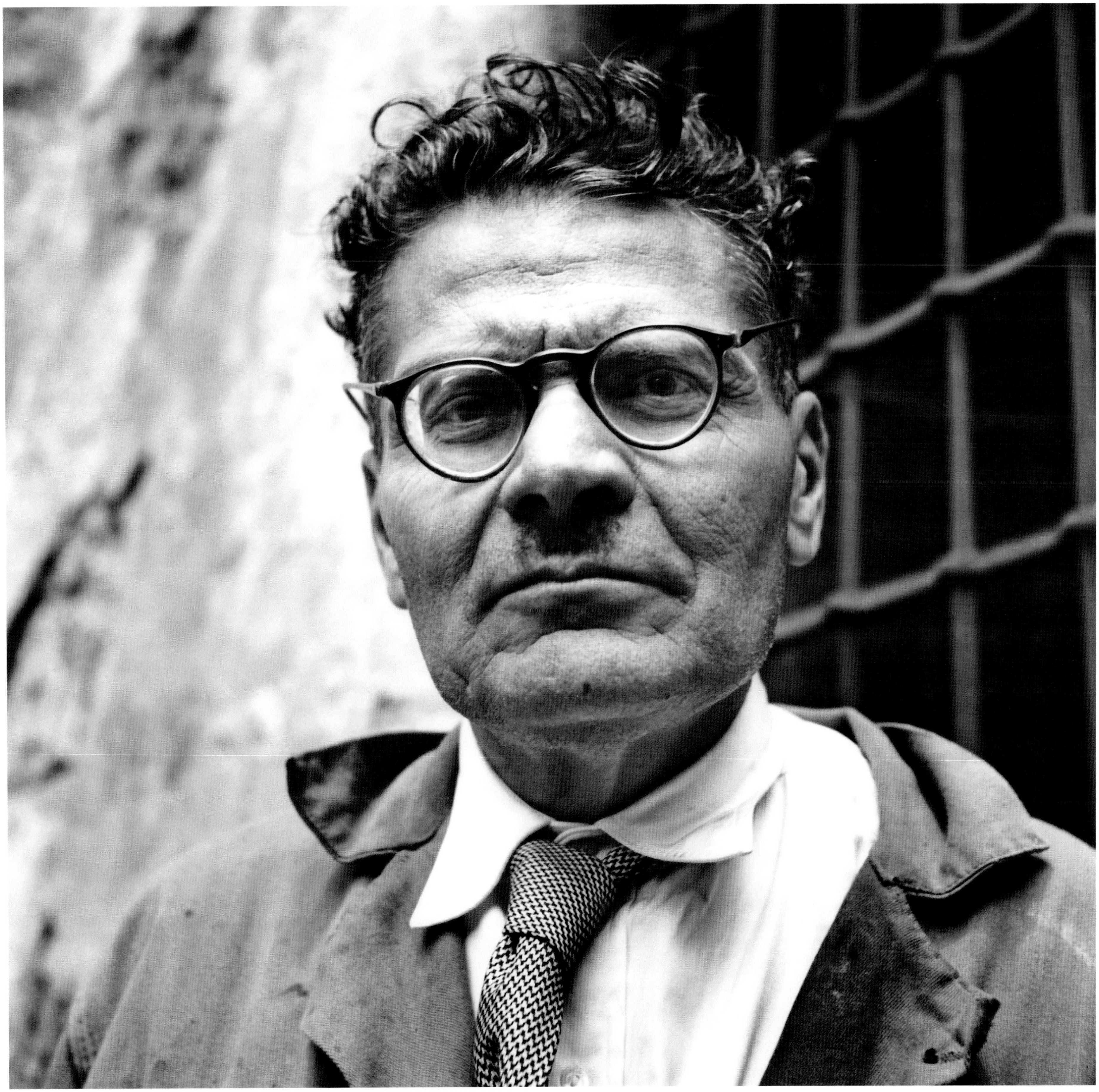

José Clemente Orozco, Mexico. 1943.

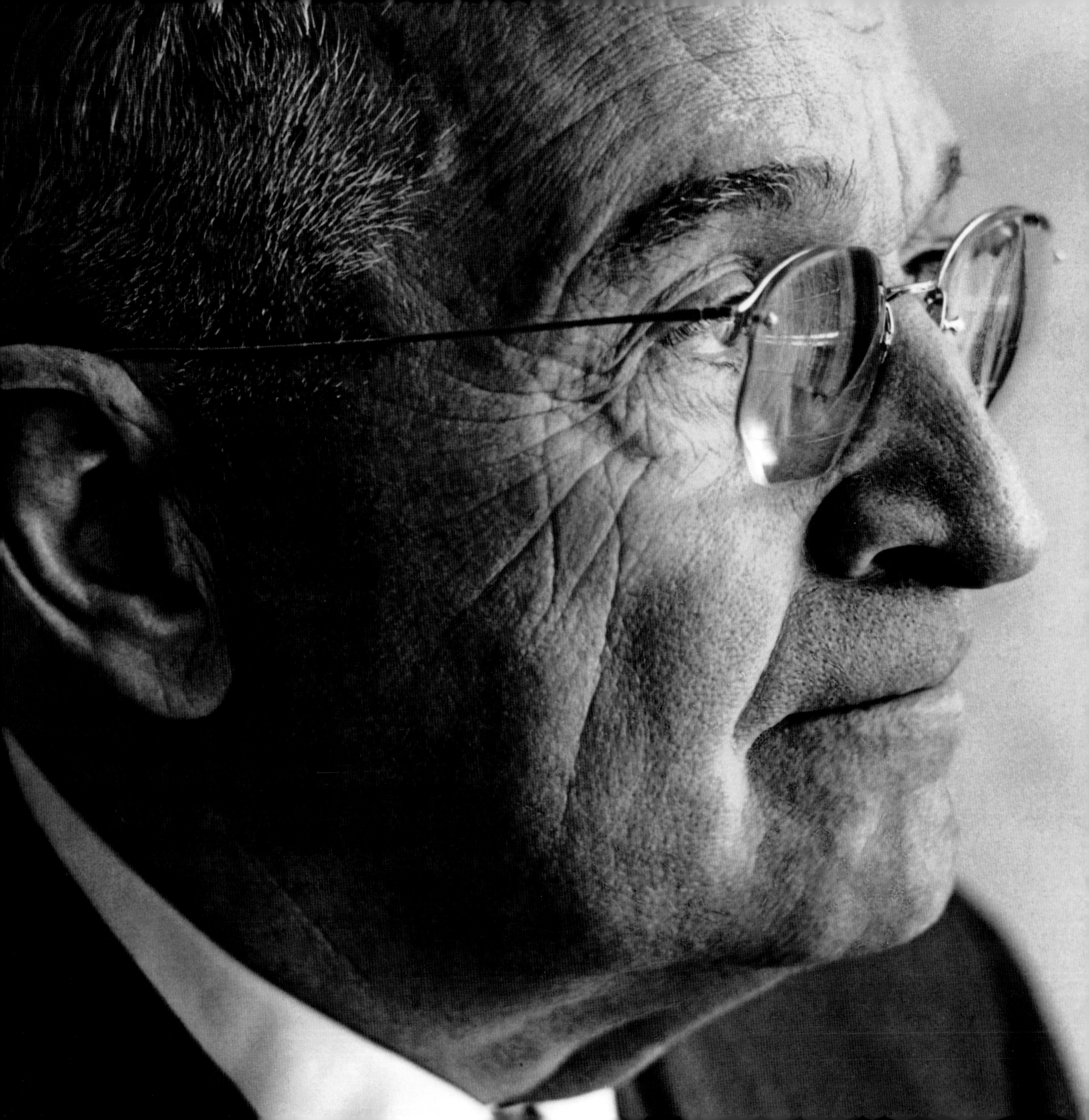

President Harry S. Truman,
New York City. Sept. 8, 1961.

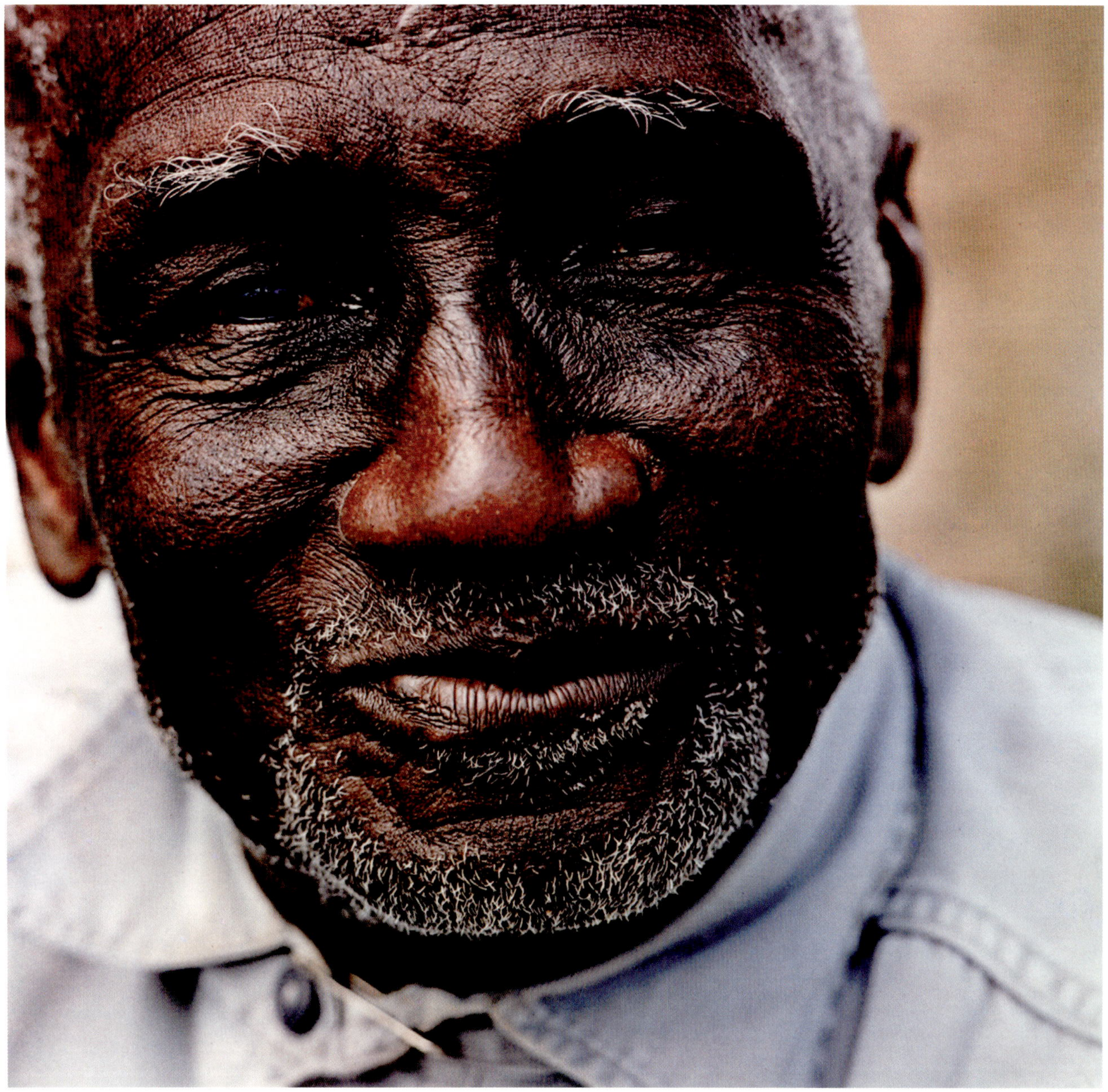

(above) Moses, the Old Wise Man of St. Croix, Virgin Islands. 1970.
(right) Coal Miner of the Ruhr Valley, Germany. 1967.

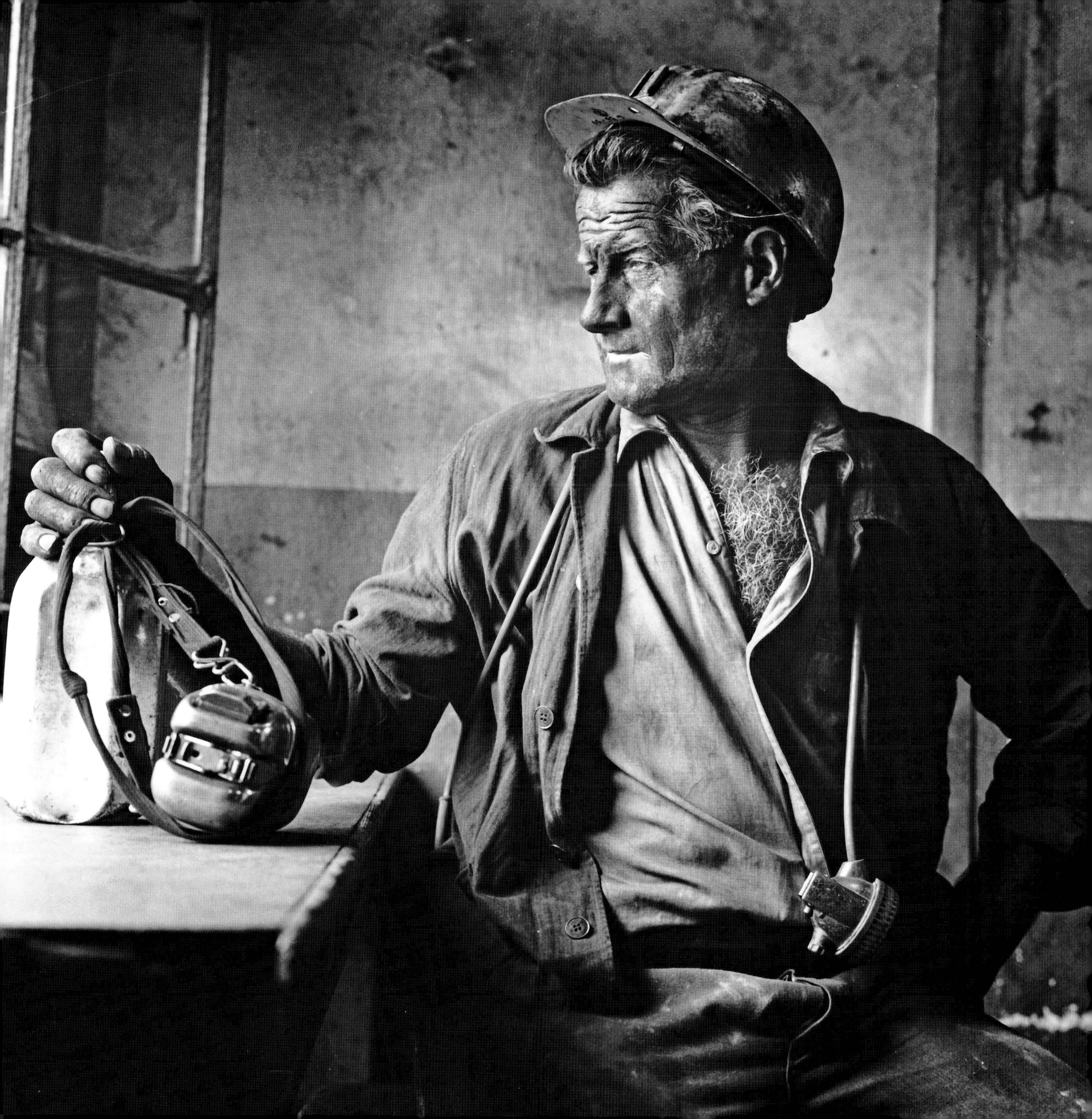

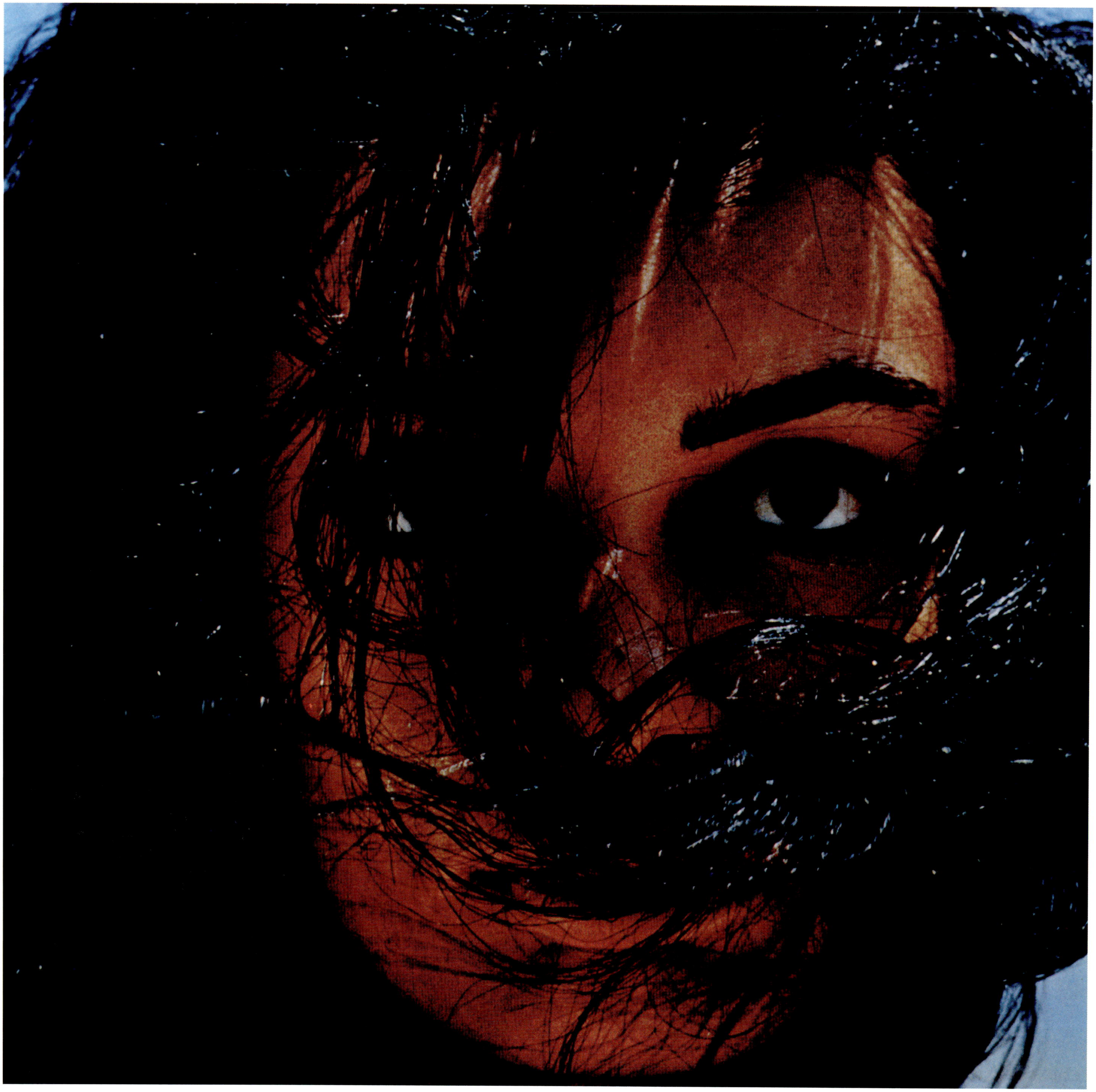

Diana, St. Croix, Virgin Islands. ca. 1968.

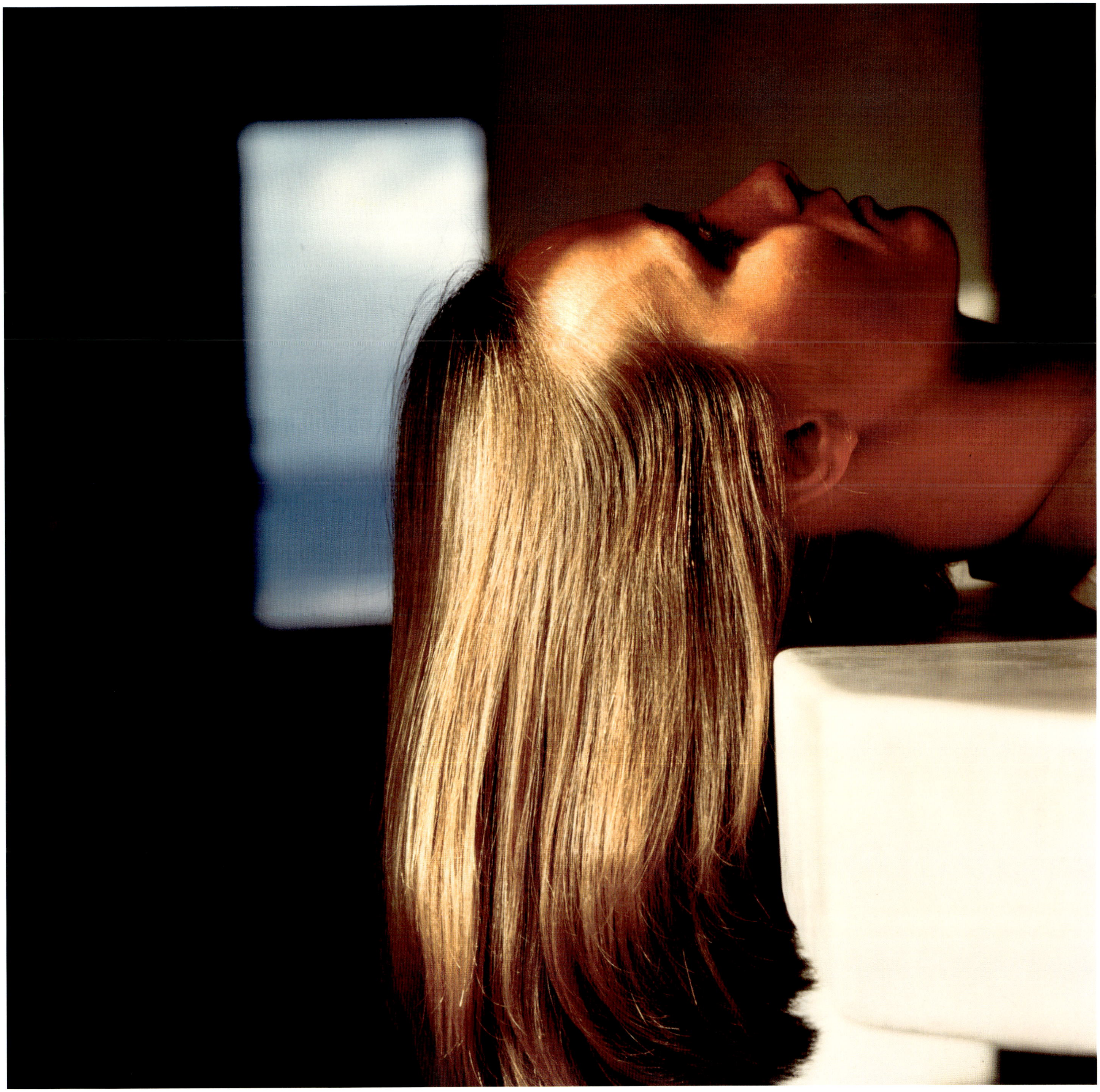

Susanne Jenkins, St. Croix, Virgin Islands. 1980.

Wisdom is the abstract of the past, but beauty is the promise of the future.

OLIVER WENDELL HOLMES

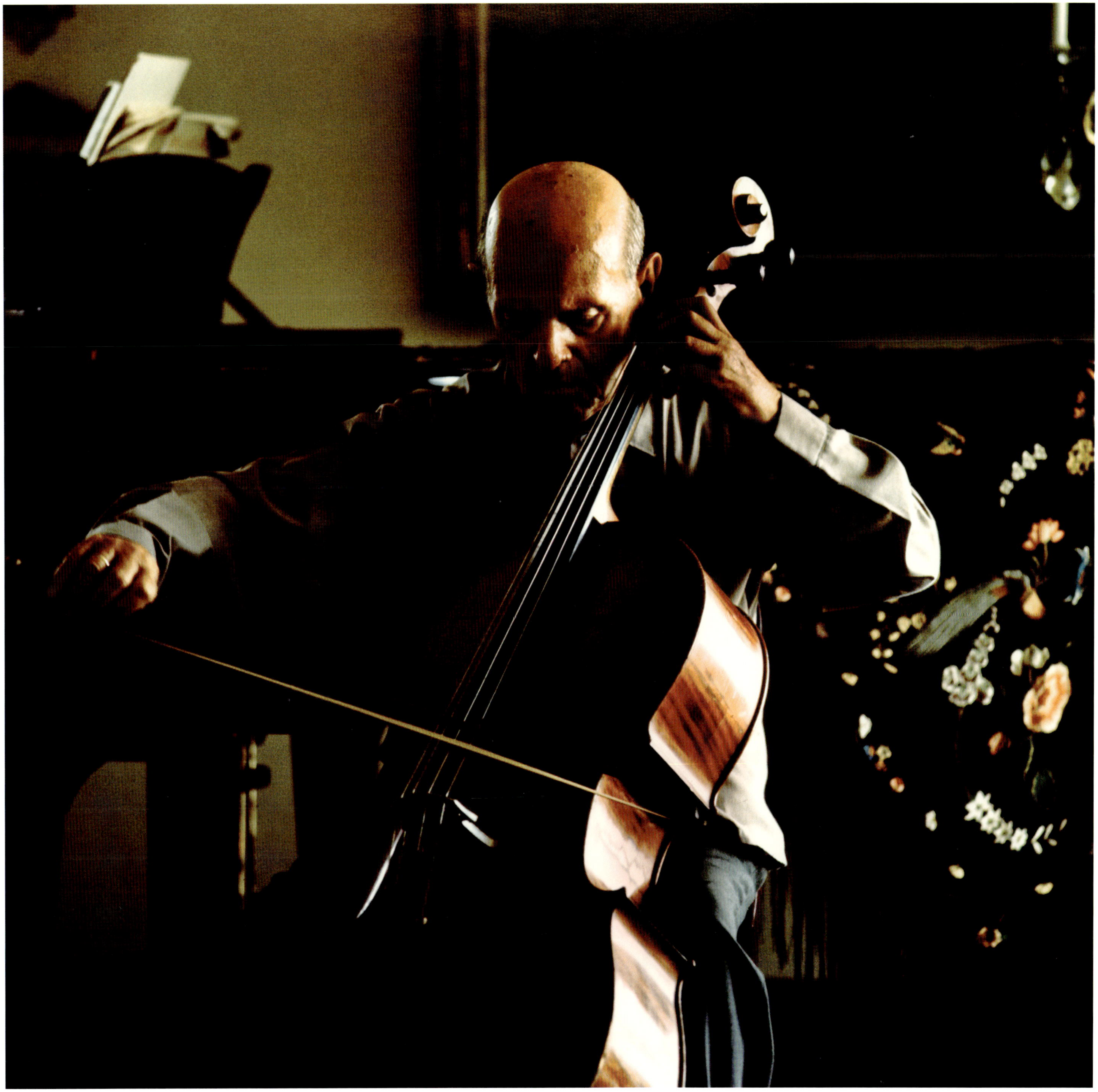

Pablo Casals Practicing in His Music Room at Calle Himalaya, Rio Piedras, Puerto Rico. 1982.

BIBLIOGRAPHY

1. *Publications by Fritz Henle: Books and Catalogues*

Manfred Schneider. *Rom. Mit 64 Abbildungen nach Aufnahmen von Fritz Henle.* Bielefeld & Leipzig: Velhagen & Klasing, 1935.

Photographs of the East by F.J. Henle: Rockefeller Center Mezzanine, November 4 to 10, 1936. New York: Burleigh Brooks & Black Star Publishing Co., Inc., 1936.

Fritz Henle. *Das Ist Japan. Volk und Landschaft.* [Text by Takayasu Senzoku. Translation by Leni Preetorius.] 1. bis 3. tausend. Harzburg: Heering Verlag, 1937.

Fritz Henle. *This Is Japan. Folk and Landscape.* [Text by Takayasu Senzoku.] Harzburg: Heering Verlag, 1937.

Kwok Ying Fung & Fritz Henle. *China. Photographs arranged and edited by Fritz Henle.* New York: Henry Holt, 1943.

Fritz Henle. *Mexico. 64 Photographs by Fritz Henle.* [Design by Alexey Brodovitch; Text by Nina Sesto.] Chicago & New York: Ziff-Davis, 1945.

Fritz Henle. *Mexico. 64 Photographs by Fritz Henle.* 2d printing. [Design by Alexey Brodovitch; Text by Nina Sesto.] Chicago & New York: Ziff-Davis, 1945.

Fritz Henle & Eliot Paul. *Paris.* [Designed by Alexey Brodovitch; Text by Jacquelyn Judge.] Chicago & New York: Ziff Davis, 1947.

Fritz Henle. *Hawaii.* [Text by Norman J. Wright.] New York: Hastings House, 1948.

Fritz Henle. *Virgin Islands.* [Text by Vivienne Tallal Winterry.] New York: Hastings House, 1949.

Fritz Henle. *Fritz Henle's Rollei. Photographs by Fritz Henle.* [Text by Vivienne Tallal Winterry.] New York: Hastings House, 1950.

Douglas A. Fisher. *Steel Serves the Nation 1901–1951. The Fifty Year Story of United States Steel.* [New York:] United States Steel Corporation, [1951]. ["Photographs of contemporary U.S. Steel operations by Fritz Henle."]

George van Riper & Fritz Henle. *Saint Croix, Virgin Islands.* [Printed by Triggs Color Printing Corp, New York. Christiansted:] George van Riper & Fritz Henle, 1952.

Fritz Henle. *Fritz Henle's Figure Studies.* [Introduction by Jacquelyn Judge.] New York & London: The Studio Publications, Inc., in association with Thomas Y. Crowell [Studio-Crowell], 1954.

Norman Hall & Basil Burton, eds. *Fritz Henle.* [Great Photographs, Volume 2.] London: Photography, [1954].

Fritz Henle. *Fritz Henle's Guide to Rollei Photography.* (With the editorial assistance of George B. Wright) New York & London: The Studio Publications, Inc., in association with Thomas Y. Crowell [Studio-Crowell], 1956.

Fritz Henle. *Fritz Henle's Figure Studies.* [Introduction by Jacquelyn Judge.] London: 1957.

Fritz Henle & P.E. Knapp. *The Caribbean: A Journey with Pictures.* New York: A Studio Book, The Viking Press, 1957.

[Erik & Jennie Lawaetz & Fritz Henle.] *St. Martin, Caribbean Island Gem: Photographs by Fritz Henle.* [Marigot?]: Island Gem Enterprise, [1958?]

Fritz Henle, with H.M Kinzer. *Mit den Augen Eines Rolleigrafen.* [Translated by Franz Pangerl.] Harzburg: Heering Verlag, 1958.

Fritz Henle, with H.M. Kinzer. *Photography for Everyone.* New York: A Studio Book, The Viking Press, [1959].

Fritz Henle & P.E. Knapp. *The Caribbean: A Journey with Pictures.* [Reissued with new material] New York: A Studio Book, The Viking Press, 1960.

Fritz Henle, with H.M. Kinzer. *Photography for Everyone.* [2d printing.] New York: A Studio Book, The Viking Press, [May 1960].

Fritz Henle. *Fritz Henle's Figure Studies.* [Introduction by Jacquelyn Judge.] New ed. New York: Bonanza Books [and The Viking Press], 1962.

Fritz Henle. *Holiday in Europe.* [Text by Anne Fremantle; Introduction by Patrick Dennis.] New York: A Studio Book, The Viking Press, 1963.

Fritz Henle. *Holiday in Europe.* [Text by Anne Fremantle; Introduction by Patrick Dennis.] London, Thames and Hudson, 1963.

Fritz Henle. *Holiday in Europe.* [Text by Anne Fremantle; Introduction by Patrick Dennis.] Canada, The Macmillan Company of Canada, 1963.

Fritz Henle. *Vacances en Europe.* [Text by Anne Freemantle; Introduction by Patrick Dennis.] Paris: Editions du Pont Royal [del Duca-Laffont], 1963.

Fritz Henle. *Vacanze in Europa.* [Text by Anne Freemantle; Introduction by Patrick Dennis.] Bergamo: Istituto Italiano d'Arti Grafiche, 1963.

Fritz Henle, with H.M. Kinzer. *Photography for Everyone.* [3d printing.] New York: A Studio Book, The Viking Press, [October 1963].

Fritz Henle. *Mit den Augen Eines Rolleigrafen.* [Text by Mike Kinzer; Translation by Franz Pangerl.] 1. bis 5. tausend. Seebruck am Chiemsee: Heering-Verlag, 1964.

Fritz Henle, with H.M. Kinzer. *Photography for Everyone.* [4th printing.] New York: A Studio Book, The Viking Press, [December 1964].

Fritz Henle. *A New Guide to Rollei Photography.* [With H.M. Kinzer.] New York: A Studio Book, The Viking Press, 1965.

Arts in the Virgin Islands. Charlotte Amalie: Virgin Islands Council on the Arts by the Caribbean Research Institute of the College of the Virgin Islands, 1967.

Fritz Henle, ed. *59th Annual National Governors' Conference / U.S. Virgin Islands 1967.* [Christiansted, Fritz Henle, 1968].

Fritz Henle. *The American Virgin Islands. A Photographic Essay by Fritz Henle.* [Introduction and captions by Ellis Gladwin.] New York: The Macmillan Company, 1971.

Fritz Henle. *The American Virgin Islands. A Photographic Essay by Fritz Henle.* [Introduction and captions by Ellis Gladwin. Special numbered ed. of 100.] New York: The Macmillan Company, 1971.

Fritz Henle. *Fotogalerie: Fritz Henle, USA. Auf der Suche nach dem Schönen. 40 Jahre Fotografie in Schwarz Weiss und Farbe.* Hamburg: Fotogalerie Staatliche Landesbildstelle, 1972.

Fritz Henle. *Fritz Henle.* [Introduction by Allan Porter.] Christiansted: Fritz Henle Publishing, 1973.

Alan H. Robinson with Fritz Henle. *Virgin Islands National Park. The Story Behind the Scenery.* Las Vegas: KC Publications, 1974.

Fritz Henle. *Casals. [Photographed by Fritz Henle].* [Afterword by Marta Casals.] Garden City, New York: American Photographic Book Publishing Co. [AMPHOTO], 1975.

Fritz Henle. *Casals.* Tübingen, Germany: WMP-Auslieferungsdienst GmbH, 1975.

Fritz Henle. *Casals.* Zurich: Neue Bücher AG, 1975.

Fritz Henle. *Casals.* Vienna: Danubia-Auslieferung, 1975.

Fritz Henle. *Casals.* Barcelona: Edicions Nauta, 1975.

L. Andrew Mannheim. *The Rolleiflex SL66 and SLX Way. With colour photographs by Fritz Henle.* London: Focal Press, 1975.

Fritz Henle. *Fritz Henle.* [Introduction by Allan Porter.] New York: 1975.

Fritz Henle. *Pablo Casals.* [Limited ed. of 100. Christiansted: Fritz Henle, 1976].

Fritz Henle. *Casals.* Tokyo: Shogakukan Publishing Co., 1977.

Alan H. Robinson with Fritz Henle. *Virgin Islands National Park. The Story Behind the Scenery.* 2d printing. Las Vegas: KC Publications, [1978?].

Fritz Henle. *Casals. Eine Bilderfolge von Fritz Henle.* Unterägeri-Zug, Sweden: Edition Sven Erik Bergh in der Europebuch AG, 1979.

Alan H. Robinson with Fritz Henle. *Virgin Islands National Park. The Story Behind the Scenery.* 3d printing. Las Vegas: KC Publications, 1982.

Fritz Henle. *Casals. [Fotografías de Fritz Henle].* [Afterword by Marta Casals; Translation by Mercedes Salisachs.] Málaga: Ediciones Sven Erik Bergh en Graficas Sorima, 1983.

Fritz Henle and Petra Benteler. *Fritz Henle.* [Introduction by Petra Benteler.] Houston: Benteler Galleries, 1983. ["…produced in celebration of the Tricentennial of German immigration into the United States…"]

Fritz Henle. *"Jubiläumskassette." [Fritz Henle und Rollei. 50 Jahre kongeniale Arbeit im Mittelformat.]* [Berlin]: Rollei Fototechnik, 1984.

Katharine R. Bailey, Gloria Bourne and Fritz Henle. *U.S. Virgin Islands: Jewels of the Caribbean.* Las Vegas: KC Publications, 1986.

Fritz Henle. *Paris von 50 Jahren.* [Texts by L. Fritz Gruber, Fritz Henle and Kurt Wettengl.] Heidelberg: Edition Braus, 1989.

Fritz Henle. *Paris 1938.* [Texts by L. Fritz Gruber, Fritz Henle and Kurt Wettengl.] Heidelberg: Edition Braus; [Paris:] Edition Hazan, 1989.

[Fritz Henle.] *Bilder aus Paris. 12 Postkarten.* Heidelberg: Edition Braus, 1989.

Fritz Henle. *United States Virgin Islands Landmarks. A Photographic Tour by Fritz Henle.* Christiansted: Virgin Islands Children's Seal Fund, 1992.

2. *Texts by Fritz Henle in Books and Catalogues*

Jacob Deschin. *Rollei Photography, Handbook of the Rolleiflex and Rolleicord Cameras* ("Chapter Sixteen: Fritz Henle on Travel," pp. 154–61). San Francisco: Camera Craft, [1962].

Jacob Deschin. *Rollei Photography, Handbook of the Rolleiflex and Rolleicord Cameras* ("Chapter Sixteen: Fritz Henle on Travel," pp. 154–61). 2d rev. printing. San Francisco: Camera Craft, [1963].

Willard D. Morgan, ed. *The Complete Photographer* v.1 ("Angle Shots and the Still Camera" pp. 188–93). New York: National Educational Alliance, Inc., 1942.

Willard D. Morgan, ed. *The Complete Photographer* v.5 ("Fashion Photography, Informal Fashion" pp. 1700–03). New York: National Educational Alliance, Inc., 1942.

Willard D. Morgan, general ed. *The Encyclopedia of Photography. The Complete Photographer: A Comprehensive Guide and Reference for All Photographers* v.1 ("Angle Shots and the Still Camera" pp. 133–138). New York, Toronto & London: Greystone Press, 1963–1970.

Colin Naylor, ed. *Contemporary Photographers* ("HENLE, Fritz"). Chicago & London: St. Martins Press, 1982.

Colin Naylor, ed. *Contemporary Photographers* ("HENLE, Fritz," pp. 433–36). 2nd ed. Chicago & London: St. James Press,1988.

Colin Naylor, ed. *Contemporary Photographers* ("HENLE, Fritz"). 3rd ed. Detroit: St. James Press, 1995.

H.S. Newcombe, ed. *The Twin-Lens Camera Companion.* New York City: Focal Press, Pitman Publishing Corp., 1949. [Other collaborators include Arnold Eagle, Andreas Feininger, Fritz Goro, Philippe Halsman, George Karger, Nelson Morris, Roy Pinney, W. Eugene Smith and Ylla.]

Claus Prochnow. *Rollei Report 1: Franke & Heidecke, Die ersten 25 Jahre* ("Vorwort" by Fritz Henle, p. 8). Stuttgart: Lindemanns Verlag, 1993.

George B. Wright, ed. *Available Light and your camera.* ("Available light around the world" by Fritz Henle, pp. 11–35). New York: American Photographic Book Publishing Co., [1955].

George B. Wright, ed. *Available Light and your camera.* ("Available light around the world" by Fritz Henle, pp. 11–35). 2d rev. ed. New York: American Photographic Book Publishing Co., [1958].

3. *Articles and Essays by Fritz Henle in Newspapers and Magazines*

Fritz Henle. "Der Palio in Siena." *Woche* (December 1933): 3–5.

Fritz Henle. "Indische Märchenbauten." [Periodical unidentified] ([1935?]): pages unknown.

Fritz Henle. "Ostern — Aber Japanisch!" *Hamburger Illustrierte* 12 (1936): 4.

Fritz Henle. "China: 8 Gesichter von 400 Millionen." *Hamburger Illustrierte* 24 [Summer 1936]: 4–5.

Fritz Henle. "Hohe Schule aüf der Bambusleiter." *Münchner Illustrierte Presse* 37 (1937): 1262–63.

[Fritz Henle.] [Advertisement.] "Photo Guide Section." *U.S. Camera*, 1, 10 (June–July 1940): 12.

[Fritz Henle.] [Advertisement.] "Photo Guide Section." *U.S. Camera*, 1, 11 (October 1940): 14.

[Fritz Henle.] [Advertisement.] "Photo Guide Section." *U.S. Camera*, 1, 12 (November 1940): 16.

[Fritz Henle.] [Advertisement.] "Photo Guide Section." *U.S. Camera*, 1, 14 (February 1941): 14.

[Fritz Henle.] [Advertisement.] "Photo Guide Section." *U.S. Camera*, 1, 15 (April–May 1941): 10.

Fritz Henle. "Pattern and Photography." *U.S. Camera* 1, 15 (April–May 1941): 44–45, 75.

Fritz Henle. "fritz henle on Shooting Color Roll Film." *Popular Photography* 23, 6 (December 1948): 74–77, 160, 162.

Fritz Henle. "High Key." *Rollei Jahrbuch der Rollei-Photographie / Rollei Annual of Rollei Photography 1953.* Vienna, Paris, London, New York (1953): 15–16.

Fritz Henle. "Karneval auf Trinidad." *Atlantis*, XXVI, 2 (February 1954): Front cover, 80–87.

Fritz Henle. "Figure Studies." *Camera*, 7, (July 1955): 344–[47].

Fritz Henle. "Travel & Camera." *U.S. Camera* 18, 9 (September 1955): 18–19.

Fritz Henle. "Travel & Camera." *U.S. Camera* 18, 11 (November 1955): 24–26.

Fritz Henle. "Travel & Camera." *U.S. Camera* 19, 1 (January 1956): 30–32.

Fritz Henle. "Travel & Camera." *U.S. Camera* 19, 3 (March 1956): 30, 38.

Fritz Henle. "Travel & Camera." *U.S. Camera* 19, 5 (May 1956): 42, 44.

Fritz Henle. "Travel & Camera." *U.S. Camera* 19, 7 (July 1956): 50.

Fritz Henle. "The Twin Lens Is Best for Me." [variant subtitle: "The Twin-Lens Reflex."] *U.S. Camera* 20, 1 (January 1957): 64–65. [Section of a larger article: "5 Experts Tell: What Type Camera To Buy," 60–68.]

Fritz Henle. "Fritz Henle talks about composing in the Square Format." *Popular Photography* 41, 1 (July 1957): 70–73.

[Fritz Henle.] "Why I Use 120." *Popular Photography* 41, 1 (July 1957): 76, 80.

Fritz Henle. "Die Inseln Saba und St. Eustatius: 10 Aufnahmen von Fritz Henle." *Atlantis* XXXI, 2 (February 1959): 69–75.

Fritz Henle. "The Human Form: Noted Lensmen Discuss Figure Studies." *U.S. Camera* 22, 3 (March 1959): 58.

Fritz Henle. "What's Wrong with a Square?" *Popular Photography* 46, 1 (January 1960): 20.

Fritz Henle. "Twelve Are Enough." *Popular Photography* 46, 2 (February 1960): 20.

Fritz Henle. "Shooting Pictures Sideways." *Popular Photography* 46, 3 (March 1960): 22.

Fritz Henle. "Can You Focus in the Dark?" *Popular Photography* 46, 4 (April 1960): 25.

Fritz Henle. "Down Where Children Live." *Popular Photography* 46, 5 (May 1960): 30.

Fritz Henle. "Two on One." *Popular Photography* 46, 6 (June 1960): 24, 101.
Fritz Henle. "Carry What You Need." *Popular Photography* 47, 1 (July 1960): 8.
Fritz Henle. "Big, Square Color." *Popular Photography* 47, 2 (August 1960): 26.
Fritz Henle. "Take Care of It!" *Popular Photography* 47, 3 (September 1960): 12.
Fritz Henle. "Just Like Watching A Movie." *Popular Photography* 47, 4 (October 1960): 26.
Fritz Henle. "How to Read A Contact Sheet." *Popular Photography* 47, 5 (November 1960): 30, 101.
Fritz Henle. "A Few Words from Readers." *Popular Photography* 47, 6 (December 1960): 40.
Fritz Henle. "Dogs, Cats, et Cetera." *Popular Photography* 48, 1 (January 1961): 28, 135.
Fritz Henle. "More about Squareness." *Popular Photography* 48, 2 (February 1961): 22.
Fritz Henle. "Tips for Bad-Weather Shooting." *Popular Photography* 48, 3 (March 1961): 16.
Fritz Henle. "How To 'Make Sure.'" *Popular Photography* 48, 4 (April 1961): 18.
Fritz Henle. "Put It in A Frame." *Popular Photography* 48, 5 (May 1961): 22.
Fritz Henle. "When Is A Subject 'Ready'?" *Popular Photography* 48, 6 (June 1961): 20.
Fritz Henle. "Keys to Non-Disappointment." *Popular Photography* 49, 1 (July 1961): 80.
Fritz Henle. "Watch the Light!" *Popular Photography* 49, 2 (August 1961): 12.
Fritz Henle. "Portrait Rapport." *Popular Photography* 49, 3 (September 1961): 20.
Fritz Henle. "How Fast Can You Load?" *Popular Photography* 49, 4 (October 1961): 14.
Fritz Henle. "Men at Work." *Popular Photography* 49, 5 (November 1961): 24.
Fritz Henle. "Wide-Angle and Tele Reflexes." *Popular Photography* 49, 6 (December 1961): 20.
Fritz Henle. "Fritz Henle Photographer." *Service*, (January 1962): 12–15
Fritz Henle. "Natural Nudes." *Popular Photography* 50, 1 (January 1962): 22.
Fritz Henle. "Landscapes: Top, Middle, and Bottom." *Popular Photography* 50, 2 (February 1962): 20.
Fritz Henle. "The Which and How of Filters." *Popular Photography* 50, 3 (March 1962): 70.
Fritz Henle. "The 'Different' Portrait." *Popular Photography* 50, 4 (April 1962): 26.
Fritz Henle. "Helicopters and Other Birds." *Popular Photography* 50, 5 (May 1962): 12.
Fritz Henle. "What photography means to me." *Popular Photography* 50, 5 (May 1962): 91.
Fritz Henle. "Children Again—By Request." *Popular Photography* 50, 6 (June 1962): 140.
Fritz Henle. "Outdoor 'Still Lifes.'" *Popular Photography* 51, 2 (August 1962): 30.
Fritz Henle. "Kodacolor—and Related Matters." *Popular Photography* 51, 3 (September 1962): 18.
Fritz Henle. "The Projected Image." *Popular Photography* 51, 4 (October 1962): 14.
Fritz Henle. "Is Composition Old-Fashioned?" *Popular Photography* 51, 5 (November 1962): 30.
Fritz Henle. "Working with Subjects in Depth." *Popular Photography* 51, 6 (December 1962): 16.
Fritz Henle. "Flash—with Forethought." *Popular Photography* 52, 1 (January 1963): 28.
Fritz Henle. "A Tripod? Yes, When You Can." *Popular Photography* 52, 3 (March 1963): 16.
Fritz Henle. "When to Depart from the Square." *Popular Photography* 52, 4 (April 1963): 20.
Fritz Henle. "Lebenslauf Eines Rolleigrafen." *Rolleigrafie*, 1 (April-June 1963): 6–13.
Fritz Henle. "Other People's Babies." *Popular Photography* 52, 5 (May 1963): 30.
Fritz Henle. "What If You're Not Seven Feet Tall?" *Popular Photography* 52, 6 (June 1963): 24.
Fritz Henle. "Animals Around You." *Popular Photography* 53, 7 (July 1963): 28.
Fritz Henle. "Reaching Four Times As Far." *Popular Photography* 53, 8 (August 1963): 18.
Fritz Henle. "Camera...Action!" *Popular Photography* 53, 3 (September 1963): 28.
Fritz Henle. "Light from Behind." *Popular Photography* 53, 4 (October 1963): 16.
Fritz Henle. "Vary Viewpoint with Sportsfinder." *Popular Photography* 53, 5 (November 1963): 56.
Fritz Henle. "TLR: Today's Portrait & Press Camera?" *Popular Photography* 53, 6 (December 1963): 40.
Fritz Henle. "Distortion for Dramatic Effect." *Popular Photography* 53, 1 (January 1964): 30.
Fritz Henle. "Now — Ten-Second Rollei Pictures." *Popular Photography* 54, 3 (March 1964): 32.
Fritz Henle. "Mutars: One Rollei Becomes Three." *Popular Photography* 54, 4 (April 1964): 32.
Fritz Henle. "Extra-Close Portraits." *Popular Photography* 54, 5 (May 1964): 34.
Fritz Henle. "The View from Eighty Feet up." *Popular Photography* 54, 6 (June 1964): 40.
Fritz Henle. "Focusing for the Next Picture." *Popular Photography* 55, 3 (September 1964): 36.
Fritz Henle. "Mode im Freien." *Rolleigrafie* (date unknown): 31–35.
Fritz Henle. [Title unidentified.] *Rolleigrafie* (March 1964): [1 p.].
Fritz Henle. "Mein Weg zum Akt." *Rolleigrafie* (date unknown): 25–27.
Fritz Henle. "Meine kleinen Freunde." *Rolleigrafie* 13 (June 1966): Front cover, 8–13.
Fritz Henle. "The Virgin Islands." *Camera* 48, 6 (June 1969): Front cover, 2–7.
Fritz Henle. "Suche nach dem Schönen. [Farbforum der Spitzenfotografen (Folde 14)]." *Westerman*, (2/1970): 52–57.
Fritz Henle. "Correspondence." *The St. Croix Avis* 114 (May 22, 1975): [1 p.].
Fritz Henle. "Amerika, Ein Thema in Variationen." *Foto Magazin* (February 1986): [1 p.].
Fritz Henle. "'Paris 1938': A Story in Pictures for 'Life' Magazine." *The Library Chronicle of The University of Texas at Austin* n.s. 48 (1989): 108–21.

4. *Photographs by Fritz Henle as Published in Books by Others*

Katharine R. Bailey and Gloria Bourne. *US Virgin Islands, Jewels of the Caribbean.* K.C. Publications, 1986.
[Miles Barth, ed.] *Master Photographs: Master Photographs from the PFA Exhibitions, 1959–67.* New York: International Center of Photography, 1988.
Best National Advertising of the Year 1949–1950, Vol. 2. Chicago: Milline, 1950.
Anita Brenner and George R. Leighton. *The Wind That Swept Mexico.* New York & London: Harper & Brothers, [1st – 4th eds.] 1943.
Anita Brenner and George R. Leighton. *The Wind That Swept Mexico.* Austin: University of Texas Press, 1971.
Anita Brenner and George R. Leighton. *The Wind That Swept Mexico.* Austin: University of Texas Press, 1996.
Casals Hall. ["Casals Album," Photographs by Fritz Henle.] Tokyo: Shufunotamo, Auftakt, 1987.
Heyworth Campbell, comp. and ed. *Camera Around the World.* New York: Robert M. McBride and Co., [1937].
Malcolm Naea Chun. *Ho'oponopono, Traditional Ways of Healing to Make Things Right Again.* Honolulu: Curriculum Research and Development Group, University of Hawaii, 2006.
Cities Service Oil Company. *Lake Charles Refinery.* [New York: 1956?].
Cities Service Oil Company. *Many Doors Are Open for Your Future at Cities Service.* [New York: 1959?].
Merle Crowell, ed. *The Last Rivet: The Story of Rockefeller Center, a City Within a City, as Told at the Ceremony in Which John D. Rockefeller, Jr., Drove the last Rivet of the Last building, November 1, 1939.* New York: Columbia University Press, 1940.
Roy Flukinger. *Photography: The First 150 Years.* Austin: Texas Photographic Society and Harry Ransom Humanities Research Center, 1989.
Tom Follet, Dick Newick and Jim Morris. *Project Cheers: A New Concept in Design.* London: Adlard Coles, 1969.
Fr[ederick]. Willy Frerk, ed. *Photofreund Jahrbuch 1938.* Berlin: Photokino-Verlag Helmut Elsner K.-G., 1937: 44.
Friedrich Grassegger and Fritz Simak. *Landscape, Two Collections. Three Centuries of Photography.* Vienna: Christian Brandstetter, 2008: 206, 209.
L. Fritz Gruber, ed. *Beauty: Variations on the Theme WOMAN by Masters of the Camera — Past and Present.* London: Focal Press, 1965: 92.
L. Fritz Gruber, ed. *Sammlung Gruber: Photographie des 20. Jahrhunderts.* Cologne: Museum Ludwig, 1984.
Frederic V. Grunfeld. *Pablo Casals.* ["Great Performers" series.] Alexandria, Virginia: Time-Life Records, 1982.
Norman Hall, ed. *Photography Year Book 1962.* London: Photography Magazine, 1961: 84.
Norman Hall and Basil Burton, eds. *Photography Year Book 1955.* London: Photography Magazine, 1954: 132.
Norman Hall and Basil Burton, eds. *Photography Year Book 1956.* London: Photography Magazine, 1955: 132.
Norman Hall and Basil Burton, eds. *Photography Year Book 1957.* London: Photography Magazine, 1956: 89.
Norman Hall and Basil Burton, eds. *Photography Year Book 1958.* London: Photography Magazine, 1957: 17.
Norman Hall and Basil Burton, eds. *Photography Year Book 1959.* London: Photography Magazine, 1958: 4.
Norman Hall and Basil Burton, eds. *Photography Year Book 1960.* London: Photography Magazine, 1959: 48.
Norman Hall and Helmut Gernsheim, eds. *Photography Year Book 1954.* London: Photography Magazine, 1953: 127, 133.
[Manfred Heiting.] *50 Jahre Moderne Farbfotografie; 50 Years Modern Color Photography, 1936–1986.* Frankfurt: Photokina, 1986.
Mackinley Helm. *Man of Fire: Jose Clemente Orozco.* New York: Harcourt, Brace and Co. 1953.
Henry R. Hope. *Georges Braque.* New York: The Museum of Modern Art, in collaboration with The Cleveland Museum of Art, 1949.
Ian James, ed. *Photography Year Book 1965.* London: Photography Magazine, 1964: 74.
Clarence Kennedy. *Studies in the History and Criticism of Sculpture.* 7 vols. New York & Northampton, MA: 1928–1932.
Ruth Wedgwood Kennedy. *Alesso Baldorinetti: A Critical and Historical Study.* New Haven: Yale University Press, 1938.
Heinrich Kreisel. *Deutsche Land, Deutsche Kunst.* Bielefeld: 1934.
Ed Lange. *Nudes in Color.* NY: Lyle Stuart, 1966.
Harold Lewis, ed., and Helmut Gernsheim, assoc. ed. *Photography Year Book 1952.* London: Photography Magazine, [1951?]: 56, 111.
Harold Lewis, ed., and Helmut Gernsheim, assoc. ed. *Photography Year Book 1953.* London: Photography Magazine, [1952?]: 127, 129.
T.J. Maloney, ed. *U.S. Camera 1940.* New York: Random House, ©1939: 142, 244, 246.
T.J. Maloney, ed. *U.S. Camera 1941: Volume II, "The Year's Photography."* [Pictures Judged by Edward Steichen.] New York, Duell, Sloan and Pearce, 1940: 88, 134.
T.J. Maloney, ed. *U.S. Camera 1942.* [Pictures Judged by Edward Steichen.] New York: Duell, Sloan & Pearce, ©1941: front dust jacket, 97.
T.J. Maloney, ed. *U.S. Camera 1943.* [Photo Judge: Lt. Comdr. Edward Steichen, USNR.] New York: Duell, Sloan & Pearce, ©1942: 118–119.
T.J. Maloney, ed. *The U.S.A. at War: U.S. Camera 1944.* [Photographs selected by Commander Edward Steichen, U.S.N.R.] New York: Duell, Sloan & Pearce, ©1943: 92.
Tom Maloney, ed. *U.S. Camera Annual 1948.* New York: U.S. Camera Publishers, ©1947: 240.
Tom Maloney, ed. *U.S. Camera Annual 1949.* New York: U.S. Camera Publishers, ©1948: 190.
Tom Maloney, ed. *U.S. Camera Annual 1951, American-International.* New York: U.S. Camera Publishers, ©1950: 282.
Tom Maloney, ed. *U.S. Camera Annual 1952.* New York: U.S. Camera Publishers, ©1951: 99.
Tom Maloney, ed. *U.S. Camera Annual 1953.* New York: U.S. Camera Publishers, ©1952: 214–216.
Tom Maloney, ed. *U.S. Camera Annual 1956.* New York: U.S. Camera Publishers, ©1955: 112.
R. Ottwil Maurer, ed. *Photofreund Jahrbuch 1939.* Berlin: Photokino-Verlag Helmut Elsner K.-G., 1938: 65.
Metropolitan Museum of Art. *2007 Calendar.* New York: Metropolitan Museum of Art, 2006.
Ruth S. Moore and David M. Hough. *Arts in the U.S. Virgin Islands. A Supplement to the Virgin Islands Council on the Arts Study Report.* [Christiansted?:] Caribbean Research Institute of the College of the Virgin Islands, 1967.
Willard D. Morgan, ed. *The Complete Photographer* v.8 New York: National Educational Alliance, Inc., 1942: 3021.
G. Müller-Gaisberg. *Volk nach der Arbeit.* Berlin: 1936.
Larraine Nicholas. *Dancing in Utopia: Dartington Hall and Its Dancers.* Alton, UK: Dance Books Ltd., 2007.
1959 Photography Annual. New York: Popular Photography, 1958: 153, 218.
[North German Lloyd Line.] *Kreuzfahrt in Mittelmeer.* [Bremen: 1931?].
PHOTO-GRAPHIC '49: Annual of the American Society of Magazine Photographers. New York: Whittlesey House, 1948.
Photography Annual, 1951 Edition: A Selection of the World's Greatest Photographs, by the Editors of Popular Photography. New York: Popular Photography, [1950]: 68, 140, 201.
Photography Annual, 1952. Chicago: Ziff-Davis, 1951.
Photography Annual, 1952 Edition: A Selection of the World's Greatest Photographs, by the Editors of Popular Photography. New York: Popular Photography, [1951]: 63, 247.
Photography Annual, 1953. Chicago: Ziff-Davis, 1952.
Photography Annual, 1953 Edition. New York: Popular Photography, 1952: 36.
Photography Annual, 1954. Chicago: Ziff-Davis, 1953.
Photography Annual, 1954: A Selection of the World's Greatest Photographs Compiled by the Editors of Popular Photography. New York: Popular Photography, 1953: 153, 218.
Elena Poniatowska. *Frida Kahlo: The Camera Seduced.* San Francisco: Chronicle Books, 1992.
Herbert Rittlinger. *Das Aktfoto, Problem und Praxis.* Düsseldorf, Wilhelm Knapp, [1960].
Alan H. Robinson. *Virgin Islands National Park, The Story Behind the Scenery.* K.C.Publications, 1974.
Rollei Jahrbuch der Rollei-Photographie / Rollei Annual of Rollei Photography: Edition 1952. Vienna, Paris, London, New York (1952): 40, 48, 71.
Rollei Jahrbuch der Rollei-Photographie / Rollei Annual of Rollei Photography 1953. Vienna, Paris, London, New York (1953): 16, 17.
Société Parisienne d'Editions Artistiques. *Nus. Photographies Originales de Savitry, F. Henle, Theda et Emerson Hall. Album No. 10.* Paris: [1950].
Otto Steinert, ed. *Akt International / International Nudes.* Munich & London: Bruder Auer Verlag, 1954.
Otto Steinert, ed. *Subjektive Fotografie 2.* Saarbrucken, Schule für Kunst und Handwerk, 1955.
Stern Magazine. *Woman. 2nd World Exhibition of Photography.* Hamburg, Gruner & Jahr: 1968.
Guido van Rijn. *Roosevelt's Blues: African-American Blues and Gospel Songs on FDR.* Jackson, MS: University Press of Mississippi, 1997.
Robert Vaughn. *In the Shadow of Trinity*: Manhattan, Kansas: Sunflower Press, 1991.
W.B. Williams, ed. and publ. *The American Annual of Photography 1953.* Vol. 67. New York, American Photography Book Department, 1953: 104, 109.
The World's Best Photographs. New York, Wise & Co., 1940: 165, 174, 250, 281.

5. *Photographs by Fritz Henle as Published in Selected Newspapers and Magazines*

The albums found in the Henle Family Archive contain hundreds of clippings and tearsheets from a wide variety of foreign and domestic periodicals. Assembled by Henle between the late 1920s and the 1950s, most bear little bibliographical reference as to the name, date or specific pagination of the illustrated article. Indeed, in too many instances Henle often saved only the copy of his reproduced images without recording their source. By rough estimate there may be close to 2,000 extant examples of Henle photographs having been reproduced in twentieth century magazines, journals and newspapers. — RF]

1928 *Westermanns Monatshefte. [Westermann's Monts-Hefte.]* (1928): [1 p.]. [This industrial landscape photograph of the steel mill outside of Dortmund was the first image of Henle's that was ever published.]

1931 *Münchner Illustriete.* [Munich] (1931): [1 p.]. [Henle's first published periodical image — *Policeman in the Rain on the Odeons-Platz.]*

Lloyd Zeitung, Monatsschrift des Norddeutschen Lloyd Bremen XXIII, 11. [Bremen] (November 1931): front cover.

1933 Lloyd Triestino. *Jubeljahr 1933.* [Trieste] (1933): front cover.

Alessandro Mombelli. "Gerusalemme Antica: Il Moriah e la Spianata del Tempio di Salomone." *L'Illustrazione Italiana* ([1933?]): [4 pp.].

1934 *Neue Woche* (June 23, 1934): Front cover.

1935 "Following the Sunlight Around the Mediterranean." *Travel* (February 1935): pages unknown. [Photographs by Fritz Henle and Paul Wolff.]

Bayerische Radio Zeitung und Bayernfunk 28 (July 7, 1935): front cover.

Umberto V. Cavassa. "Gioia de crociera." [Periodical unidentified] (1935): [12 pp.].

Grete Margaretha. "Das bunte Palermo." [Periodical unidentified] (1935): [4 pp.].

1936 "At the Foot of Mt. Fuji." *NIPPON* 6 (1936): 22–23.

"The Photographers of Japan." *Fortune* XIV, 9 (September 1936): 16–17. [Henle ms. note in his collection copy: "My first assignment for U.S.A. — my new country."]

"The Gentlemen of Japan." *Fortune* XIV, 9 (September 1936): 59–66, 166–72.

"No Left Turn." *Fortune* XIV, 9 (September 1936): 95–106.

1937 Fritz Rumpf. "Symbol im Spiel." *die neue linie* 5, VIII (January 1937): 45–47, 99.

Globe (January [1937?]): Front cover.

Lloyd Zeitung XXIX, 5 (May 1937): Front cover.

News-Week (August 28, 1937): Front cover.

"The Japanese: The World's Most Conventional People." *LIFE* 3, 9 (August 30, 1937): 41.

The Fight (October 1937): Front cover.

"The American Legion Takes New York City." *LIFE* 3, 14 (October 4, 1937; 23–36.

"People." *LIFE* 3, 16 (October 18, 1937): 48.

"Life Goes to a Party, With Café Society at the Opening of two Night Clubs." *LIFE* 3, 16 (October 18, 1937): 114–120.

"Life on the American Newsfront: Hairdressers and Milliners Battle over Curls." *LIFE* 3, 17 (October 25, 1937): 34.

"Movies: Danielle Darrieux Acts for U.S. with Her Mouth." *LIFE* 3, 17 (October 25, 1937): 59–61.

"*LIFE's* Pictures." *LIFE* 3, 17 (October 25, 1937): 112.

"The Game: An Old Pastime Which Is Sweeping America in New Versions." *LIFE* 3, 19 (November 8, 1937): 89–90.

"And Many A Lightship Lad." *LIFE* 3, 20 (November 15, 1937): Front cover.

"Anything Goes as A Hat for A Woman." *LIFE* 3, 21 (November 22, 1937): 82.

"Memo To: Walter Wanger, Subject: 52nd Street; Photographs for *LIFE* by Fritz Henle." *LIFE* 3, 22 (November 29, 1937): 64–67.

"1937 Closes with Big Apple." *LIFE* 3, 25 (December 20, 1937): 32.

"Life Goes to a Party: With the children of Hollywood for the Children of Spain: Photographs for *LIFE* by Fritz Henle." *LIFE* 3, 25 (December 20, 1937): 70–72.

"Deanna Durbin Has A Birthday Party." *LIFE* 3, 25 (December 20, 1937): 74.

"Alle Puppen Tanzin." *Illustrieter Rundfunk* 51 (December 1937): 35.

1938 "Hollywood Keeps Fit — Or Else." *LIFE* 4, 2 (January 10, 1938): 24–25.

"Letters to the Editor: American Creation." *LIFE* 4, 6 (February 7, 1938): 2.

"Texas High-School Girls." *LIFE* 4, 10 (March 7, 1938): Front cover.

"One American High School: The Thomas Jefferson of San Antonio." *LIFE* 4, 10 (March 7, 1938): 22–29.

"Mexico: Can A Socialist at Home Be A Good Neighbor Abroad?" *LIFE* 4, 15 (April 11, 1938): 51, 55, 57–58.

"Life looks at Summer Sports Clothes." *LIFE* 4, 19 (May 9, 1938): 17, 20, 21, 24, 25.

"Fascism: Inside Italy There Is Also the Corporative State." *LIFE* 4, 19 (May 9, 1938): 33.

[Title unidentified: Article on Hollywood stars.] *The Bystander* (June 8, 1938): [2 pp.].

The Illustrated Sporting and Dramatic News (June 17, 1938): Front cover.

"Danielle Darrieux. She came from France to become the rage of Hollywood." *LIFE* 5, 1 (July 4, 1938): 39. ["Recognizing in Danielle Darrieux a new type of beauty, *LIFE* sent Photographer Fritz Henle about New York with her."]

"Released for Publication." *LIFE* 5, 4 (July 25, 1938): 54.

"Cardinal Hayes Entombed in Own Cathedral's Crypt." *LIFE* 5, 12 (September 19, 1938): 19.

Noel F. Busch. "A Loud Cheer for the Screwball Girl." *LIFE* 5, 16 (October 17, 1938): 49, 51.

"Modern Living: A New Epoch Sets in for Muffs; History Shows They Presage War." *LIFE* 5, 17 (October 24, 1938): 64–65.

"American Art comes of age." *LIFE* 5, 18 (October 31, 1938): 29.

"On Parade: America's Favorite Industry." *LIFE* 5, 20 (November 14, 1938): 24.

"Pitt's Unfinished Cathedral." *LIFE* 5, 20 (November 14, 1938): 52–53.

"Palace Show for Princesses' New Dolls." *Weekly Illustrated* (December 10, 1938): [1 p.].

"At Curtis Institute Great Teachers Nurture Talent." *LIFE* 5, 24 (December 12, 1938): 54–55.

"Make A Bow for Your Hair." *The Daily Mail* (December 23, 1938): [1 p.].

"Tasco. Erlebnis einer mexikanischen Stadt." *Hamburger Anzeiger* ([1938?]): [2 pp.].

1939 "Damon Runyon Says These Miami Girls Have the Glamor New York Debs Lack." *LIFE* 6, 2 (January 9, 1939): 10–11.

"Educated Like A Rich Man's Son Marsh Prefers to Paint Poor Men." *LIFE* 6, 2 (January 9, 1939): 24.

"Modern Living: Men on Southern Beaches Vie with Girls in Colorful Apparel." *LIFE* 6, 3 (January 16, 1939): 41.

Morris Gilbert. "Crosstown, New York." *Radio Times* (January 20, 1939): 11.

"Modern Living: Washington's Peruke Sets A Style." *LIFE* 6, 6 (February 6, 1939): 37.

"Cruise Girls at Paradise Beach." *LIFE* 6, 9 (February 27, 1939): Front cover.

"Two Little Girls on A Cruise." *LIFE* 6, 9 (February 27, 1939): 48–55.

"Sports: Patty Berg at College Still Lives for Golf." *LIFE* 6, 21 (May 22, 1939): 46, 48.

"Life goes bicycling with young socialites up in Maine." *LIFE* 7, 3 (July 17, 1939): 70–73.

"Beautiful Before Breakfast!" *The Leader* (July 22, 1939): 27.

"Diana Barrymore." *LIFE* 7, 5 (July 31, 1939): Front cover.

"[Summer Theater:] Diana Barrymore Acts in Royal Family Style." *LIFE* 7, 5 (July 31, 1939): 56.

"Summer Theater: Off-Stage Comedy." *LIFE* 7, 5 (July 31, 1939): 60.

"Sports: Pretty Girls Set Records at National Swimming Meet." *LIFE* 7, 7 (August 14, 1939): 58–59.

Noel F. Busch. "The Week the War Began: *LIFE* presents a retrospective close-up of the last days of an American era." *LIFE* 7, 12 (September 18, 1939): 74.

"War & Fashions." *LIFE* 7, 17 (October 23, 1939): Front cover.

"Modern Living: War & Fashions: Its effect on women's styles is great but unpredictable." *LIFE* 7, 17 (October 23, 1939): 49–52.

"Life goes to Dali's new Ballet: A surrealist 'Bacchanale' with a mad Bavarian and a Venus in white tights." *LIFE* 7, 22 (November 27, 1939): 90–93.

"'Angels' of 'Negro Heaven.'" *The World's Womankind.* (1939?): [1 p.].

"Jeu nesse Americane: Beauté. Grace. Fraicheur, dans un college du Texas." *Regards* (1939?): Front cover; pages unknown.

"Die Grosse Chinesische Mauer." *Hamburger Anzeiger* (1939?): Front cover.

1940 "Life goes on a Skiing Weekend, in the White Mountains of New Hampshire with girl who can't ski." *LIFE* 8, 8 (February 19, 1940): 86–89.

"Salon Section: Men and Guns." *Popular Photography* VI, 2 (February 1940): 46.

"Season's Choice: The Ballet Bows to the Golden Horseshoe." *Dance* 7, 4 (March 1940): 12–13.

"The Annual Ballet Ball." *Dance* 7, 4 (March 1940): 14–19.

"The Two Newest Ballets of Kurt Joos." *Dance* 7, 4 (March 1940): 28–33.

"Miami & Miami Beach: Biggest U.S. winter resort has biggest boom. Photographs for *LIFE* by Alfred Eisenstaedt; color by Fritz Henle." *LIFE* 8, 10 (March 4, 1940): 60–67.

"Nightmare Inspires Ballet." *Everybody's Weekly* (March 9, 1940): 22–23.

"Modern Living: Bonnets with Fruit, Long Jacket Suits for Easter." *LIFE* 8, 12 (March 18, 1940): 69–70.

"White Collar Girl: Research notes for Ginger Rogers' film version of Christopher Morley's best-selling novel, Kitty Foyle." *LIFE* 8, 13 (March 25, 1940): 81–87. [Joint assignment with Alfred Eisenstaedt.]

Theatre Life (April 1940): Front cover.

"Modern Living: Summer Styles, Fashion Swings to simplicity as Paris Concentrates on War." *LIFE* 8, 21 (May 20, 1940): 63–65. [Joint assignment with Alfred Eisenstaedt.]

"1940 Fair Features Fun & Folksy Informal Charm." *LIFE* 8, 22 (May 27, 1940): 32–33. [Also features photographs by Eliot Elisofon.]

Hazel K. Wharton. "Lead A Model Life." *Better Living* (June 1940): 14–17.

"Any Place the Old Flag Flies. [A photo lyric of the U.S.A....]" *U.S. Camera* 1, 10 (June–July 1940): 22–50. [Includes 4 Henle photos: 26, 33.]

Edgar Laytha. "House of Fifty Nations." *Harper's Bazaar* (August 1940): 82–83, 100.

["Furs."] *Harper's Bazaar* (August 1940): 86–87.

"Leaves from Freshmen Bibles." *Harper's Bazaar* (August 1940): 90–91.

"Vacations: Yellowstone 'Savages' Work for Their Fun." *LIFE* 9, 6 (August 5, 1940): 68–69.

"Modern Living: New Hats Restore Foreheads and Eyesight to Women." *LIFE* 9, 6 (August 5, 1940): 82–83. [Also features photographs by Francis Miller.]

"Modern Living: College Girls in Men's Clothing, Masculine Togs Invade Campus." *LIFE* 9, 14 (September 30, 1940): 41–42.

[Advertisement.] Agfa Ansco. *Popular Photography* VII, 3 (September 1940): [2].

["Salon Section:] Vacation." *Popular Photography* VII, 3 (September 1940): 42.

"Salon Section." *Popular Photography* VII, 4 (October 1940): 43.

Stanley Marcus. "You Buy Furs..." *Harper's Bazaar* ([October?] 1940): 15–17.

"This Is Work at Colorado Springs Fine Arts Center: It is an art students' paradise." *LIFE* 9, 15 (October 7, 1940): 65–67.

"Modern Living: Football flowers: These Variations Are for Exhibitions." *LIFE* 9, 16 (October 14, 1940): 54.

"Radio City Rockette." *LIFE* 9, 23 (December 2, 1940): 75–77.

["Salon Section: Prize Winners, Black-and-White."] *Popular Photography* VII, 6 (December 1940): 69.

1941 *Cue: The Weekly Magazine of New York Life* (January 18, 1941): Front cover.

Grover Theis. "Ten Thousand Skippers: Yachting Goes Democratic." *Saturday Evening Post* 213, 30 (January 25, 1941): 16–17, 67–69.

[Advertisement.] Agfa Ansco. *Popular Photography* VIII, 2 (February 1941): [2].

"Life on the Newsfronts of the World." *LIFE* 10, 13 (March 31, 1941): 36.

"*LIFE*'s Pictures." *LIFE* 10, 15 (April 14, 1941): 21. [A portrait of Andreas Feininger — to accompany Feininger's picture story on New York City.]

"People." *U.S. Camera* 1, 15 (April-May 1941): 34–35.

Glamour (July 1941): Front cover.

"U.S.A. Adolf Dehn Depicts It in Words and Watercolors on His Coast-to-Coast Trips." *LIFE* 11, 6 (August 11, 1941): 40.

1942 "A.B.C.'s: Camera and Picture-Taking Terminology......" *Minicam Photography* 5, 6 (February 1942): 44 [Uncredited photograph].

"Pictures of the Month." *Minicam Photography* 5, 6 (February 1942): [54].

U.S. Camera (March 1942): Front cover. [Evelyn Frye in bathing suit].

Look (April 1942): Front cover. [Color version of Evelyn Frye in bathing suit].

"Salon Section." *Popular Photography* X, 4 (April 1942): 43.

"Busman's Holiday." *Harper's Bazaar* (April 1942): unpaged.

[Article unidentified.] *Harper's Bazaar* (April 1942): 41.

"Salon Section: Beach." *Popular Photography* X, 5 (May 1942): 42.

U.S. Camera (June 1942): Front cover.

"Salon Section: Ranch." *Popular Photography* X, 6 (June 1942): 42.

"Fine Pictures. Let-Down by Fritz Henle." *U.S. Camera* V, 7 (July 1942): 34.

Bob Hope. "Off the Hope Chest." *Harper's Bazaar* (July 1942): 16–17, 68.

"Irving Berlin's Soldier Show Rehearses on Broadway." *Harper's Bazaar* (July 1942): 34.

"The Keys to the City." *Harper's Bazaar* (July 1942): 38–39.

Peggy LeBoutillier. "A New Man in Your Life — the County Agent." *Harper's Bazaar* (July 1942): 54–55.

"The Ormsbee Family Is Doing Its Share in the Nation's War Effort." *The Burlington Free Press and Times* (August 5, 1942): [1 p.].

"Salon Section: Pets." *Popular Photography* XI, 2 (August 1942): 49.

"Off Islanders." *Harper's Bazaar* (September 1942): 64–67.

"High School Technique." *Harper's Bazaar* ([September 1942?]): [1 p.]. [Photographed at the Hockaday School in Dallas, Texas.]

"Salon Section." *Popular Photography* XI, 4 (October 1942): 50.

America's Alertmen I, 39 (November 30, 1942): Front cover.

"Anna Mary Robertson Moses [Grandma Moses]." *Harper's Bazaar* (December 1942): 43.

"[Fine Pictures.] Balancing the Budget by Fritz Henle From O.W.I." *U.S. Camera* V, 12 (December 1942): 28–29.

"At Ease!" *Minicam Photography* 6, 4 (December 1942): [22–23].

"Glamor Girl Flyers Are 'Pin-Ups' for B-17 Crews." *Air News, The Picture Magazine of Aviation* ([1942?]): 34–35.

1943 "Be Indispensable." *Harper's Bazaar* (January 1943): page unknown.

Sue McDaniel. "Models Teach Flying." *Minicam Photography* 6, 8 (April 1943): 48–49.

Joseph Wechsberg. "So You're Going to Italy — pictures Johnny Doughboy will find." *Minicam Photography* 6, 8 (April 1943): 64–67, 97.

"City of Citizens." *Harper's Bazaar* (April 1943): 55–[56].

"Fine Pictures. The Mail Hour by Fritz Henle for O.W.I." *U.S. Camera* VI, 4 (May 1943): 31.

"A Parachute Is A Man's Last Chance — the Waves make it a good one." *Harper's Bazaar* (July 1943): 28–31.

"You'd have no Harper's Bazaar if women hadn't taken the place of men in these civilian jobs." *Harper's Bazaar* (several months, 1943). [A multi-issue series.]

[Title unidentified: Article on Mexico in WWII.] *Coronet* (August [1943?]): [6 pp.].

"Los Mexicanos Estan Listos!..." *Hoy* ([1943?]): [6 pp.].

Gloria L. de Mola. "La Tierna Arcilla." *Norte* ([1943?]): 26–27, 60.

1944 "Mexico at War." *Mayfair* (February 1944): [1 p.].

Serge Koussevitzky. "American Composers." *LIFE* 16, 17 (April 24, 1944): 60.

"How to Teach Your Child to Swim." *Harper's Bazaar* ([July?] 1944): 62–63.

Baby Bazaar (July 1944): Front cover.

"Paris the Eternal." *The New York Times Magazine* (August 20, 1944): 8–15?

"Salon Section: Ideas for Vacation Pictures." *Popular Photography* XV, 2 (August 1944): 42.

Junior Bazaar ("College Issue," Fall 1944): Front cover.

Edgar DeEvia. "When the Lights Go on Again...." *Popular Photography* XV, 6 (December 1944): 47.

"Take Your Subject Outdoors." [Photographs by Fritz Henle.] [*Photography?*] ([1944?]): 24.

1945 Bob Hawk. "Photoquiz." *Look* 9, 1 (January 9, 1945): 11.

"Inspired by South America." *Look* 9, 1 (January 9, 1945): 42-43.

Bob Hawk. "Photoquiz." *Look* 9, 2 (January 23, 1945). 11

"Land of Plenty." *Look* 9, 2 (January 23, 1945): 25.

Alfred E. Phelps. "The Look Clinic: Understand Your Arthritis." *Look* 9, 3 (February 6, 1945): 72.

Bob Hawk. "Photoquiz." *Look* 9, 4 (February 20, 1945): 10.

"Salon Section: Pictures in Motion." *Popular Photography* XVI, 3 (March 1945): 44, 45, 49.

Mademoiselle ("What's New Number," March 1945): Front cover.

"First Permanent." *Look* 9, 6 (March 20, 1945): 66 & 68-69.

Mademoiselle ("Bride's Number," April 1945): Front cover.

U.S. Camera (April 1945): Front cover.

"Salon Section: Keynote — Tranquility." *Popular Photography* XVI, 4 (April 1945): 38–39.

"Outdoor Props." *Popular Photography* XVI, 4 (April 1945): 50–51.

Admiral William F. Halsey, as told to Frank D. Morris. "A Plan for Japan." *Collier's* (April 28, 1945): 18–19+.

Bob Hawk. "Photoquiz." *Look* 9, 9 (May 1, 1945): 15.

"Should 2 ½-Year-Old Johnny Go to Nursery School?" *Look* 9, 10 (May 15, 1945): 82.

"Salon Section: Five Photographers...1. Fritz Henle's Mexico." *Popular Photography* XVI, 6 (June 1945): 38–41, 100.

Parade Magazine (June 3, 1945): Front cover: "Sign of Summer."

Mademoiselle ("College Number," August 1945): Front cover.

Nina Sesto. "La Guerra comenzó en China...y en China terminará." *Norte* (September 1945): [2 pp.].

Ernest Dichter. "Look's Personality Clinic: Inhibition." *Look* 9, 24 (November 27, 1945): 21.

[Leonard Coulter. "Salon Section:] Americana Salon." *Popular Photography* XVII, 6 (December 1945): 45–46.

Richard Watts Jr. "China." *Harper's Bazaar* ([1945?]): [2 pp.].

John M. Maki. "El Problema Japones." *Norte* ([1945?]): [1 p.].

1946 *Mademoiselle* ("Latin-American Number," March 1946): Multiple pages ["Henle...took most of the photos" — Editor].

George R. Clark. "Pictures, Pictures...Pictures." *Popular Photography* XVIII, 4 (April 1946): 63.

Norte (May 1946): Front cover.

Elle (April 16, 1946): Front cover.

Elle (April 23, 1946): Front cover.

Peter Samarjan. "Eye Pictures." *Popular Photography* 19, 2 (August 1946): 57–59.

"Take It Easy! Photographs from Monkmeyer." *Minicam Photography* 9, 12 (August 1946): [62–63].

Frank Fenner, Jr. "...darkroom Pictures." *Popular Photography* 19, 4 (October 1946): 63.

Norman Harkness. "What Size Negative...?" *Popular Photography* 19, 5 (November 1946): 37.

Bill Cartwright. "Vagabond Pictures." *Popular Photography* 19, 5 (November 1946): 59, 65.

1947 ["Table of Contents."] *Popular Photography* 20, 1 (January 1947): [4].

Virginia Pope. "Fashions for the Tropics." *The New York Times Magazine* (January 12, 1947): 38–39 [6 photos].

"Cotton Convertibles." *Mademoiselle* (January 1947): [1 p.].

Thomas Wolfe. "Go, Seeker." *Charm* (February 1947): [1 p.].

Bruce Downes. "...backlighted Pictures." *Popular Photography* 20, 3 (March 1947): 88.

"Pictures." *Popular Photography* 20, 6 (June 1947): 66, 73.

"Pictures of People." *Popular Photography* 21, 3 (September 1947): 69, 71.

"Nine to Five Pictures." *Popular Photography* 21, 5 (November 1947): 71.

"Children in Pictures." *Popular Photography* 21, 6 (December 1947): 71.

1948 "Pictures in Winter." *Popular Photography* 22, 1 (January 1948): 64–65.

Gilbert C. Close. "How to make and sell Stock Photos." *Minicam Photography* 11, 7 (March 1948): 86.

"[Hawaii]." *Holiday,* 3, 4 (April 1948): Front cover and pages incl. 26–32, 41–43, 120.

"Contents." *Minicam Photography* 11, 10 (June 1948): 2.

"Hawaii. Aufnahmen von Fritz Henle." *Atlantis* (July 1948): 306–11.

"Sunlight Pictures." *Popular Photography* 23, 1 (July 1948): 69.

"The Virgin Islands." *House & Garden* (September 1948): pages unknown.

"Pictures." *Popular Photography* 23, 4 (October 1948): 72, 79.

"Holiday Salon." *Popular Photography* 23, 6 (December 1948): 98, 100, 102, 114.

1949 "People in Pictures." *Popular Photography* 24, 1 (January 1949): 62–63.

"February Photographs." *Minicam Photography* 12, 6 (February 1949): 76.

"Oil Is Where You Find It." *TW* ((September 11, 1949): 8–9 [7 photos].

"My Favorite Picture of 1949." *Popular Photography* 25, 6 (December 1949): 78.

1950 Eric Johnston. "For A New Approach to the Labor Issue." *The New York Times Magazine* (January 29, 1950): 7.

Empire (January 1950): Front cover.

"books about photography." *Modern Photography* 13, 6 (February 1950): 124–125.

World Petroleum (March 1950): Front cover.

"Rough Weather round the Leewards." *Picture Post* (April 22, 1950): 20–23.

Picture Post (May 6, 1950): Front cover.

"Vacation Preview: A Pictorial Feature." *Popular Photography* 26, 6 (June 1950): 70.

"Water Witchery." *Modern Photography* 13, 10 (June 1950): 30–31.

Travel (November 1950): Front cover.

Modern Photography 14, 4 (December 1950): Front cover.

1951 Lloyd E. Varden. "is pictorialism killing photography?" *Modern Photography* 15, 4 (April 1951): 38–39.

"Photographer's Vacation." *Modern Photography* 15, 6 (June 1951): 61, 63.

George Boardman. "The Heat's On...Hot Weather Do's and Dont's [*sic*]." *Modern Photography* 15, 7 (July 1951): 56.

W[olfgang] Suschitzky. "Personality Plus — Sunlight." *Photography* 6, 8 (August 1951): 16–20.

["Popular Photography 1951 Picture Contest. Color:] Third Prize." *Popular Photography* 29, 6 (December 1951): 76–77.

["Popular Photography 1951 Picture Contest. black & white.]" *Popular Photography* 29, 6 (December 1951): 83.

1952 "Crystal Jubilee Portfolio: A selection of memorable pictures from the past fifteen years: 15th Year: Fritz Henle." *Photography* 30, 5 (May 1952): [81–82]. ["*Wyoming Ranch*...rates tops with our readers. We've received sheaves of letters asking for copies of it, and it is reproduced here in a gorgeous gatefold, suitable for framing."]

Hans Neuburg. "Die Photo-Weltausstellung in Luzern / The World Exhibition of Photography in Lucerne / L'Exposition mondiale de la Photographie à Lucerne." *Camera* 31, 6/7 (June/July 1952): 190–225.

Joe Franklin. "7 Keys to Depth." *Modern Photography* 16, 10 (October 1952): 54–[59].

Jacquelyn Judge. "Henle's First Movie..." *Modern Photography* 16, 11 (November 1952): 90–92, 94, 96, 100.

"A Gallery of Photographs with Human Interest." *Photography* 7, 12 (December 1952): 21–32.

Travel (December 1952): Front cover.

1953 Peter Gowland. "New photo books: Rollei Photography." *Modern Photography* 17, 5 (May 1953): 38, 96.

[Advertisement.] National Educational Alliance, Inc., *Encyclopedia of Photography. U.S. Camera* 16, 5 (May 1953): 41.

"Coffee Break with the editors: Calypso Carnival..." *Modern Photography* 17, 11 (November 1953): 26.

1954 "1954 Picture Contest. [color:] Fourth Prize." *Popular Photography* 35, 6 (December 1954): [116].

"Die Nymphe. Fotostudien von Fritz Henle, New York." [Periodical unidentified] ([1954?]): pages unknown.

1955 "Fritz Henle: Figure Studies." *Camera* 34, 7 (July 1955): 344–47.

1956 *Photography* (January 1956): Front cover.

John Scofield and Charles Allmon. "Virgin Islands: Tropical Playland, U.S.A." *The National Geographic Magazine* 109, 2 (February 1956): 201–32.

Photography (June 1956): Front cover.

1958 *Newsweek* (January 6, 1958): Front cover.

PSA Journal, 24, 7 (July 1958): Front cover.

1959 *195 Magazine* (February 1959): Front cover.

1960 [Advertisement]: "Rollei." *Popular Photography* 46, 4 (April 1960): 101.

"Yes, They Take Baby Pictures." *Infinity IX*, 6 (June 1960): 12.

1961 "Pictures That Say Travel." *Popular Photography* 48, 5 (May 1961): 58–67.

Town & Country ("Virgin Islands, U.S.A." issue, September 1961): Front covers, inside cover, and many pages throughout the issue.

Service (October 1961): Front cover.

Foto Blickpunkt (November 1961): Front cover.

1963 *Popular Boating* (November 1963): Front cover.

1964 Marion Gough. "Go now. Stay later." *House Beautiful* (January 1964): [1 p.].

1965 *The Continental Magazine* 5, 2, (May-June 1965): Front cover.

Rewe Post (September 11, 1965): Front cover.

1968 *The Catamaran and Trimaran Magazine* (July 1968): Front cover.

Rolleigrafie, 20 (March 1968): Front cover.

Rolleigrafie (October 1968): Front cover.

1969 *The Catamaran and Trimaran Magazine* (January 1969): Front cover.

1970 *Westerman* (February 1970): Front cover.

Signature (February 1970): Front cover.

1972 "FSA." *Vermont Life* (Autumn 1972): 28–32.

1973 "The Virgin Islands — A Troubled Paradise." *US News & World Report* (November 5, 1973): 79–80.

1976 "Pablo y Marta Casals: Fotografías de Fritz Henle." *Humboldt* 61 (1976): 69–73.

1977 "Movie Shows Love, Fear." *The Virgin Island Daily News* (February 4, 1977): [1 p.].

Virgin Islander 2, 2 (December 1977): Front cover.

[Advertisement]: Antilles Air Boats. "Our Islands Are More Than Pretty Pictures." [Periodical unidentified] (December 14, 1977): 31.

1978 *Virgin Islander* 2, 3 (July/August 1978): Front cover.

1980 "Proud People, Proud Heritage." *The Virgin Islands Daily News* [50th Anniversary Edition] (August 1, 1980): B-1.

1982 *Directory [1982]*. U.S. Virgin Islands Telephone Corporation: Front cover.

1987 *Kölner Wochen* (April 6–12, 1987): Front cover.

1989 Paolo Constantini. "Helmut Gernsheim." *Contemporanea* (September 1989): 76–80.
"Homer Bryant — Profile of A Dancer." *The Daily News of the Virgin Islands* (September 10, 1989): 12–13.

1990 *Foto Design + Technik* (February 1990): Front cover.
[Advertisement]. Ken Lieberman Laboratories Inc. "Fritz Henle: Comment on Photography." *ASMP Bulletin* 9, 12 (December 1990): unpaged.

1992 "Snap Shots: Spoiled cream of the square-format crop." *Popular Photography* (July 1992): 8.
Victor Flores Olea. "La Fascinación del otro: fotógrafos extranjeros en México." *México Desconocido* 190 (December 1992): 38–45.

2002 Nancy Price Graff. "Images of Vermont 1936–1942." *Vermont Life* LVII, 1 (Autumn 2002): 42–47.
Phyllis Tuchman. "Frida Kahlo." *Smithsonian* (November 2002): 50–60.

2004 *Art & Antiques* 27, 8 (September 2004): S2.
Art & Auction 27, 1 (September 2004): 43.
Art & Auction 27, 2 (October 2004): 24.
ARTnews 103, 9 (October 2004): 28.
ARTnews 103, 10 (November 2004): 28.

2006 Nadia Ugalde Gomez and Juan Rafael Coronel Rivera. "Frida Kahlo." *Editorial RM* (October 2006): [1 p.].

6. *Films by Fritz Henle*

The American Virgin Islands. (1950–52). [Recut and re-released as *Virgin Islands U.S.A.*]
Carnival in Trinidad. (1951–52). [Re-released with variant titles: *Carnival* and *Calypso Carnival.*]
Shango. (1951–53).
Yanvallou: Dance of the Snake God Dambala. (1951–53). [Print preserved by the National Film Preservation Foundation.]
Crackers by the Billion. (1952–53). [Produced for the National Biscuit Company.]

7. *Solo Exhibitions of Works by Fritz Henle*

1936 Photographs of India by Fritz Henle. Cleveland Museum of Art, Cleveland, Ohio, U.S.A., March 19–April 22, 1936.
Japan. Mitsubishi Department Store, Tokyo, Japan.
Photographs of the East. Mezzanine, Rockefeller Center, New York City, New York, U.S.A., November 4–10, 1936. [Sponsored by Burleigh Brooks, U.S. Agent for Rolleiflex Camera, and Black Star Publishing Co., Inc.]

1937 Fritz Henle, Photographs [of Japan and China]. Rockefeller Center, Lobby, New York City, New York, U.S.A.
[Exhibition title unidentified.] M.H. de Young Museum, San Francisco, California, U.S.A.
Thirty Oriental Photographs. Memphis Academy of Art, Memphis, Tennessee, U.S.A. [1937?].

1938 Fifty Photographs of the Orient. Photographic Salon, Balboa Park, San Diego, California, U.S.A., January 1938. [Sponsored by the San Diego Photographic Art Society.]

1943 Contemporary Mexico. National Exhibition Service, American Federation of Arts, New York City, New York, U.S.A. [Exhibition traveled to various Chapters of the AFA.]

1945 Mexico: Photographs by Fritz Henle. Cleveland Museum of Art, Cleveland, Ohio, U.S.A., December 4, 1945 – January 3, 1946.

1948 [Hawaii.] Corner Gallery, American Museum of Natural History, New York City, New York, U.S.A.

1949 Mexico: Photographs by Fritz Henle. Cleveland Museum of Art, Cleveland, Ohio, U.S.A., March 31–April 6, 1949.
Hawaii – Photographs by Fritz Henle. Baltimore Museum of Art, Baltimore, Maryland, U.S.A.

1950 Hawaii. American Museum of Natural History, New York City, New York, U.S.A.

1952 Fritz Henle. George Eastman House, Rochester, New York, U.S.A.

1953 Photographs. The Gallery of the Camera Club of New York, New York City, New York, U.S.A.

1954 Caribbean. Smithsonian Institution, Washington, D.C., U.S.A.

1957 [Mexico.] Cleveland Museum of Art, Cleveland, Ohio, U.S.A.

1960 American Virgin Islands in Color. Government House, Christiansted, St. Croix, U.S. Virgin Islands.

1961 Caribbean Journey. Museum of the University of Puerto Rico, San Juan, Puerto Rico, November – December 1961.
Caribbean Journey. Government House, Christiansted, St. Croix, U.S. Virgin Islands, December 12–17, 1961.

1962 [Exhibition title unidentified.] Staatliche Landesbildstelle, Hamburg, Germany.

1963 The Fritz Henle Show. The Camera Club of New York, New York City, New York, U.S.A., November 19 – December 10, 1963.

1965 Exhibition of Photographs by Fritz Henle. Virgin Islands National Bank, Christiansted, St. Croix, U.S. Virgin Islands.

1967 Rollei Werke, Braunschweigh, Germany.

1969 Virgin Islands. City Hall, Copenhagen, Denmark, August 1969.
Virgin Islands. Hamburg, Germany, August 1969.
Virgin Islands. Braunschweigh, Germany, September 1969.
Virgin Islands. Cologne, Germany, September 1969.
Virgin Islands. Ballroom, Government House, Christiansted, St. Croix, U.S. Virgin Islands.
Virgin Islands. Ballroom, Government House, St. Thomas, U.S. Virgin Islands.
[Fritz Henle: 50 Color Photographs of the Virgin Islands]. Photographers Gallery, New York Coliseum, New York City, New York, U.S.A., May–June 1969. [Held in conjunction with the Photographic Society of America's Photo Expo '69 — The Universe of Photography. Henle gave a lecture on "Virgin Islands, U.S.A." during the PSA International Conference, June 6–8, 1969.]

1970 Virgin Islands. Munich, Germany.
Virgin Islands. Milan, Italy.
Virgin Islands. Paris, France.
[Exhibition title unidentified.] Institute of Culture, University of Puerto Rico, San Juan.

1971 Fritz Henle Fotografo. Museum of the University of Puerto Rico, San Juan, Puerto Rico, March 2–19, 1971.
Fritz Henle Fotografo. Institute of Culture, San Juan, Puerto Rico, Opened February 5, 1971.
Fritz Henle Fotografo. Ponce Museum of Art, Ponce, Puerto Rico.
The Virgin Islands: A Photographic Essay. Santo Domingo Museum, Convento de Santo Domingo, Instituto de Cultura Puerterriqueña, San Juan, Puerto Rico, February 5–March, 1971.
The Virgin Islands: A Photographic Essay. Denmark, Summer 1971.
The Virgin Islands: A Photographic Essay. Germany, Summer 1971.
The Virgin Islands: A Photographic Essay. Milan, Italy, October 1971.
The Virgin Islands: A Photographic Essay. Rome, Italy, November 1971.
The Virgin Islands: A Photographic Essay. Paris, France, December 1971.
The Virgin Islands: A Photographic Essay. Government House, Christiansted, St. Croix, U.S. Virgin Islands, December 9–12, 1971.

1972 The Virgin Islands: A Photographic Essay. London, England, January 1972.
Fritz Henle, USA. Auf der Suche nach dem Schönen. 40 Jahre Fotografie in Schwarz Weiss und Farbe. Fotogalerie Staatliche Landesbildstelle, Hamburg, Germany, February 1–29, 1972.
[Exhibition title unidentified.] Rollei Werke, Braunschweigh, Germany.

1973 Virgin Islands. Coliseum, New York City, New York, U.S.A.

1974 Photographs by Fritz Henle. New York Cultural Center [in association with Fairleigh Dickinson University], New York City, New York, U.S.A., May 16–July 7, 1974. [The earlier working title for the exhibition was Fritz Henle: Photographer in Retrospect.]
Fritz Henle: Master Photographer. Trinity University, San Antonio, Texas, U.S.A., April 2–6, 1974.

1975 Photographs by Fritz Henle. Rampart Gallery, New Orleans, Louisiana, U.S.A., August 2–31, 1975.

1976 Fritz Henle: Retrospective. Galeria de las Americas, San Juan, Puerto Rico, May–June 1976.

1977 [Fritz Henle, Photographs.] Thousand Year Celebration, Wolfenbuttel, Braunschweigh, Germany.
[Exhibition title unidentified.] Rodale Gallery at Allentown Art Museum, Allentown, Pennsylvania, U.S.A., October– November 11, 1977.

1978 [Fritz Henle, Photographs.] West End Work Bench Gallery, Fredericksted, St. Croix, U.S. Virgin Islands, Opened March 17, 1978.
Fritz Henle Retrospective. Trinity University, San Antonio, Texas, U.S.A.

1979 Fritz Henle: Color. Trinity University, San Antonio, Texas, U.S.A.

1980 Fritz Henle, A 50 Year Retrospective. The Witkin Gallery, New York City, New York, U.S.A., April 23–May 31, 1980.
Fritz Henle: Color. Michener Gallery, The University of Texas at Austin, Austin, Texas, U.S.A.
Fritz Henle: Casals. Michener Gallery, The University of Texas at Austin, Austin, Texas, U.S.A.
[Fritz Henle?]. Art Museum of the University of New Mexico, Albuquerque, New Mexico, U.S.A.

1981 Fritz Henle. Galerie Foto-Arts, Basel, Switzerland, September 8–October 20, 1981.

1982 Fotografis: Pablo Casals. Fotografix, Österreichische Länderbank, Vienna, Austria, January 11–29, 1982.
Images. Chapman Graduate Center Great Hall, Trinity University, San Antonio, Texas, U.S.A., April 1982. [An exhibition curated by Henle of a selection of his own prints juxtaposed with facsimile prints from the Photography Collection of the Harry Ransom Center, The University of Texas at Austin.]
[Fritz Henle.] The Gallery on Company Street, Christiansted, St. Croix, U.S. Virgin Islands, February 26–March 1982.

1983 Fritz Henle. Benteler Galleries, Inc., Houston, Texas, U.S.A., March–April 1983. [Held in conjunction with the Houston Fotofest.]

1984 [Fritz Henle]. Fotomuseum, Münchner Stadtmuseum, Munich, Germany, May–July 15, 1984.

1985 [Exhibition title unidentified.] Kunsthaus, Zurich, Switzerland.

1986 Fotografis. Meisterwerke internationaler Fotografie. Kunstforum Österreichische Länerbank, Vienna, Austria.
Fritz Henle: Amerika, Ein Thema mit Variationen. Museum für Kunst und Kulturgeschichte der Stadt Dortmund, Dortmund, Germany, July 11–August 10, 1986; Amerikanische Botschaft, Bonn, Germany; Amerika Haus, Hamburg, Germany, October 9–29, 1986; Kodak AG, Stuttgart, Germany; Rollei Fototechnik, Braunschweig, Germany, 1986–87. [Exhibition traveled in collaboration with the American Embassy, Bonn.]

1987 Diego Rivera y su Mexico — a través del ojo de la camera, mit Fotografien von Fritz Henle. Centro de Arte Reina Sofia, Madrid, Spain.

Images of the People of Hawaii. Bernice Pauahi Bishop Museum, Honolulu, Hawaii, U.S.A., March 1987.

[Fritz Henle.] Museum Ludwig, Cologne, Germany, April 1987.

1988 Amerika. Ein Thema in Variationem. Fotomuseum Burghausen, Munich, Germany, June 11–August 14, 1988.

Amerika. Ein Thema in Variationem. Stadtbücherei Tannenbusch, Bonn, Germany, August 23–September 16, 1988.

1989 Fritz Henle: Paris 1938. Museum für Kunst und Kulturgeschichte der Stadt Dortmund, Dortmund, Germany, June 23–August 27, 1989; Universitätsbibliothek, Heidelberg, Germany, October 27–December 16, 1989; Kulturinstituten, Hamburg, Germany, November–December 1989. [Exhibitions traveled by the Goethe Institute to 20 other locations.]

Fritz Henle: A Life devoted to Photography. Little Gallery, Estate Whim Plantation Museum, St. Croix Landmarks Society, Frederiksted, St. Croix, U.S. Virgin Islands, February 12–May, 1989.

Amerikanischen Impressionen. AmerikaHaus, Stuttgart, Germany, August 18–September 29, 1989.

Fritz Henle: Amerika — et tema med variationer. Museet fur Fotokunst, Odense, Denmark, March 17–April 23, 1989.

September 17 — St. Croix after Hugo Through the Lens of Fritz Henle. Old Apothecary Hall, Christiansted, St. Croix, U.S. Virgin Islands, December 23, 1989–January 1990.

1990 Fritz Henle: Fotografien von 1928–1988. Lichtbild Galerie, Ingolstadt, Germany.

Fritz Henle: Paris 1938. Kiel, Germany, January–February 1990; Kulturforum, Neuss, Germany, March 1990; Mainz, Germany, April 1990; Bremen, Germany, May 1990; Hamburg, Germany, June 1990; Tübingen, Germany 1990.

Paris 1938: Fotos von Fritz Henle. Studio DuMont, Cologne, Germany, October 2–26, 1990.

Pablo Casals. Museo Pablo Casals, San Juan, Puerto Rico, Opened May 23, 1990.

1991 Pablo Casals. Plaza de las Américas, San Juan, Puerto Rico. May 26–June 29, 1991.

1992 Thema für Frauen. Fotogravien von Fritz Henle. Studio DuMont, Cologne, Germany, September 16–October 25, 1992.

Fritz Henle: Amerika ein Thema in Variationem. Räumen des "club parterre," Gotha, Germany, August 7–September 4, 1992.

1994 Fritz Henle (1909–1993): Die Quadratur der Schönheit. Retrospektive für den Fotografen Fritz Henle. Museum für Kunst und Kulturgeschichte der Stadt Dortmund, Dortmund, Germany, February 5–April 10, 1994.

1996 Fritz Henle: A Life in Photographs. Maria Henle Studio, Christiansted, St. Croix, U.S. Virgin Islands, December 13, 1996–January 14, 1997.

2004 Fritz Henle / Mexico: Vintage Photographs by Fritz Henle. Throckmorton Fine Art, New York City, New York, U.S.A., September 23–November 27, 2004.

8. *Group Exhibitions Including Photographic Work by Fritz Henle*

1937 Photography 1839–1937. [Curated by Beaumont Newhall.] Museum of Modern Art, New York City, New York, U.S.A.

1938 Third Rollei Salon. Rockefeller Center, New York City, New York, U.S.A., May 2–8, 1938.

First International Photographic Exposition of the Guild of Photographic Dealers. New York City, New York, U.S.A.

1948 This Is the Photo League. New York City, New York, U.S.A.

American Society of Magazine Photographers First Annual Exhibition. Pepsi-Cola Center, New York City, New York, U.S.A., November 15–31, 1948.

1949 Popular Photography Prize Winning Picture Contest Exhibition. New York Museum of Science and Industry in Rockefeller Center, New York City, New York; The Franklin Institute, Philadelphia, Pennsylvania; Marshall Field and Company, Chicago, Illinois; The Higbee Company, Cleveland, Ohio; Bullock's Downtown, Los Angeles, California, U.S.A., March–April 1949.

1951 7th Annual Popular Photography Traveling Salon. Kodak Information Center in Grand Central Station and International Business Machines Building, New York City, New York [and various traveling sites], U.S.A., 1951–52.

1952 The World Exhibition of Photography / Weltausstellung der Fotografie. Art Museum, Lucerne, Switzerland, May–August 1952.

1954 Subjektive Fotografie 2. [Curated by Otto Steinert.] Schule für Kunst und Handwerk, Saarbrucken, Germany, 1954.

1956 Images in Oil: Photographs from Cities Service Company Photo Library. George Eastman House, Rochester, New York, U.S.A., Opened June 21, 1956

1959 Photography at Mid-Century: 10th Anniversary Exhibition. George Eastman House, Rochester, New York, U.S.A.

1961 Photography As Fine Art III. Minneapolis Institute of Arts, Minneapolis, Minnesota, U.S.A., June 14–September 3, 1961. [Exhibition traveled.]

1962 [Places throughout the world visited by our buyers.] Bloomingdale's, New York City, New York, U.S.A., Opened September 1962.

1963 Photography As Fine Art IV. Metropolitan Museum of Art, New York City, New York, U.S.A., May 16–September 30, 1963. [Exhibition traveled.]

1965 Photography As Fine Art: The Museum Directors' Selection. Kodak Pavilion, New York World's Fair, New York City, New York, U.S.A., May 20–June 16, 1965.

1967 Photography As Fine Art V. Metropolitan Museum of Art, New York City, New York, U.S.A., March 14–June 11, 1967. [Exhibition traveled.]

1968 Woman. 2nd World Exhibition of Photography. [*Stern Magazine*], Germany, 1968.

1970 Infinity 70: ASMP 25th Anniversary. New York Cultural Center, New York City, New York, U.S.A., January 20–March 7, 1970.

1980 Body Electric: Color. Squibb Institute, Princeton, New Jersey, U.S.A.

1981 Farbe im Photo: Die Geschichte der Farbphotographie von 1861 bis 1981. Agfa-Gevaert Foto-Historama, Leverkusen, Germany, June 11–August 2, 1981.

Fritz Henle and Ferenc Berko. [Curated by Helmut Gernsheim.] Matthews Center, University Art Collections, Arizona State University, Tempe, Arizona, U.S.A., March 1–22, 1981.

1983 The Henle Family. Reichhold Center for the Arts, St. Thomas, U.S. Virgin Islands, February 3–March 31?, 1983.

The Henle Family Art Show. College Art Gallery, St. Croix, U.S. Virgin Islands, December 1983.

1984 Sammlung Gruber. [Curated by L. Fritz Gruber.] Museum Ludwig, Cologne, Germany.

1985 Das Aktfoto. Fotomuseum im Stadtmuseum, Munich, Germany; Museum für Kunst und Kulturgeschichte der Stadt Dortmund, Dortmund, Germany.

1986 Diego Rivera y su México: a través del ojo de la cámara. Detroit Institute of Art, Detroit, Michigan, U.S.A., February 12–April 17, 1986; Philadelphia Museum of Art, Philadelphia, Pennsylvania, U.S.A., June 2–August 10, 1986; Museo del Palacio de Bellas Artes, Mexico City, Mexico, September 29, 1986–January 4, 1987; Centro de Arte Reina Sofía, Madrid, Spain, February 18–June 4, 1987; Staatliche Kunsthalle, Berlin, East Germany, July 23–September 20, 1987; Hayward Gallery, Arts Council of Great Britain, London, England, October 29, 1987–January 10, 1988.

50 Jahre Moderne Farbfotografie: 50 Years Modern Color Photography, 1936–1986. [Curated by Manfred Heiting.] Photokina, Frankfurt, Germany, September 3–9, 1986.

1987 Henle 4: Recent Works by Fritz, Maria, Tina and Martin Henle. Christiansted, St. Croix, U.S. Virgin Islands, Collage–Apothecary Hall Upper Courtyard, January 23–February 7,1987.

Deutsche Lichtfildner–Wegbereiter der zeitgenössischen Photographie. Museum Ludwig, Cologne, Germany, February 4–March 29, 1987.

Nutidige Kunstnere: Dansk Vestindien For Og Nu. Anneberg-Samlingerne, Anneberg, Nykobing Sjaelland, Denmark, April 30–October 4, 1987.

Vom Landschaftsbild zur Spurensicherung. Museum Ludwig, Cologne, Germany, August 26–October 18, 1987.

1988 Master Photographs from the "Photography in the Fine Arts" Exhibitions, 1959–67. [Curated by Miles Barth.] International Center for Photography, New York City, New York, U.S.A., 1988. [Exhibition traveled.]

1989 Photography: The First 150 Years. [Curated by Roy Flukinger.] Laguna Gloria Art Museum, Austin, Texas, U.S.A.

1990 Photography 150. [Curated by Roy Flukinger.] Leeds Gallery, Harry Ransom Center, The University of Texas at Austin, Austin, Texas, U.S.A.

2002 Looking Back at Vermont: Farm Security Administration Photographs, 1936–1942. Middlebury College Museum of Art, Middlebury, Vermont, U.S.A., September 12–December 1, 2002.

2004 Focus Mensch: Menschenbilder aus der Photosammlung Helmut Gernsheim. [Curated by Claude W. Sui.] Reiss-Engelhorn Museum, Mannheim, Germany, October 12, 2003–May 16, 2004.

Men of Mexico: Photographs by Manuel Alvarez Bravo, Hector Garcia, Edward Weston, Fritz Henle, and Gerardo Suter. Throckmorton Fine Art Gallery, New York City, New York, U.S.A., August 4–September 17, 2005.

2005 Permanent Collection. [Curated by Ricardo Viera.] Zoellner Arts Center, Lehigh University, Bethlehem, Pennsylvania, U.S.A., December 1, 2005–December 1, 2007.

2007 Frida Kahlo: Images of an Icon. Tampa Museum of Art, Tampa, Florida, U.S.A., October 21–December 16, 2007.

One Shot Each, Humor Belyst. [Curated by Finn Thrane.] Museet for Fotokunst Brandts, Odense, Sweden, 2007.

Frida Kahlo Centenary. Museo de Arte Contemporaneo de Monterrey AC, Monterrey, Mexico, August 30–September 30, 2007; Casa de la Cultura, Monterrey, Mexico, October–November 2007.

2008 Fritz Henle & Berenice Abbott: Paris–New York. Kicken Gallery, Berlin, Germany, June 14–August 30, 2008.

9. *Permanent Collections with Photographs by Fritz Henle*

Agfa Foto-Historama, Cologne, Germany.
Alfred Stieglitz Center, Philadelphia Museum of Art, Philadelphia, Pennsylvania, U.S.A.
Art Institute of Chicago, Chicago, Illinois, U.S.A.
Bernice Pauahi Bishop Museum, Honolulu, Hawaii, U.S.A.
Bildarchiv Preussischer Kulturbesitz, Berlin, Germany.
The Brooklyn Museum, Brooklyn, New York, U.S.A.
Breitenbach Collection, Photo-Museum, Munich, Germany.
Center for Creative Photography, University of Arizona, Tucson, Arizona, U.S.A.
George Eastman House, Rochester, New York, U.S.A.
Graphic Arts Department, Detroit Institute of Arts, Detroit, Michigan, U.S.A.
Harry Ransom Center, The University of Texas at Austin, Austin, Texas, U.S.A.
Historama, Agfa-Gavaert, Leverkusen, Germany.
International Center for Photography, New York City, New York, U.S.A.
J. Paul Getty Museum, Santa Monica, California, U.S.A.
Landesbildstelle, Hamburg, Germany.
Latin American Library, Tulane University, New Orleans, Louisiana, U.S.A.
Menil Museum, Houston, Texas, U.S.A.
Metropolitan Museum of Art, New York City, New York, U.S.A.
Museum für Kunst und Kulturgeschichte der Stadt Dortmund, Dortmund, Germany.
Museum Ludwig, Cologne, Germany.
Museum of Fine Arts, Houston, Texas, U.S.A.
Museum of Modern Art, New York City, New York, U.S.A.
Mystic Seaport Museum, Mystic, Connecticut, U.S.A.
New Orleans Museum of Art, New Orleans, Louisiana, U.S.A.
The Nimitz Library, U.S. Naval Academy, Annapolis, Maryland, U.S.A.
Northlight Gallery, School of Art, Arizona State University, Arizona, U.S.A.

Prints and Photographs Division, The Library of Congress, Washington, D.C., U.S.A.
Photographic Archives, Ekstrom Library, University of Louisville, Louisville, Kentucky, U.S.A.
Reiss-Engelhorn Museum, Mannheim, Germany.
San Antonio Museum of Art, San Antonio, Texas, U.S.A.
San Francisco Museum of Modern Art, San Francisco, California, U.S.A.
Smithsonian Institution, National Museum of American History, Division of Photographic History, Washington, D.C., U.S.A.
Southwest Collection, Texas Tech University, Lubbock, Texas, U.S.A.
University Art Museum, University of New Mexico, Albuquerque, New Mexico, U.S.A.
Virginia Museum of Fine Arts, Richmond, Virginia, U.S.A.
Zoeliner Arts Center, Lehigh University, Bethlehem, Pennsylvania, U.S.A.

10. *Texts on or about Fritz Henle in Books and Catalogues*

1937 Beaumont Newhall. *Photography 1839–1937.* New York: Museum of Modern Art, 1937.

1957 Norman Hall, ed. *Photography Today*. London: 'Photography' Magazine, 1957. [Henle ms. note on title page reads "May 1958"]

1969 "Fritz Henle's New Perspectives: 'Mr. Rollei' and the SL 66. Credo of a 'Convert.'" In: Franke and Heidecke. *40 Jahre Rollei Fotografie*. [Braunschweig: 1969].

1979 Fritz Kempe et. al., eds. *Fotografie 1919–1979, Made in Germany: Die GDL Fotografen*. Frankfurt: 1979.

1982 Helmut Gernsheim. "HENLE, Fritz." In: Colin Naylor, ed. *Contemporary Photographers*. Chicago & London: St. Martins Press, 1982.
Richard Pare. *Photography and Architecture: 1839–1939.* Montreal: Canadian Centre for Architecture, 1982.

1983 Bill Jay. *Photographers Photographed*. Salt Lake City: Gibbs M. Smith, Peregrine Smith Books, 1983.

1984 Helmut Gernsheim. *A Concise History of Photography*: 3rd rev. ed. New York: Dover, 1984.

1985 Michèle and Michel Auer. *Encyclopédie des Photographes de 1839 a Nos Jours: A–K*. Hermance: Editions Camera Obscura, 1985.

1986 Karl Steinorth. "Fritz Henle. Beruf: Rolleigraph." In: Karl Steinorth, ed. *PROFIFOTO Geschichten. Sonderdruck aus PROFIFOTO, 1983–1986. [Berlin?]: 1986.*

1987 Reinhold Misselbeck. *Vom Landschaftsbild zur Spurensicherung*. Cologne: Museum Ludwig, 1987.

1988 Helmut Gernsheim. "HENLE, Fritz." In: Colin Naylor, ed. *Contemporary Photographers*. 2nd ed. Chicago & London: St. James Press, 1988.

1989 James Enyeart, ed. *Decade by Decade: Twentieth-Century American Photography from the Collection of the Center for Creative Photography*. Boston, Toronto & London: Bulfinch Press, Little, Brown and Co., 1989.

1990 Studio Dumont / Kölner Stadt-Anzeiger. *Fritz Henle — Paris 1938: Fotografien*. Dortmund: Museum für Kunst und Kulturgeschichte der Stadt Dortmund, 1990.

1994 Brigitte Buberl, ed. *Fritz Henle 1909–1993. Die Quadratur der Schönheit*. [Foreword by Brigitte Buberl; Texts by Helmut Gernsheim, Günter Metken and Enno Kaufhold.] Dortmund: Museum für Kunst und Kulturgeschichte der Stadt Dortmund; and Heidelberg: Edition Braus, 1994.

1995 Helmut Gernsheim. "HENLE, Fritz." In: Colin Naylor, ed. *Contemporary Photographers*. 3rd ed. Detroit: St. James Press, 1995.

1996 "Henle, Fritz." In: Jane Turner, ed. *Dictionary of Art Online*. ©1996.

2003 [Claude W. Sui, ed.] *Helmut Gernsheim: Pionier der Fotogeschichte, Pioneer of Photo History*. [Mannheim: Reiss-Engelhorn Museum,] Hatje Cantz, [2003].

2004 Maria Henle, "Fritz Henle." In: *Fritz Henle / Mexico: Vintage Photographs*. New York: Throckmorton Fine Art, 2004.

11. *Articles and Reviews on or about Fritz Henle in Periodicals*

1934 Leopold Schreiber. "Fritz Henle, Heidelberg." *Gebrauchsgraphik* 11 (November 1934): 57–61.

1937 F.A. Gutheim. "Shadows on Celluloid." *Magazine of Art* 30 (March 1937): 166–171.
"*LIFE*'s Pictures," *LIFE* 3, 17 (October 25, 1937): 112.
"*LIFE*'s Pictures," *LIFE* 3, 20 (November 15, 1937): 21. ["The front cover is a picture of assistant engineer Hamilton taken for *LIFE* on the U.S. *Lightship Portland* by Arthur Griffin."]
"*LIFE*'s Pictures," *LIFE* 3, 21 (November 22, 1937): 106. ["The cover for the November 15 issue was taken by Fritz Henle not by Arthur Griffin as stated."]

1938 Hazel Boyer Braun. "Comment About Art and Artists." *The San Diego Evening Tribune* (January 15, 1938): [1 p.].
"Henle's Camera Registers Artistry of the Ballet." *The Magazine of Light* (February [1938?]): 22[–23].
"*LIFE*'s Pictures," *LIFE* 4, 10 (March 7, 1938): 61.
"People in Mexico seen in photographs by Fritz Henle." *Magazine of Art* 31 (June 1938): 340–43.

1939 "*LIFE*'s Pictures," *LIFE* 6, 9 (February 27, 1939): 72.
"Letters to the Editor: Girls on a Cruise." *LIFE* 6, 12 (March 20, 1939): 2. ["One pretty girl delights a photographer; two pretty girls overwhelm him; but gosh, two pretty girls and twelve whole days to snap at them and the poor guy's bound to throb all over! Your Fritz Henle sure gets the breaks." — Robert E. Wilson, North Grafton, Mass.]
"Announcing the Winners of the Popular Photography Prize Photo Contest: Black & White: 42." *Popular Photography* V, 6 (December 1939): 176.

1940 "Notes on the Salon Section." *Popular Photography* VI, 2 (February 1940): 76.
"Notes on the Salon Section." *Popular Photography* VII, 3 (September 1940): 78.
"Notes on the Salon Section." *Popular Photography* VII, 4 (October 1940): 78.
"Prize-Winners in the Popular Photography 1940 Picture Contest." *Popular Photography* VII, 6 (December 1940): 147.
"Notes on the Salon Section: Black-and-White: 21st Prize." *Popular Photography* VII, 6 (December 1940): 143.

1941 "Women Fliers, Fritz Henle Photographs American Air Beauties." *U.S. Camera* IV, 4 (October 1941): 72–73.

1942 "Fritz Henle Photo-Globe-Trotter Settles For Fashion And The American Scene" ["Aces" series]. *U.S. Camera* V, 2 (February 1942): 55–59.
"Cover Photograph." *U.S. Camera* (March 1942): 61.
"Notes on the Salon Section." *Popular Photography* X, 4 (April 1942): 74.
"Notes on the Salon Section." *Popular Photography* X, 5 (May 1942): 62.
"Simplicity is Henle's Keynote." *Minicam Photography* 5, 9 (May 1942): [56]–63.
"Cover Photograph." *U.S. Camera* (June 1942): 77.
"Notes on the Salon Section." *Popular Photography* X, 6 (June 1942): 80.
"Photographers, Amateur and Professional, and Contributors to U.S. Camera. *U.S. Camera* V, 7 (July 1942): 4.
"Notes on the Salon Section." *Popular Photography* XI, 2 (August 1942): 78.
"Six Years and China fights on!" *Minicam Photography* 6, 1 (September 1942): 70–[71].
"Notes on the Salon Section." *Popular Photography* XI, 4 (October 1942): 72.
"Pat Fitzgerald as six Ace photographers see her." *Minicam Photography* 6, 4 (December 1942): [24–29], 95.
"Mexico, Old and New." *Bulletin* ([1942?]): 326.

1943 "Photographs for Victory...The O.W.I. Photographers Show Democracy Working and Fighting." *Minicam Photography* 6, 5 (January 1943): 50–61.
Chen Yi. "The Courage and Beauty of China." *The New York Times Book Review* (July 18, 1943): BR7.
"China. Fritz Henle Selected and Arranged the Photographs. Text by A Young Chinese-American Kwok Ying Fung." *U.S. Camera* VI, 8 (November 1943): 12.

1944 "Mexican Life. Antonio Reynoso and Fritz Henle Express What They Feel Concerning the Beauty and Rhythm of This Country." *U.S. Camera* VII, 3 (April 1944): 25–27, 56.
Norris Harkness. "Simplicity. Fritz Henle's fashion shots prove that the easy way is often the most effective." *Popular Photography* 15, 2 (August 1944): [36]–38, 93–94.
"Notes on the Salon Section." *Popular Photography* XV, 2 (August 1944): 64.
"Notes on the Salon Section." *Popular Photography* XV, 6 (December 1944): 88.

1945 Society of Magazine Photographers. "The Magazines." *Popular Photography* XVII, 2 (August 1945): 102.
Mary Ellen Slate. "The Magazines." *Popular Photography* XVII, 3 (September 1945): 98.
Jacquelyn Judge. "Models Shoot Photographers." *Popular Photography* XVII, 4 (October 1945): 59.
Mary Ellen Slate. "The Magazines." *Popular Photography* XVII, 4 (October 1945): 102.
"Notes on the Salon Section." *Popular Photography* XVII, 6 (December 1945): 62.
Mary Ellen Slate. "The Magazines." *Popular Photography* XVII, 6 (December 1945): 110.

1946 Mary Ellen Slate. "The Magazines." *Popular Photography* XVIII, 3 (March 1946): 72, 156.
"Memo from the Editor." *Mademoiselle* ("Latin-American Number," March 1946).
John R. Whiting. "Candid Shots by the Editor." *Popular Photography* XVIII, 4 (April 1946): 32.
Mary Ellen Slate. "The Magazines." *Popular Photography* XVIII, 5 (May 1946): 16.
"Notes on the Picture Section." *Popular Photography* 19, 2 (August 1946): 82.
"Notes on the Picture Section." *Popular Photography* 19, 4 (October 1946): 76.
John R. Whiting. "Candid Shots by the Editor." *Popular Photography* 19, 5 (November 1946): 32.
"Notes on the Picture Section." *Popular Photography* 19, 5 (November 1946): 78.
"Photographic Yule Cards and Calendars Available." *Popular Photography* 19, 5 (November 1946): 108.

1947 Jacquelyn Judge. "Men Who Love Paris, Fritz Henle and Elliot Paul combine pictures and text in a handsome book about their favorite city." *Popular Photography* 20, 1 (January 1947): 60–61, 94.
"Notes on the Picture Section." *Popular Photography* 20, 3 (March 1947): 88.
"Bahama Sunshine." *U.S. Camera* (April 1947): 51–54.
Mary Ellen Slate. "The Magazines." *Popular Photography* 20, 4 (April 1947): 183.
Mary Ellen Slate. "The Magazines." *Popular Photography* 20, 6 (June 1947): 16.
"Notes on the Picture Section." *Popular Photography* 20, 6 (June 1947): 66, 73.
Robert Fuhring. "The Magazines." *Popular Photography* 21, 1 (July 1947): 140, 142.
Ralph Samuels. "To photographer Fritz Henle — Paris Is People." *Minicam Photography* 11, 2 (October 1947): 60–[67], 144.
"Notes on the Picture Section." *Popular Photography* 21, 3 (September 1947): 84.
Jacquelyn Judge. "The World and Fritz Henle." *Photography* Fall 1947: [61]–65, 138–140.
Robert Fuhring. "The Magazines." *Popular Photography* 21, 4 (October 1947): 153.
Ira S. Glick. "Singing Faces." *Popular Photography* 21, 5 (November 1947): 58–59, 100.
"Notes on the Picture Section." *Popular Photography* 21, 5 (November 1947): 88.
"Notes on the Picture Section." *Popular Photography* 21, 6 (December 1947): 178.

1948 "Notes on the Picture Section." *Popular Photography* 22, 1 (January 1948): 86.
Robert Fuhring. "The Magazines." *Popular Photography* 22, 2 (February 1948): 163.

Robert Fuhring. "The Magazines." *Popular Photography* 22, 4 (April 1948): 177.
"Guest of Honor----No. 2----Fritz Henle." *Photography* n.s. 3, 1 (May/June 1948): 24–25.
"Notes on the Picture Section." *Popular Photography* 23, 1 (June 1948): 90.
A.R. Sutherland, Jr. "The Magazines." *Popular Photography* 23, 2 (August 1948): 144–45.
"Winners of 2nd Special Monthly Awards in the 1948 Popular Photography Contest." *Popular Photography* 23, 3 (September 1948): 47.
"The Magazines." *Popular Photography* 23, 3 (September 1948): 131.
"Notes on the Picture Section." *Popular Photography* 23, 4 (October 1948): 90.
Frank Fenner, Jr. "Candid Shots by the Editor." *Popular Photography* 23, 5 (November 1948): 40.
"Outstanding Photographs in Color and Gravure by Blumenfeld, Karsh, Henle, Kargas..." *Popular Photography* 23, 6 (December 1948): Front cover.
"Notes on the Picture Section." *Popular Photography* 23, 6 (December 1948): 148, 168.
Frank Fenner, Jr. "Candid Shots by the Editor." *Popular Photography* 23, 6 (December 1948): 48.
Jacob Deschin. "Picture Books. Travel Photography by Henle — Other Guides." *The New York Times* (September 12, 1948): [1 p.].
Barnet Bildersee. "On making photo-essays." *Popular Photography* (1948): [1 p.].

1949 "Notes on the Picture Section." *Popular Photography* 24, 1 (January 1949): 76.
"New Books." *Popular Photography* 24, 1 (January 1949): 134.
Roy Pinney. "Magazine Photography." *U.S. Camera* (February 1949): 12.
"How These Pictures Were Made." *U.S. Camera* (February 1949): 61.
Doris Birnbaum. "The Magazines." *Popular Photography* 24, 2 (February 1949): 147.
"The Prize Winners in the Popular Photography 1948 Picture Contest." *Popular Photography* 24, 3 (March 1949): 198.
Doris Birnbaum. "The Magazines." *Popular Photography* 24, 5 (May 1949): 135.
Roy Pinney. "Magazine & Advertising Photography." *U.S. Camera* (June 1949): 10.
Doris Birnbaum. "The Magazines." *Popular Photography* 24, 6 (June 1949): 18.
Edna Bennett. "Choosing your enlarging paper." *Minicam Photography* 12, 11 (July-August 1949): 66–[73], 128–129.
"Fritz Henle." *Service* (October 1949): unpaged.
"New Books." *Popular Photography* 25, 4 (October 1949): 116.
Doris Birnbaum. "The Magazines." *Popular Photography* 25, 5 (November 1949): 18, 20.
"'My Best of 1949' Pictures in Color and Gravure by Bruehl, Coster, De Dienes, Frissell, Henle, Keppler..." *Popular Photography* 25, 6 (December 1949): Front cover.
"Notes on the Picture Section." *Popular Photography* 25, 6 (December 1949): 104.
"New Books." *Popular Photography* 25, 6 (December 1949): 170.
Roy Pinney. "Magazine & Advertising Photography." *U.S. Camera* (December 1949): 16.

1950 "The Camera Artist Strikes Oil." *Service* (April 1950): [17]–22?
Jacquelyn Judge. "Fritz Henle — What Makes Him Click." *Popular Photography* 26, 5 (May 1950): 34–39, 220–21.
"Notes on the Picture Section." *Popular Photography* 26, 6 (June 1950): 88.
Roy Pinney. "Magazine & Advertising Photography." *U.S. Camera* 13, 6 (June 1950): 12.
Doris Birnbaum. "The Magazines." *Popular Photography* 27, 1 (July 1950): 10.
Roy Pinney. "Magazine & Advertising Photography." *U.S. Camera* (August 1950): 12.
"Photography Unlimited — Starring Hawaii." *U.S. Camera* 13, 10 (October 1950): 52.
J[acquelyn] J[udge]. "beauty around the world: Hawaii by Fritz Henle." *Modern Photography* 14, 4 (December 1950): 44–[45]. ["With these two pages by Fritz Henle, *Modern Photography* inaugurates a series devoted to showing our readers the beautiful women of the world."]
"Prize Winners in the Popular Photography 1950 Picture Contest — Black-and-White." *Popular Photography* 27, 6 (December 1950): 186.

1951 "How these pictures were made." *U.S. Camera* (March 1951): 63.
Roy Pinney. "Magazine & Advertising Photography." *U.S. Camera* 14, 4 (April 1951): 8.
"'To What Vacation Spot Would You Return for Pictures this Summer?'" *U.S. Camera* (July 1951): 42-54.
"U.S. Camera Presents......a portfolio of outstanding industrial photographs made by Fritz Henle on special assignment for a 50th anniversary picture record of United States Steel Corporation." *U.S. Camera* (September 1951): 57–62, 103.
J[acquelyn] J[udge]. "beauty around the world: Trinidad by Fritz Henle." *Modern Photography* 15, 9 (September 1951): 40–41
"Picture Section: Paris." *Modern Photography* 15, 9 (September 1951): [50]–51, 53, 56–[57].
"Darkroom tips from Seven pros." *Popular Photography* 29, 4 (October 1951): 50, 52, 100.
"Prize Winners in the Popular Photography 1951 international picture contest. color: third prize." *Popular Photography* 29, 6 (December 1951): 127.
"Prize Winners in the Popular Photography 1951 international picture contest. color: fifty prizes." *Popular Photography* 29, 6 (December 1951): 127.
"Prize Winners in the Popular Photography 1951 international picture contest. black & white: fifty prizes." *Popular Photography* 29, 6 (December 1951): 127.
"Meet the prize winners in our 1951 international picture contest." *Popular Photography* 29, 6 (December 1951): 157, 182.
"Technical Data on Contest Winners." *Popular Photography* 29, 6 (December 1951): 210, 211.
"Prize Winners in the Popular Photography 1951 international picture contest. black & white: 70 prizes." *Popular Photography* 29, 6 (December 1951): 217.
"Prize Winners in the Popular Photography 1951 international picture contest. black & white: 100 prizes." *Popular Photography* 29, 6 (December 1951): 218.

1952 "Industrial Portfolio. Work by Fritz Henle." *American Photography* 46 (February 1952): 62–67.
"Crystal Jubilee Portfolio: A selection of memorable pictures from the past fifteen years: 15th Year: Fritz Henle." *Photography* 30, 5 (May 1952): [64], 80[–82].
"Notes on the portfolio." *Photography* 30, 5 (May 1952): 235–36.
Hans Neuburg. "Die Photo-Weltausstellung in Luzern / The World Exhibition of Photography in Lucerne / L'Exposition mondiale de la Photographie à Lucerne." *Camera* 31, 6/7 (June/July 1952): 190–225.
Max A. Wyss. "Grosse Namen in der Photographie / Great names in photography / Les grands noms de l'art photographique." *Camera* 31, 6/7 (June/July 1952): 226–45.
Bill Cannon. "Picture File on Oil." *U.S. Camera* 15, 10 (October 1952): 50–51, 106.
Jacquelyn Judge. "Henle's First Movie...What It's Like to Turn from Stills to Moving Pictures..." *Modern Photography* 16, 11 (November 1952): 90–92, 94, 96, 100.
"Prize Winners in the Photography 1952 international picture contest. black and white: 70 prizes." *Photography* 31, 6 (December 1952): 194.
"Prize Winners in the Photography 1952 international picture contest. black and white: 100 prizes." *Photography* 31, 6 (December 1952): 195.

1953 "New Books." *Photography* 32, 2 (February 1953): 106.
"Dance to the Calypso! Fritz Henle in Trinidad." *Art Photography* 4, 9-45 (March 1953): 34–37.
"New Books." *U.S. Camera* 16, 3 (March 1953): 30.
"Candid Shots by the Editors: 'Mr. Rollei' Makes a Movie." *Photography* 33, 6 (December 1953): 34.

1954 H.M. Kinzer. "Fritz Henle's Figure Studies." *Photography* 34, 5 (May 1954): 58–59, 132.
"Fritz Henle: Foto Presenterar Tre Uppslog Bilder av den Amerikanske Stjärnfotografen." *Foto* 16, 7 (July 1954): 18–23.
"Images and Inspirations." *Modern Photography* 18, 10 (October 1954): 62–65.
"Meet the prize winners in our 1954 international picture contest." *Photography* 35, 6 (December 1954): 62, 64.
"Prize Winners in the Photography 1954 international picture contest. color: fourth prize." *Photography* 35, 6 (December 1954): 153.
"Prize Winners in the Photography 1954 international picture contest. color: 50 prizes." *Photography* 35, 6 (December 1954): 153.
"Technical Data on the Pictures: Fourth Prize—Color." *Photography* 35, 6 (December 1954): 205–06.

1955 "Form and Inspiration." *Photography* (January 1955): 21–25.
Ed Hannigan. "Editor's Notebook." *U.S. Camera* 18, 10 (October 1955): 62.
"Prize Winners in the Popular Photography 1955 International Picture Contest. Black & White." *Popular Photography* 37, 6 (December 1955): 209.
"Oil." *Applied Photography* 5 (1955): [1]–3, 6–[7].

1956 George B. Wright. "Books in use: Christmas—or nine fair books in a pear tree: For the discriminating." *Modern Photography* 20, 1 (January 1956): 131–32.
"Fritz Henle — Master of '120.'" *U.S. Camera* 19, 2 (February 1956): Front cover.
"Five Famous Photographers." *U.S. Camera* 19, 2 (February 1956): 65.
Willard Clark. "Fritz Henle: Master of Twin-Lens Reflex." *U.S. Camera* 19, 2 (February 1956): [70]–73.
Ed Hannigan. "Editors' Notebook." *U.S. Camera* 19, 3 (March 1956): 58.
Herbert Keppler. "How Peter Basch and Fritz Henle use creative Composition and Cropping." *Modern Photography* 20, 4 (April 1956): 58–67.
"Fritz Henle: One Man and A Rolleiflex." *Photography* (December 1956): 24, 28–35, 72.

1957 John Wolbarst. "Henle's Guide to Color Exposure." *Modern Photography* 21, 7 (July 1957): 72–77.
"Henle. Know your model, use daylight: two basic rules for successful figure studies." [Periodical unidentified] ([1957?]): 48–53.

1958 H[erbert] K[eppler]. "New Photo Books." *Modern Photography* 22, 6 (June 1958): 28.

1959 Ray Shorr. "Grapevine." *Infinity* VIII, 9 (November 1959): 24–26.

1960 "Books." *Infinity* IX, 3 (March 1960): 17.
Arnold Eagle. "Switch to Motion Pictures?" *Infinity* IX, 10 (October 1960): 18–21.
"The Rangefinder: Traveling travel expert." *Popular Photography* 47, 5 (November 1960): 47.
C[harles] R[eynolds] "Books: Photography for Everyone." *Popular Photography* 47, 6 (December 1960): 148.
Fth. "Fritz Henle." *Elegante Welt* (1960): 46–51.
"Mr. Rollei: Fritz Henle. Porträt eines Unbeirrbaren." *Foto Magazin* III ([1960?]): 45–49.
Karlheinz Thiergart. "Reise nach Irland." *Foto Magazin* III ([1960?]): [1 p.].

1961 Charles Reynolds. "Photographic Style. What is it? How can it be developed? Who has it? How much is it worth?" *Popular Photography* 48, 2 (February 1961): 43–44, 96–100.
"Kender de Mr. Rollei — Alias Fritz Henle." *Foto Magazin* IV ([1961?]): 38–39.

1962 "Fritz Henle Photographer." *Service* (January 1962): 12–15.
Bill Stuart. "Grapevine." *Infinity* XI, 8 (October 1962): 30.

1963 "Grapevine." *Infinity* XII, 1 (January 1963): 29.
Jacob Deschin. "Abstracts in Color: In Fritz Henle Show." *The New York Times* [Sunday Edition] (December 1, 1963): [1 p.].

1964 Lou Jacobs, Jr. "Reviews: Holiday in Europe." *Infinity* XIII, 4 (April 1964): 16, 30.
H.M. Kinzer. "Focus on Fritz Henle." *Popular Photography* (November 1964): 142–149, 192.
H.M. Kinzer. "I fokus: Fritz Henle." *Popular Photography*: Svensk Edition (November 1964): [32]–33, [1 p.].

1965 Regina Benedict. "Grapevine." *Infinity* XIV, 5 (May 1965): 35.
H[erbert] K[eppler]. "Books in Review." *Modern Photography* 29, 9 (September 1965): 40.
Karlheinz Thiergart. "Great Britain. Fotografiert von Fritz Henle." *Foto Magazin* (October 1965): 48–51.

1966 "Fritz Henle. Una Vita per la Fotografia." *Notiziario Erca Cine-foto-ottica* (April 1966): 10–12.

1967 M.A. Matzkin. "Closeups — Parade Movies Need Them. That's how Fritz Henle filmed 'Calypso Carnival.'" *Modern Photography* (February 1967): 82–83, 94.
"The Editors: 'Mr. Rollei' Makes a Movie." *Modern Photography* (February 1967): 34.
"Fritz Henle — master photographer." *Port of Mobile* (December 1967): 30–33.
"Fritz Henle: Wanderer zwischen Kontinenten." ["Reise Mit Der Kamera" series] *Foto Magazin* X ([1967?]): 68–73.

1968 "A Declaration of Conscience." *Infinity* XVII, 1 (January 1968): 6–7.
Beaumont Newhall. "Fritz Henle: Portfolio with Text." *Infinity* XVII, 3 (March 1968): 4–11.
"Governors' Conf. Activities in V.I. Shown in Book of Photographs." *The St. Croix Avis* 80 (June 5, 1968): 1, 12.
Rae Murphy. "Grapevine." *Infinity* XVII, 7 (July 1968): 32–33.

1969 Rae Murphy. "Grapevine." *Infinity* XVIII, 5 (May 1969): 34.

Alan Porter. "People. Places: Pictures." *Camera* 48, 6 (June 1969): 1.
"Fritz Henle: Lebens-Rente in Schwarz-Weiss." *Foto Magazine* XII (1969): [1 p.].

1970 "He Clicks with the Islands. Caribbean Says Cheese For Resident Lensman." *The Daily News of the Virgin Islands* (January 3, 1970): 6.
"The World Sees The Virgin Islands Through The Camera Of Fritz Henle." *The St. Croix Avis* 40 (February 19, 1970): 13.
Julia Scully. "Fritz Henle: 4 Decades at the Top." *Modern Photography* (March 1970): [62]–71, 107.
"Caribbean — Inselparadies der Träume." *Rolleigrafie* 28, 3 (March 1970): 30–35.
"Coffee Break with the editors: Youth Will Out..." *Modern Photography* (December 1970): 8.

1971 "Fritz Henle Exhibit In Puerto Rico." *The Virgin Islands Daily News* (January 23, 1971): 15.
"Henle Photo Exhibit Friday." *The San Juan Star* (February 4, 1971): [1 p.].
Fred Clarke. "Henle: 'Anyone Can Take Good Pictures.'" *The St. Croix Avis* (March 16, 1971): 1–2.
"Noted Photographer Publishes Photo Essay On The Islands." *The Virgin Islands Daily News* (October 26, 1971): 15–16.
Phyllis Battelle. "Assignment America." *The St. Croix Avis* (December 1971): 7.

1972 Freck Hart. "Famous Lensman Was Always In Focus." *The San Juan Star* (February 6, 1972): 27.
Horst Buckholz. "Impressions of The V.I." *Caribbean Sun* (February 13-26, 1972): [1 p.].
"Fritz Henle." *Westermann Monatshefte* (February 1972).

1973 Norman Rothschild. "Portfolio Review in Brief—The American Virgin Islands." *Popular Photography* (February 1973): [1 p.].
"Fritz Henle: Photographer in Retrospect." *The Daily News of the Virgin Islands* (May 5, 1973): 22.
"V.I. Academy of Arts And Letters Cites Local Residents." *The Daily News of the Virgin Islands* (August 28, 1973): 11.
"Henle's Casals Album To Be Photographic Poem." *The San Juan Star* (October 28, 1973): 32.

1974 Jacob Deschin. "Fritz Henle on Pablo Casals." *The Photo Reporter* 4, 6 (June 1974): 1–2, 4.

1975 Freck Hart. "Henle's Casals." *Sunday San Juan Star Magazine* (August 3, 1975): Front cover, 8–9.
Irving Desfor. "Camera Angles." *Associated Press Newsfeatures* (1975): unpaged.
[Advertisement.] "Pride Is Beautiful." *The St. Thomas Daily News* (ca. 1975): unpaged.

1976 Connie Underhill. "Henle Retrospective." *Sunday San Juan Star Magazine* (May 30, 1976): 8-9.
Evelyn Kieran. "Dateline Travel: Curable case of islomania." *PSA, The California Magazine* (May 1976): 16–17.

1977 "Sensitive photo exhibit." *The Morning Call Weekender* (October 8, 1977): [1 p.].
"(Some of) Fritz Henle's Best." *The Daily News of the Virgin Islands* (December 29, 1977): 12–13.
Robert Henry. "Fritz Henle." *The St. Croix Avis* ([1977?]): [4 pp.].

1978 Carolyn Bengtson Mark. "Photographer Henle captures life." *The Austin Citizen* (May 5, 1978): B1.

1979 "Fritz Henle: Un 'Rolleigraf' de Alemania en el Caribe." *Humboldt* 70 (1979): 46-55.
Mike Cox. "'Decisive moment' key to photo success." *Austin American Statesman* (Sunday, May? 1979?): [1 p.].

1980 Ed Hirsch. "Fotograf Fritz Henle: Alias Mr. Rollei." *Foto Magazin* (March 1980): 26–31.
"Fritz Henle Retrospective Opens in New York." *The Virgin Islands Daily News* (April 25, 1980): 19.
Grace Glueck. "Art: Fritz Henle, Witkin Gallery." *New York Times* (May 2, 1980).
Grace Naismith. "Who, What, Where." *Overseas Press Club Bulletin* (May 15, 1980).
"La galleria dell'immagine: dall'estero: New York: 50 anni di fotografia di Fritz Henle alia Witkin Gallery." *il diaframma* 250 (July/August 1980): unpaged.
"Fritz Henle...Master Photographer." *The Virgin Islands Daily News* [50th Anniversary Edition] (August 1, 1980): B-14, B-15.
"National Endowment for the Arts 1981 Photographers' Fellowships." *Afterimage* 8 (December 1980): supplement, 1–8.

1981 BWW. "Ein Leben Mit Der Rollei: Fritz Henle." *Professional Camera* 3, 81 (March 1981): 44–[48?].
Gary Grayson. "Fritz Henle. The art of a photographer." *Virgin Islander* (April 1981): 19–21, [53].
"Der Photograph Fritz Henle." *Feuillleton* 41 (September 26, 1981): [1 p.].

1982 "Fritz Henle, Artistry On Exhibition." *The St. Croix Avis* (February 1982): [1 p.].

1983 "Henle Family Show Held Over." [Periodical unidentified] (1983): [1 p.].

1985 "About Members." *ASMP Bulletin* (January 1985): 1.
Carolyn Elliott. "Henle's photos featured in exhibit." *San Antonio Light* (April 3, 1982): [1 p.].
Ellen Wallenstein. "[The] Medium Is The Message. Fritz Henle's Perspective." *Photo District News* (May 1985): [1 p.].
"Fritz Henle at 75—'Mr. Rolleiflex' keeps the square format alive and well in the sun-soaked haven of St. Croix." *Popular Photography* (1985): [1 p.].

1986 Rainer Wanzelius. "In Dortmund hatte Fritz Henle seine allererste Dunkelkammer." *Dortmunder Rundschau* 159 (July 12, 1986): [1 p.].
"'Mr. Rollei' fotografierte 1929 zum Abschied Dortmunds Hafen." *Dortmunder Zeitung* 158 (July 12, 1986): [1 p.].
"Komponist der Mattscheibe: Museum Hansastrasse zeigt 'Variationen' in Fotos von Fritz Henle." *WAZ* 159 (July 12, 1986): [1 p.].

1987 Venetia Harvey. "Art is a part of life for the Henle family." *The Virgin Island Daily News* 57th year, 14889 (January 24, 1987): 1.
"Henle Photograph Display Reveals Unique Images of People of Hawai'i." *Ka 'Elele: News of Bernice Pauahi Bishop Museum* 14, 3 (March 1987): 4–5.
"Profile of an extraordinary island resident." *Island News* 1, 5 (Sept/Oct 1987): 1, 3, 8.

1988 Ann-Kathrin Akalin. "Die Welt im Ausschnitt seiner Kamera: Amerika-Impressionen von Fritz Henle in der Stadtbücherei Tannenbusch." *Bonn General-Anzeiger* (August 25, 1988): [1 p.].
"I sort og hvidt: Dedikation fra Pablo Casals." *Morgenhavisen Jyllands-Posten* (October 8, 1988): 11.
Walter Hönscheidt. "Die Rolleiflex wird 60: Das nicht alltägliche Jubiläum der zweiäugigen 6 x 6–Spiegelreflexkamera." [Periodical unidentified] ([1988?]): [1 p.].

1989 [Dave Oliphant.] "The Fritz Henle Collection at the Harry Ransom Humanities Research Center." *The Library Chronicle of The University of Texas at Austin* n.s. 48, [1989]: 86–107.
Dr. Kurt Wettengl. "Die Meisterreportage des Fritz Henle: 'Paris 1938.'" *foto-scene* ([September?] 1989): 28.
"Neue Bücher." *DGPh Intern* 3, 89 (March 1989): 134.
Berend Berke. "Paris als Bühne des Lebens." *Dortmunder Rundschau* 144 (June 23, 1989): 4.
"Fotos von Fritz Henle aus dem Jahr 1938 im MKK: Wie ein Dortmunder Paris sah." *Dortmunder Rundschau* 144 (June 23, 1989): 4.
Sigrid Karhardt. "Zum 80. Geburtstag von Fritz Henle. Glanz und Elend des Paris 1938 mit der Kamera eingefangen." *Dortmunder Zeitung* 144 (June 23, 1989): [1 p.].
"'Mr. Rollei' kehrt mit 110 Bildern heim: Fotos des 80 jährigen Fritz Henle im Museum." *WAZ* (June 23, 1989): [1 p.].
Doris Pieper. "Fotoaustellung: Paris 1938. Momentaufnahmen einer verlorenen Menschlichkeit. Dortmunder Museum ehrt den Fotopionier Fritz Henle." *Die Glocke* (June 24–25, 1989): [1 p.].
Roland Gross. "'Mister Rollei' in Paris: Schnappschüsse von 1938." *FAZ* (August 4, 1989): [1 p.].
"Fritz Henle. Paris vor 50 Jahren." *Photo Technik International* 5, 89 (Sept/Oct 1989): 69–75.
Heide Seele. "Der Mensch im Zentrum des Interesses: Fritz Henles Ausstellung 'Paris 1938' in der Universitätsbibliothek Heidelberg." *Rhein-Neckar Zeitung* (October 31, 1989): [1 p.].
Heide Seele. "Mr. Rollei ist ein steter Gast in Heidelberg." *Ausstellung Aktuell* (November 1989): 8–9.
Fredreka Schouten. "Beauty among the ruins." *St. Thomas Daily News* (December 22, 1989): [1 p.].
"Again, 'last classic photographer' Fritz Henle is the toast of Paris." *VICA news*, II, 1 (Winter 1989–90): 6–7.
"Henle organizes photograph archive at UT Austin." *Texas Libraries* 50 (Winter 1989–90): 122–23.
Zt. "Fritz Henle, der Mann mit vier scharfen Augen." *Foto Magazin* ([1989?]): 6–9.
"Meet the Rollei's Master." *Popular Photography* (1989): 72–73.

1990 "UT safeguards Henle's work." *Distinct* (January 10, 1990): 6, 8.
Helen Tackett. "Collection acquires Henle's master prints." *On Campus* (January 22–28, 1990): 2.
"Prints by artists in D.C. exhibit selling well." *VICA news* (Summer 1990): [3 pp.].
Bernhard Schaub. "Der Bildreporter mit einem Herzen für die Menschen." *WAZ* 146 (June 26, 1989): [1 p.].
Daniel Alexander Schacht. "Flaneur mit der Kamera: Fritz Henles [*sic*] Fotografien aus dem Paris der Vorkriegszeit." *Hannoversche Allgemeine Zeitung* (July 28, 1990): 8.
Terri Guttilla. "Interview with Fritz Henle." *ASMP Bulletin* 9, 8 (August 1990): 1, 5, 10, 12–13.
GRU. "'Mr. Rollei' und seine Fotografien." *General-Anzeiger* (August 11–12, 1990): [1 p.].

1991 John Wood. "Caribbean Connoisseur." *Modern Maturity* (December 1991–January 1992): 14.

1992 wop. "Die Kunst, den Schnappschuss zu gestalten: Fritz Henles [*sic*] amerikanische Impressionen sind in der Stadthalle Marzig zu sehen." *Saarbrücker Zeitung* (January 18, 1992): [1 p.].
"Amerikanische Impressionen: 'Mr. Rollei' Fritz Henle stelit in der Stadthalle aus." *Neues aus Merzig* (January 22, 1992): unpaged.
JoD. "Einfühlsame Kamera: studio Dumont zeigt Bilder von Fritz Henle." *Kölner Stadt-Anzeiger* 217 (September 17, 1992): [1 p.].
Billy Vaughn. "Outstanding Islanders. Fritz Henley [*sic*]: The man with magical eyes." *St. Croix Avis* 231 (October 4–5, 1992): 4.

1993 [Bent Rasmussen?] "1909–Fritz Henle–1993." *Caribbean Impressions* 5, 8 (February 25, 1993): unpaged.
Suzanne Goldstein. "Portfolio: Fritz Henle." *The Picture Professional* XXIII, 1 (Spring Issue 1993): front cover, 22–25.
Anna Auer. "Fritz Henle. '31.1.1993.'" *Mitteilungen der PhGW* (June 1993): 14.
Helmut Gernsheim. "Fritz Henle ist tot." *DGPh Intern* 1/93 (1993): 6–7.

2005 Paul Gardner. "Fritz Henle: Throckmorton Fine Art." *ARTnews* 104, 2 (February 2005): 134.

2007 Herbert Keppler. "Picture Progress." *Popular Photography* (March 2007): [2 pp.].
[Maria Henle.] "Retrospective: Photographer Fritz Henle 1909–1993." *Art Fusion* 2 (Spring–Summer 2007): 12–[16].

ACKNOWLEDGEMENTS

In photography...you will spend the rest of your life learning to see light. It will not take long to learn all about the camera, but you will never come to the end of discovering about the effects of light itself. The only rule is to watch the world about you, all the time, even when you have not got a camera in your hand....

FRITZ HENLE

From 1978 onward, it has been my privilege to work with Fritz Henle on a number of enterprises, primarily on what became the Henle Master Print Collection at the Harry Ransom Center. In the process of assessing his work, we were fortunate to have many good discussions, debates and reviews not only about the subjects of his work and his thoughts about their creation, but also and always with an anecdotal narrative and insightful analysis of his interpretations and feelings about the imagery. He evaluated every one of his photographs on the basis of several aesthetic, historical, emotional and personal factors.

Not to mention beauty. Beauty always played a role. We discussed the nature of what made something beautiful, whether or not the effect was permanent or transitory, and how each photograph's beauty might be impacted or transformed by the vagaries of style and taste as well as the insistence of time itself. The question of beauty — perhaps unanswerable but certainly, like light itself, always present — was one that occupied Henle's spirit and persona for all his years.

Therefore, I am obligated firstly and always to thank Fritz himself for sharing all those perspectives with us and for giving me the foundation from which to begin this investigation into his life and his art.

I must begin these acknowledgments by extending my thanks to Fritz Henle's immediate family: Marguerite and her children — Maria, Tina and Martin — who have shared their time, reflections and passion for this husband/father/artist. They have welcomed me into their homes, allowed me complete access to Fritz's archives, and shared their time and memories with me. I could not have completed this work without their commitment, patience and friendship. My only regret is that Maria was summoned to heaven's atelier before we completed this work.

The fundamental commitment for the production of this book and the compilation of its accompanying exhibition comes from the Judy and Steven Gluckstern Family through their Lucky Dog Foundation, which has been steadfast and essential. Additional support has also come through the Robin and Danny Greenspun Family and their Culture Dog Foundation. I am also grateful to Kathryn Clubb of The Ajax Group of Companies for all her assistance and time.

The administrative support for this project stems from three directors of the Harry Ransom Center: Thomas F. Staley, our present director, who has seen to the continued, active support and completion of this book and exhibition; his predecessor, Decherd Turner, who provided the necessary endorsement for Henle's Master Print Project and protection for the archive during a time when it was threatened with destruction; and Carleton Lake, then acting director, who first welcomed the photographer and encouraged the adoption of his plans for the project.

The staff of the Photography Department at the Ransom Center has once again provided the critical first line of support for me throughout this project. They are David Coleman, Linda Briscoe Myers, Deborah Smith, Franki Hand, Mary Alice Harper and Kristin Ware. To that primary roll should also be added the Ransom Center's Chief Photographer, Pete Smith — who mastered all the photoduplication work for this publication — as well as our Photographic Conservator, Barbara Brown.

The production of this volume is the creative labor of several individuals whose talents and expertise have been of incalculable assistance. DJ Stout and Julie Savasky of Pentagram have overseen the design and production of this volume with their customary excellent creativity and understanding of the artist and his work. Together with editor Dana Frank, they have been of tremendous aid in helping me present Fritz's story with clarity and order. On the UT Press side, Jim Burr served as humanities editor of the work, and he and associate director Dave Hamrick have provided solid insight and advice from the beginning. Among the others who have assisted from the Press have been Nancy Bryan and Laura Young Bost. In addition, I am also once more indebted to my own dependable team of editors/researchers/colleagues who have helped me throughout this project to challenge my assumptions, choose the good questions, find the true answers and employ the correct words: James B. Colson, Julianne Newton, April Rapier, Rick Williams and W. Russell Young.

I am also immeasurably grateful to a number of Fritz Henle's friends and associates who extended their hospitality during my visit to the Virgin Islands and, in many instances, were even patient enough to sit through a video interview. These kind individuals include Diego Conde, Mary Simpson, Erik and Jenny Lawaetz, Mona Doane, David Lawaetz, and Paul Voytershark.

Among the many professionals who have assisted with advice and guidance — not to mention never staring at me awry when I asked them to define "beauty" — I wish to particularly thank the staffs of the George Eastman House — notably Alison Nordstrom, Rachel Stuhlman, David Wooters, Rick Hock, Joe Strubel, Jessica Johnston, Patrick Loughney and Daniel Wagner — and of the Center for Creative Photography at the University of Arizona — Britt Salvesen, Amy Rule, Leslie Calmes, Trinity Parker and Marcia Tiede. Thanks are also due to Verna Curtis and Beverly W. Brannan of the Library of Congress, as well as to the public service staffs of the University of Oregon and University of Washington libraries. Individuals who have also been of particular help have been Steve Clayton, Giuli Cordara, Marita Holdaway, Jim Hughes, Rudolf Kicken, Jo Leggett, Gail Meyers, Arthur Ollman, Orville Robertson, Karen Sinsheimer, Claude S. Sui, Mary Virginia Swanson, David Travis, Anne Tucker, Peg Wallace, Ruth Weaver, Bill Wright and Stephen Yates.

Members of The University of Texas community who have been of great assistance in helping us with the completion of this publication and its exhibition include Robert Abzug, Annette Carlozzi, Donna De Cesare, Leslie Ernst, Kurt Heinzelman, Jesse Otto Hite, Lee Loden, Lawrence McFarland, Linda Peterson, Sheree Scarbrough, Cheryl K. Snay, and William Stott.

I must certainly honor the outstanding staff and employees here at the Ransom Center. Among the many individuals, past and present, who have facilitated the creation of this book and exhibition and/or whom the Henle family wishes to thank for their important assistance over the past number of years are Helen Adair, Debbie Armstrong, Linda Ashton, Lisa Avra, Eric Beggs, Tom Best, Mary Baughman, Mary Beth Bigger, Ron Brynaert, Barbara Carr, Stephen Cooper, David Dibble, Alicia Dietrich, Wyndell Faulk, Pat Fox, Oliver Franklin, Bob Fuentes, Tom Galyean, Bryan Garcia, Ken Grant, Gil Hartman, Cathy Henderson, Hsiao-Ju Huang, Jim Janknegt, Sally Leach, Christine Lee, Beverly Lewellen, Mary Lopez, Anthony Maddaloni, Peter Mears, Jeff Melton, Jill Morena, Sue Murphy, Mary Sue Neilson, Rich Oram, Olivia Primanis, Nan Ratnayake, Sonja Reid, Callie Shelton, Danielle Sigler, Hayley Simms, Jim Stroud, Lisa Talen, Jean Townsend, Lee Tran, Tracy Tran, Margaret Tenney, Jen Tisdale, Darnelle Vanghel, Steve Wilson, Richard Workman, John Wright, Frank Yezer, Lan Zhang and Daniel Zmud.

Finally, my love and thanks go to my own family, Martha and Erica, who have offered their constant and unwavering support throughout the many years that we have all been deeply moved by Fritz's song.

ROY FLUKINGER
Senior Research Curator
Harry Ransom Center
The University of Texas at Austin
September 2008